Paths of Stones
A Family Journey
1900 – 2024

Paths of Stones

A Family Journey
1900 – 2024

Cynthia Dickstein

HenschelHAUS Publishing, Inc.
Milwaukee, Wisconsin

Copyright © 2024 by Cynthia Dickstein
All rights reserved.

First printing: April 20, 2024

Published by
HenschelHAUS Publishing, Inc.
Milwaukee, Wisconsin
www.henschelHAUSbooks.com

ISBN (hardcover): 978159598-961-1
ISBN (paperback): 978159598-962-8
LCCN: 2023940146

Cover photo: The author and her father on Cadillac Mountain, Maine, ca. 1950

Printed in the United States of America.

Dedication

To my parents, who did the best they could

*To their parents and all the immigrants who left their homes
for an unknown country and did the best they could*

And to Frank.....simply the best of the best

"An invisible thread connects those who are destined to meet, regardless of time, place, and circumstance. The thread may stretch or tangle. But it will never break."

—Ancient Chinese Proverb

Table of Contents

Preface i
Introduction iii

Part One
1. Glubokoye, Russia 1
2. Coming to America 7
3. Growing Up in Scranton, PA 11
4. The Other Dicksteins 19

Part Two
5. My Childhood 45
6. Growing Up 51
7. It Was the Sixties 63
8. After College 73
9. Dad's Illness and Death 87
10. After Dad 93

Part Three
11. Exchange Programs 1980, Poland and Russia 99
12. 1982 Russia, Mongolia 113
13. 1983 and NESNE 139
14. Natasha 145
15. 1984, 1985 NESNE 151
16. 1986, Sasha 169
17. 1987, NESNE, Women/Politics 183
18. 1988, Uzbekistan 191
19. 1989, Marriage & More 205
20. 1990, Lithuania Fights for Independence 223

Part Four
21. Family 247
22. 1991, The Coup & After 253

23. Glubokoye 283

Part Five
24. Sofya's Life 305
25. 1993/2nd Visit to Glubokoye 323
26. 1993, Health Update 337

Part Six
27. Israel 343
28. Partisans 353
29. Nachama and Yale 357
30. Secrets 365
31. 1994, Last and 20th Trip to Russia 367
32. Robert 373
33. Dealing with the US Government 377
34. 1996, Cambridge, Massachusetts 385

Part Seven
35. Iran 393

Part Eight
36. Talk Show Host 411
37. Mystery Solved 415
38. Si 419
39. Michael 431
40. Sofya Turns 100 433
41. The Adventures 437
42. Putin 449
43. Write the Story 451

Afterword 455
Family Tree 463
Simon's Sayings 465
Glossary of People 467
Glossary of Terms and Abbreviations 477
Bibliography / Works Cited / Recommended Reading 481

Acknowledgements 487
About the Author 489

Preface

In December of 1910, when William Howard Taft was President, my 10-year-old father Simon (Schlaime), three of his siblings, and my 42-year-old grandmother Socia Zalmanovna Dickstein, sailed out of Hamburg, Germany in steerage on the USS *Moltke*. They disembarked twelve days later on January 11th, 1911, at Ellis Island, the last of my father's immediate family to leave Glubokoye (sometimes called Glubokie or Glubok), their Russian shtetl, for America.

With them were two little girls, listed on the family passport as my father's siblings, but they were not. He thought they might have been his cousins, but he was just guessing. Although I inherited the passport, it was over 100 years after their arrival in America, by pure and improbable happenstance, that I learned the identities of those two girls.

Many of my family's stories, many of my stories, took place in Russia, a country rich with its own drama, with its own disturbing, yet captivating past. A past created by facts, falsehoods, and fantasy, much the same as our own unique lives were shaped, and the lives of those people on that passport.

Like so many immigrant families, my father's relatives had a difficult life, both in Russia and in America. Once here, they worked hard, sent their children to college, and ran successful businesses. Perhaps their stubbornness helped. They were very stubborn, painfully stubborn, but maybe it was their birthright, since their Ashkenazi name came from the German Dickenstein, which translates to 'thick' or 'fat' stone.

But as obstinate as they were, they also always maintained their sense of humor, a uniquely Yiddish sense of humor.

When my grandmother, my Bubbe, told my Aunt Ida that if she didn't stop giving away her money, there would be nothing left to buy clothes to bury her in, Ida snapped back "Then I'll die in summer, so you shouldn't have to buy me so many clothes."

When my Uncle Harry answered the phone one day at his home in Scranton, PA and learned that it was his good friend, the local undertaker calling, Harry declared, "I'm not ready for you yet" and promptly hung up on him.

Sadly, the undertaker has called on Ida and Harry, my father, and the rest of his brothers and sisters. There is no one left in my father's immediate family with a first-person memory of living in their Russian town of Glubokoye, or of immigrating to America and creating a life here.

But I have their stories, and stories of an extended family. The extended family I found by accident. The extended family I found in ways that almost defy belief.

With branches not only in the US, but in Israel and in Russia, my relatives included some who perished in the ghetto of Glubokoye at the hands of Hitler's army, some who were partisans who fought that army in the woods, some who were executed by Stalin, one who starved to death during the Siege of Leningrad, and two who were passengers on the *Exodus*, the ship with Holocaust survivors that was turned away from Palestine in 1947 by the British Royal Navy.

For those who came before me, those who suffered and sacrificed so that the next generation's stories could have happy beginnings and endings, I have gratitude beyond measure. The least I can do for them, the only way I can thank them, is to share their stories.

Those family members who stayed behind in the Old Country, their narratives are important, too, and those narratives cannot be told without discussing the history of Russia and the Soviet Union, and the path it has been on since 1900.

And finally, my story. My father's bed was the top of an iron stove in the countryside in Russia; I have a wonderful home with a comfortable king-size bed in Tucson, Arizona. The longest distance to get from where he slept to where I now sleep was travelled by him.

I've tried to live my life in ways that would make him proud, in ways that would honor my family and the journey they took, the hardships they endured. So I have written here about my life also, to show, within a generation, how different our lives were, our pleasures, our struggles, how the dreams of those immigrants' for their children have come true for many. I am but one.

Introduction

In the late 1880s, the majority of the world's Jews lived within the borders of the Russian Empire. In 1900, out of a population of 128 million, there were five million Jews in Russia, the largest Jewish community in the world in the biggest country in the world. Born in April of that year, my father, Schlaime Dickstein, later to be called Simon, was one of them. Three years before his birth, according to a census, Jews in his shtetl numbered 3,917, 70.4% of the area's population.

Average life expectancy in Russia then was 40 years, six years less than in America, but the mortality rates for those living in a Jewish community were twice as high as those in non-Jewish communities.

At that time, wealthy aristocrats owned the best land and there was only a small middle class that lived in the cities. The majority of people lived in the countryside, sustaining themselves through agriculture. Those peasants, 50 million of them, more than half the country's population, had been serfs until they were freed on March 3, 1861. Four years, by the way, before America began freeing its slaves.

My father's family was part of that peasant population. They lived in a shtetl in the Pale of Settlement in western Russia, where Russian law confined the Jews and where Christian boys routinely threw stones at Jewish boys and tossed manure through open Jewish windows. In fact, all but 300,000 of Russia's Jews lived in the Pale of Settlement. Russian law was actually the Tsar's law. Catherine the Great first decreed the Settlement on December 23, 1791, to keep Jews out of the cities. From 1882 on, no Jews could own land. The Pale existed in various reconfigurations until it was abolished on March 20, 1917.

On March 13, 1881, Tsar Alexander II, a reformer, was assassinated in St. Petersburg by a bomb wrapped in a handkerchief. Both his son, Alexander III, and his grandson, Nicholas II, witnessed his murder. Russians blamed the Jews. They rioted, beat and killed Jews, destroyed their property, and launched a new wave of anti-Semitism that continued for decades. Those violent riots were called pogroms.

Zvi Gitelman, in his book *A Century of Ambivalence,* wrote "The pogroms were marked by indescribable cruelty and face-to-face brutality. Men were buried up to their necks and then killed by the hooves of horses driven over them, or were literally pulled apart by horses driven in opposite directions. Children were smashed against walls in view of their parents; pregnant women were a favorite target, their unborn children killed while their mothers helplessly watched on. Thousands of women were raped and hundreds were left insane by their experiences."

These pogroms came to the shtetls, including my father's town of Glubokoye, which was part of Poland until 1793 and then again between 1921 to 1945.

But in 1900, under Russian rule, the ruthless monarch Tsar Nicholas II displayed a somewhat ambivalent attitude about the pogroms. The Tsar wrote in a police report, "I am glad in my heart when they beat the Jews, but it cannot be permitted." But he did permit it.

Not only did Nicholas II permit it, in 1903 his secret police, the *Okhrana*, the forerunner of the KGB, forged an anti-Semitic document called "The Protocols of the Elders of Zion," falsely stating that Jews were plotting global domination by taking control of media and financial institutions. It spread throughout the world, was and still is available in many languages, and to this day is believed by some to be the truth.

Between 1901 and 1910, somewhere between one and two million Jews left Russia. They left to avoid being drafted into the army—where Jews were to serve for 25 years if they survived that long—or to flee the restricting and often dangerous anti-Semitism, or simply in search of a better life. Most immigrated to America, known as the Golden Sanctuary, along with eight to nine million people from many other countries. They were immigrants who toiled in sweatshops, spinning mills, and coal mines. Immigrants who found prejudice and poverty. Immigrants filled with both hope and fear.

By the end of the 20th century, the population of the former Russian Empire and Soviet Union had gone from over five million Jews to about 600,000 Jews.

In 1900, the year of my father's birth, at the International World Fair in Paris, a Russian engineer named Konstantin Persky first used the word "television" to talk about the exciting new concept of image transfer for distance.

According to *National Geographic Magazine*, 1914, the Russian Jews were called "Those Who Follow the Mosaic Creed" (meaning those who believed that Moses wrote the Torah, the first five books of the Old Testament.)

In her 1938 book, *Comrades and Citizens*, Seema Allan stated that because the Jews couldn't have property, "they did what was left—became traders and artisans. They drifted from place to place, with no roots, and were thus called *Narod Vozdukha*, or "People of the Air."

When my family left Russia, they put down their roots, primarily in Scranton, PA. I was born 35 years later in Binghamton, NY. Our stories here reveal that we escaped being "People of the Air."

Part One

Chapter 1
Glubokoye (Hlybokaye), Russia

"Remember, remember always, that all of us, and you and I especially, are descended from immigrants and revolutionists."
—Franklin D. Roosevelt (1882 – 1945)
32nd President of the United States

Our home town of Hlybokaye

"The worst things that ever happened to us because we were Jews happened once a year, when Russians were drafted and several hundred at a time had to march five to seven miles to the train station to join the army. They would get drunk, sing, and every time they saw someone Jewish, they'd shout, "There's a Jew, let's get him." When they passed a Jewish home, they yelled and threw stones at it. My mother then had to rush to stuff our money in the bottom of the flour barrel, to close our wooden shutters so that the windows wouldn't be broken, and to make us take cover under the tables and chairs. Iron bars protected our door.

Once, two men robbed and killed many people in our area. With knives, they murdered a whole family that lived near us. My mother warned us to be on the lookout for strangers. Those men were on their way to our house when the Tsar's police caught them. We all stood outside and watched as they were put in chains and marshaled down the road into town.

Something else. My father made vodka and often the Cossacks with their whips and swords, who were loyal to the Tsar and who we Jews hated, came to buy it from him. Once, they were very drunk when they came and so my father refused to sell to them. They retaliated, and he was bruised and bloodied, badly beaten when they left. We always thought it affected his heart and was probably what caused him to die so young. Or maybe it was pneumonia. Of course, we'll never know for sure what it was that took him."

"Daddy, tell me more about Russia, please. Do we still have family there? Did any of our relatives die in the Holocaust?"

When I was a young child, I never tired of asking my father to tell me the stories of his life in the Old Country. I'd sit next to him on the sofa, tuck my legs under me and off to one side, rest my head on his chest after he put his arm around my shoulders, and listen. When I got older, I still wanted to hear the stories.

My father: It was only ten years, 1900—1910, that my father lived on the outskirts of Glubokoye, a small town about 120 miles northeast of Minsk, on or near Koprick-ayasse Street. But I had lots of curiosity and he had lots to tell.

"We don't have any family there anymore, and we didn't lose anyone to Hitler. I had six siblings and we all came to America. My mother had two babies before me who died, at birth I think.

"Glubokoye, also known as the Deep, had about 5,500 people when I was a kid and was in the state of Vilna or Vilna Gubernia. Nobody ever mentioned Moscow. We called ourselves Litvaks, but we didn't speak Lithuanian, only Russian and Yiddish."

"What were your parents like?" I asked.

"Your Bubbe Socia—you were five when she died—was tiny, about 5 feet 2 or 3 inches tall, maybe 125 pounds. Her marriage to my father in 1885 was arranged by their fathers who were friends. One day, when she was 15, her father simply told her to put on her best clothes because she was going to be married that day, to a boy only a year older, at 16.

"When my oldest brother Sam (for whom my parents bought papers and medical records for from a sickly man named Wexler so that Sam wouldn't be drafted into the military in Russia) went to America in 1904 and settled in Scranton, Pennsylvania. It was because my mother had family there in the pants manufacturing business. There were families of her Alperowitz relatives with changed names, the Alperins, the Alperts, and the Halperins.

"My father was tall, about six feet, 175 pounds or so. A handsome man with a Van Dyke beard, he was very strict and he was definitely the boss in the family.

"*Catsella* (his Yiddish nickname for me, means kitten: The usual spelling is *Ketzele*, but I want to use his spelling here, to see it as it was in all his letters and cards to me - "Dear Catsella"), I never saw my parents kiss, hug, or express any affection to one another, and I don't remember my father playing with any of us when we were kids. In fact, I don't think I ever saw him laugh.

"We didn't have much for clothes, mostly lots of hand-me-downs. I wore only a long shirt, no underwear, and I never had a pair of shoes. We had to cut burlap bags to wrap around our feet. During the cold winters, I had a large coat with rope tied around my waist. Three of us slept in our house with feather beds on top of the oven; others slept on the dirt floor or on the one bed.

"There were three rooms—a big entry room with a hole for the chicken coup under the floor, a kitchen and a dining room. No bathroom. Not even an outhouse. We went outdoors, in the back of the house. The pigs cleaned up after us. We also had a few cows and goats, which along with the chickens were for our own personal use. And two horses. No pets.

"One of the horses was white and when he was old, I remember one night it got so cold that my parents brought him indoors to spend the night. We rode that horse all over the place, with no problems, unless we came to a fence. Repeatedly, the horse would bump into whichever fence he was faced with and it was some time before we finally figured out that the horse was blind.

"One day, my father and my brother Harry had gone to market and on the way home, they had sheep in the wagon that they hadn't sold. A pack of wolves pursued them and to keep the wolves from attacking, they had to throw one sheep at a time out of the wagon.

"We bathed in the river running near the house. In the winter, we didn't really bathe, only washed our faces and took the equivalent of sponge baths. As for food, we ate mostly meat, vegetables, potatoes, cabbage, and turnips. My mother made her own black bread. No desserts or pastries. I never saw ice cream until I came to America.

"I think the town was about one mile or so from our house, which was in the country. We didn't have any neighbors—no Jews living nearby—only our Russian landlord who was about 100 yards away. I don't know his name.

"Since there was nobody living near us, I didn't really have any friends. I did know some kids at the *Kheyder*, the boys' school which was almost a two-mile walk from our house and where we studied just Hebrew and the Talmud. Only my brother Herman, a couple years younger than me, and I could go. Every one else had to work. We went from early morning to 5:00 PM. On occasion, one of my older brothers would give us a ride with the horse and sleigh, but usually we had to walk. My mother packed us a few slices of black bread and gave us a few kopeks each to buy a bottle of pop.

"The private tutor, or *melamed*, was a rabbi, not married, who was probably somewhere between 55 and 65 years old. His thick, long, gray beard made it hard to tell his age. He had a samovar for tea, which he drank all day long. Once during lunch break, when he fell asleep, some of the 12 to 15 kids in the school went and got burdocks and put them in his beard. He jumped up and down mad, but nobody told who did it. We also used to ride his goats, something else that angered him.

"When it was time to go home, it was usually dark and we had to pass a cemetery, with only a wooden lantern and candle inside for light. I was so scared of the cemetery I ran past as fast as I could, which wasn't too fast when there was a lot of snow, but even when there wasn't snow, I had to slow down to wait for Herman to catch up. Frankly, I always found him annoying.

"After supper, we usually sat on top of the oven and picked feathers off their stems to make pillows and mattresses. Bedtime was usually between 8:00 and 8:30 PM.

"We didn't play much. Sometimes, when my mother was milking the cows, we did fool around with the goats and calves. And we occasionally swam for fun in the river in the summer. But we did get into mischief. The landlord had acres of peas in pods. Some of us would put on big shirts, tie a rope around our waist and sneak into the field. We couldn't be seen because the peas grew so high. We picked them, stuffed them in our shirts, and never got caught. My mother knew and didn't like it, but she wasn't going to throw away food.

"I spent most of my time with your Aunt Ida, only a year and some months older than me. She was dark like a gypsy, and my mother drummed it into our heads that the gypsy caravans stole kids and that we had to be careful. In fact, she told us they stole everything that wasn't nailed down. The caravans from Romania usually had four to five wagons. The gypsies wore earrings, red or green blouses and dresses, always bright colors. A few times, caravans did call Ida over to them, and each time I grabbed her hand and dragged her away as fast as I could.

"We weren't religious, didn't wear yarmulkes, but we did always keep the Jewish holidays. Those were the only special occasions I remember. There was certainly prejudice against the Jews. Our landlord didn't treat us badly, but others did. My older brother Harry often took me with the horse and wagon for three to five days to call on farmers to buy chicken, ducks, eggs, whatever was available, so that he could take them to the market for resale. We used to go to rich farmers' places and before they would even talk or do business with us, we had to bow and kiss their hands. The Russian farmers looked down on peasants, and it was even worse if the peasants were Jewish.

"Once our landlord had a big party with lots of food and music. Alone, I stood and stared through the fence for a long time. And I vowed right then and there that when I grew up, I would have only one child, so that I could afford that kind of life.

"In 1907, when I was seven and my father was 40, he immigrated to America. In New York City, he became a fruit and vegetable pushcart peddler and went by the name Herman or sometimes Hyman.

"He was there only about three years. I don't remember the day he left, but I do remember when we learned that he had died. I was out in the pasture with our two horses and was bringing them up to the top of the hill when I saw a crowd of people at the house. We had gotten a notice from my brother Sam. My mother was sobbing and carrying on something awful. I cried too when I found out. We all cried."

> **In 1703, Tsar Peter the Great began building St. Petersburg. He used forced labor—Swedish prisoners, from the Great Northern War, and serfs. Because conditions were so difficult, he insisted that the city be built of stone. There are about 100,000 corpses lying beneath the city. Construction was completed about 10 years later and the Tsar then moved the capital of Russia from Moscow to St. Petersburg.**
>
> **In January of 1905, unarmed workers went to the Tsar's Palace in St. Petersburg to petition for bread. His troops fired into the crowd, killing about 100 and wounding many more. This massacre became known as Bloody Sunday. There followed strikes and uprisings and mutinies until October, when the Tsar allowed the establishment of a multiparty system and a national parliament with limited powers called the Duma, but so limited that the autocracy eventually regained full control within less than a year. The Revolution failed, but had succeeded in conducting 690 anti-Semitic pogroms, which killed more than 3,000 Jews. ……".**
>
> —*Antifa, The Anti-Fascist Handbook* by Mark Bray,
> Melville House Publishing, 2017

Paths of Stones

Socia Dickstein, my grandmother, with her children Simon, Mirke, and Herman (ca. 1907)

Passport to bring family, 1910

Chapter 2
Coming to America

"Tis time, my friend, 'tis time! The heart to peace aspires:
Day follows day; the rolling stream of hours
Crumbles the banks of being, and you and I
Had thought to live, and yet, behold, we die.
Though joy forever flees, peace stays and concentration.
For long now has it been my consolation,
Hard-driven slave, to plan rebellious flight
To some far sanctuary of work and chaste delight.
—Alexander Pushkin (1799–1837)
Russian poet

Not long after my grandfather died, my father's oldest brother Sam sent for the rest of the family, minus my 16-year-old Aunt Fanny, who had already come to America alone two years earlier. So in January of 1911, my 42-year-old little Bubbe took my father, three of his siblings, and the two little girls passing as her daughters out of Russia. On her own.

They first travelled by train to Hamburg, Germany. To save the price of two tickets, my father and the smaller Herman hid under my grandmother's long skirt, but my father remembered that it was very uncomfortable there because they had to sit on

The SS *Moltke*, Hamburg America line

the hot steam pipes under the seats. They were too afraid to complain, so they sweated and squirmed until the conductor had come by and collected all the tickets.

The family brought with them very little luggage, only a few clothes, and a large, solid brass Russian samovar. But they also brought something else with them, something far more valuable. Their strength of will.

"My mother, who was very afraid to cross the ocean even before we left Russia, spent the entire voyage seasick in bed, in the ship's hospital. The rest of us were in steerage, in the bottom of the ship, where when I could look out, I saw only green water. There were people from many different countries, all clothed like peasants. I didn't even have any shoes on the ship.

"The sea was very rough, so rough that everybody prayed, afraid that the boat wouldn't make it safely. Herman and I shared an upper berth and one day he got seasick. He leaned over the side of the bed and threw up, directly onto the shiny baldhead of the man in the lower berth, who at that moment was bent over trying to see past his big belly to lace up his shoes. You can imagine the man's reaction. And mine— I about choked trying not to laugh out loud.

"Another day, I got very thirsty and went looking for water. I wandered upstairs to first- or second-class, saw a chef in his tall white hat and apron with a pot that he was filling with water out of a faucet. As soon as he left, I ran over, put my mouth to the faucet, and took a very long drink. But it was seawater, and soon I was throwing up, too.

"We had our meals at long tables with benches. Big five-gallon crocks were set down on the table with salty herring, potatoes, and prunes. People ate with their hands, like animals, because there were no plates or silverware, so everyone had to grab food as best they could. And it smelled really bad.

When the SS *Moltke* reached New York City and people caught sight of the Statue of Liberty, a gift from France, everyone began to smile. I imagine they were all grateful and relieved.

Emma Lazarus wrote the words inscribed on the base of the Statue of Liberty in 1883, although because of lack of funds, the statue wasn't dedicated until 1886. Part of the inscriptions reads:

"Give me your tired, your poor,
Your huddled masses yearning to breathe free,
The wretched refuse of your teeming shore."

In fact, by 1860, the rise of Jewish immigrants to America was accompanied by widespread anti-Semitism. At the time that those words appeared on the Statue, the populace considered the "wretched immigrants" to be the Eastern European Jewish refugees. According to the November 11, 2019 *New Yorker*, "… In the early 1900s, the novelist Henry James was disgusted by the people he saw "swarming" on New York's heavily Jewish Lower East Side, who reminded him of 'small, strange animals…snakes or worms."

"Once at Ellis Island, across the room, we saw my brother Sam signing some papers at a desk. Then he took us all to Scranton, all except the two young girls who settled somewhere in NY. I don't know whatever happened to them."

> **It is estimated that almost 40% of all Americans can trace their ancestry back to someone who immigrated through Ellis Island. Categories of exclusion were created which included health, glaucoma, lice, radical political leanings and criminal backgrounds. But only 2% of 13 million were turned away. The center began receiving immigrants January 1, 1892. Immigration decreased significantly in 1924, due mainly to the Immigration Act of that year, which limited the number of immigrants from any country to 2% of those from that country already settled in America.**
>
> **Ironically, also in 1924, Native Americans were finally granted citizenship—and I am compelled to add, in the very country that was stolen from them!**
>
> **Ellis Island was officially closed in November of 1954.**

Without speaking a word of the language, and with probably very little idea of what to expect, my family arrived in an America where in early 1911, there were only 144 miles of paved roads, where only 6% of all Americans had graduated from high school, yet 18% of households had a full-time servant or domestic help, where the average working wage was 22 cents per hour. And where drugs such as morphine, marijuana, and heroin were all available over the counter at pharmacies.

Like other immigrants before and after them, they made their way in their strange new home in a manner that I can only call heroic, with no idea what the future would bring for them, their new country and their old country.

Chapter 3
Growing Up in Scranton, Pennsylvania

"...the bestiality of the Romanov Family – those pogrom-mongers who drenched Russia in the blood of Jews, workers and revolutionaries..."
—Vladimir Lenin (1870–1924)
Communist revolutionary

"What was your first impression of America, Daddy?" I asked.

"I was disappointed to see an indoor toilet. I thought that Americans were very dirty to go to the bathroom inside. And near the kitchen yet. I really didn't like it and just couldn't understand why the toilet wasn't outside."

Over the years, I asked my father more and more questions. I wanted to know everything. And a year before he died, I recorded him as he told me yet again and in yet more detail about his life in Russia.

"Your Bubbe soon met a man, a widower, and married him, to make the burden lighter on your Uncle Sam. Joseph Dinner. Herman and I lived with them, but he was a real miser. He used to go to the saloon where you could get a big glass of beer for five cents and along with it, a free lunch of herring, pretzels, and cheese. He'd eat lunch, then load up his pockets with food for supper. He was worth some money and used to peddle dry goods from house to house. He had a daughter but sent her to live with his son in Patterson, NJ.

"He used to pick on my mother a lot and he didn't want to keep me. Bubbe told him that I wasn't going anywhere, that he'd go before I did. Once he threw a towel at her. I picked up a heavy soup ladle and I threw it at him. Hit him in the forehead. He grabbed a chair to hit me with, but I took a swing at him and gave him a black eye, which kept him out of work for several days.

"After that, I decided I'd better move out. I was twelve years old. People my mother knew rented me a room on the second floor of their home, clean, with a separate entrance. For one dollar a month.

"I went to school during the day and sold papers at night. I figured out that I could go to the theatre and work there until the late show let out at 11 PM. When it did, I'd hold just two or three papers. Often somebody would feel sorry for me and buy all of them. As soon as that person was out of sight, I'd run around the corner and grab two or three more. That's how I got rid of them quickly.

"But the entrance to my room was off an alley, which was muddy and dirty and had no lights. After I got back from the theater, I would stay on the street 10 or 15 minutes before I could get up enough nerve to run down the alley to my room. I would count to ten over and over and then chicken out each time. Finally, when I took off running, I was hoping that the iron gate to the house would be open so that I wouldn't lose any more time. Once I almost tripped over a drunk man and woman who were lying in the mud. As I ran by, the man hollered, "Hey buddy, you wanna be next?"

"But even when I got to my room, I was scared. It was still dark. The lights were from gas jets and my hands shook until they came on and I could close the door. But that didn't do much good for long, because then I would be scared again when it was time to turn the lights out. My main ambition in life then was to somehow get to bed before the room got dark.

"I cried myself to sleep every night and would wake up with the pillow soaked. I think I lived there like that for about six months. When your Bubbe asked how I was doing in the room, I always said everything was fine because I didn't want her to worry. I even didn't tell her when I checked myself into the hospital when I was very sick with what they told me was scarlet fever. You know, somebody should write a book about my life.

"Anyway, after that first six months, I then went to live with and work for my aunt, delivering orders from her store. She was my mother's brother's wife. My bedroom was a closet, about three and a half feet wide, maybe seven feet long. There were shelves over the cot and the door was left open for air. The first few mornings when I woke up, I hit my head on the shelf, having forgotten it was there.

"This aunt had no kids living in the house; they were all grown and on their own. I got up at 4:30 or 5:00 in the morning to go to market with a pushcart and came back around 6:00. I would have to deliver orders until 8:00 or 8:30, come home, have breakfast, then go to school. After school, I delivered orders again until supper, around 8 PM. Whenever there was time, she sent me outside with a big basket to go collect her customers' empty milk bottles. I was afraid then, too. Of the dogs.

"Now I have to tell you about the eggs. Three meals a day, two eggs each meal. Because my aunt's hands were so dirty, I wouldn't let her cook for me. I fried the eggs myself. But she told me I had to take my eggs out of the storage crate. Those were awful, so when she wasn't around, I would switch two of the fresh eggs for two in storage and remember where I put them. I had to remember because she always watched to see where I took the eggs from, but she never caught on, even though once in awhile a customer would complain about bad eggs.

Growing Up in Scranton, Pennsylvania

"I lived with that aunt for about a year, then moved in with my sister Fannie. She took Herman in, too. I think I quit school around then and got several different jobs. First, as an usher in the Academy Theatre in Scranton where they had Stock Company Road Show Plays. Stayed there until I was about 17 years old. Then as a sales clerk at Rosenberg Brothers Clothing Store on Pennsylvania Avenue, then two other local places until I becuase a salesman for Leeds Woolen Mills in Pittston, PA.

"In the meantime, my brother Sam, after first working for my mother's relatives in an overall factory, started his own manufacturing business, Anthracite Overall Company. My brother Harry became his partner. They also bought out Star Clothes in Norwich, NY and set Herman and me up in business there in 1923. We ran it until the stock market crashed in 1929, when we had to sell out. But we didn't lose too much, and were able to pay back Sam and Harry.

"During that time, when I was 24, I married Leona (Weiss). On August 31, 1924 to be exact, in Syracuse, when she was 22. We had a Jewish wedding and then we lived with Sam and his wife Sadie for a while. I became a US citizen on April 7, 1926 and Mort was born on July 14, 1926."

"Leona's brother Milton had a shoe store and hired me after we closed Star Clothing. Then, in 1933, Milt told me I should consider the insurance business, that he had recommended me to the manager of Metropolitan Life Insurance in Binghamton. It was during the Depression, but agents were making good salaries, so I went to work there. When we moved, I had $13 in my pocket, owed $985 to the bank, and your brother Mort was seven. But I stayed with Metropolitan until 1965, when I retired.

"Leona and I separated in 1941 and were divorced in 1944. I enlisted in the army on November 27, 1942, and served as a clerk and Private 1st Class in the Army Air Corps for six months, was discharged on May 27, 1943. I could have been out sooner, but my commanding officer kept me in exactly six months, so that I could qualify for medical care with the VA. I married your mother in 1944, and you know the rest."

While my father was growing up, learning to speak English with no trace of an accent, creating his life in America, Russia, which had the largest proportion of illiterates of any civilized country, was about to create a new chapter in its story, to eventually play a major part on the world stage.

World War 1, from 1914-1918, resulted in about 20 million deaths worldwide, including soldiers and civilians. More than 50,000 were Americans, but Russia lost an estimated 2-3 million lives, 500,000 of them Jews. (In 1914, there were 13 million Jews in the world and half of them lived in Russia.)

The British army lost 50,000 Jewish soldiers and the German army 100,000. Yet in 1917, in spite of the number of Jewish soldiers in combat,

there was so much anti-German feeling that Europeans attacked Jews with German names and conducted anti-Jewish riots.

* * *

Now, a necessary, interesting, and brief Russian history, or at least as brief as I can make it. Opposition to the war was fierce in Russia and contributed to the Tsar's unpopularity. By summer of 1915, resources and food were depleted and there were strikes and food riots. The Bolshevik Party opposed the war.

That August, the Tsar took command of the Navy, leaving behind much power in St. Petersburg in the hands of the Tsarina and Grigori Rasputin, the self-proclaimed mystic and holy man. Those two did nothing to improve the situation and in fact they angered the people even more.

In late 1906, Rasputin had begun acting as a healer for Alexei, the Tsar's and his wife Alexandra's son who suffered from hemophilia. He gained considerable influence with the Tsarina, but many considered him a charlatan.

In December of 1916, several from inside the Royal Court collaborated in a plot to murder Rasputin. One of the Monarchist princes invited him, along with other princes, to his palace where he served him cyanide-laced chocolates and Madeira wine with poison. Rasputin was a large man. It had no effect on him.

Consequently, the princes simply shot him. Several times. Rasputin ran outdoors, into the snow, stumbled, was beaten and kicked by the princes and shot many more times. When he was finally dead, they wrapped his body in chains and dumped him into a nearby canal. He was later found because a shoe had dropped off his foot and been overlooked at the shoreline.

By the third year of WWI, there was rationing. Hungry crowds roamed the streets, threw stones at police stations and through shop windows, and banged on doors, desperately searching for food.

On February 22nd, International Women's Day, 90,000 women and men rioted, yelled for bread, and demanded an end to the war and to the monarchy.

In March, realizing he had lost control, the Tsar abdicated, thus ending the Romanov Dynasty. His hated police were abolished, and a provisional government, under the liberal-minded leadership of Minister

Alexander Kerensky, was agreed upon. The United States was the first country to officially recognize this provisional government.

But this did not end the unrest. Violent crime turned the people of St. Petersburg into victims, and the Provisional government was unable to protect its citizens.

Vladimir Lenin, sensing that the timing was right, returned from a decade of self-imposed exile in Western Europe. After travelling eight days from Switzerland, through Germany, Sweden and Finland, he arrived in Finland Station in Petrograd, where he was met by Stalin. Once in Petrograd, Stalin, then editor of the newspaper Pravda, protected Lenin when necessary by moving him from house to house while Lenin set about organizing his fellow Bolsheviks, based on his interpretation of the writings of philosopher Karl Marx (a descendant of rabbis).

The provisional government had abolished the Pale of Settlement and given women the right to vote in 1917, (three years before America granted women's suffrage). But then came the October Revolution, when, under Lenin's leadership, the Bolsheviks took power.

Two months later, after a vote that established the Bolsheviks' Revolutionary Government based on workers' control of production and the rights of peasants to own land, the government established by law equal rights for men and women in work and marriage, the right to divorce, to maternity support, free universal education and the decriminalization of homosexuality.

Sounds good, doesn't it? But then, Lenin appointed Felix Dzerzhinsky to create the Cheka, the secret police, the forerunner of the KGB. And the Bolsheviks soon established a police state, a dictatorship.

Lenin, whose maternal grandfather was Jewish (a well-kept secret during his life) spoke out against anti-Semitism and wanted to appoint Leon Trotsky as Minister of the Interior, but Trotsky declined because he knew that his enemies would attack him because he was a Jew.

Interesting fact. Before Bolshevik rule, in June of 1917, Great Britain sent writer Somerset Maugham, who was already working for the British Secret Service Intelligence, later known as MI-6, to Russia. His mission – to prevent the Bolsheviks from seizing power. Some believe that that mission included killing or having Lenin killed. He failed on both counts, obviously.

Lenin was more successful with his murderous missions. After they had been arrested and held in isolation for almost a year, ex-Tsar Nicholas and his family were executed the night of July 16-17, 1918, under Lenin's order, with bullets and bayonets. Their bodies were dumped into a mineshaft and sprinkled with sulfuric acid, to make it difficult to identify them. They weren't discovered until 1979.

In addition to the 2-3 million lives lost during World War I, Russia's Great Famine of 1921-1922, the worst natural disaster in Europe since the Black Plague of the Middle Ages, resulted in at least five million deaths, perhaps as many as eight million, due to famine and the resulting typhus spread by lice and cholera. The famine was caused primarily by drought and the policies of the Bolsheviks.

To understand how truly gruesome it was, one needs to know that butcher shops sold human flesh and many ate corpses. Some mothers had to make the horrific decision to kill their own children, especially babies, to feed their other children. (During an earlier Russian famine, from 1601-1645, one could knowingly buy in the market pies made of human flesh.)

Lenin asked the US for help and Herbert Hoover, at the time Secretary of Commerce under President Warren Harding and also head of the American Relief Association, launched what has been called the greatest humanitarian operation ever, perhaps saving more lives than anyone who has ever lived. He actually thought the food aid might stop the Bolsheviks and lead to regime change but it was reported by PBS's American Experience, The Great Famine, that the US aid may have actually saved the Soviet regime instead of overthrowing it.

The country was known as Soviet Russia until 1924 when it became the Union of Soviet Socialist Republics (USSR). Lenin died in 1924 and against his wishes, Joseph Stalin took control of the Soviet Communist Party. Lenin had survived an assassination attempt when he was 38 and never had the bullet to his lung or the one at the base of his neck removed. He had three strokes in the two years before he died of a massive cerebral hemorrhage. However, because he also had seizures, which are unusual in stroke patients, according to the NY Times of May 8, 2012, there are those who suspect that he was poisoned, most likely by Stalin.

Stalin's birth name was Joseph Dzhugashvili, but he changed it to Stalin because in Russian Stalin meant "Man of Steel" and he thought that he would thus be perceived as a man of strength. For the following four years, there was much infighting and shifting of political positions. He consolidated his rule by creating a police state of paranoia, cruelty and murder, by reviving anti-Semitism, blaming Jews for Bolshevism and the Revolution, and creating Communism as we knew it.

But that wasn't enough for the pathological, sadistic Stalin. Until he died in 1953, this small man, 5 feet 4 inches, with scars on his face from small pox, with a webbed foot and a withered left arm that was shorter than his right, a result of an accident when he was 12, and with maybe unequaled paranoia and brutality in a world leader, conducted a reign of terror with purges, persecutions, executions, torture and a manufactured famine. During the purges of the 1930's, it has been estimated that between 600,000 to 1,750,000 people were killed, all who Stalin thought or imagined were traitors or disloyal.

Others died from famine and starvation. He created a forced famine in the Ukraine from 1932-1933 to destroy the kulaks, the wealthy farmers who had owned a lot of land, although all peasants suffered. He did that to collectivize privately held land and to make the landowners scapegoats for his failures. Many were exiled to labor camps where they were killed. The total number of deaths from the famine is estimated to be 7,000,000.

In 1934, Stalin formally established in Eastern Siberia, in an area called Birobidzhan, a Jewish Autonomous Region. Because it is remote, Jews did not want to go there and it never became a center for Jewish life. Today fewer than 10% of its inhabitants have Jewish roots.

World War II began in 1939, and lasted until 1945. During that time, Russian soldiers and civilians suffered almost unimaginable losses. An estimated 60 million worldwide died in that war, 6.3 million of them Jews. According to *Izvestia*, the USSR lost 26,452,000 soldiers and civilians, almost half of all the war's deaths. Other Russian journalists and politicians say there were over 40 million casualties, both civilian and military.

It is impossible to know the real numbers of unnatural deaths that Stalin was responsible for during his 30-year rule. It is widely estimated that it was between 20-60 million, (not counting military deaths). Dissident writer Alexander Solzhenitsyn claimed with certainty that it was closer to 60 million.

It could be argued that Stalin was responsible for his second wife's death too. On November 9, 1932, after a fight at a dinner party when he angrily demeaned her opinions, she went into her bedroom and shot herself.

While he was alive, the populace referred to him as Uncle Joe. Today, Russian school textbooks refer to him as a great leader.

Chapter 4
The Other Dicksteins

"As in nature, as in art, so in grace; it is rough treatment that gives souls, as well as stones, their luster"
—Thomas Guthrie (1803–1873)
Scottish preacher and philanthropist

My father said I knew the rest, and I do. His life wasn't wonderful, not the parts that followed, or the parts he left out of his narrative. How much do you, the reader, want to know? How much should I, the daughter, the half-sister, the niece, the cousin, reveal? And which is more important, family loyalty or truth?

My grandfather
Chaim Lazar Dickstein
(1867-1910)

My "Bubbe" (grandmother)
Socia Alperowitz Dickstein
(1863-1951)

Paths of Stones

Before I decide that, let me tell you about my father's immediate family, and what they did with their lives in the new country.

Bubbe's Russian passport, issued on December 15, 1910, listed her as Sosia or Sosha Zalmonovna Dickstein. (The ship's manifest listed her as Sasche.)

Age: 42 years old (But elsewhere it says she was born in 1869)
Jewish
Place of Birth: Kyrenetskaya
Bourgeois
Occupation: Mishanka, or farmer
Widow
Sister named Rochel or Rachel Krauss
Hometown, Gluboka
US destination: Son Sam Dickstein's home, Rose Street, Scranton, PA.

My brave little grandmother settled in Scranton, became Sarah, and lived in America for 45 years, speaking no English, only Yiddish. She smoked cigarettes and tried to blow the smoke away whenever any family approached. Bubbe never worked, but at some point, she bought a building, against the advice of her sons Sam and Harry. She lived in a multi-level apartment on the top floor, while on the first floor was a furniture store. When she eventually moved out, the health department condemned the building and when one of her grandchildren went to investigate, he saw that each room had a bath and plumbing. Evidently, it had been a house of prostitution at one time.

After her 22-year marriage to my grandfather, my Bubbe married four more times, twice to the same man. She outlived all her husbands and because she had so many wedding bands, she was nicknamed the "Ring Lady" in the Jewish Home in Scranton where she spent her last years. One of her husbands, Joseph Dinner, was the father of two brothers who married Bubbe's daughters Ida and Fannie, so they were not only sisters, but sisters-in-law. He was the man my father punched. Bubbe later married another man named Cohen, but she quickly divorced him because "his ideas were too young." One husband was someone named Morris Chaim Yasseen. I never met any of them.

Family lore states that Bubbe's grandfather had three wives, four sons (three of whom were rabbis) and two daughters, and he lived to 103 years old. Her father Zalmon (Solomon) Alperowitz had four or five wives and 19 children, and a half-brother, Chaim Yosef (Hyman Joseph). I only know with certainty that her father died in Scranton, PA in 1919 at age 72, that his son Louis Alperin died at age 66 in 1956 and ran the pants factory, and that Bubbe had a sister Anna, a brother Abraham, and a half-brother

The Other Dicksteins

Solomon who died in Scranton at age 72 in 1929. There was no mention of any other siblings.

When I was little and Bubbe had by then moved into the Home, we often went to visit her. One time, I remember we walked down a long hall that smelled like a dusty old attic to find her seated on a bench by a window. The sun was so bright behind her that she was visible only as a small silhouette as we approached her. I scampered up to her so that I could snuggle on her lap, but I remember being very careful because she was so very tiny and frail.

Her health was fine until at age 87, she got up in the middle of the night to go to the bathroom, opened the wrong door, and tumbled down a set of stairs. Apparently she didn't live much longer after that, and in 1951, early in the morning of July 1st, Socia bat Zalmon (daughter of Zalmon) died at age 88.(Her death certificate and gravestone states July 1st as her date of death; other documents list the 5th. There is also some discrepancy over the year of her birth, as was common with many immigrants then. She is listed in various places as being born in 1863, 1864, 1866, and 1869. Her last name on my father's death certificate was Alpert, shortened from the original Alperowitz)

My father said I couldn't attend her funeral, telling me I was too young. I didn't just ask to go, I demanded!

"I'm a big girl. I am five years old now!"

I convinced him.

After the private viewing for the family, they closed the casket. As we were walking away, I ran back and asked them to please open the casket again so that I could see her one more time. They did that for me. Thus, I was the last family member to see her, and I was so very proud of that.

Only recently, I learned that my grandfather was born in or around 1867. When married, every year in the spring, he planted cherry trees to harvest in the fall. One year, a severe storm ruined his plantings and he lost everything. That apparently was the motivation for him to move to America. He was first booked on the SS *Patricia*, scheduled to sail for America on August 16, 1907. For some reason I've been unable to determine, his name was crossed off on that ship's manifest, and he instead sailed in steerage almost two weeks later out of Hamburg on the SS *Blucher*, which arrived in NY on September 9th. That manifest listed his occupation as tailor, his fare paid for by Sam Dickstein.

He had with him a six-year-old Szepsie Rosin, listed as my grandfather's nephew and described in the manifest as fair skinned, blue eyed with freckles. His father Yoschel Rosin was living at the same address as my Uncle Sam. I still haven't found out the relationship we had with Szepsie or Yoschel.

Miriam (Mirke) Dickstein
(1889 – 1913)

My father called my grandfather Herman, but I found a 1910 census that has him listed as Hyman, age 43 and a boarder at 69 East 114th Street, NY, the same address Fanny went and where her uncle Josef Rosen lived. I know he died in 1910, but have not been able to find a death certificate for him.

Mirke Dickstein is a bit of mystery. Hours and days of research revealed little information about her. No documentation of her coming to America, no definite name for her here, no marriage or death records. Her sister Ida told me that she went by the name Miriam in America, and that she moved to Oak Forest, Illinois, where the family says she died from tuberculosis in 1913 when she was about 24 or 25 years old. Her siblings all said, "Such a shame, she was the pretty one."

Samuel (Shmula or Schmula) Mesa
April 15, 1886 – April 6, 1956

My uncle Sam, the oldest child, 14 years older than my father, came to America in 1904 and went to Scranton. After working for his Alperin cousins, in 1910 he founded the Anthracite Overall Company in the 200 block of Franklin Avenue. He later moved his plant to Pennsylvania Avenue, and then became co-owner of another business called Loaf-eez, as well as the Lackawanna Pants Manufacturing Company.

It was he who brought all of his family to America. And who saved two relatives, young girls, from Auschwitz. I know no more details except that one fled to NY and the other to Israel.

Sam petitioned to become a naturalized citizen of America on July 12, 1910, after signing the Declaration of Intention that stated he renounced his allegiance to Nicholas II, Emperor of all the Russias and that "I am not an anarchist: I am not a polygamist nor a believer in the practice of polygamy…"

My uncle had three sons—George, Howard, and Stanley—and he was very active in the Jewish community and was very generous to that community. Sam once told Stanley, "I don't know how much I will leave you in worldly goods, but I do know that

The Other Dicksteins

you will never go down the street and have people say, "There's the son of that son-of-a-bitch Sam."

Sam and his wife Sadie appeared to have a good marriage, although when he got frustrated, he would say to her, "You're like a cow that gives a whole bucket of the sweetest milk. And then kicks the pail over."

Sam died from heart failure on April 6, 1956 after spending four weeks in the hospital. His obituary stated: "He was a philanthropist, a prominent worker and contributor to every worthwhile civic campaign, especially the United Jewish Appeal. He served as treasurer of the 1940 drive of the UJA and was listed in the 1941 edition of the Builders of Scranton." He was a member or served on the Board of Directors of many Jewish organizations: Temple Israel, B'nai B'rith, the Jewish Home, Zionist Organization of America, Israel Lodge, Jewish Community Center, and the Jewish Federation, to name some, as well as non-Jewish organizations, such as the Scranton Lodge of Elks.

Fanny (Frumpke)
May 31, 1894 – November, 1972

I was ten years old when he died and had not seen him often, mostly at weddings and bar mitzvahs. I don't know how religious he was. But I do know I thought he had a kind face.

(My uncle Sam was not the Samuel Dickstein who served in Congress from 1923-1944, became a New York State Supreme Court Justice and sold secrets to the Russians for $1,250 per month from 1937 to 1940. As far as I know, there is no familial relationship.)

Again, there is missing information: I couldn't find any ship's manifest for Fanny. She apparently came to America alone in 1908, when she was around 14. Supposedly, for safety reasons, she pretended to be the daughter of a woman with six children.

In the 1910 census, Fanny is listed as living in Manhattan as a boarder with a family named Litman, and employed as a garment worker. I'm guessing that she married her first husband, Frank Dinner, in 1912 or 1913, since her daughter Esther was born in 1913 and her son Louis in 1916. Dad and his brother Herman were living with them during the 1920 census.

On December 17, 1933, Fanny remarried Frank, a year after she was divorced from him on December 23, 1932. At some point, they divorced again and he died in 1954. Her third marriage was to James Reichel, a cousin, son of Nathan and Anna Alperowitz (my grandmother's sister). They were together only about a year before they divorced.

Her fourth marriage was to Sam Dinner, her first husband's brother. I'm told this was her happiest marriage and they were together until his death.

(To clarify, my grandmother married the father, Joseph Dinner; her daughter Fanny married his son Frank, twice, and then later his son Sam; her daughter Ida married his son James.)

When I was young, I saw Aunt Fannie, who was six years older than my dad, the most of all my father's siblings. Thus I knew well her daughter Esther and son Louis, and kept in touch with them until each of them died.

We often went to Fanny's home on Madison Avenue in Scranton, or her house on Lake Winola. Because she bought and sold antiques, I loved looking at her beautiful things. And I especially loved to sit on her porch overlooking the lake, on the comfortable white wicker furniture, listening to her and my father speak Yiddish.

What I loved most about my Aunt Fannie? Her delicious, creamy scrambled eggs. Still the best ever!

As a small child in Russia, born in the Belarus town of Dokshytsy 16 miles south of Glubockoye, Harry was about two to four months old when he got sick and then died. Or so they thought. The family prepared for the burial, and at the home, according to *shemira*, the Jewish tradition of sitting with a dead body until it is buried, a male guardian, or *shomer*, watched over his body, which had a candle beside it. The man saw the candle flicker, put his head down to Harry's chest, heard his heartbeat, and went running for help.

Harry lived, but he didn't talk or walk until he was three years old. And no one ever knew what happened.

Harry (Handel or Gendel) Feb 3, 1896 – June 10, 1984

When he arrived in America, Harry first lived with his relative David Alperin and began working as a tailor, making overalls for miners in his brother Sam's Anthracite Overall Co. They got an army contract to make khaki uniforms during War War I. When the war ended and then the mining business waned, together they started Loaf-Eez sportswear for women, especially tall women.

(In Brooklyn in 1915, Harry married his first wife, Eva Reichel. She was also his first cousin, the daughter of his mother's sister. Eva died on January 9, 1960. One year later, he married his second wife, Ruth Smith Shapiro. She died in 1979, five years before Harry.)

The Other Dicksteins

Harry and Eva had three children: Miriam, Herbert and Shirley. While Miriam and Herb worked with their father, Shirley became quite accomplished on her own. She first played the piano, then the harp. Two days after her graduation from Cornell, where she majored in music and literature, she enlisted in the WAVES and was given the task of teaching aerial gunnery to Navy flyers, "… because I was so good in math, which plays a big part in aiming and firing weapons at moving targets."

Shirley and her husband Seymour Hollenberg had only one child because she had had a ruptured tubal pregnancy, and their first child, Abraham, born in August 1948, lived only four days before he succumbed to pneumonia. Their second son David did his undergraduate work at Columbia, and then his graduate study in architecture at the University of Pennsylvania. His son Matt is a professional musician who I haven't seen since his bar mitzvah, but who I am happy to be in touch with on Facebook.

Shirley Dickstein Hollenberg
(1923 – 2013)

When Shirley was young and in the car with her father, they drove past a depressing place called the School for the Friendless. It made a deep impression on her. After her son David went to high school, she began volunteering at that same school, renamed Friendship House, a social services program for children with social, emotional, and mental health problems.

Forty years later, she was still a volunteer, and also a board member and a benefactor. In 2003, a 3,100 sq. ft. building was dedicated to her, called the Shirley Hollenberg Early Childhood Center.

Shirley, the cousin I was closest to, lived a month short of 90 years. She began all her letters to me with "Honey" and she signed all those letters "Kisses, love you so much."

Her father, like Sam, was very involved in the Jewish community. He was named in 1981 in the *Who's Who in World Jewry*. In 1951, he was part of a small reception committee at the Scranton airport that greeted Israel's ambassador to Washington, D.C., Abba Eban, who later became Israel's Prime Minister.

Harry's achievements were also read into the congressional record by Congressman Joseph McDade on March 14, 1974, for having been given the B'nai B'rith Americanism Award. McDade stated, "For nearly 50 years, Harry Dickstein gave himself tirelessly to the betterment of his community.

(Some years later, McDade was arrested on a beach in Florida for exposing himself. I love doing research.)

Harry was also president of the Scranton campus of Penn State and his children established the Harry Dickstein Memorial Scholarship at Penn State "for children with a financial need who demonstrated academic achievement, leadership in high school activities, and contributions to the community."

Although he liked supporting Jewish organizations, Harry had little use for religion. To him, it was a social function, not philosophical. As for his philanthropy, his mother said that if he didn't get his name in the paper, he'd never give away any money.

Harry liked the cold weather, not hot. He hated cigar and cigarette smoke, played gin rummy and pinochle, loved to fish, and preferred fresh bread to chocolate.

Apparently he also liked women. When I was a freshman in college at Syracuse, one of my friends from high school invited me to the University of Pennsylvania for Homecoming Weekend and fixed me up with a date. I took the Greyhound bus, a nine-hour ride that had only a brief layover in Scranton, but long enough for me to get out and walk around. A block from the station, I spotted a familiar face in topcoat and hat. It had been a while since I had seen him so I ran up to him, calling out "Uncle Harry!" He grabbed me and gave me a big hug and kiss. I smiled and thought, "How nice." And then, it became obvious he hadn't heard my greeting.

"Now, who are you?" he asked.

I also don't think Harry and my father liked one another much. Harry came to visit my dad while he was dying. He walked into the apartment, looked at my feeble, failing father sitting on the sofa, and said, "You know vat? Can you imagine, at my age, I still have all my teeth!

The rest of their conversation was not memorable.

There is an old Yiddish saying, *Ale tseyn zoln dir aroysfaln, nor eyner zol dir blaybn af tsonveytik*— May all your teeth fall out but one remain as a toothache.

Now that sounds like my Aunt Ida! My Aunt Ida, who had an answer and a solution for everything. Once, while she was visiting her daughter during Yom Kippur, a day of fasting in the Jewish faith, Ida reached into the refrigerator to get some breakfast. Her daughter Esther told her that she couldn't eat. Ida insisted that she wasn't interested in observing the religious holiday. Frustrated by her mother's stubbornness, her daughter said, "Mom, when in Rome, you do as the Romans do."

Ida (Chaika) Dickstein
(1899 – 1987)
Buried in the Knollwood Park/Mt. Judah Cemetery, Row "M" in the back near the fence.

Ida said no more, shrugged, and retreated to her bedroom, only to reappear at the top of the stairs half an hour later, a suitcase in each hand.

"What are you doing?" her daughter stammered.

"I don't like it in Rome," Ida replied, "I am going to Paris."

She ate, of course.

When I was a child, my parents used to take me to the Bronx and drop me off at Ida's 181st Street apartment for the weekend, where I was the one who wouldn't eat— I wanted only tuna fish and only got gefilte fish. When I was older, we visited Ida in Miami Beach—or Miami "Bitch," as she pronounced it—(later called *Shtetl* by the Sea in the 1970s and 1980s, because so many Jewish retirees settled there since it was so affordable after the economic downturn in the 1970s). Miami "Bitch" was where she lived for fifty years, and where we went to dinner at Juniors, Pumpernicks, sometimes Wolfies, or the Rascal House on Collins Avenue, and then ate the yummy pastries we bought from a nearby Jewish bakery. We always made sure there were leftovers for Aunt Ida's refrigerator.

After my father died, I continued to visit Ida whenever I could. On one trip to Miami in May of 1985, she wasn't feeling well. Her eyes were swollen and her head dropped to her chest often. She'd lost 25 pounds, but her stomach was bloated and she had trouble with her bowels. She was weak. At one point, she said, "It's terrible to be so sick". Her eyes filled and she put her head down.

Yet she still had her sense of humor. As we sat outside her front door at her 11th Street apartment and watched the neighborhood in motion, she pointed to a car on the street and said, "Look at that car. They steal everything here, even the headcups."

And when a heavy woman walked by, braless, with a massive chest, Aunt Ida remarked, "There she goes with her two bullets".

But this visit, she was more serious than usual, too. She told me again about her daughter Esther's stroke that left her half paralyzed. "And I have to live to see that," she said, shaking her head, tightening her lips. (Aunt Ida didn't live to see that her granddaughter Miriam, Esther's daughter, became afflicted with Parkinson's Disease and died from it in 2020.)

After about an hour, she had to go lie down. I sat alone outside, looking at the skyline, the Art Deco buildings, listening to the Spanish voices and the loud music on car radios, remembering all the times I had come to Miami Beach with my father.

I was afraid I wouldn't see Aunt Ida again, but when I visited a few months later, she looked much better and was in great spirits.

That's why when she told me she had tried to commit suicide, my mouth dropped open.

"You know," she said, laughing, "I tried to kill myself last spring, soon after I saw you. I put on my nicest nightgown, put a note on the kitchen table telling everybody I loved them and if I could do anything for them from the other side, I would. Then I took eight sleeping pills—I had taken one once and slept for two days and the doctor said they were a mistake and I should throw them out—that's all right for him to say, he didn't spend $10 for them—and went to lie down. And you know what happened? An hour later, I had to get up to go to the bathroom. You see, even the devil doesn't want me."

The Aunt Ida I loved was back, in good form, and we were going to lunch!

Ida dressed up in her best clothes, elegant shoes with no nylons, and although it was 75 degrees outside, her mink stole.

"Won't you be hot?" I asked.

"Listen, I can't be fancy so often."

Aunt Ida on a hot day in Miami Beach

She suggested Wolfies for lunch because it was close, but I told her to think of someplace nicer, somewhere she couldn't get to on her own. We decided to go to the Fountainbleu Hotel. I had spent a New Year's Eve there in 1965 and it was impressive then. But the service this day was awful—the roast beef tough. Neither of us liked the macaroni salad, but when I returned from making a telephone call, it had disappeared from my plate. Aunt Ida didn't believe in waste.

"I eat a lot now, for the worms. They should have a party when I die. Let's get dessert," she said.

She came back from the buffet table with crème puffs, orange layer cake, cherry crumb cake, and strawberry-pineapple cheesecake, and bless her, she ate every one. With her last bite, like someone who had just completed a monumental task, she put down her fork, looked up, and decisively declared that she was ready to go home.

"So soon?" I asked.

"Listen, I'm tired, I'm not used to eating so much. How much did it cost? Six dollars. Six dollars for all this food! It was worth it, even though it wasn't so good."

I asked her if she'd like to walk around the hotel. "I can't walk. It's my shoes. You know, I bought them ten years ago, for $28. They're good shoes but I never wore them. I got to wear them; they match my dress. But they hurt my feet."

So we sat on a bench in the lobby for a while and she talked about the family.

"Seven of us who always tried to outdo one another. But I loved your father the best. He had a miserable life, we all did, but he had it the hardest of all of us. Nobody helped him, even when he was a twelve-year-old kid, living alone in a new country. He was so clean, so handsome. It's a shame he had to die like that, from that ugly cancer. I miss him."

She started to cry. Me too. After wiping my tears and blowing my nose, I said, almost in a whisper,

"Aunt Ida, tell me about Russia."

"Russia, *bist meshugeh*? Are you crazy? Who wants to remember such a hard life!

"We had chickens who lived under the stove in the house, laid their eggs there, and we had to crawl under it to get them. And when the Russians soldiers got drunk, they would break our windows and we all had to hide under couches. Our landlord took care of us, but the Russians didn't like the Jews.

"I think my grandfather was born in the town of Voropayevo and my Aunt Anna settled there with her husband, Naathan Reichel, before they came to the US, maybe in 1906.

"And I remember the name Alpert, grandparents I think, but I never met them. When they died, we inherited only pots and pillows.

"But everybody did alright in this country. You know there's only three of us left now. But all my brothers and sisters, they made a lot of money and they saved a lot of money. It was spending it they didn't do so good. Only me, I gave mine all away."

When it was time to leave, the parking lot attendant brought the car and started to help her in.

"Oy, be careful," she said. "Be gentle vit all deez crème puffs."

As we got closer to her apartment, she said "You know, the mirror should break from how ugly you get when you get so old. And I used to be pretty. I even had my nose fixed. But I just live from day to day now. You know something else? Sometimes you have to be lucky to die. Every night I want to just go to sleep and not wake up."

In April of 1986, Aunt Ida got her wish. I got a call from an Officer William Young of the Miami Beach Police. When I returned the call, the police told me what I feared. My Aunt Ida had lived her last day. My wonderful Aunt Ida had become case number 86-24973. Cause of death: arterial sclerotic cardiovascular disease.

But she died as she wanted—in her sleep.

A few years later, I wrote a piece about her for the *Boston Globe*, because Ida Shapiro was a real character, an original, and as genuine a person as one could ever meet. She worked hard her whole life. Ran a grocery store in Scranton, a boarding house in the Bronx, a restaurant. Said that some days she couldn't even go to sleep because she drank so much coffee, 17 to 18 cups a day. But she sent both her kids to college.

I still have the letter she wrote to my father when she learned that he had cancer. "I didn't sleep for two nights when I found out you were sick. If there is a heaven, you will go because you had so much hell here on this earth. You are my favorite brother, and you had it the hardest of all of us."

My father replied, "Ida, I was delighted to hear from you. The mere fact that we haven't written to each other much doesn't mean I haven't thought of you often. As to my sickness, don't worry. I don't. I've lived my full life. Age 77 is a great deal longer than most people live and the way I feel is it is just as natural to die as to be born. When I see some of the old people my age, the way they look and get around, I would rather be dead than alive. I'm not used to that kind of life. To sit around in a rocking chair is not my kind of life."

Each visit I made to Miami, I kept a record of what Ida said, because even back then I thought that with each generation, we would lose more and more of that *shtetl* mentality, the wisdom, and the strength that enabled so many like her to address life head-on, with no embellishments or excuses, and certainly no pretense. But with humor, most definitely that humor I mentioned earlier. I think you might get to know her better from her own words:

- "We had a slaughterhouse in Russia, and a general store where we sold the meat, with a partner. Then, my father went to America. He was good-natured, but had a mean temper and he used to beat me up pretty bad when I did bad things. Once so bad I had to stay in bed for a week because I stole some cherries.
- "My mother, who was beautiful, I think she had a sweetheart.
- "On the ship to America, we got very little food in steerage. I was 12 then and I used to go work with the sailors. I peeled potatoes and then hid bananas, apples, and pears in my apron so that I could bring them to my family.
- When we got to America, my stepfather didn't want me living with him and my mother, so I went to NY when I was 13 and worked for 25 cents a day in a house, cleaning, washing dishes, for a dressmaker in New York. I went to school for a half-day, then she even had me making silk flowers besides the housework, had me working day and night. Finally I wrote my mother and told her to come get me or I would commit suicide. So next I went to live with my brothers Harry and Sam.
- I didn't like America at first. I wanted to go back to Russia, where I used to wander freely in the fields and pick berries and mushrooms.
- I had only one dress and every Sunday, I washed and ironed it.
- You see these photos on the wall; this one is after I had my nose fixed.
- Once an engineer was in love with me, he was so handsome, like a doctor he looked.
- I don't know where I learned to do all I did. I made rugs, knitted, worked hard to put my kids through college. You see these dolls sitting on the sofa? I bought them naked and made all their clothes.

The Other Dicksteins

- Not long ago, I got lost. Nobody speaks English here. I asked and asked for directions and they kept saying, "Do you speak Spanish?" I got so mad, I finally shouted back to one, "Do you speak Jewish?"

- They should mix the races; there would be more peace on earth.

- What's on TV? Oy, on Sunday you have to live with Jesus. Can't they let him rest in peace? I hate the priests and the rabbis, *gonifs* (thieves) all of them, all they want is money.

- You must help those who don't have. What, I'm going to take it with me. I have what I need, a refrigerator filled with food, a nice apartment. I give to the Cubans, and especially to the ones who work so hard.

- My mother said I was the dumb one, that I would give everything away. Is it so dumb to help people who need it so badly?

- I'm 85 years old next month and I don't depend on nobody. But, it's a lonely life. I feed the cats. There is one that follows me back and forth here. Somebody should take a picture of it. I bet they'd get paid $35.

- So smart this cat, she sits down on the curb looking up, waiting for me to come. I feed her early in the morning, so the neighbors won't see and get mad. My mother always said, "If it is a living thing, it has to eat."

- I'm too stout now, but what else do I have? No children here, no friends, only the cat is my friend, and that's only if I feed him, so what else can I enjoy but to eat?

- You know, I'm not so stupid. At the Roney Plaza Pub, they have the best breads. I get dressed up, I take a cab and I eat there once a month. I tell the waitress she'll get a better tip if she should bring me an extra loaf of rye and a quarter pound of butter. Nobody would think to do what I do. I cut the loaf in half, put all the butter inside, then when I get home, I take the butter out. What, I should let it go to waste?

- My brother Herman, that *mamzer* (bastard), you think he could take me out to dinner once in awhile. He has a hotel here, he's a millionaire. Obligations he has, he says, and then he says he doesn't bother nobody. I told him that's the trouble with him, that he doesn't bother with anyone. Me he should bother a little more.

- And you think an education makes a difference? Herman went to college. Let me tell you something—college doesn't give you brains. You got to be born with character, and he doesn't have any, education and all!

- My sister Fanny, my brother Sam, they were angels."

- Harry, my brother Harry, I call him Hitler.

- Your father had a hard, hard life. That's why he was so stingy. Nobody ever gave to him. You were the light in his life, but he wasn't nice to your mother, or his first wife. He didn't treat his women right. But he suffered; we all suffered.

- I don't know how my family got so stingy. Thank God I'm not like that, and thank God they can't take it with them. They'd be worse.

- The doctor told me I'd never walk again, I have such trouble with my feet. But I walk. I don't give up.

- You see that woman across the street, the one with the tennis racquet? She's going to exercise. She exercises every day, she's strong like iron. You know what, exercise, schmexercise, she'll still die!

- You don't need a man. You know what they are like, most of those men? Like the dogs I see on the street, running from one female to the next, sniffing them all.

- My mother married a Dinner when she came to America. Joseph. When he died, she cried. I asked her," What, he was so good to you, that mamzer, that you cry because he's gone?" "No," she said, "I'm crying he didn't die sooner."

- When I was 18, I married his son James, my sister Fanny married two of his sons. So my sister and I were sister-in-laws, too. And, we each named our daughters Esther. But none of those Dinner guys were any damn good. My mother said, in Yiddish, and this isn't very nice, but it's funny ...."*What do you think, from shit can come honey?*"

- And then my mother married her third husband, somebody named Cohen, then Jasseen. She was really happy with Jasseen; he was a wonderful person. They lived together about 12 years until he died, and she never married again.

- She was religious, kept kosher. None of us kids kept kosher, so I told her, when we all die, you'll go to heaven and be alone and we will all be in hell because we are not kosher. Aren't you going to be lonesome, won't you want to see your children? "I'm too old already to change," Bubbe said.

- I left my first husband once. He was no good, but I had to go back because of my daughter. When I went to work in the factory, I left her with a Christian family. They didn't take care of her. I went to pick her up and her back was burned. So I went back to my husband, and then I had my son. Later, I divorced him.

- I was 19 when I had my daughter Esther and 23 when Harry was born, both in Scranton. Later I moved to the Bronx where I had a rooming house, 42 rooms, six apartments with seven rooms each, three floors. All by myself, without a husband. I even spoke Portuguese to the tenants. It was too much work. I worked only for my kids so that one day, they could work even in the White House. I sent my daughter to nursing school, gave her jewelry and antiques, piano lessons. And my son I sent to college.

- But my second husband, Eugene Shapiro, oh how he loved me. A little crazy, he had an operation in the head before I met him. I didn't know; they experimented on him like a monkey. He had—what do you call them when you get excited—seizures. I went to the doctor and said I'd give him anything if he could make my husband well. The doctor told me if he were well, he wouldn't treat me so good.

- You know, when I came home and said my feet were tired, he would wash them, massage them, and then kiss them. Can you imagine a man who could love you so much?

The Other Dicksteins

- Men need someone to care for them. I wasn't so giving. I was kind of cold-blooded, but I was lucky, I found a man who was crazy, so he was crazy about me.

- I've had other boyfriends since, some nice ones. They're all right until they want me to go to bed with them. I won't let them touch me. I need that at my age?

- It's a shame to get so old, so ugly. I look in the mirror and envy your father. I hope he's got it better on the other side than he had it on this one. Me, I can hardly lift my arms to get my dress on, I have to take cortisone shots for my arthritis, but thank God, I don't need nobody.

- I don't know. I got two dead feet, arthritis, no teeth. You give me a hat and a broom and I could fly.

- People ask if I feel good. Just what d'you think can feel good when you're 87?

- "I'm afraid this will be the last time you see me," says Aunt Ida, as I give her a hug and a kiss. "No," I say, "you're not even sick."

- "No," she says, "but when I wake up in the morning, I'm dead."

I met my Uncle Herman only once, in December of 1965 when my father and I visited him in Miami Beach. Herman was shocked to see us; he and my father hadn't spoken in 40 years. I believe he was kind of the black sheep in the family, because no one had anything nice to say about him or had much to do with him, including my father. In fact, the entire family was not happy when he divorced his wife Lydia, a professional singer, after 40 some years. Their one daughter, Lorna, stopped talking to him after the divorce. I don't know if or how long their estrangement lasted. Herman was the only one who was college educated, paid for by Sam and Harry, and he did visit Aunt Ida in Miami Beach on occasion. He had TB when he was younger, lost a lung, and went to the sanatorium in Liberty, NY. After that, he stayed with my Uncle Harry's family in Scranton for a couple of months to more fully recover. My sweet cousin Shirley, kind to everyone, called him a disgusting person.

When he got better, he went to work for Anthracite Overalls. He then lived in Los Angeles for a while, where he worked in real estate. His in-laws lived in Florida and he moved there around 1960 and bought a hotel in Miami Beach on 17th Street. I think he also owned two other small ones. In retirement, he lived at 2301 Collins Avenue.

Herman had a long torso and short legs. He also had a deep voice. I was told he was very glib. That he was a smooth talker. And that he was a show off who drove a big, flashy Cadillac. When he was a paperboy, he often sold to people who drove Pierce Arrows and he always wanted one. By the time he could afford it, they stopped making that classic car.

I remember only that on our visit, my father asked him to cash a check for him and Herman said no. From the look on my father's face, I surmised correctly then that that was the last time I'd see Herman.

Back: Sam, Ida, and Harry. Middle: Herman, Simon
Front: Fanny with baby Esther, my Bubbe, Mirke
(Between 1912 and 1914)

Simon (my father), Aunt Ida, my Bubbe, Aunt Fanny, Uncle Harry (ca 1950)

My half-brother Mort
(July 14, 1926 – July 17, 2008)

I have two sepia baby photos of my half-brother Mort. The pictures aren't dated, but seated upright in a chair wearing a blousy top and leggings, he looks to be about five to seven months old. In one of the photos, he is leaning to his right, peering away from the camera, with a big smile on his face. In the other photo, he is sitting up straight with a serious, sad, seemingly suspicious look on his face.

On one of the pictures, his Hungarian Jewish mother Leona had written "my baby."

Two words, *my baby*. And I wonder. How is it that one of those pictures inspired her to write what she did in the corner? How did she know to write on the image that represented the person her son would become?

I can only imagine his 25-year-old mother's dreams for him, her hopes for a happy life for him, for herself and for her husband. For her family.

I do know, whatever those dreams might have been, that they didn't come true.

When she got pregnant again, after Mort was born, my father insisted she have an abortion. I suspect she wasn't happy about that. Their marriage formally fell apart in 1942 when Leona sued for divorce or for at least a separation on the grounds of cruel and inhuman treatment. She accused my father of adultery, based on a letter she found in his briefcase.

Only 16 years old, Mort testified at the divorce trial on his mother's behalf, saying he saw his father and another woman embracing. Without a jury, the judge ruled in my father's favor, dismissed the complaint and denied both actions—the divorce based on the fact that adultery hadn't been established to his satisfaction and the separation because "actual physical violence is denied by the defendant. If any violence occurred, I am convinced that it was insignificant and probably mutually inflicted." The judge also implied that Mort testified on his mother's behalf because he was living with her and she was most likely less strict with him regarding his privileges and conduct than his father.

Pretty clear what that judge's bias was!

Mort was convinced our father had paid off the judge to rule in his favor.

Two years later, in May of 1944, my father went to Reno and got what was at the time a standard Nevada divorce from Leona. This time, he sued on the grounds of cruelty and desertion based on the fact that she didn't appear or answer a summons or submit a plea. (In 1931, Nevada legislated a quickie divorce after only six weeks of residency, shorter than any other state in the country and earning Reno the title of "The Divorce Capitol of the World.")

And four months later, he married my mother, Marcella Matruski. (The family's original name before they changed it was Matuszewski.)

In the meantime, when Mort was 16, he left home, lied about his age, and enlisted in the Navy on December 28, 1942. He was assigned to a ship called the USS *Blair* and stayed in the Navy until he was released June 8, 1945. Named Mortimer

My parents' wedding photo
(September 9, 1944)

Harold at birth, Mort at some point changed his first name to Morton, Morty for short, after getting in countless fights in school with boys picking on him because of his name.

He married Marilyn Hink on December 25, 1947, when he was 21 years old. They moved to New York City. His mother lived in the same building as they did for several years, one apartment on the 5th floor, the other on the 7th at 113th and Broadway. Since Leona received no money from my father after the divorce, she worked as a nanny/maid for a while, supposedly at one time for famous gossip columnist Hedda Hopper.

In time, they moved back to Binghamton and it became clear that Leona was not right in her mind. She feared that people in the radio could hear her; she pounded nails around the perimeter of the front door to make herself safe from those she imagined were out to get her. Eventually, she was diagnosed as paranoid schizophrenic, and Mort had to commit her to the local asylum. She died some years later in 1962 at age 60 from breast and lung cancer and is buried at West Lawn Cemetery in Johnson City, NY.

My half-brother and I weren't particularly close, and in fact, I always say I was an only child. Twenty years is a big difference. We never lived together, and thus he was more like an uncle to me. I think love is too strong a word, but I was fond of him. And I treasure the one letter I ever got from him, addressed *Dear Sis* and signed *With Love*.

Now I realize just how little I knew Mort. Once, when I was home from college on semester break, he brought out an accordion and started to play. I got teary-eyed. Not only was he good, I never knew he played the accordion. I don't know what his favorite food was, what made him happy, what made him fearful, what made him laugh. I don't know why he didn't encourage any of his children to go to college. None of them went.

I do know that like me, he had dessert after breakfast; his favorite dessert was strawberry shortcake. I do know that he quit smoking the day actor Yul Brenner died from lung cancer. I can say with certainty that he talked a lot, a real lot, and that he was not a kind father or husband, even had no affection for his dog, a black lab named Eric he used for hunting. I do know that he liked to hunt and fish, and that while deer hunting, he once accidentally shot a fellow hunter in the shoulder and shattered his clavicle. And that he was too nervous, too quick to anger, too quick to raise a hand, a belt, or even a fist.

His youngest child, David, told me that his father never beat him. "He only slapped me in the face a couple of times. I would put my hands up to protect myself and he would say, 'Put your hands down, I won't hit you'. I'd put my hands down and he would slap me again."

But at least he was a Democrat.

Mort and Marilyn had four children. Martin, Renee, (who, four years younger than I, has always been like my sister), Vincent, and David (whom Renee and I love), and a rocky marriage.

Nephew David Dickstein, Mort's son

Niece Renee and the author

Sadly, but not so unusual in many families, Renee and I are estranged from Martin (Butch) and Vince, but that, along with their parents' miserable marriage, is a story for another time.

And Mort and our father also had a complicated, certainly not a devoted, relationship. "He never showed me any affection when I was young," Mort told me.

"Did he hit you much?"

"No, because I was so afraid of him I stayed out of his way. When I was in grade school, we went to a lake. He put me up on the dock and then told me to jump and he would catch me. When I did, he didn't catch me. He put me up there again and for the second time, told me to jump, promising me that he would catch me that time. I did, and he didn't. Yet again, he put me on the dock and then swore he would catch me if I would jump this one last time. I, of course, didn't want to, but I finally did. And for the third time, I splashed down into the water. He then picked me up, stared me in the face, and said, 'That will teach you to never trust anybody, not even your own father.'

Chilling, to know my father believed that and felt the need to convey that belief to his child at such a young age.

The Other Dicksteins

Dad and Mort (ca 1960)

He did get Mort a job working for Metropolitan Insurance Company, in the Security Mutual Building on Exchange Street in Binghamton. They were the top two salesmen in the office, sometimes in the state.

When all of us kids were young, we often went to Chenango Park for picnics, or on summer vacations together, usually to Cape May, NJ, or Sylvan Beach on Oneida Lake, so father and son could fish for pike. At Sylvan Beach, I was either at the arcade playing skee ball or sitting on my favorite boulder on the sand where I used to watch the sunset on the lake. I also used to watch the Canastota fighter Carmen Basilio train in front of the Hotel Oneida. He was a world champion in both the welterweight and middleweight divisions and who began his professional career in 1948 in Binghamton. In 1989, the International Boxing Hall of Fame officially opened in Canastota to commemorate native son Basilio's accomplishments.

And for years, my parents, Mort, and Marilyn played canasta, often into the middle of the night. I guess that would be something Mort enjoyed.

Yet my father complained that Mort never called him "Dad," only yelled out "Hey" in the office when he wanted Simon's attention. And I heard repeatedly the story of how 13-year-old Mort came to my father's apartment when he and Leona were separated and stole some chicken from his freezer to take home to his mother. I don't think forgiveness was a Dickstein family trait.

Mort did tell me that my father had been an excellent basketball player when he was young, and won many medals. I never knew that. He also told me that our father and a friend of his used to cheat at cards.

"They worked out a system, wrote away for marked Bicycle cards, and during the Depression, he used to win $15 to $20 a week. One time, they went to Utica and took the Mafia. When they returned, he was so afraid the gangsters would be wise to them that he started wearing a little pearl-handled pistol in a shoulder holster. He would do anything to make a buck, and then wouldn't spend any of it. He wouldn't even buy me long pants for my own Bar Mitzvah," Mort shared with me.

"And I never liked the way he treated my mother, yelling at her, staying out late, running around."

In later years, father and son used the same lawyer and at some point, inexplicably, the lawyer told Mort that he had been left out of his father's will. Mort approached our father, they had a brief conversation, and that was the end of their relationship. They never spoke again.

One of the few heart-to-heart conversations I had with Mort was when, after they had been estranged for a decade or more, I told him our father was dying. But I didn't say "our father" because it never felt like we shared him, even when they did have a relationship. But I was anxious to see how he would react when he heard the news. He didn't. He remained absolutely stone-faced as I told him the details. And there was no deathbed reconciliation.

As he aged, Mort gradually became perceptively paranoid. He had always been healthy but in his 70s, he was diagnosed with lung cancer, which they caught early. But it was after the surgery that he became so mistrustful. He believed he never had cancer in the first place, that the doctors misdiagnosed him and operated on him only for the money. And gradually, he forgot things, wandered away from home, and once even took the lawn mower out instead of the snowblower to clear the sidewalk. Then he was diagnosed with Alzheimer's.

Mort died at home in 2008, age 82, in his bed, his father's bed, the pineapple bed I had given to Mort and Marilyn after my father died. My last image of Mort is from a photo of him in pajamas, barely standing, shortly before his own death. Looking sad and suspicious. Lost and confused.

Part Two

Chapter 5
My Childhood

"A man's destiny stands not in the future but in the past."
Havelock Ellis (1859 – 1939)
Physician, writer, and social reformer

I was born in 1946, in Binghamton, NY, the first year of the Baby Boomers, and the year the Cold War began between the USSR and the US.

Binghamton, originally the site of a Tuscarora Indian village razed by British General Henry Clinton during the American Revolution and named for a land baron who never laid eyes on the town. Where in the 1860 mastodon bones were discovered on Susquehanna Street. In 1866, home of Binghamton Cylinder Oil, later renamed Valvoline Oil. Binghamton, famous for-cigar making and called the Parlor City because it was a neat showplace, like an old-fashioned parlor.

Binghamton, along with Johnson City and Endicott, was part of the Triple Cities. Binghamton, home to Rod Serling of *Twilight Zone* fame; Jack Sharkey, the heavyweight boxer who won the title from Max Schmeling in 1932; Billy Martin, manager of the NY Yankees five different times, (both Whitey Ford and Thurman Munson and others of note played for the Binghamton Triplets, the Yankees farm team located in Johnson City, and Babe Ruth is said to have been hired to write columns for the Binghamton Press newspaper), home to a World Checkers Championship in 1914, and to the 1918 Kentucky Derby-winning race horse Exterminator, who lived there the last three years of his life.

Binghamton, one of the stops on the Underground Railway, where City Hall is now located. Site of a Gothic Revival building called the NY State Inebriate Asylum, established in 1858 as the first hospital in the US dedicated to the treatment of alcoholism, which in 1879 became the New York State Asylum for the Chronically Insane and then in 1890, Binghamton State Hospital. Burial place of John Wilkes Booth's daughter, Ogarita Booth Henderson, a stage actress who died at age 32 in 1892 and who was buried in Binghamton's Glenwood Cemetery.

Binghamton, home of Ross Park, the fifth oldest zoo in the nation (1875). Home of the Spiedie, comprised of cubes of marinated meat—chicken, port, beef, or lamb—placed on a skewer and char-grilled before being served on Italian bread or a hoagie roll. Home, along with Endicott and Johnson City, of Endicott Johnson factories, which made almost all of the shoes and footwear for the US Army in both world wars. Home of Ansco Film. And in 1889, home of a little factory on Water Street called Bundy Time Recorder, Co., later called IBM. (According to Edwin Black in his book *IBM and the Holocaust*, Crown Publisher, 2001, IBM formed a twelve-year alliance with Nazi Germany, enabling them to efficiently identify, catalogue, round up, and transport Jews by using IBM's Hollerith punch card machines.)

And in the 1920s, Binghamton was home to the New York State Chapter of the Ku Klux Klan.

Until I was five, we lived at 19 Crandall Street, in a second-floor, one-bedroom walk-up apartment with a mahogany staircase, built in 1910, across the street from the railroad tracks. My first memory of anything was of me standing in my crib. The room was very dark and a person tiptoed in to peek at me. I knew I was sick. My mother told me that that happened when I was two years old, when I had measles.

And I remember wanting to go to my grandmother's (my mother's mother) funeral and being told I was too young. I don't remember too much about her, just that at her home there was always the smell of fresh oranges and the sound of a clock that ticked very loudly. And outside, along the back driveway, burrs on the bushes that always managed to attach themselves to my clothes.

The Crandall Street neighborhood of my childhood is now unsafe, the site of a lot of crime. Shootings and stabbings, even a murder, across the street two drug houses that the city closed down, and sex offenders are listed as living on the street.

But, it was nice enough when we lived there and I have mostly good memories of my time at that apartment. I remember being read my favorite book, *Wynken, Blynken and Nod*. I remember Sunday morning walks with my father; I remember lying next to him in the living room on the sofa with its yellowed doilies, listening to *The Shadow* and *Johnny Dollar* on the four-foot-tall cathedral radio; I remember sometimes he would fall asleep on my arm and I would be afraid to move for fear I would awaken

My Childhood

him; I remember lying in bed quietly so I wouldn't wake my parents, because I slept in the same room as them.

I remember once a cute mouse ran across the kitchen floor; I remember being allowed to go out and walk alone around the block picking up horse chestnuts; I remember walking around that same block, ringing people's doorbells so that I could hand them their newspapers, which had been lying on their stoops; I also walked alone the half-mile or so to and from kindergarten at Horace Mann School, which I attended only a half-year before they promoted me to first grade.

I remember kneeling down on the front sidewalk, putting a stone in the palm of my hand and holding it out to a squirrel to see if she would come. She did and I was so happy, even though she ran off when she saw it wasn't food. I remember winters lying in our yard, staring up at the night sky while I made angels in the snow.

And I remember sitting on the ground across the street almost every day, excitedly waiting for the trains to come by so I could wave to the engineers.

I also remember my parents arguing in that place.

When we moved, it was to 22 Jerome Avenue, a two-bedroom house close to Thomas Jefferson Elementary School on the west side of town. Nearby streets were named after musicians: Schiller, Schubert, Beethoven, Mozart, Handel, Goethe.

My mother started cooking Jewish food—cholent, kugel, latkes, and we ate a lot of gefilte fish and herring and sour cream. And she made delicious fruit pies, including always a small one just for me with my initials carved into the crust.

My house on the left, 22 Jerome Avenue, Binghamton, NY

I came home for lunch at noon every day to again listen to the radio, this time with my mother, to learn if *Helen Trent* could prove that romance can live in women 35 and over, and if *Our Gal Sunday*, a girl from a little mining town in the West, could find happiness as the wife of a wealthy and titled Englishman.

The house had what I thought then was a big backyard; at least it seemed very big when I was very little and had to rake the leaves with my father. Unenthusiastically.

But that yard also held some wonder for me in summers. Nightly displays of fireflies. Or lightening bugs, as we called them then. (I now know that there are 2,000 species worldwide, that they belong to the beetle family, that the light comes from under their abdomens, that their lights represent the search for a mate, and that an adult firefly has a lifespan of only about two months. And that they are now facing extinction due to habitat loss, artificial light, and pesticides.) Back then, yes, I caught them in a jar, with holes punched in the top so they could breathe. But I always let them go. And the little girl I was asked herself—were they all a family, could they feel and find happiness?

Maybe I began my search for happiness at five when I took ballet and tap-dancing lessons. But any dreams of prima ballerina were gone by 1958, when I was dancing to "Bird Dog" and "Witch Doctor."

In third grade, I came home from school reporting that I could take music lessons there.

"I'd love to play the flute," I told my father.

"No, you don't want to play the flute; it will give you big lips," my father told me.

"Oh. Ok, what about piano?"

"No, you don't want to play the piano."

"Why not?

"You can't take it with you if you want to play music for someone."

"Oh. Ok, what about….."

"You know what you want to play? The violin!"

"Oh."

And so I began my short-lived career as a violinist. I started taking lessons from a teacher who lived around the corner from me, Marianne Wallenberg, and then in high school from the school's instructor (who often tried to feel my breasts, but at least didn't insist when I moved away from his reach. I never told my father, afraid he would have killed the man.) Apparently I was a pretty good musician. I played a solo in front of my high school (while wearing a bright red corduroy dress with a full, scratchy crinoline underneath). I was concert-mistress of the high school orchestra, and always got As in the state competitions.

When I wasn't practicing and still young, I spent a great many hours by myself on the merry-go-round at Recreation Park, one of six Herschell carousels in the Binghamton area placed on the National Registry of Historic Places. Installed in 1920, it has 60 jumping horses, two chariots, and the original 51-key Wurlitzer Military Band Organ. And when I find myself in Binghamton now, it is the first place I go.

Also, I roller skated around my neighborhood or rode on my tricycle with a tennis ball in one pocket, which I repeatedly bounced off of the back of our house, and a deck of cards in the other, because I would often play rummy or Old Maid with our Russian neighbor, Mrs. Haletsky, on her front porch. And I diligently practiced, not only my

My Childhood

violin, but the game of Pick Up sticks, or Clothes Pins in the Bottle, which meant that I usually won when they were played at birthday parties.

I was free at a young age to be outside for hours by myself, to find ways to entertain myself at an age that today gets parents arrested for leaving their children alone in a park. Occasionally I get asked if I was lonely, being an only child. I don't think I was, after all, we only know what we know. I think I got bored sometimes, but I also developed confidence and independence, and an appreciation for solitude.

On wintery Sunday mornings, my father took me ice-skating, or in the summer to watch the Yankees farm team, the Triplets, who played in nearby Johnson City field until 1968. Or swimming at a local creek. And almost every night, after dinner, we sat together and had ice cream. Strawberry was his favorite, so it was mine, too.

A nostalgic merry-go-round ride at Recreation Park

They said it was the bright red snowsuit that saved me. I had wandered away from a company clambake and made a beeline to the end of the dock, where I leaned over to get a closer look at the water that was gently lapping at the pilings. Then I fell in. To this day, even though I was only three, I remember it well. The sensation of being submerged with my eyes open wide. The slow, swaying motion of the tall reeds. The silence that enveloped me.

The men had been outside, minding the fire in the pit, while the wives were inside the lakefront cottage, seeking refuge from the brisk November air. One of my father's co-workers happened to spot my hood bobbing in the water. It was he who raced over and pulled me out. I wasn't scared at all.

The following summer, my father took me fishing to Oneida Lake, one of the Finger Lakes in upstate New York. He loaded the boat and then began to attach the outboard motor while I sat patiently on the dock, legs dangling and swinging over the edge.

"Now don't fall in," he warned.

I did. Not from clumsiness, but curiosity. From bending forward to get a closer look. I wasn't scared then either. I seemed to be drawn to the water like the sailor to the call of the Sirens. Whenever I was near it, I couldn't wait to get in it. I was never afraid.

Baths used to be a favorite thing to do, too. In part, because of the game. My mother would shape an animal out of shampoo on top of my head; I would then try to guess what it was. On a good day, she let me go through a long list. *Monkey? Donkey? Bat? Cat? Rat?* And on and on, until finally I'd giggle and shout out something like "himmopamatus" and she'd smile and say "Yes, how did you know?"

But over time, she had less and less patience for the game, and one day, she wouldn't play at all. That day, she was rough when she washed my hair, and I squirmed and whined that she was yanking it. I started to cry and repeatedly tried to pull away.

"If you don't sit still, I'll drown you!" she yelled.

I screamed. I crawled out of the tub, ran from the bathroom, down the mahogany wooden staircase to the front door of the Crandall Street place, flung it open, threatened to run outside naked, and refused to come back up the stairs till she promised I wouldn't have to get back in the tub.

I was suddenly afraid of water.

So after that, even on the hottest, most humid, most oppressive summer days, when we went to the local swimming hole to cool off, I was too scared to go in any deeper than my knees.

My father gently began to tackle my fear. First, he talked me into letting him hold me by the waist while he lifted me in and out of the water, taking care never to get my face wet. Then, promising not to let go, he placed his strong arms under my back and held me as I floated. Finally, after many weeks, he came up with a strategy to overcome the biggest hurdle—to get me to put my head underwater.

"You scrunch your eyes shut," he said, "and with my hands, I'll cover your mouth, your nose, and your ears. I promise, not a drop of water will get in anywhere."

At first, I stubbornly refused. But finally his patience and the trust he had earned won out. I did it, and it wasn't long before I was dunking my head under all by myself.

When I was nine in the summer of 1955, my parents took a 33-day trip to tour the Canary Islands, as well as Madrid, Seville, Tangiers, and the Rock of Gibraltar. They flew over on July 24th and returned on a seven-day cruise on an Italian liner, the *Cristoforo Colombo*. They won the canasta tournament on board the ship and their trip warranted a small notice in the *Binghamton Press*. I stayed with Mort and Marilyn and toured their backyard in search of four-leaf clovers.

Yet, in spite of these activities, the life represented in the TV show *Ozzie and Harriet* and the current nostalgia for the 1950s, that decade wasn't a more innocent time, not for the culture and not for my family.

The New York State government put out a pamphlet in 1950, (which I still have) "You and the Atomic Bomb—What to do in Case of an Atomic Attack." It seemed that everyone was afraid of the Communists. In grade school, we had to practice both Duck and Cover air raid drills, when we hid under our desks or lined up against the wall in the

My Childhood

hall in the event that we were bombed by the Soviets. (I'm sure those precautions would have been most effective against explosions and the ensuing radiation.)

And across the street from my elementary school, a man once called me over to his car. And there was his "thing," totally exposed. I didn't run, I didn't say anything. In fact, I think I was pretty nonplused. I did tell my parents though, and they alerted the school.

One Christmas season at the same school, I found myself with a dilemma. "Daddy, I know I'm Jewish. What do I do when everybody in class sings Christmas carols?" He thought for a minute and then told me I could sing too, as long as I didn't say the word Jesus. Like it is a swear word, I thought to myself.

Children who are born with a talent are born facing a direction. When I was a young adult, I was frustrated because I didn't know what I wanted to do with my life. But as I look back now, I can see how those invisible threads the Chinese spoke of were drawing my map. I just didn't know then that I was following it.

As a young person, I was drawn to older people and loved hearing the stories of their lives. When I played cowboys and Indians with neighborhood kids, I always wanted to be the Indian. I thought they were more interesting. I had a collection of international dolls, and I wanted to visit all the places they came from, especially Russia. As I got older, I didn't know what kind of work I wanted to pursue, but I knew I wanted a meaningful life, not simply a lucrative one. Definitely not an ordinary one. I wanted adventure. After I got over my fear of water, I was pretty intrepid, other than my extreme dread of snakes and worms, but I remember being very afraid of living a boring life.

And I wanted to have connections with people, connections that were strong and enduring.

The most exciting thing I did in Binghamton was go to Wittig's Ice Cream Parlor, where I got sundaes in a tulip glass for 45 cents. A few times, we drove to Florida and I saw the "colored" pea pickers in the fields, the "colored only" signs at water fountains and restrooms, and the chain gangs, none of which I found exciting. Depressing, actually. (And only recently did I learn that during Jim Crow years, it is said that Blacks were not allowed to eat vanilla ice cream except on July 4th.)

When I was ten years old, I asked my parents repeatedly if we could please move to where Aunt Ida lived, to New York City, the exciting city. NY was where everything screeched—the traffic, the newspaper boys, and the animals at the Bronx Zoo. New York was all about noise, and eagerness, and the smell of horses in Central Park, and of the subways and the alleyways filled with broken wine bottles and stale urine, and of bagels and blintzes and cheesecakes at the deli's around Delancey Street, on the lower East Side where my grandfather had peddled his goods with his pushcart.

The answer was always "no."

In 1948, Stalin began his campaign against cosmopolitanism, targeting Jews in particular. The Doctor's Plot, between 1948-1953, when Stalin accused a group of mostly Jewish doctors of killing or plotting to kill political leaders, resulted in 37 doctors being arrested, 17 of whom were Jewish. Some were tortured.

During the night of August 12, 1952, 13 prominent Jewish writers, five of them who wrote in Yiddish, were executed in their cells in Lubyanka Prison in Moscow, accused on bogus charges of espionage and treason. The event came to be called the Night of the Murdered Poets. Ironically, all were members of the Jewish anti-Fascist Committee formed by Stalin while fighting the Nazis.

On March 5, 1953, Stalin died. Official cause was a stroke, although as I mentioned earlier, some theorize that Stalin was poisoned. With warfarin, or rat poison, by Lavrenti Beria, previously head of Stalin's Secret Police, and three other members of the Politburo, because they were concerned that his behavior was going to lead to a war with the United States.

After his death, those doctors still imprisoned were freed and exonerated by Beria, who assumed power for a brief time, before he was arrested in June, found guilty of treason and terrorism (with no real proof) and killed in December. He was however known to be sadistic when it came to torture and to take pleasure in beating and raping women, especially young girls.

Nikita Khrushchev, having positioned himself well, became head of the Communist Party, the most powerful man in Russia. In 1953, on August 12, the USSR tested the world's first transportable hydrogen bomb. On March 31, 1958, the Soviet Union, under Khrushchev, announced that they would unilaterally stop nuclear testing. But their arsenal continued to grow.

In America in 1957, Native Americans were finally allowed to vote in all states.

And in 1965, President Lyndon Johnson passed a law preventing discrimination and Blacks were finally allowed to legally vote.

Chapter 6
Growing Up

"Every heart has its own skeletons."
Leo Tolstoy (1828 – 1910)
Russian writer, from the novel *Anna Karenina*

In 7th grade, after reading about Anne Frank, I started my own diary. Even addressed it "Dear Kitty," as she did. She wrote things like "I see the eight of us with our secret annex as if we were a little piece of blue heaven, surrounded by heavy black rain clouds."

I wrote…..

1958: Went shopping and bought hair rollers, deodorant, pink pop-it-beads, and a book of 25 games of solitaire. Had beets (ugh!) for dinner. Got some new Topps Baseball cards for my collection. I love the Brooklyn Dodgers and Duke Snyder is my favorite player. Visited Grandpa with Mom at his room in the Bolebruch Hotel on Clinton Street.

And then I listed all my "How to dispose of unwanted food" tricks.

1) Put bread crusts behind stove
2) Put vegetables in mouth and then spit out in napkin
3) Put food in mouth and then go to the bathroom and spit it out in the toilet
4) Put food under plate until Daddy leaves the table
5) Spread food around plate to look like less and then talk more so that Daddy won't notice.

1959, 8th grade: Somehow I got straight As and became concert master of the orchestra. But Mom and Dad are fighting more. I'm starting to bite my nails, sometimes get hives and also bad headaches. If the headache is at night, I chew on the corner of my pillow for the little relief it gives me. Mostly I side with Mom.

I found solace in reading. At the dinner table when I could get away with it, and in bed under the covers with a flashlight. I read so much that my mother once yelled, "If you don't stop reading, don't get out of that chair and go outside and play, you're going to be an invalid when you grow up!"

But in grade school, she took me to the nearby public library and I took out ten children's books, the maximum allowed. And then returned the next day for ten more.

I also had my father's Army songbook, published in 1941, and I read and sometimes sang to myself the 67 songs. My favorites were the "Battle Hymn of the Republic" and the "Marine's Hymn."

From the Halls of Montezuma
To the shores of Tripoli
We fight our country's battles
On the land as on the sea....

I paid no attention to the mentions of Christ or the Lord or the battles. I just liked the rhythms.

When I got older, I read horse stories, Albert Payson Terhune's dog stories, and Nancy Drew mysteries, every one. Also my mother's Agatha Christie novels. Then I moved on to more serious books. *Catcher in the Rye*, *1984*, *Brave New World*, and *Animal Farm*, books by Thomas Hardy and Dostoyevsky, books about the Holocaust, books from my enrollment in the Book of the Month Club.

When I wasn't reading, I was asking my parents for a pet. First a monkey—I really, really wanted a monkey—then a dog, then a cat, a rabbit, even a turtle. But mostly I wanted a dog when I understood that a monkey wasn't reasonable. I begged for a dog. Any kind of dog. Repeatedly. The answer was always "no."

As a teenager, I was one of 2,800 people who saw Dick Clark in July of 1963 when he emceed a rock-and-roll concert in nearby Johnson City. My first album purchase from the Colombia Record Club was "Chances Are" by Johnny Mathis. I wore tube and sack dresses, felt skirts with sequined poodles, starchy crinolines, short shorts, and a pony tail, and I carried first my autograph hound and then my autograph book with me everywhere.

And one evening, as I was getting undressed after an evening out at the Dutchess Bar with my fake ID, (which I didn't really need because they let just about everyone in and served us all), already down to my bra and panties, I spotted a face peering in at me through the blinds in my bedroom. Now that scared me. I ran into my closet, scrunched down in the corner, and started yelling "Daddy!" But my yells came out in whispers, and by the time I had the sense to race out to the living room to tell my father what happened, the guy was running away and had already reached the far end of the block.

When the patrol car arrived, for some reason, the officer took me into the front seat of his car to ask me what happened. He then told me if I saw the guy again, I should continue to slowly undress, but at the same time, calmly let my parents know he was there so they could call the police. The Peeping Tom would then be caught in the act when the police arrived.

Growing Up

When I told my father the plan, he yelled, "I don't care what that schmuck of a cop said, you will not do that, not ever!"

The police eventually did come back, but for other reasons.

During high school, I took four years of Latin, joined the Russian Club, the Literature Club, and was a color guard. My father had dreams of my attending Julliard School of Music. I had dreams of boys. Singer and teen idol Bobby Rydell especially. And I knew that while I had practiced hard and had good technical skills, I had no real talent, no real passion for it, and so I put my violin down shortly before I went to college. I still have it, only now it is in a frame, on my bedroom wall, where I can look at it, touch it, and think of it fondly as one thinks of so much from their youth, so much that was so important then, so much that is long gone now.

During my high school years, the Cuban Missile Crisis had the country on edge, and the assassination of President John F. Kennedy had the country in mourning. I cried, too, as I watched his funeral on TV. And I saw anti-Semitism in action. During one of the campaigns for election of my high school class officers, too many kids did and said bad things about the Jewish candidates. Called them dirty Jews. Drew swastikas. Even criticized the kids campaigning for the Jewish kids.

Anti-Semitism surfaced in America in the 1890s, when poor immigrants were seen as a threat to Americans' way of life. The Emergency Immigration Act of 1921 imposed a quota system that was clearly preferential to those with Nordic backgrounds.

Because I had been pushed ahead in grade school, I graduated mid-term, on February 4th, 1964. And because I planned to be an English major in college, I took Freshman English at Harpur College, which later became SUNY Binghamton. Because of that class, I qualified to take Sophomore English as a freshman at SU. It was Chaucer, at 8 AM. That ended my English major; I had no interest in or love of Chaucer or 8 AM classes.

At a book fair on the Harpur campus, I saw the title *Civil Disobedience*. I had no idea what that was, but as I look back, I recognize that as the beginning of my interest in politics. But the most important political book I've ever read is Howard Zinn's *A People's History of the United States*." I think it should be required reading for every high school student.

I have fun memories from high school. The Beatles arrived on the scene and I was transfixed the first time I listened to "I Want to Hold Your Hand" on the radio. And I modeled for two local department stores. I went to buy a bathing suit at McLean's Department Store in 1962 and they asked me to model in one of their fashion shows. I did, and in return, I earned a $10 gift certificate and dinner. I also remember that the guy who represented Catalina bathing suits was a little too friendly, although not overly pushy. And I modeled for Drazen's women's store without incident, as part of my sorority (Theta Sigma) fashion show at the Arlington Hotel. I also became editor of the newspaper at the Jewish Community Center.

On Sundays, my parents and I often took rides to Scranton, usually to see my Aunt Fanny, who always made me laugh. On February 9, 1963, we went to Scranton for a Bar Mitzvah and I wrote this in my diary.

> *"At the reception there was this lady cousin of Daddy's—Mrs. Stanley Feld, called Dora. She's worth over a million dollars. She's so sharp. I did the Twist with her. She even wears wigs."*

Apparently the 16-year-old me was quite impressed with her. Little did I know then that 50 years later I would meet her daughter Dana.

However, some memories from then aren't so wonderful. During high school, my parents' fights grew more frequent and more violent. I think for my father, my mother was simply "eye candy" before the term was ever heard.

My mother was a beautiful woman. Polish Catholic, she was baptized in Blossburg, PA, her birthplace, on the 21st of September, 1923, six days after her birth. Both her parents, born in Poland, were not happy about her marriage to my father. Because he wasn't Catholic and because he was almost 24 years older than her. She became a lapsed Catholic.

As I've mentioned, I was brought up Jewish, went to Sunday School at Temple Concord, the Reform temple. My father however told me that all religion was nonsense, but he also told me how accomplished the Jewish people were and stressed the importance of my identifying with them, of being proud of that part of my heritage.

I used to get angry in later years when other Jews implied I wasn't really Jewish because my mother wasn't. That was, of course, Jewish law then, but it made no sense to me that that should be the criteria, not the fact that I was raised as and identified as Jewish, not the fact that I had grown up hearing Yiddish and eating Jewish food. And not the fact, most importantly, that I was proud of being Jewish.

Finally, in 1983, I was legitimized when the Reform branch of Judaism through the CCAR (Central Council of American Rabbis) passed a resolution that recognized patrilineal descent to define a Jew without requiring conversion. In fact, Reform Judaism.org states that "up to the Rabbinic period (70 – 500 CE), we find little trace of the principal of matrilineal descent. The Bible in fact seems to recognize a purely patrilineal descent, regardless of the identity of the mother."

My mother had many wonderful qualities. She was kind and generous and loving, and totally devoted to me when I was young. But my father was very insecure and he constantly belittled her. He complimented her on her cooking and her housekeeping, things that would keep her close to home, but told her how stupid she was and how inept she was at anything else. Then she started drinking and seeing other men. And I grew to disrespect her and also to be terrified of becoming her, of being weak, of being married to someone who would also make me a prisoner in my own home.

I had been a daddy's girl from the beginning, even when I sided with my mother after one of their fights. As a child of two or three, if it was before dark, I ran up the driveway to greet him when he came home from work. Or, if I was already in bed, I couldn't fall asleep at night until he came in and gave me a good night kiss.

I teased him a lot. When I commented on his high forehead, he told me that years ago, some thought that was a sign of intelligence. It was one way the Nazis believed they could identify Jews. I joked that his nose, not his forehead, would have given him away. Laughing, he said, "You're right. If I had a nose full of nickels, I would be a rich man."

He had lots of sayings:

- Can you imagine, I have to have the same birthday as Hitler?
- Don't do me any favors.
- I need this like a hole in the head.
- Now I don't have to work anymore.
- Too light for heavy work and too heavy for light work.
- You can't shave a mosquito with a monkey wrench.
- Time marches on.
- Let's get the show on the road.
- Another country heard from.

And he was the one who told me "the facts of life" when I was in high school.

"Catsella, don't let any boys touch you. Not because you could get pregnant; we could fix that, but because they won't respect you and you will lose your reputation after they tell all their friends, because you could catch some diseases, and finally, at this age, they don't know what the hell they are doing so while they will enjoy the sex, you won't. Wait till you find someone who will give you pleasure, too."

His attitude toward sex was definitely unusual. One night while we were away in a hotel, and I was in the cot next to my parents' bed, my mother caught me masturbating. Horrified, she yelled at my father… "Look what she is doing!"

"So what…let her have a good time."

That closeness and love between us continued until his death, but it wasn't uncomplicated or without conflict or intermissions.

He was very proud of his hair, wavy, thick, only slightly gray as he aged. He was conservative, always wore a suit and tie, topcoat and hat, saying he never wanted me to be ashamed of his appearance. He never went barefoot, indoors or out, and always wore rubbers on his shoes if it looked like rain.

But I think it was his mouth that revealed his personality: thin lips, tightly kept in place, reflected his self-discipline and determination. I don't remember him laughing often; he didn't place much value on pleasure. Critical, stubborn, and proud, he didn't trust anybody, and was uncomfortable if someone tried to do something nice for him, I think because he felt he would then owe the person.

At home on Jerome Avenue, he took very good care of our house. Repaired the crumbling corners of the concrete steps, painted the kitchen yellow, watered and mowed the lawn, cared for the roses and rhubarb he so proudly planted. If only he had taken such good care of my mother.

While his older brothers were active in their Jewish community, my father became assimilated. He bragged that he spoke with no accent, even though he came from the Old Country, and he signed his name with a flourish. He also saved money every way he knew. Walked five blocks in bad weather rather than feed a parking meter ("It's good exercise.") and waited for the movies to come to TV ("I have to sit in a crowded theater and listen to people cough when I can see it in the comfort of my own home?") His sense of security rose and fell with the Dow Jones Average, and he never sold a share of stock, believing that to be the secret of making money in the stock market.

With that money, he was able to realize two dreams: the trip to Europe and the purchase of a Cadillac. His first one was white but the second one, the big one he drove while wearing his fedora and smoking his Owl cigar, the one I inherited and had to drive around Cambridge, MA while scrunched down, because of my embarrassment, was solid gold, inside and out.

But education was something he was pleased and proud to spend money for. There was never a question or doubt that I was college-bound. Once he drove me and my friend past Philadelphia Sales, a rundown discount store on Clinton Street in Binghamton (that smelled of butter because they had a free popcorn machine that lured people in) and told us that working there for a living would be our fate in life if we weren't college material. He stressed good grades, I tried for all As. He said he hated a liar. I never lied. He told me that I was a special person, and I believed him.

When I was little, he taught me how to count to 100 in Yiddish. In later years, he took me to Bache and Company, the local stock brokerage firm, to try to get me interested in putting dollar signs in front of those numbers. It didn't work. And then he tried to turn me into a Republican. That didn't work either, not even a little, and we had many arguments about candidates, issues, civil rights, women's rights, and my rights.

I rejected many of his values. Unlike most of the Jewish immigrants from Eastern Europe who were primarily progressives or socialists, he was a Barry Goldwater Republican. (He did tell me, however, that if I were a boy and going to be drafted for Vietnam, he would send me to Canada.)

He had a stubborn pride that didn't ever allow for compromise or apology. And he wasn't kind to animals.

My father was very domineering and as I grew up, it was a tough balancing act to continue to love him, yet develop into the person I was becoming as opposed to the person he wanted me to become. I wanted to keep being a daddy's girl, yet I also fought to be my own person. And I had to reconcile my love for him with his abuse, both physical and emotional, of my mother.

My mom rebelled against his dominance and their marriage eventually ended in a bitter, ugly divorce. When I was in junior high, my mother insisted that I go with her almost every night "for a walk." That walk was to the liquor store several blocks away on Main Street, so that she could buy a pint of Gallo white wine for 54 cents, which she hid from my father in my bedroom closet.

And once she took my best friend Arlene Nelson and me to New York City so that she could pawn her stone martin fur stole. The small allowance my father gave her was never enough for her cigarettes, her wine, and the clothes that she bought for me that my father didn't think I needed. They most often came from Philadelphia Sales. (The irony —for class notable, I was voted best-dressed girl at high school graduation.)

For 20 years, Mom hadn't been allowed to drive, (my father wouldn't teach her to drive, but he made a big point of teaching me) handle money, or make important decisions; she was only to cook, clean, and look beautiful. And fight. I remember well the screaming and yelling, the hitting and punching; the time her face was swollen and bruised, eyes red and puffy from crying; the time he cried after he hit her, telling her how sorry he was; the times when I was little when I would just hide scrunched in the corner of my closet with my fingers stuffed in my ears and tears running down my cheeks; the times when I was older and tried to stop them. They stopped fighting for a while, until I was in high school.

Then sometimes all of us were fighting. One day, they would fight. The next day, it would be my mother and me. The day after that, my father and I would argue. It was difficult to keep track of who wasn't speaking to whom, and more difficult to determine whose side I was supposed to be on, or how to not be on either side. Sometimes I felt sorry for my mother, other times for my father. The silent treatment was in effect often, sometimes lasting a month or more. It was difficult to sleep. Either I would lie awake waiting for them to start fighting, or I would fall asleep and have nightmares, always of me running away from something or somebody.

My mother said she was dealing with nerves from menopause. Once she got so "nervous," she hit me repeatedly, threw me in my room without supper, and then threw all my clothes out in the backyard. (She hit me often but as I got older, I either ran out of the house or fought back.) Another time when she and my father were having an argument, she picked up a lamp and threw it at him. "Now look what you've done," he said, pointing to the broken lamp. "That's what you get for buying cheap light bulbs," she yelled back.

Sometimes during a physical fight, she called the police. When they arrived, while she was visibly shaken, my father calmly explained that she drank too much and often acted out like this. The police always took him at his word. I wasn't a daddy's girl then.

Nor, so upset after times like that, could I turn to my books for comfort, so I either called Arlene or went to her house. She had actually witnessed arguments between my mother and me or my mother and my father. So she knew, she understood, she listened. She was my dear, dear close friend. And she still is. Sixty years after we met and became friends, I recently watched her granddaughter Sara's bat mitzvah on Zoom.

The marriage really began to fall apart when the problems went beyond fighting.

My father started sleeping on the cot in the remodeled attic, where he had his desk.

Arlene Nelson Sahr,
high school best friend

Growing Up

My mother started staying out late. Out drinking with other men, my father told me. When it was late at night and she still wasn't home, he locked her out of the house. I'd sometimes later hear tapping on my bedroom window, then her quietly calling for me to let her in. I was afraid to, afraid not to. Sometimes I put the pillow over my head and pretended I was asleep. Sometimes I tiptoed to the window and told her I was just too frightened of my father's anger if I opened the door for her. I never found out where she went afterward.

Once, I picked up the phone and heard a man say, "I'd like to take a shower with you, honey."

"This is her daughter," I shouted before I hung up.

I never told that to my father, but by then, I was no longer siding or sympathizing with her.

My father hired private detectives from Levey Investigation and Detective Service based on State Street in Albany, NY to follow her. They filed reports and he actually gave me those reports to read.

> *March 6, 1964*
> *Female subject: Age 40*
> *Height: 5'9"*
> *Weight: 160*
> *Hair: Blonde, permanent*
> *Very good dresser, wears large earrings, usually carries large pocketbook*
> *Doesn't wear glasses, except sunglasses*
> *Likes to drink, usually liquor*
> *Constantly smokes cigarettes*
> *Likes to dance*
> *Wears light tan cloth coat, or dark brown coat cape collar, also has crème color coat with a mink collar.*

The investigators came to Binghamton 17 times that year to put her under surveillance from March to August. They got the license plates of the various cars she entered and then the names of the men who owned them. A couple times, they saw that a man was allowing her to drive, giving her a lesson. Mostly they followed her to various bars in town, but a few times they witnessed my mother and a man having sex in his car. Once, while on another job, they unbelievably spotted her in Albany with a man, followed them to a motel, and got photos.

In 1965, my mother sued my father for a divorce and his lawyers issued a subpoena to me to testify at trial in his defense on December 6th. The presiding justice, Robert O. Brink, not only did not allow me to testify, he also sent me out of the courtroom and into his chambers, where I couldn't hear the proceedings. Alone, I found a glass and put it up to my ear and against the wall, having read somewhere that that made it easier to hear things going on in an adjoining room. Disappointed, I couldn't hear much, only mumbling.

After my father's detectives gave their damning testimony, the court broke for lunch, and my mother, no doubt humiliated, didn't return for the afternoon proceedings, so her case was dismissed.

My father then sued her for divorce six months later, on the grounds of adultery. My mother did not show up for that special hearing either. On July 5, 1966, the divorce was granted by the same judge, who

> *"ordered, adjudged and decreed that this judgment ....shall become final three months after entry and filing. ... Upon this judgment becoming the final judgment, the said marriage shall be dissolved and the plaintiff shall hereby be divorced from the defendant and it shall be lawful for the plaintiff to marry again the same as if the defendant were dead, but it shall not be lawful for the defendant to marry any person other than the plaintiff during the lifetime of the plaintiff except by express permission of the Court."*

Shall not be lawful for the defendant to marry any person other than her ex-husband without the permission of the Court! This was part of an 18th-century New York State law, the only state that required a spouse to prove adultery as the only legal reason for divorce. I didn't read the divorce decree until sometime in the 1990s. I immediately called the Binghamton Courthouse to see if that draconian ruling was still on the books. I was told that it had been done away with in the fall of 1967, when four other grounds for divorce were granted. So the necessity to get the court's permission to remarry was gone not long after their divorce. And I am sure my mother never knew.

Because of the adultery, after 22 years of marriage, she didn't receive a penny of settlement or alimony. She was, however, entitled to part of my father's Social Security, and with that and jobs in the ticket booth of the Crest Theater, at the S&H Green Stamps store, and finally as a clerk in Ben's Clothing shop in Johnson City, she was able to support herself.

My father showed me the detectives' reports, and when I confronted my mother about them, she told me that she couldn't take it anymore, that everything had to be my father's way, that money was his sickness, more important to him that she was. And that she always resented the fact that he wouldn't allow her to have any more children after me.

That wasn't an adequate explanation to the teenage me, and because of her behavior, there were a few years that I didn't speak to her. At the time, I was so mad at her that I didn't realize that I was experiencing a loss too. I was losing my mother.

Growing Up

One day, Mort took me aside and asked me a simple question. "How would you feel if she committed suicide while you weren't communicating?" I understood, and was grateful to him for stepping in.

Mother and I "made up" shortly after that. I stopped biting my nails. She visited me after I had moved to California years later and we went to Hawaii together. She always laughed at the TV show *I Love Lucy*, but I remember seeing my mother experience real-life joy only twice. While visiting me in Los Angeles, my good friend Corky took us to Santa Monica and insisted that my mother take off her shoes to walk barefoot in the grass overlooking the highway and the ocean below. She actually giggled. And when we were in Hawaii, she rode the waves on a rubber raft and laughed non-stop as the waves repeatedly returned her to shore. But my feelings were never the same, even when I was old enough to understand what had driven her behavior. I wasn't angry anymore, but I didn't feel any love either. I didn't feel anything. And by that time, she was drinking so much that it was impossible to have a mother-daughter relationship. Any relationship.

It was only after both my parents had died that I began to recognize the reality of their marriage, began to see things other than in black and white. There were times I felt sorry for my mother, other times for my father. I had judged my mother pretty harshly, and naively, and I regret that.

My mother had been the youngest child; she had five brothers who all outlived her. Did she suffer some kind of abuse as a child? Three of the brothers were also alcoholics.

And if she had married someone other than my father, would she still have become one? I wondered about that a lot, yet I do know that there was nothing I could have done to stop the momentum of the destruction of their life together and of her very being. But I believed that regardless of their behavior, they loved me. And I believe that now.

However, they both remain unforgiven for not getting me a dog!

Of course, there are many things that I am grateful to them for. Very important, especially in this age of helicopter parenting, the independence I was given when very young. I was expected to entertain myself. Unlike most children now, I didn't have play dates scheduled, no siblings, no one knowing where I was every minute of every day. My mother was afraid for me to climb a tree, but there was no over-protectiveness in terms of where I wandered when I went out to play. As long as I was home by whatever time they told me, there were no restrictions except that I was not to cross any busy streets.

On my first morning in kindergarten, I asked my mother why all the kids were crying and clinging to their mothers. She told me they were afraid. I couldn't understand why they weren't as excited as I to go to school.

Feeling very grownup, I said, "Mommy, you can go home now, I'm a big girl."

Of course, that's what my father told me after they were divorced and he sold our house, when he also sold all my belongings—cherished toys from childhood, my record and baseball card collections, all my dolls, anything and everything that I hadn't taken to college with me.

"You're a big girl now; you don't need toys."

Chapter 7
It Was the Sixties

*"....Like a white stone in the depths of a well,
One memory glimmers deep within my soul.
I can't, I don't want to fight its spell,
Joy and pain together make up its whole...."*
Anna Akhmatova (1889 – 1966)
Russian poet

It was 1965. I had just completed my freshman year at Syracuse University, where I spent ten days in the infirmary with mononucleosis and where I was just beginning a search for certainty. My cousin Jimmie, my mother's nephew, was a career Marine, a five-year veteran heading for Viet Nam. His plane, which lifted off from Irvine, California's El Toro Marine Air Base, hit a mountain on Loma Linda Ridge just after takeoff and with a full tank of fuel, exploded on contact. Eighty-four servicemen died. There were no survivors and, as I learned decades later, no intact bodies. The Marine Corps did its best to have a complete body, but one man could and probably did have parts of others in the casket. I'm grateful I didn't know that as I watched Jimmie's coffin being carried into the church for his funeral.

Four years older than I, Jimmy and I had spent a lot of time together while I was in high school; he always came to see me when he came home on leave or before he was being posted out of the country, like in Cuba. Mostly we took rides, talked, or once in a while, stopped somewhere for a drink.

Corporal James Matruski
(May 11, 1942 – June 25, 1965)

A week before the crash, I had cleaned and organized my bedroom and thrown out letters I had received from everyone. I saved only two cards from him, one from Camp Lejeune and the other from Okinawa. The day he died was the first day I truly understood how fragile our lives are, how suddenly they can change, and how important it was for me to have something left of a loved one. I had saved gifts Jimmy had sent me, but it was his words I wanted. Since then, I have not thrown out one letter or card from anyone I care about. I won't embarrass myself by revealing how many boxes, filed and labeled, I have hidden away throughout the house.

On June 25th, 2015, 50 years to the day after the crash, there was a California memorial gathering for family of all those who died that day. We got special permission to visit the actual crash site, high on the mountaintop. I was the only one of Jimmy's relatives there. Most of us brought a stone with the name of our lost person printed on it, which we all placed in a circle on the flat surface of a small boulder at the site. I took a long time to choose mine from outside our Tucson home. After, we meandered alone, most of us in silence. I imagine everyone was thinking about the last time they saw their loved one, and about how fast 50 years goes by.

James Matruski

Memory Stones with names

The next day we attended a dedication ceremony for the new memorial kiosk in the historic hanger in Orange County's Great Park. Outside, after the speakers had finished, we all stood quietly for the Missing Man formation fly-over by military jet fighters.

I didn't realize it at the time, but I was coming of age during the decade of drugs and discontent, of protest and rebellion, of assassination, and a loss of faith in the future.

I went to hear Stokely Carmichael, the head of the Student Nonviolent Coordinating Committee (SNCC), speak on campus in March of 1967. Had I known that three years later he would say, "I have never admired a white man but the greatest of them was Hitler" and that his opinion about women's place in the movement should only be prone, I probably wouldn't have gone. But that same year, conductor Leonard Bernstein held a party for the Black Panthers, and I was naively proud, imagining that a coalition of Blacks and Jews could do much to advance the position of Blacks in America and perhaps even diminish the enduring anti-Semitism that had been so viciously stoked by Catholic Priest Charles Coughlin in the 1930s and by Henry Ford who believed that Jewish financiers were responsible for WWI.

The following month, I went to a demonstration at Manley Field House where racist, pro-segregationist George Wallace, then governor of Alabama, spoke to a crowd of about 4,200. I had no optimistic illusions about Wallace and went mainly out of curiosity to hear for myself just how racist he was. I was pleased to see anti-Wallace demonstrators with Confederate flags, some wearing white hoods to symbolize the KKK, booing him loudly.

Those college years, I didn't get involved in the anti-Vietnam protests; it was civil rights that I cared about passionately, that aroused my anger and my sense of right and wrong. I read Eldridge Cleaver, Frantz Fanon, Claude Brown, Malcolm X, and Ralph Ellison, prophets of the Black Movement. At the same time, I was a big fan of Motown. The Temptations song, "My Girl," remains to this day my favorite song ever.

My college freshman roommate read bridal magazines and wanted to be a bride. I read sociology and anthropology and fantasized about being Margaret Mead. And I took a geology class and started collecting stones. I also did some more modeling, for a photographer who took pictures for a spread in the University's newspaper and in 1967, in a campus bridal show. Ninety tried out and eight of us were chosen to wear wedding gowns in the Bridal Fair, sponsored by *Bride and Home Magazine*. I joked with my friends that it was probably the only time I would wear a traditional wedding gown. I was right.

But I had no real professional dreams or plans, no idea of what I wanted to do after college. All I knew was that I wanted to do many things, didn't want to be tied down to one job my whole life. Mort had suggested that I might want to become a divorce lawyer, because many women would feel more comfortable with a female attorney. He made a good point, but I certainly didn't want to spend the greater part of each day with people who were angry and fighting with one another.

Often, when I felt uneasy because I didn't know what I wanted to do, I went to Crouse College and sat on the big boulder outside. I wanted to be alone to contemplate my future. When it was time to go back to my dorm, I stopped and stared at the monumental mosaic mural on the east wall of Crouse—of Saco and Vanzetti, done by artist Ben Shahn. I never tired of thinking about the injustice done to them and that led me to decide that whatever profession I chose, it would be one what would be of benefit to society.

I ended up majoring in sociology and for a while considered social work. Once, when I was in elementary school, I came home to find a black boy about my age on our front steps, working on a puzzle. His father was painting our house. I sat down to help with the puzzle and shortly after, a neighbor came by with her five-year-old daughter,

Anna Mae. The little girl looked at us and shouted "Mommy, look how dirty that little boy is." Even then, I was mortified.

When I was a young child, I didn't understand why people didn't like Negroes. My reasoning was that when they hurt themselves, they cried just like us. So why did White people not like them?

In high school, my sorority, Theta Sigma, admitted the first Black girl, and I chose her to become my little sister. She did. In college, I took a class that required students to interact with young children from the nearby Black community. Mine was an adorable five-year-old boy named Devon. For an entire semester, I saw him on Saturdays, and always tried to come up with things to do that would be fun for him. At Christmas time, my two roommates and I got a Christmas tree and I brought him to our apartment to help us decorate it.

"Ya know what," he said to me afterwards. "When I get older, I'm gonna buy you a beautiful red velvet dress for Christmas."

"Oh, Devon, that is such a sweet thought. Thank you. And what would you like for Christmas?"

"I'd like to be White like you."

Devon, about five years old

I had no words. And he didn't understand my tears.

On April 8, 1966 *Time* magazine published an article on the demise of religion, with a black cover with bright red letters saying *Is God Dead?* It was a cultural moment, and led to many late night discussions in campus dorms. My answer was yes. He (and why not she?) had actually never been alive for me, and I haven't changed my mind since. It is nature that I turn to for solace and support.

One summer, my father and I went to the Concord Resort in the "Borscht Belt" in the Catskill Mountains. I think his motivation to spend money on that was his hope that I might find a nice Jewish husband there. He insisted that I participate in a bathing suit contest and I tied for first place with another girl my age.

On Christmas breaks, I flew to Miami Beach to spend time in hotels there with my father, although my greater motivation was probably to get a tan to take back to school. As soon as I awoke, I was out on a lounge chair. And not too long after that, my father came to the pool in his bathing suit and flip-flops, carrying a glass of freshly squeezed orange juice for me. Every morning that we were there.

But that winter break after the Concord, the day before New Year's Eve, I met a guy on the beach who was staying at the Fontainebleau. He invited me to spend New Year's Eve there in the Boom Boom Room with him and his brother and his date. My father wasn't pleased that I got "picked up" on the beach, but was impressed about where I was going. The most remarkable thing about that evening—his brother's date was the gal from the Concord, the one who tied with me for first place in the bathing suit contest.

The summer between junior and senior year, my roommate Linda Winer and I spent two months travelling around Europe on Fodor's $5.00 a day. When I broached the possibility of the trip with my father, he agreed. Readily. And besides paying for the trip, he even went out and got me a new camera and film. Frankly, I was surprised, but thrilled.

We visited the Anne Frank House and the ovens at Dachau, the Nazi's first concentration camp, established in 1933. (According to Dachau's own records there were 206,206 prisoners, 31,951 of whom died. It is of course impossible to know exact statistics, but most estimates are close to these numbers.) I remember being very angry when I saw a large cross there, and the Chapel of the Agony of Christ Carmelite Convent. Benefactors who contributed to the building

College roommate and travel companion, Linda Winer

of the convent said it was an effort to make amends for the evils perpetuated there. Still, the Agony of Christ, at a concentration camp mostly for Jews? Only recently did I learn that many priests were also prisoners who perished at Dachau.

The memorial there states that it is "a testimony to sufferings endured…and a warning to the living today and all time to come. A warning that evil is always in man, and that he must fight against it at all times."

We also went into East Berlin, where the military at Checkpoint Charlie made me take off my large Audrey Hepburn-style sunglasses, where they pushed mirrors under the bus to make sure no one was hiding and trying to enter illegally, where the many, many bullet holes were visible in the buildings, and where flags hung from every single window, a sight so chilling to me that I immediately understood the dangers of nationalism and vowed I would never fly a flag. And I haven't.

Highlights of our trip were visits to every museum in every city, the fact that I turned 21 in Salzburg, Austria, and the fact that we laughed a lot, especially when Linda (whom I still call Winer) decided I needed tips on how to be seductive! We literally laughed our way through eight countries, creating unique experiences and memories that have kept us close to this day.

I lost my fear of boredom. She lost her camera case out the train window as we were rolling through the Alps and her virginity in Amsterdam.

When we returned, my father was anxious to see the photos. He was only half kidding when he said "What, I got you all that film so you could take pictures of dogs and ducks?"

It Was the Sixties

* * *

Abortion was illegal back then. Winer was fine, but that fall, after our trip, our roommate Bonnie got pregnant. I located a Dr. Adams, who was well known in the underground for doing safe abortions. The story, and I don't know if it was true, was that he had lost his daughter to a back-alley abortion and so he dedicated himself to providing safe procedures for other desperate women. When he died, Dr. Adams was written up in *Time* magazine.

Bonnie was nervous, so I called and made the arrangements, and with two friends, on December 1, 1967, we drove to the Aztec Diner in New Jersey, (Clifton, if I remember correctly) where a woman met us at 8:15 PM and took her away. When she returned about a half-hour later, we checked into a local hotel for the night and drove back to Syracuse the next day. She passed the fetus in our bathroom. We spent a few quiet moments staring at it, alone with our thoughts.

Another friend had a terrible experience with an abortion that year. Delia, who we called Dee then, had left home during high school, shortly after her mother committed suicide when she learned her husband was having an affair with her best friend. Dee's high school boyfriend Kevin was at Syracuse, in the Sigma Alpha Epsilon (SAE) fraternity and was a friend of mine because I was a little sister in Sigma Alpha Epsilon, the fraternity he belonged to. Dee got pregnant and Kevin arranged for an abortion in New York City, in a tenement walk-up. When Dee came back to SU, she had to check herself into the hospital, where she was for ten days. There was some question about whether she could ever have children or not. I was fond of Dee the moment I met her; we have had lots of adventures together and to this day, I love her dearly. More about Delia later.

Terry Sage

If I drank at all then, and it was rare, it was only vodka and grapefruit juice. During my senior year, I also smoked marijuana for the first time. It took persistence to teach me how to inhale, I had never smoked cigarettes, but I learned, taught by a guy I was dating whose stage name was Terry Sage, a singer at the piano bar at Soo Lin's Restaurant on Erie Boulevard. Whenever I came in, he sang love songs, which I liked to imagine were to me. I may have been right, because we began dating and I spent the night of December

22nd, before winter break of my senior year, with him. He was indeed the man my father had told me to wait for.

I got back to my campus apartment about an hour before my father arrived to take me home. We went out to dinner that night and out of the blue, he asked "So, Catsella, are you still a virgin?" I looked down at my watch to give myself a few seconds. When I looked up at him, I smiled. "No, not of as about 12 hours ago."

"Well, I'm surprised you waited this long!"

But what really defined my college experience and much of my life after was the fact that I had fallen in love freshman year. I took one look at Michael Villari, tall, blond, Greek-god gorgeous, and I was hopelessly, helplessly gone. Storybook swept away. We dated for almost two years. He became president of the fraternity Sigma Alpha Epsilon (SAE). And he introduced me to his family, who lived not far away from campus, in the small, mostly Italian town of Canastota, known for its rich muck lands, perfect for growing onions and potatoes.

Michael Villari

And I loved his family, too. I always like to say that I slept with his sister Marie before I met her. The first time during freshman year that Michael and I skipped out on curfew, we went to his house. His mother opened the door and in spite of it being the middle of the night, graciously let us in and led me to a bedroom where 14-year-old Marie was sound asleep. I crawled in and she awoke the next morning to find a strange girl in her bed. We laughed then, and still laugh about that now when we get together. It was the beginning of what would become a supportive and enduring friendship.

But after a while with Michael, I got scared. It was happening too fast. He was talking about marriage. I was too young. I was afraid of becoming my mother. I still had to find my adventures. I broke up with him. We did, however, see each other off and on before we graduated. Senior year, February of 1968, we went to hear Timothy Leary speak on campus about the value of LSD. President Nixon labeled Leary the most dangerous man in America because of his drug use and the fact that he spoke of its therapeutic potential at so many venues, especially college campuses. He actually was arrested for both and spent time in 36 prisons worldwide.

It Was the Sixties

But he had a convert in Michael. As we were walking away at the end of Leary's talk, he said he was going to take it. I begged him not to, said it would be a mistake because I thought he had an addictive personality. I lost that debate, and he began a downward drug trajectory that was painful to watch. But my relationship with Michael evolved and he was always in my life, always an important part of my life.

Until 2013, when he wasn't.

Chapter 8
After College

"There will always be rocks in the road ahead of us.
They will be stumbling blocks or stepping stones;
it all depends on how you use them."
Friedrich Nietzsche (1844–1900)
German philosopher

After graduation, Winer and I decided to move to Boston together. During the summer, we worked cocktails on Cape Cod and then found an apartment on Commonwealth Ave. I first applied for a job as a private detective, only to be asked dismissively by the interviewer, "What is a nice Jewish girl like you doing looking for a job like this?" Probably trying to be Nancy Drew, I realized some years later.

Shortly after, I found a job as an advertising and public relations assistant for a British company, the Ealing Corporation in Cambridge, where I met Kathy Holmes. We became friends, at first out of necessity, to have an ally in our defense of the inappropriate behavior of our boss. Mostly, we thought he was a fool, but that didn't make his conduct acceptable. He often, but not always, drank a lot and seemed, like an elementary school kid, to find it amusing when he grabbed a hat or another belonging of ours and wouldn't return it. One Friday, when he was in NY on business, he called the office and ordered one of us to come to the City. When we hung up, Kathy said "I'm not going." I said "I'm not going."

We went together.

Paul was already somewhat drunk when we arrived, and then more so after we went out to dinner. By the time we got back to our hotel, he was weaving and stumbling. Kathy and I hurried to the door of our room, but before we could get it open, Paul lunged and grabbed each of us. We managed somehow to wriggle out of his grip, push him away, get the door open, and run inside. After pounding on our door for some time, he then called us every half hour, slurring, insisting we see him. Finally we phoned the front desk and told them not to put through any more calls from his room.

The moment when I realized Kathy and I were going to be not just friends, but *great* friends, as we are to this day, was that night after the phone stopped ringing, when she said "Can you imagine? He is so incompetent that he couldn't even assault us without getting it backwards. He grabbed your ass and my boobs!"

We sneaked out of the hotel early the next morning. Neither of us could have been described back then as shrinking violets, yet we were concerned that he would be so embarrassed that he might fire us on Monday. He didn't. But to this day, we don't understand how it never occurred to us to report him. That's just the way it was back then.

Some months after Kathy had come out as a lesbian and after I had a difficult time with a guy I was dating after Terry, I naively asked her if she thought there was any chance I could become a lesbian. I was truly fed up with men. She wasn't helpful. "No, you are hopelessly heterosexual."

Terry came often from Syracuse to see me on the Cape and we went to the Newport Jazz and Folk festivals, and when we were in Boston, to the Jazz Workshop and Paul's Mall on Boylston Street. We were together for about two years and it was always fun and he was gentle and kind, but the long distance relationship was too hard to maintain. And again, I was restless, not ready to settle down. My adventures were still waiting. We saw one another now and then over the years and I'm happy to say that we are still in touch today, sharing fond memories.

I enjoyed Boston and I got to spend more time with Dee. She lived in Provincetown that summer after graduation with her boyfriend Albert, working as a chambermaid. Dee, who came from an upscale part of Chicago and whose family was very wealthy—a chambermaid! She then also moved to Boston. It was with Dee and Albert in 1969 that I had my first serious drug experience, one that in retrospect was also my funniest. Years before it became widely available with the name Ecstasy, Albert had the pure form of MDMA, sometimes called a "love drug." The three of us took it. The two of them then went into one bedroom and I went into mine. Alone. Desperate for someone to hug or hold. I may be the only person who has taken Ecstasy and spent the night alternately fondling and mauling her pillow! (Ecstacy is now being studied as a cure for PTSD.)

And Kathy and I, under unusual circumstances, joined the more than 400,000 people at Woodstock. She had a broken leg in a full cast and I was physically drained, having just lost 15 pounds from colitis. I guess you could say we were determined. We had to park a long way from the stage, so we decided to stay only one night, but we got to see Country Joe McDonald, John Sebastian, and Santana, and to participate in a once-in-a-lifetime historical musical event, which people even (or perhaps especially) today find impressive. When same-sex marriages became legal, Kathy and her partner Ronnie Copeland got married. Both became college professors.

After College

Kathy Holmes and Ronnie Copeland, Married June 4, 2004

Then, about a year after I had gone to Boston but was back home on a visit, my niece Renee, still in Binghamton and freshly graduated from high school, asked, while we were having a drink at the Belmar Bar on Main Street, if I wanted to move to Los Angeles. Since I had always been "California Dreaming," I said yes. Winer decided to stay in Boston and stick with her job at Garber Travel, where she became vice president and remained until she retired forty years later.

I quit my job at Ealing and went to work serving cocktails at a club on Boylston Street called Factory East to make more money. After work one evening, I went with the bartender to the after-hours Pioneer Club, which often didn't close until 5:00 or 6:00 in the morning. You had to be a member to be admitted and if you carried a gun, it had to be checked at the entrance.

The club was the haunt of many musicians like Duke Ellington, Louis Armstrong, and Billy Holiday, who often performed, as well as lawyers, politicians, journalists, athletes, and even Mafia types. Owned and operated by Blacks, both Blacks and Whites hung out there. It was a Boston institution, having opened as a club in 1903. During Prohibition (1920-1933), beer was served. Sadly, in 1974, the building was demolished and one of Boston's irreplaceable cultural establishments with its unique history disappeared into the dust.

In December of 1969, Renee and I drove across the country. The high point was our time in Chicago where we spent an evening at the original Playboy mansion. It had opened in 1953; on the outer door, a brass plate touted the Latin inscription *Si Non Oscillas, Noli Tintinnare* ("If you don't swing, don't ring").

My friend Dee had recently moved from Boston to Chicago, needed a place to live, and so took a job as a Playboy bunny, where she paid very low rent to stay in one of the bunny dorm rooms. Bathing suits were stacked in a basket for anyone who wanted to swim in the pool, and food was available 24 hours. We didn't swim, we didn't eat, but we did talk. And laugh. A lot.

Renee and I found an apartment on 4th Street in Santa Monica, where we met neighbors Cleve ("Corky") and Lynne, who had a beautiful female shepherd husky named Chris. Kathy came out and lived with us for a few months before she decided she wanted to return to New England.

The same day I had met Michael the summer before college, I met a girl named MaryAnne Setticase, whom I liked immediately. After graduation, she had moved to Santa Monica, which was why Renee and I chose to go there. MaryAnne and I roomed together one year in college and I often went home with her to Canastota. She had an incredible mother, one I looked forward to seeing always. She was very kind to me and I truly loved her.

Mary and MaryAnne Setticase

MaryAnne and I went roller-skating on the Los Angeles sidewalks before it was a trend—when only kids did it—and we called each other when we had organized our closets and cupboards, so that the other could come, look, and nod approval. We enjoyed the nude beach at Topanga. We occasionally took psilocybin (magic mushrooms) and smoked weed, hash, and Thai sticks together, too. Once while very high, I saw images of clothespins dancing to music in a lettuce field. In the same field, there were small circular clusters of consciousness, rows and rows of them, each imagining human lives, creating new ones when one was gone.

We went together to Corky and Lynne's Buddhist wedding, at the Nicheren Shoshu Myohoji Temple at Etiowanda, CA. They had a daughter, Christina, who became a physician. Sadly, Lynne died several years ago. Fifty years on and Corky and I are still close friends.

And MaryAnne and I, to this day, call one another "sister."

After College

Corky and Christina Ford

Before I left California in 1977, I also lived in Topanga Canyon, West LA, and Brentwood. In Brentwood, my next-door neighbor was a young B-movie actress, Tiffany Bolling. Her boyfriend was Jason Williams, the star of the erotic spoof movie *Flesh Gordon*, made in 1974. Our apartment walls weren't very soundproof, so I can tell you without question that they did a lot of rehearsing.

Renee and I rented the Canyon house, with its knotty pine living room and a fireplace. We looked out over rolling hills, trees, a pasture with horses, and coyotes that wandered by our bedroom windows in the mornings. There were no streetlights and we used butane gas for heat. The landlord, who lived next door, was an engineer; a hippy band lived across the street, and Hell's Angels' motorcycles often roared up and down the road. Coincidentally, Dee had also moved to Los Angeles with her first husband, a very handsome man named Terry, who unlike "my" Terry, turned out to be not a very nice man. Abusive. And Dee left him.

Late one night, when I was driving home in the silence of the canyon, I first heard Roberta Flack's "The First Time Ever I Saw Your Face." I had to stop the car. To listen. To lean over the steering wheel, to close my eyes, and to give myself over completely to that beautiful song.

I always knew I wanted to attend grad school, but didn't know what career I wanted to pursue. While I took the time to decide, I worked cocktails in Marina del Rey to support myself for a while, then chose to go to graduate school in 1971 at California State University, Los Angeles. It was one of only three schools in the country that offered a master's program in "Orientation and Mobility," a profession specific to blindness and low vision that teaches people safe, efficient, and effective travel skills.

The first university program for the profession was established in 1968. Two of the three of us in the program at that time were sent for a three-month internship at the VA Rehabilitation Center in Palo Alto.

Mark and Niza Uslan

Ken Kesey, author of *One Flew Over the Cuckoo's Nest* (1962), was inspired by his voluntary participation there in a government-funded study on the effects of psychedelic drugs.)

My fellow student Mark Uslan and his wife Niza made that time at school very enjoyable. I ate often at their apartment, took a painting class with them (I was absolutely the worst one in the class), and Mark and I compared notes on problems and progress with our students. These days, we are comparing notes on the memoirs we are writing.

My first young student

My most challenging student was a guy named Woody, who at 28 had lost his eyes in Viet Nam. It was his third stay at the Center; he couldn't cope, periodically had breakdowns, was diagnosed as manic-depressive, schizophrenic, and psychotic (all at once, depending on which psychologist I talked to). After I had worked with him for two months and was feeling very good about the progress he was making, with no warning, he broke again (incontinent, vulgar, threatening suicide) and was placed in the psychiatric ward for a week. When he was released, staff admitted that he was "one of our failures," he cried and asked me why no one could help him. Then I cried with him because I didn't have an answer either.

After I received my master's degree, I was hired by the Braille Institute in Los Angeles.

Besides teaching adults, I pioneered a program for children eight to twelve years old, much younger than mobility students generally were.

It was also there that I began writing for publication; my first two pieces were in professional journals. And I created a course about blindness to teach at UCLA adult ed (which unfortunately didn't get a large enough enrollment for me to actually teach it). The day the course catalogue arrived, I noticed that the person just above my course description was a Karen Coen. I immediately called the school to confirm my suspi-

Karen Coen

cion. I was right. We had lost track of one another when we went to college, but it was my friend Karen from high school. We became even closer friends and she introduced me to the joy of hiking (remember, I was terrified of snakes, so the joy part didn't come for a long time). We had opposite outlooks on where we went to find peace and we debated them often. She always turned to nature; back then I turned to art and reading, things created by man to balance all the bad that our species is capable of.

Karen, only five days older than I, died young, at age 50, from colon cancer. To this day, I regret that I can't tell her that I gradually came around to her side of the debate. Or thank her for introducing me to the music of Leonard Cohen.

I spent many, many hours at Café Figaro on Melrose, with its Tiffany lamps, chessboards, newspaper walls, and menus, and Papa Bach's bookstore on Santa Monica Boulevard. (Whenever I was in San Francisco, City Lights Bookstore was my first destination, as it is still.) I joined the Los Angeles County Museums Graphic Arts Council. I defined myself as a secular humanist and joined the American Humanist Association. And I made my first political contribution. To Democrat activist Tom Hayden in his 1976 primary run for state senator. The first of many losing candidates I've backed over the years.

My Sheba

And, I got my dog!

She was a rescue terrier mix I named Sheba, who, in spite of having been to obedience school, had a stubborn mind of her own. But no matter how frustrated I got with her, I loved that little girl. She and Corky and Lynne's dog Chris were great friends. When Sheba was a year old, I had some friends over and she ran out of my apartment one night when I opened the door to let someone in. Seconds later, I heard car brakes screech, a thump, and her yelp. She came running back to the apartment and I had a moment of incredible relief until she crawled behind the sofa and simply lay there.

Corky, Tiffany and I raced to my car; they piled into the back seat while I drove as fast as I could. Corky held Sheba on his lap and Tiffany gave her mouth-to-mouth resuscitation. By the time we got to the emergency vet, she had died of internal injuries. My only comfort is that she died in the arms of someone she and I both loved and who loved her. I still have her red collar and tags. For years, whenever her four-legged friend Chris saw my car, she ran up to it, stood on her hind legs, put her front paws on the window, and frantically searched inside for Sheba.

Renee moved back and forth to and from Binghamton a couple of times over a few years. I stayed on, and we had a lot of fun while in California together. One late night, as a lark in matching bathrobes, we drove to Grauman's Chinese Theatre and for fun, walked barefoot on all the celebrity's handprints and footprints on the Hollywood Walk of Fame.

Living in the Los Angeles area was a great place to come of age. And I liked my work. One of my students was a close friend of Katharine Hepburn's. I enjoyed meeting the star and enjoyed playing with her dog; her peanut butter cookies were quite delicious. Of course, the many celebrity sightings were fun. But none as exciting as meeting Frank Sinatra and actually going to his house.

My friend Dottie, whose last name was Rizzo, met Jilly Rizzo, Frank Sinatra's close associate, in Palm Springs and they laughed over the fact that they shared a last name. Rizzo told Dottie if she ever wanted to go to Pips, a private club in LA, which was THE club at the time, to tell them she was his niece so she could get in. One night, she and I were driving around, bored, looking for something to do, and on the spur of the moment, we decided to go to Pips. We weren't dressed for it—we looked like two timid secretaries—and we were in her car, with its back seat all chewed up by her dog Charley.

When she gave her name at the door, the hostess replied, "Oh, wonderful, he and Frank are inside." Dottie panicked and whispered, "Let's leave."

"Oh no, we're going in," I declared, eyes wide with anticipation.

And go in we did. We joined Sinatra, Rizzo, Bing Crosby's brother Bob, Dean Martin's son Ricci, and comedian Pat Henry. They were all very nice to us, although I

After College

didn't like Henry very much. When it was time to leave, they invited us to Frank's house. Jilly said he'd drive in our car so we wouldn't get lost.

"No, no," I said, "thanks, we'll be fine following you," embarrassed for him to see Charley's doggy handiwork. We did fine and somewhere high up in Beverly Hills, were graciously greeted at the door by Barbara Marx. Sinatra went into the kitchen to make pasta for all of us (white sauce, delicious!). At one point, he and I talked about Sylvan Beach, and the fact that he had played the clubs there early in his career. He didn't say whether it was DeCastro, Forest, or Lakeshore or all of them. When it was time to go, we got a whispered tip from Crosby, who gave us the name of a horse to bet on at the track the next day.

So of course, we went. To the track the next day! Bet on the horse to win! It came in second.

Michael, my first college boyfriend, and I saw each other while I was in California. Once, Renee and I went to San Francisco and made a surprise visit to his house in the hills overlooking Berkeley, where we met his bull mastiff, Ernie. Michael brought out some cocaine and the requisite $100 bill, which, when he passed it rolled to Renee, she tried to light. It was the first time she had done coke. He told us he was smuggling drugs and making a lot of money at it. A real lot of money. I wasn't sure whether to believe him or not, although he had an impressive collection of coral and beautiful Oriental rugs.

And once he visited me in LA. I took three days off from work and we spent them in my apartment, doing cocaine, listening to the Bob Marley "Legends" album he brought me. There was a moment after we were intimate that I held him, felt him, wanted only good for him. In my bed, and in my body, I loved him, and I cried. Because I knew that he was too absorbed in the highs, that he was out there all by himself, and that while we would always be important to one another, we would never meet in that place where we could share a life.

Not too long after that, he ended up back home in Canastota with his parents, his six-foot body weighing about 88 pounds. Around that time, I dreamed that I was at an outdoor table with a friend. When I looked up, I spotted Michael on a nearby music stage. I started to wave to him, and then heard a shot. He fell. I panicked. Ran through the crowd, shoving people away, trying to reach him, but already knew he was dead. I woke up scared and depressed.

Again, it was the 1960s and early 1970s. Many of us were following Leary's mantra: "Turn on, tune in, and drop out." I didn't want to drop out, but I wanted to try things. Except heroin, which I knew enough about to be afraid of. In addition to what I mentioned doing with MaryAnne, I did some coke, some free-basing. I never worried about becoming addicted. I liked my life too much to let that happen. And, I was already addicted—to chocolate.

I did have one LSD trip. An amazing trip! What I remember most about it was the feeling that if I died right then, it would be all right. It wasn't that I had a desire or urge to die, just a simple realization that there was something bigger, something universal, and I was a part of that, too. I felt that way one more time, many years later, without drugs. In Outer Mongolia.

I haven't taken illegal drugs in decades (with one exception, the night Donald Trump was elected President in 2016, and the weed was most definitely NOT for pleasure). My drugs of choice and enjoyment now are champagne and ice cream.

My father wrote to me regularly while I was in California, signing off with "Isle of View" written in the margins. He always said he wished I weren't so far away. And he always included some advice, adages I'd heard since I was little, like "You can lead a horse to water but you can't make him drink." Which made me think of Michael.

Once, when *Fiddler on the Roof* was made into a movie, I arranged to have Renee, who was then back in Binghamton, buy two tickets, mail them to me, and then I mailed them to my father as a birthday gift. He loved the movie he said, "Life in Russia was just how it was portrayed on screen."

"But don't ever do that again, Catsella, because I can get the tickets cheaper as a senior."

In 2018, the play *Fiddler on the Roof*, directed by Joel Grey, was performed in Yiddish at the Museum of Jewish Heritage in New York City. It was translated for the audience on a screen, into both Russian and English. I was surprised at how many Yiddish words and expressions were familiar to me, no doubt from listening to the many conversations between my father and his sisters.

In 1971, before I started graduate school, when I had the freedom and the finances to be away for a long time, Winer and I travelled again. We took a trip to Greece and then Israel. After the first two weeks, she went back to Boston and I stayed on alone in Jerusalem. (More about that part of the trip later.) Then it was on to Istanbul, then to London.

On the flight from Tel Aviv to Istanbul, I sat next to a guy who told me he knew of a good place to stay there. "Just tell me that it is clean," I said. He reassured me it was. It turned out to be a 3rd-class hotel, 60 cents a night. When we arrived, the innkeeper asked if I wanted clean sheets. (So, there are people who would say no?) Anyway, I said yes, and then he took us to our room, a room with four beds, two of them occupied by guys already sleeping. My new friend and I took the other two beds. There was only a communal toilet, no shower. Even though the 1960s were technically over, culturally they weren't, and traveling then, at my age, was sort of like being at Woodstock. Everybody was your friend, so it felt quite comfortable and safe there in that hotel—a hotel, I might add, unlike any I've stayed in before or after.

After College

Because there were no showers, I went to the public Turkish baths. After I paid my $1.50, I entered a marble room with ceilings at least two stories high, huge round marble slabs in the center, and ornate faucets and sinks along the walls. I walked in naked, as was the norm, and was approached by a fat, toothless, bare-bosomed woman wearing only a pair of boxer type underpants. It turned out she was in charge of my care. She washed my hair at one of the wall sinks, then took me by the hand and led me to the marble disc. She pointed, I lay down, and she began her real work. With a sponge that felt like barbed wire, she scrubbed and scrubbed until she drew blood, and throughout she kept asking me, with what I was sure was her one word of English, "Good? Good?" smiling her toothless smile and nodding her head up and down. I managed a weak "yes," and tried to explain that she didn't have to scrub quite so hard.

After three days in my cheap hotel, where all the residents sat around a large table smoking dope every night, (one of them, a young guy from Austria, was making his way around Europe wearing *Lederhosen* and carrying a shopping bag with a big, round chunk of heroin), I exchanged my jeans for a silk blouse, gabardine pants, and high-end leather boots, and checked into the Hilton. Twenty dollars a night, the cheapest Hilton in the world at the time. I was ready for a real bathroom and privacy.

But before I left my optional clean sheets behind, the guy I met on the plane, whose name I can't remember, took me to visit a friend of his, a Turk who had a room in a different hotel. The hash came out and every hour, the hotel manager knocked on the door and came in carrying a tray with a cup of hot tea for each of us. I had one each time, seven in all, and remember being very impressed with this ritual, as well as grateful for the liquid to soothe my dry throat. I also remember that for most of that time, I was curled up in a corner, absolutely stoned, absolutely silent.

That evening, we took a drive and parked high up in the hills, overlooking the Bosphorus Strait. Just beautiful. Suddenly, there in the middle of nowhere, there was a knock on the car window, a small forehead and two small eyes barely visible above the door, some words spoken in Turkish, and minutes later, pizza. To this day, the best pizza I've ever had.

After a week in Istanbul, I headed to London for a totally different experience. I stayed in a nice B&B, did the usual sightseeing, beginning with a visit to both houses of Parliament. While there, I met a member of the House of Commons and actually went out with him a few times, to dinner and theater.

And a friend from Los Angeles, Royal Marcher III—Roy—was in London at the time and he suggested I go with him to meet some of his friends. He arrived in a chauffeur-driven Rolls Royce to pick me up and take us to the private helicopter that was going to fly us to a summerhouse somewhere in the countryside outside of the city. Roy told me his friends, Gordon White, the pilot, and James Hanson, were wealthy bankers. (I had already figured out the wealthy part after the Rolls and the helicopter.)

After sitting around the house for a while with them and the two women I assumed were their wives, we all went out to a local pub for dinner. The aircraft took us back to the city that evening. I was appropriately impressed at the time, but was stunned when I started writing this book and googled White and Hanson to find out which bank they had been with.

Gordon White and James Hanson were actually ruthless corporate raiders who created the British conglomerate called The Hanson Group. They had a 30-year partnership. Ironically, one of their eight acquired companies in the US was Endicott Johnson, the shoe company in my Triple Cities (Binghamton, Endicott, and Johnson City) that produced almost all the shoes for American soldiers in both WWI and WWII. According to their obituaries, White dated Ava Gardner, Grace Kelly, Liz Taylor, Susan Hayward, and more (*LA Times,* Aug 25, 1995). Hanson also dated in the same circles and was once engaged to Audrey Hepburn. They were worth billions of dollars.

Although I didn't know it then, I was a very long way from Binghamton.

Winer and I travelled again in 1975 to the Yucatan, where I climbed 79 feet to the top of the Temple of Kukulcán (El Castillo) at Chichen Itza (closed to climbers in 2006, after a woman fell to her death during her descent) and fought off an onslaught of mosquitoes. When Winer flew back to Boston, I flew into Mexico City to meet Eloy.

Eloy, whom I had met in LA and spent five years with. Pleasurable and painful years. The pleasure was being with him, looking at his handsome face, his mischievous grin, his capacity for joy. We went to Mexico together, drove through rural areas where I was overwhelmed by the textures, the clarity, the simplicity, the bright colors of the country. Tall pink flowers waved in the breeze; tall, straight cactuses grew even straighter up the mountains; beehives, thatched roofs, dirt floors, hammocks; and animals—dogs roamed, cows lumbered, roosters strutted, and turkeys paraded across the narrow roads. All to create a canvas onto which the people made imprints of their lives through their daily tasks. Fathers walked with bundles of wood on their backs, plowed with oxen, carried machetes, sat by the dusty roadsides waiting for buses. Mothers were the artist Francisco Zuniga's women: black shawls, long black braids, and wide black eyes in round, ingenuous faces; women who walked slowly beside their children, little sons who peed by the road, and little daughters who carried littler babies in their stick-like arms.

In Taxco, where Eloy was born, we visited his mother and sister. His uncle prepared at his farm a goat barbeque and proudly displayed the sacrificed goat's skin in a tree overhanging the outdoor table where we ate. Just above my head.

In Guadalajara, we visited the Orozco murals at the orphanage; in Cuernavaca, we saw more art at the Hotel Las Mañanitas: Cuevas, Siquieros, Nierman and three bigger-than-life Zuniga bronzes that shared the garden with live peacocks and parrots. All the Mexican artists I had loved long before I met Eloy.

After College

In Acapulco, at night, overlooking the dark, vast expanse of shimmering blue water, we stood naked on the balcony of our hotel, held one another, and were silent as we listened to the waves hitting the beach.

In Mexico City, we fought the noise and the crowds and went to the Museum of Anthropologia where the Mayan Rain God was depicted creating life through his tears.

But despite the good, I decided my tears over Eloy were draining me of life. The painful part? He was unorganized, often untruthful, almost always unreliable. He was not a good partner. And he drank too much. I hadn't been able to save my mother, or Michael, and I knew I couldn't save Eloy. I could see the future. I walked into it without him.

Simon Dickstein, my father
(April 20, 1900–June 23, 1977)

Chapter 9
Dad's Illness and Death
(1976 –1977)

"Parents rarely let go of their children, so children let go of them. They move on……It is not until much later…..that children understand; their stories, and all their accomplishments, sit atop the stories of their mothers and fathers, stones upon stones, beneath the waters of their lives."
—Mitch Albom (1958–), American author

"You don't want to end up in a sick bed with a healthy head."
That was another of my father's favorite sayings. Little did he know that that is exactly what would happen to him.

After the divorce, he sold our house and moved into a two-bedroom apartment on Mitchell Ave., not far from Binghamton General Hospital. He was proud of his housekeeping – did his own laundry, ironed his own shirts, did the grocery shopping and cooking. He even had his own recipe for chicken soup. Minus the matzo balls.

At 76, my father was still a good-looking man. He had aged well and people often guessed he was ten years younger. He liked that, and most always replied, "You know what the Good Book says: when you're green, you grow, and when you're ripe, you rot." He was strong. His gait was still deliberate and decisive. And he loved to dance; he carried his patent-leather dancing shoes with him all the time, in the trunk of his car, "just in case".

So when I got a letter from Fran (Collingwood), who for the past seven years my father had referred to as his lady-friend, telling me that he was in the Veteran's Hospital in Syracuse, I was anxious, but not too worried. When I called him though, I knew how bad it was as soon as he started to talk. I knew even before he told me that the doctors said they couldn't remove or replace or repair his malignant liver.

I flew to Binghamton the next day, Thanksgiving Day. Three thousand people were feared dead in an earthquake in Turkey, American people were excited that there were football games on TV. Neither mattered to me. All that existed for me was that man in that hospital bed.

All of our daily activities are so insignificant in the face of death. The day before the flight, I went shopping in Beverly Hills. And then, the next day, instead of wondering what dress to buy, I wondered who was going to be proud of me when my father was gone. Who was really going to care about my life and what I did with it?

On the flight, a stewardess walked by holding a baby, crying for its father.

I will be forever grateful to a stranger named Dean Dorsey, who sat behind me on the flight. Who saw my tears, started talking to me, bought me a drink. A vodka and orange juice, two of them in fact, and then some wine. He was full of life, and energy, and conversation. He made me laugh and I felt much better. And then he left, at the layover in Chicago, and the desperation returned.

I sat in front of a Fannie May candy shop inside the airport, waiting for my connection, and wondered how Mort would respond when he heard.

And I remembered I forgot to pack my toothbrush.

It was a sarcoma. With classic Dickstein practicality, my father refused surgery, saying it was senseless since it wouldn't provide a cure. He did initially agree to chemotherapy when the doctors told him that without it, he'd have about two months, with it, maybe up to six months. But then, he started asking questions.

"Will I lose my hair?" and they said "yes."

"Will it make me very sick?" and they said "yes."

Then he asked if they thought it was worth it, and they didn't know what to say.

Five days later, he decided against it. "It's not worth it for a few torturous months. I don't want to live a half life."

There is one benefit to a terminal illness instead of a sudden death. Time. Time for me to tell him how grateful I was for his love and care, his support and encouragement, and that I would miss making him proud of me. Time for him to tell me that he felt good knowing he was leaving me financially secure so that I wouldn't have to worry and fear as he had when he was young, so that I wouldn't have to be dependent on anyone.

And time for him to tell me more.

"In spite of all the hard times with your mother, I would do it all over again because of you."

"Well, Catsella, my only regret is that I won't see your children."

I told him I wasn't having any.

"You haven't had an easy life. Live your life the way you want to. You are grown up enough now to do what you want to do. Just be happy."

I told him I'd try.

"You might better stay at your job if you like it rather than worry about making more money and risking not liking what you do."

That surprised me.

But then, "Now, don't spend a lot of money on clothes. You look great in clothes, so you don't have to buy expensive ones."

Uh, okay.

When he was in the hospital, which he was three times over the seven months I was in Binghamton, Fran and I drove the 80 miles to Syracuse to visit him every other day. When he was home, she brought dinner every night and we often played pinochle.

He was still able to shower, with my assistance. I took off his pajamas, helped him into the tub, adjusted the water temperature, put soap on the cloth, and then stood staring at the closed shower curtain, listening to the ping of the water against that faded plastic, against the tiles, against the rubber mat. I'd hear him lather the washcloth with soap—Ivory, the only soap he ever used. I'd hear his labored breathing. I'd hold my breath. And wait, silently begging "Please, please, whatever it is that determines our lives, please don't let him fall." No one listened.

Because often, he did fall. The first time, I was asleep on the sofa when I heard a cry and then a loud thud. I got weak, dizzy, turned hot and cold at the same time as I ran into his room to find him stretched out flat on his stomach on the floor.

"Lie still for a few minutes, so you can catch your breath," I said, fearing that I was going to faint. I finally got him up onto the bed, put a cold towel on his face, and then we just lay quietly, holding one another, shaking.

After a while, I searched under the bed for his dentures. I found them amidst a pile of dust balls. He went into the bathroom to wash them off and I saw him staring at his face in the mirror for what felt like a long time. Then he shuffled into the kitchen to make his oatmeal for breakfast, the oatmeal he had eaten every morning for most of his adult life.

Another day, he fell at a gas station. The attendant gave him a really funny look, no doubt thinking Dad was drunk. And then again in the bathtub. I struggled always to get him on his feet after the falls, and somehow managed. I also struggled to put the tight white elastic support stockings on his swollen legs every morning.

He didn't hurt himself until the last collapse, when he crashed into the toilet. I found him wedged in between the bowl and the wall, with one arm on the seat and one on the toilet-paper roll, trying to pull himself up. He broke two ribs then and was readmitted to the VA.

When Fran and I went on our hospital visits, we first had to walk past Admitting, where the mostly old men sat and waited in a long row, their heads relaxed against the wall, their eyes closed. Or they leaned forward and stared at the floor, elbows rested on their knees, hands clasped. Many had nicotine-yellowed fingers and dirty nails on hands that shook. Some were amputees in wheelchairs or on crutches; some were on stretchers with IVs, and all seemed to have pasty gray complexions and hacking coughs.

The smell. The sick smell combined with dead cigarettes and cigars in overflowing ashtrays made the air heavy and close. Generally, at that point, I had to take a stick of gum. To help my queasy stomach. To help hold back the tears.

Each time Dad came home from the hospital, he remarked how good it was to be in his own bed, the antique mahogany poster bed, with elegantly carved pineapples at the top. When I was young, I called it the pineapple bed. His wish to die in it was not to be.

I looked through his things in preparation. I found his address book, found my page with every address since college. Nine different ones. Mrs. Williams' boarding house in Hyannis, 1086 Commonwealth Avenue, and 1870 Beacon Street in Boston, and the rest in California. He used to tell me, "You know what the Good Book says. It's not a tragedy to stay in one place for a while."

I also found the instruction sheet from the funeral home. He had made all the arrangements and didn't want me to spend money on a fancy funeral, or any funeral, for that matter.

"I don't want any flowers when I can't smell them."

No newspaper notices, no committal services, no embalming, only cremation. I asked if those were still his wishes. He said "absolutely" and then told me of his conversation with the funeral director. After everything was discussed and the cost agreed upon, my father got up to leave and the man said that there was one last detail. He needed to know what Dad wanted done with his ashes.

"You carry them with you in the trunk of your car."

The director's eyes widened, and then my father told him, "The first time it snows and you get stuck, you should scatter the ashes under the tires, and that, my friend, will be my last good deed on earth."

And he told me whom to contact when the time came: his sister Ida, his niece Esther, his brother Harry. But not that mamzer Herman!"

I thought of death a lot during the time I was in Binghamton for him. Would I get cancer too? I was very conscious of my body, aware of every sensation. I examined my breasts every day, as well as checked a mole on my back that my mother had always worried about.

By then, my niece Renee had married, gotten divorced, and had a two-year-old daughter. Holding and hugging and playing with that sweet little toddler, Tambi, was my greatest comfort. And my boyfriend Terry, from my senior year in college, was another comfort. He came to Binghamton one day and spent the night with me while my father was in the hospital. For that one day, with his arms around me, wrapped in his kindness and tenderness, I lost my anxiety.

I also went to bookstores to find a manual on how to do it, how to be the caretaker, and most important, how to deal with my father's impending death. I didn't find any books. I did learn that throughout human history, people needed to believe in some kind of afterlife. Half a million years ago, Neanderthals placed food and flint implements in graves. The Old Stone Age men, the Cro-Magnons, also buried food and weapons, as well as ornaments. The belief in reincarnation has been present in almost all simple food gathering and fishing and hunting civilizations.

More modern religions promise to provide an afterlife for the worthy, but modern science gives us facts and no faith, and renders man insignificant in space and time. And our society doesn't teach us to accept death. On the contrary. Not that long ago, children who lived on farms saw animals live and die. Parents and grandparents died at home and children saw it all. The family would dress the body. The death was natural, a part of living, not ugly, not scary, not something to be hidden.

Today, we have hospice care, which wasn't available when my father was dying, but even now, most dying still takes place in hospitals and nursing homes, all part of a technological process complete with hall monitors, beeping machines, and a way of speaking that implies something other than the reality. People even have a hard time saying someone died, as if it were impolite, or worse. Instead, we hear "they're gone," "I lost him," "she passed away."

My Dickstein family has always said "died."

On the evening of June 23rd, Fran and I stayed at the hospital until early evening, until my father told the nurses to tell us to go because there wasn't anything more we could do. We actually stayed another hour, but he was drifting. He kept putting his blanket in his mouth, and when I asked why, he looked at me as if I was very stupid and said, "What does it look like I'm doing? I'm eating my strawberry shortcake." I hesitated, because I didn't want to ruin his enjoyable illusion, but then I told him what he had always told me, that it would ruin his appetite for dinner. That he listened to.

When it was time to leave, I leaned over, gave him a kiss goodbye, and said "I love you, Daddy."

He whispered, "I love you, too."

At 10:30 that night, I got the call from his doctor, who told me my father had "expired" from primary sarcoma of the liver. (Because "expired" is a kinder word than died?)

Four days later, Simon Dickstein was cremated at Vestal Hills Memorial Park. I picked up his ashes the next day, my birthday. He was Box 52770. I was 31.

Fran and I said our final goodbye to him on July 20th, at App's Livery and Boat Rentals on Oneida Lake, on the north side of the lake in Cleveland. The place where my father always rented his boats to go fishing.

The day was oppressively humid. The sun looked like a full moon behind a curtain of haze. A young couple sat at the end of the jetty and smoked grass while embracing one another. We sat away from them with our backs to the marina, holding each other too, hoping no one would see what we were about to do. The music for this simple ceremony: the low drone of distant motors, the gentle push of the water against the rocks, the cries of the gulls flying single file along the shore. And there, where my father had spent so many happy hours, we let him go, let him drop gently to his peace.

When he died, this man from the Glubokoye shtetl who had only burlap to wrap around his feet for shoes when he was young, left, before taxes, an estate of almost half a million dollars. And a solid gold Cadillac.

>**February 1956—Khrushchev gave a speech denouncing Stalin's dictatorship**
>
>**October 14, 1964—Khrushchev was removed from power**
>
>**September 11, 1971—Khrushchev died at age 77**

Chapter 10
After Dad

*"...each heart is made of a different stone—
no two feel alike nor break the same way ..."*
—John Geddes (1936–), author of *A Familiar Rain*

It would be 13 years after my father's death when I learned that we did indeed have family in Russia and that we did indeed lose some during the Holocaust. Apparently my father was too young when he left Russia to remember relatives or to understand the familial relationships back in the old country.

And then it would be 20 more years before I learned who those two little girls on the passport were, in one of the most extraordinary events in my life.

But first, I needed to learn how grounded I could be without my father. I never gave myself the chance. I decided to move back to Boston, to be nearer to Renee and Tambi, the family I felt closest to. Emotionally exhausted from his illness and death, physically exhausted from quitting my job in Los Angeles, selling my car, and the move itself, I rushed into marriage six months after my father died. Leon and I were married at the Colonnade Hotel, under the huppah, by the rabbi from Temple Ohabei Shalom and I became Cynthia Jacobs. My dear friends Arlene, Winer, and Dee were there to share the moment.

I took a job as Administrator for the Department of Ophthalmology at Mass Eye and Ear Infirmary (MEEI), Harvard Medical School, working closely with Claes Dohlman, MD, who turned 100 in 2022 and who, known as the "Father of Modern Corneal Science," is one of the most highly honored ophthalmologists in the world. I also taught part-time at Mass Association for the Blind.

After three years of marriage, I realized that my husband and I were there for each other only symbolically. He had married me shortly after a woman he had been with for five years broke things off with him; I married him thinking I could heal with him.

Leon was an excellent father, but I had to struggle against his growing need to control me and wondered why I had run so fast toward what I feared most. What was not symbolic, what was very real, however, was my love for his three sons. His youngest, Steven, still lives in Boston and every time I go back East, I look forward to

Leon's sons: David, Steven, and Barry

having dinner with him. Our relationship has been ongoing for more than 40 years. Our conversations are intimate and seamless and our connection is strong, as is my perpetual love for him.

Besides Leon's sons, I inherited something else of great value: his friend Debby Brown. Still my friend now. I adored her from the moment we met.

Leon was an attorney and the divorce took a long time to negotiate. Seven weeks after it was final, he died suddenly from a heart attack at age 48.

I always thought it somewhat odd that my father's first marriage was to a Leona, and mine was to a Leon. And then, one day, as I was struggling to understand the failure of my marriage, I wrote this poem.

Still Life in Motion

*As a child, I yanked sundresses and corduroy jumpers off hangers and buried
myself in a violent attempt to shut out the shouts.
Two thin fingers struggled, time after time,
To plug ears and to dry a face impressed and imprisoned by tears.
As a woman, I found another closet where I thought I could
Hide from the everyday echoes, from the stalking shadows.
A safe place, a traditional place, a comfortable room.
But a room soon filled with familiar resentments, and gloom.
And there I remained, in my splendid silk and my lovely lace.
Until the day I looked at my husband and saw my mother's husband's face.*

During the short time we were married, before I went to MEEI, I worked at Perkins School for the Blind. Since it was part-time, I decided I also wanted to do some

After Dad

volunteer work. In 1979, I walked into the Boston office of Citizen Exchange Council (CEC), a New York-based non-profit, non-governmental organization that for 16 years had promoted professional exchanges between citizens of the US and the Soviet Union. The mission was to encourage greater mutual understanding at all levels of both societies in the hope of thus reducing the possibility of nuclear confrontation, a very real fear during the Cold War.

On January 27, 1958, the first Soviet-American agreement was signed to promote exchanges, and initially most were initiated and conducted under the auspices of each government. In 1979, President Carter refused to renew the Agreement on Cultural Relations between the two countries because of the Soviet invasion of Afghanistan. Funding for academic centers for Soviet studies declined significantly. Gradually private individuals, organizations and churches began to support projects to improve US-USSR relations, in the hope that by exposing citizens of each country to one another, they could promote understanding and knowledge of the positive aspects of the other's culture, and thus encourage peace and even disarmament. (See *US Soviet Exchanges – The Kinds of Exchanges That Have Taken Place; What Works: How Can They Be Made More Effective?*) by Sarah C. Carey, August 18, 1983, Institute for Soviet American Relations.)

During the interview, I said I would do anything but type or ask for money. When the director, Natasha Bourso-Leland, learned of my background, she asked if I would like to organize and then lead a program for the blind to the Soviet Union. I could not have been more surprised or happy. I led my first delegation to Russia the following year.

In the years to come, after CEC closed its Boston office, several of us exchange specialists did not want to stop our work and we founded a non-profit 501©3 New England group, ASCE—American Soviet Cultural Exchanges. We soon after changed our name to OASES, the Organization for American Soviet Exchanges, because it became clear that we were involved in much more than just cultural exchanges.

I became the ASCE/OASES president and traveled to Russia 20 times, creating, leading, and directing professional exchanges between such diverse groups as journalists, police officers, firefighters, doctors, physical fitness professionals, women in politics, to name just a few. (Without the aid of a fax machine or email or the ability to speak Russian!) American participants had meetings with their counterparts, visited schools, training centers, and workplaces. And Russian delegations that visited the US had the same type of meetings and conferences here with their professional peers.

The journalism exchange, the first of its kind between the Cold War enemies, continued for 12 years, until after the fall of Communism. It gave me the opportunity to interview Eduard Shevardnadze, Prime Minister under Premier Gorbachev, and to meet with editors of major Soviet newspapers, including *Pravda*.

The last of those international journalism programs involved a trip to Tehran, Iran, in 1998, where I interviewed Shirin Ebadi, future Nobel Peace Prize winner. I never dreamed during the 1979 Iran Hostage Crisis that I would go to the country in an official capacity in fewer than twenty years.

Every exchange was an adventure; every exchange taught me something new; every exchange gave me gratification. But most importantly, although I didn't realize it immediately, I was following my thread.

Part Three

Chapter 11
Exchange Programs
1980—Poland and Russia

"Give me a piece of old stone/let me find myself again ...."
Adam Wazyk (1905–1982), Polish Jew
From *"A Poem for Adults"*(1955)

POLAND

In March of 1980, the Cold War was colder than usual. The USSR had invaded Afghanistan to assume political control a few months earlier. (The Soviets didn't leave until 1989) and in response, the US had already cut back on trade and cultural agreements and refused to participate in the Olympic Games which were to be held in Moscow that year. That month, I led a special education program to Russia; my group of 26 was comprised of teachers, rehabilitation specialists, six people who were blind, and two who were deaf. The group was to meet with therapists, educators, and policy-makers in Poland and the USSR.

At a time of increased international tension, when the two superpowers could destroy one another many times over, many angry Americans were ready to abandon any attempts to affect important dialogue with the Soviets. They dehumanized them, lumped them all together as the enemy, and ignored the good that can come from mutual understanding. In a letter to Citizen Exchange Corps, then Secretary of State Cyrus Vance stated that it remained the policy of the Carter administration to encourage meaningful contact between the American and Soviet individuals, and "to avoid dismantling the framework of exchanges and cooperative activity developed with such great effort over the years."

En route to establish that type of meaningful contact in the USSR, all the more important with the recent demise of détente, I had arranged for a stop in Poland for a few days. Since my mother's family was Polish, it felt appropriate for me to visit the two countries of my ancestors.

The most impressive of our visits to schools and workplaces for the handicapped in Poland was the Institute for the Blind in Laski, twelve miles north of Warsaw. It was founded in 1911, the year my father arrived in America, by a nun who herself was blind. I was captivated by the simplicity and the warmth of the facility. Different children's groups played music or sang for us. Their rooms, with pink paisley bedspreads, hardly looked lived in because they were so neat, and the lunchroom was delightfully cheerful, with lampshades decorated with hearts and smiling faces. In the ladies room, a bar of soap hung on a string in a net bag, and one towel was there to dry your hands. At the time, some 300 children were in residence with 100 or so nuns living and working there.

Their chapel, built in 1925, was the most moving place of Christian worship I'd ever seen. The chandeliers, ceilings, and walls were made entirely of wood, the pillars of tree bark, the altar supported by a tree trunk. Tree trunks also held up statues of Christ. There were only eight rows of pews on the brick floor, divided in two by the narrow aisle down the middle. Separate from the rows were small individual praying pews, where a few nuns were seated, their heads bowed beneath crosses on the walls.

During World War II, 700 people were killed on the Laski grounds, and Hitler himself made an appearance.

Long after this visit, I learned that wooden synagogues had also been built in the 17th and 18th centuries in Poland. And in Lithuania, Belarus, and Ukraine. Typically they were painted and carved inside, with arches and multi-tiered roofs. The paintings were of zodiac symbols, Hebrew text, animals, arabesques, and floral designs. Art historian Stephen S. Kayser called these buildings "a truly original and organic manifestation of artistic expression—the only real Jewish folk art history." Most were destroyed by the Nazis, but a few survived.

In the early 1970s, contemporary American artist Frank Stella, himself a Catholic, created a series of paintings called the "Polish Village Series," to evoke the memory of those old synagogues.

After saying goodbye to the children of Laski, we were able to walk the cobblestone streets of Warsaw's Old Town. We passed stone staircases and archways, saw both Chopin's monument and the church that holds his heart. In the tiny courtyard of St. Martin's Church, in the center of the totally rebuilt Old Town, is the only tree still standing in all of Warsaw that survived Hitler's flamethrowers.

At the site of the Warsaw Ghetto, there was no sign of the anguish that was once as much a part of the landscape there as the air that sustained the ghetto, no sign of the 400,000 people who had been torn from the fabric of their lives, thrown into confinement there in an area of only 1.3 square miles, forced to brand themselves with the yellow Star of David, forced to identify themselves as something less than human in the eyes of those who would later shove them into boxcars of trains, boxcars that were so crowded that there was barely room to breathe, boxcars which transported them to the concentration camps, to a hell no sane soul could have ever imagined.

Exchange Programs: 1980—Poland & Russia

Only some 60,000 of those 400,000 were alive in the ghetto when the Uprising occurred on April 19, 1943. It is estimated that 7,000 were killed during the almost month-long fighting, and that the remainder were sent to Treblinka, Majdanek, and various labor camps, where most were eventually "eliminated." Three million Jews lived in all of Poland before the war. Most did not survive the Holocaust.

At the ghetto, we saw the monument to the memory of the Polish Jews. It was made of stone imported from Scandinavia, stone that Hitler had intended to be used for a monument to himself, intended to be a testament to the power and glory of the great leader of the Third Reich.

And we went to another place that also served as a memorial: a small 100-year-old synagogue that was no longer open. Outside, we had the good fortune to run into a man who had a key to the padlock on the wooden doors. Curiously, there was still electricity, and bare bulbs illuminated the bas-relief of the walls, the scrolled columns, and Gothic arches. Dust adorned what had once been a beautiful *shule*. Abandoned on the floor were several old prayer books, in both Hebrew and Yiddish. I convinced the man to sell one of them to me for $5. Afterwards, I worried about how to get it out of the country through both Polish and then Soviet customs.

That evening, the group was invited to the home of a Polish Jew, Aleksander Najmanowicz, whom one of our group met on the street earlier in the day. Although his wife was not Jewish, and his sons had not been raised Jewish, Aleksander had many paintings on his walls that reflected his heritage, paintings of marriages and musicians in the old *shtetls*, of Jewish men and women who danced, who laughed, who were happy. He told us that there were currently only around 1,000 Jews in Warsaw, most of them assimilated. "On Yom Kipper, (the holiest of days for all Jews), only 100 or so go to temple. In Moscow, many more attend services every Saturday morning, but the KGB is always there."

Aleksander, a sad, soft-spoken man, had lost his entire family in Treblinka. He himself left Poland during the early days of the war, believing it to be dangerous for Jews. When I asked him why his family hadn't departed when he did, he said few thought the whispered rumors about what Hitler was doing were true. Plus, they were used to anti-Semitism; it had always been there, kept alive by those who believed myths. One such myth states that there was Polish blood in matzo, because for every batch baked, the blood of a young Gentile boy was used instead of the blood of a lamb. Poles had even killed Jews before the war, by gruesome means, including stoning.

Aleksander actually found safety working as a building engineer in Russia, another country that did not treat its Jews well. I thought about that as our train rolled along toward the USSR. Crossing the border to Russia was easy, once the train changed wheels. (The tracks have a different size gauge than those in Poland. Nicholas I, who ruled Russia from 1825 to 1855 built the first railroads and bowing to xenophobia, intentionally designed them to guard against easy access to the country by foreigners.)

But our entry into the country was more than easy. When we stopped at the border, an American woman in my group leaned out her compartment window and waved to a Russian woman on a nearby train. Impulsively, she handed a rose to one of the grease-covered railroad workers walking along the tracks and motioned for him to take it over to the woman. A few moments later, the Russian woman sent him back with a two-kopeck coin. "For good luck," he mumbled through a toothless grin, as he handed it up to the American. As each woman smiled and threw a kiss, the Russians and Americans who had been watching quietly from their own windows began to wave and shout hellos to one another.

At the same time, I worried about my customs declaration form, which required all visitors to list how much money they were carrying into the country, as well as valuables such as jewelry. I had a ring I was bringing in to give to someone and didn't know whether to "forget" to declare it or declare it and deal later with the consequences of no longer having it.

The ring had been given to me by a 43-year old woman named Galina to take to her mother in Moscow, whom she expected to never see again. Galina was a speech pathologist living and working at the Fernald School in Boston who was able to tell me a lot about education for the deaf in Russia, information I needed to prepare for the trip. She also provided me with the names of schools we should visit and people in the field we should meet. I was very grateful to her and more than happy to do this small favor for her, especially after she told me a bit about herself.

Galina had married a Jewish man in the USSR who, because he periodically protested the arrest of dissidents, was ultimately fired from his job and put on trial. Galina's brother-in-law was asked to testify and refused. (Because of that, he had been under surveillance by the KGB for the past 12 years; I didn't learn about that part until my return to Boston.)

Galina's husband Ilya was labeled as a dissident and sentenced to prison, sent first to Lefortovo Prison in Moscow. When released, he continued his dissident activity and was re-arrested two years later and sent to prison in Tashkent, Central Asia, and then to Siberia. He was forced to work outside in both climate extremes with very little clothing on. He came back after three years a broken man. Galina said that the prison system so breaks your spirit that to move from chair to chair is a big undertaking.

Ilya was unable to find work because the KGB would not give permission to any employer to hire him. Furthermore, once a week he was called in by the KGB and asked to make a public statement that he had been wrong. He refused. They wanted him to leave the country, but he was unable to muster up the strength to go through the bureaucratic procedures, and Galina could not have done it herself because she was not the head of household. Ultimately, her husband's despair drove him to commit suicide in 1973. He jumped off of an 11th-floor balcony.

At the time, Galina had a four-month old daughter and an older son and through Jewish Family Services, was able to come to America. She left Russia with bread and vodka, having been taught that these things didn't exist outside of Russia. She said it had been a sudden culture shock, arriving in Vienna, Austria, and seeing all the wonderful pastry.

"Leaving the Soviet Union was like running from a burning building, knowing nothing or where or how you'd end up, knowing just that you must get out," she told me. "Once in America, you become as a child, having to learn how to do everything. First, the language problem. I was afraid of the telephone when it rang. Then other things—the bank, learning to drive a car, etc. For several years, I existed as if in a dream."

Amnesty International reported that between 1975 and 1980, 400 people were known to have been imprisoned in Russia because of their political or religious views. They suspected the number of dissidents in Soviet jails was actually much higher. And two months before my trip, the human rights activist, dissident, and nuclear physicist, father of the Soviet hydrogen bomb, Andrei Sakharov, and his wife Elena Bonner, were sent into internal exile in Gorki.

After hearing so many stories about the difficulty of Soviet customs, we all prepared ourselves for the worst. At the border checkpoint, a young boy in uniform came into our compartment, checked our passports and visas, collected our declaration forms, and simply inquired if we had any magazines. I gave him a copy of *House Beautiful* and, smiling, he left us alone immediately.

I opted to declare the ring and to worry about its absence later.

"Who are these Russians? No one can say with certainty. But if their perception of America is as flawed as we believe it is, then our perceptions of the Soviet Union just could be flawed, too. In the absence of any real dialogue, the same old fears and doubts continue to dominate our relationship."
—Walter Cronkite, American Broadcast Journalist
(1916–2009)
New York Times, Sunday, June 14, 1981

RUSSIA

Once we were on our way again, I spent a long time staring out the window in the waning daylight. I looked out at the small villages and at the people. People whose breath was visible, people who walked along the tracks carrying lanterns, people who passed by the white birch trees, people who were carrying net bags with bread and whatever else they had managed to find for supper, people who were heading to the warmth of their small wooden homes.

The Cossacks were there too, but of course they were Soviet soldiers now, soldiers with loaded rifles that cast ominous shadows in the dirty snow, soldiers who no longer threw stones at Jewish homes, but who had far more sophisticated means of aggression.

I felt I was heading home too, but for the first time.

At Brest, I had to interrupt thoughts of my father and the Russia of his youth. The train stopped to enable us to change dollars into rubles, so that we could eat dinner in the dining car. But we couldn't find the bank. With only a few minutes to spare, I went off alone, did find it, and convinced a woman there to change $50. Suddenly another woman came up to me, grabbed me by the arm and pulled me to the train.

In English, she said "Hurry, the train will leave without you. Which car are you in?" I knew where my car was, but not its number, so I replied " I don't know."

"Number 11," she said, "get on quickly."

Clearly someone or ones were officially assigned to keep an eye on us.

When we arrived in Moscow, we checked into the Cosmos Hotel. Brand new, built for the Olympics, it was impressive. Porters brought our bags to our rooms, and we had a quick dinner of greasy potatoes, mystery meat, and mineral water. As soon as we could break away from the group, my interpreter, Veronica Worth, and I took the Metro to Red Square. Natasha had advised that it was much more impressive to see Red Square for the first time at night. She was so right.

Veronica and I had to walk for a few blocks beyond our Metro stop. The streets were deserted and it was snowing. We crossed a road illegally—one was supposed to use the underground passages—and a lone soldier in the distance yelled to us. Before he could ticket us, I ran up to him, put on my "naive" face, a big smile, and breathlessly and excitedly asked him where we could find Lenin. He looked disgusted and it was obvious that he thought we were "stupid" Americans. But it worked. He gave us directions and no reprimand.

While we waited for the 1:00 AM changing of the guard in front of the granite Lenin's Tomb, we spoke with a soldier named Victor, who immediately proposed to Veronica, saying he desperately wanted to come to America. Needless to say, in spite of Victor's deep, intense, beautiful blue eyes, Veronica turned him down. He agreed to let me take his photo, but another soldier saw us and said he would smash the camera if I took the picture.

At precisely 12:55 AM, we heard footsteps crunching the snow, echoing across the Square. The soldier guards, two of them, came out goose-stepping from behind one of the Kremlin gates. That is the thing that stood out the most for me about Russia—so

Exchange Programs: 1980—Poland & Russia

many military, so young, so everywhere. The innocence on their boyish faces contrasted dramatically with the trepidation affected by their uniforms—polished leather boots, long woolen coats, fur hats with red stars in the center, and the loaded rifles.

There we were, in Red Square. Lenin at rest in front of us; St. Basil's and its famous onion domes to our left; GUM, the large department store behind us; red stars lit above us on top of the spire towers of the Kremlin; and the heavy snow creating white caps on our heads, turning even our eyebrows bushy white.

Red Square. Soldiers. Snow. The Communist country, occupying one-sixth of the earth's surface, founded on the unfulfilled principle "from each according to his abilities, to each according to his needs." I was finally in Russia, the Russia I had dreamed of visiting since childhood.

The next morning, after only a few hours sleep, we went to the showplace synagogue on Archipova Street, the only one in Moscow, the only one the Soviets allowed to operate, to prove that they did indeed tolerate religion. Unlike the one in Warsaw, this ornate building had stained glass windows, huge menorahs, a beautiful ark for the Torah, and was very well maintained. Twelve old men dressed in black sat around a table reading, studying, waiting for the Sabbath service to begin at 10:00 AM. I spoke to a short, older woman who was the *shamus*, the keeper of the temple.

More Yiddish than I knew I understood came back from my childhood, since she knew no English and I no Russian. Later, also in Yiddish, I talked to a tall, good-looking man with a red star on his lapel. He asked me many questions, and all of those I was able to understand. I answered honestly. When we finished speaking, an elderly Jew with a long white beard grabbed my attention by bumping into me. As he caught my eye, he glanced over at the tall man, and almost imperceptibly, shook his head. I understood the warning. I had been speaking to one of the KGB infiltrators Alexander had warned us about back in Warsaw.

When we left the temple, we got our first real look at Moscow on our city tour. The Kremlin. The Tomb of the Unknown Soldier. The Bolshoi. The Tretyakov Museum was most frustrating because we had only one hour to see 57 rooms, with wonderful items in each. The collection of icons was impressive, but I especially liked the paintings, many depicting the old Russia I had always imagined. As is typical, each museum room had a keeper, usually a woman, who took her job very seriously, watching out for the smallest infraction. And she was usually short, wore heavy woolen stockings, flat black shoes and a *babushka*. (*Babushka* is a term used to describe both a headscarf and an old woman.)

We drove by KGB Headquarters (where I would be received formally, inside, by the KGB some years down the road.) But throughout the city, most impressive was the number of people and posters. Everywhere we looked there were long lines of Muscovites, so many with gold teeth, in front of whatever store had goods to sell that day, or old men wearing chests full of war medals at the taxi stands or trolley stops. Huge propaganda posters covered entire sides of buildings and extolled the values and virtues of working for the collective good. Glory to Labor! Glory to Lenin! Glory to the Communist Party!

Other posters hailed the upcoming Olympics. Everywhere we went, be it the stadium where they were to be held or our hotel dining room, people angrily asked us why the US had cancelled its participation in the games. We tried to explain it was because of the USSR's invasion of Afghanistan, and then we tried not to get involved in long discussions. Often people pressed us to discuss our upcoming primaries and presidential election, and often we heard them say confidently "Kennedy (Teddy) means peace, he will keep us out of war." Of course, he lost the Democratic nomination to Jimmy Carter.

Sometimes, they had another agenda. We were approached several times and asked if we could change some dollars for rubles, or if anyone in the group would sell jeans, for which they were willing to pay $110. Or the watch I was wearing—would I consider trading it for two jars of caviar and 20 rubles? It was tempting, but we didn't want to risk it.

We were the only group of Americans in Moscow at the time, and our purpose was professional, not political. And we knew that most of the Soviets didn't really understand why the US was boycotting the Olympics. For the decline in US-Soviet relations, Party boss Leonid Brezhnev had blamed the American "imperialists" because of their aggressive interference in Afghanistan, and he repeatedly told his people that he took their military into Afghanistan only because its leadership had beseeched the Soviet Union for assistance.

As for our professional program, visits to schools or training centers for the deaf or the blind were very informative and we were graciously received, given tours, food, and gifts made by the students or residents. Often they provided entertainment and we reciprocated by singing "It's a Small World" or "This Land is Your Land". But I was most proud in particular of two of my participants. One totally blind woman sang and played the guitar, and a totally deaf woman recited a poem she had written about her world of silence.

Our stay in Leningrad, built by Peter the Great to be modeled after Amsterdam and often referred to as the "Venice of the North," was more relaxed. We were lucky to get a room with a view of the water, so we looked out at the Neva River and the battleship *Aurora* that was moored directly in front of our window. Built in 1903, the ship fought in the Russo-Japanese War, and in October 1917, it has been said that a shot from one of her guns signaled the beginning of the assault on the Winter Palace and the October Revolution.

Exchange Programs: 1980—Poland & Russia

The Neva was frozen every day in the morning, but began to break up as the day went on. I took solitary walks alongside the riverbanks. I'd stop, close my eyes, and listen to the forceful sounds of the floating ice as it cracked and collided with other chunks. And I thought of Tchaikovsky, who tried to commit suicide once by standing in the cold water of the Neva in the hopes of freezing himself to death.

The city tour leader told us that Leningrad had 101 islands and 620 bridges, took us to the Peter and Paul Fortress and the huge Hermitage Museum, where there have been guardian cats since 1747 to keep mice and rats in check. Nowadays, since there is poison for the rodents, the cats are more of a tradition. They wander the basements, the grounds, and the garden, but are not allowed in the galleries.

The tour also took us to the Nevsky Prospekt with its Dom Knigi, or House of Books, where I bought two volumes of Pushkin, in English. While I stood there with my money in my outstretched hand, the cashier seemed preoccupied and somewhat curt. But when she realized I was American, she stopped what she was doing and said, "It's a pity you are not coming to the Olympics."

"Yes, it is, isn't it?" I replied.

"Well, never mind," she said, and a far-away look came over her face. She suddenly leaned toward me and lowered her voice. "It really doesn't matter, nothing else matters so long as we have peace, so long as we don't kill one another."

And then, just outside the door to the store, a poorly dressed man approached us. "Have you a light?" he asked in broken English, holding out a cigarette.

We said "no" and he stepped closer.

"Do you maybe have some old newspapers or books, anything is alright?" he asked.

We took a chance, hoping he wasn't a KGB man, and offered him some newspapers we had brought with us. He did not seem to expect this so soon, and he hesitated a moment before replying, "Maybe it would be better not to. Look, if you are here again, here is my address and phone number."

Suddenly, a frightened look came over him. "Maybe … it's just better not to," he said, grabbing the slip of paper out of my hand. "I once gave my address to an American tourist. As he was leaving the country, the Customs officials found it and the KGB came to question me. Let's forget it."

He shook our hands quickly and disappeared into the crowd.

That evening, our dinner was at the Sadko Restaurant, well known for receiving groups of tourists. Besides us, there was a large group from Canada, and one from Yugoslavia. After a meal of champagne, wine, punch, vodka, and some unmemorable food, we started applauding and interacting with each group. The balalaika band got us all singing to "America the Beautiful," "Frere Jacques," "She'll be Coming 'Round the Mountain," even "Jingle Bells." Soon, every person marched single file through the restaurant to "When the Saints Come Marching In." Finally, one of the members of our group and I got up and danced the Hora. I got so dizzy circling as we danced that I reeled across the stage and fell down. I couldn't stop laughing and had no real option except to get up, smile, and take a bow.

Another evening, we were fortunate to be invited to the private home of Valery and Nadia, friends of Natasha. Because Soviet citizens were not allowed inside the hotels for foreigners, and all guests had to show identification before entering, Valery met us outside the hotel, where he greeted us with a wide grin and a firm handshake before taking us by taxi to his home in one of Moscow's high-rise suburbs.

His building looked impressively new from the outside, although not yet complete because there was no landscaping, only mound after mound of dirt. Inside, in the halls and stairwells, we were shocked to see how old and dilapidated it actually was.

As was the custom, we took off our shoes and chose a pair to step into from the many provided at the door for this very purpose. The first thing I noticed about their place was the great number of books and records. The second was the peeling wallpaper. What surprised me most, however, were the pictures of Mickey Mouse and Sleepy, one of the seven dwarfs, painted on the wall above the bathtub. They had a beautiful antique table and chairs and an authentic icon, yet the apartment would have been considered poverty level in the States.

This couple considered themselves lucky to have three rooms and a private kitchen and bath for themselves and their two children. Most Russians lived in one room and shared common kitchens and baths with several other families. (We were told that many who shared bathrooms had their own portable seats to fit over the toilet.) Thus, most families had only one to two children because it was so difficult to get adequate housing. The housing shortage resulted in a three to four year wait before the state assigned an apartment. For those who could afford to buy one, the wait was usually nine to ten months and 40% of the cost of the apartment had to be paid in cash. The remainder was paid off either monthly or annually over 25 years, with no interest. Our Intourist guide said that the average price for two rooms in Moscow was 4500 rubles, for a three room flat it was 5800 rubles. Our dollar exchange rate for one ruble was $2.60.

Valery was charming and warm. He had blond hair, a bright complexion, was a handsome man who laughed often. In contrast, the very obviously religious Nadia was drawn, tired, haggard and without makeup. We sensed a deep unhappiness that her strong religious faith could not alleviate. She complained all evening about how difficult their life was, saying that it was especially so for women, who had to stand in line daily to obtain basic necessities. Stores regularly and recently ran out of staples like soap and thread. Coincidentally I had both in my purse, which at the last minute I had picked up in my hotel room in NY. I gave them to her, and she absentmindedly smelled the Camay soap all evening. Their soap was harsh, more like lye.

Exchange Programs: 1980—Poland & Russia

Valery was a researcher at the University. His work was on electric brain waves. He did some studies on ESP a while back, and concluded that people read other's emotional states, but not their thoughts. He told us that he had been asked to join the Communist Party, and had so far been able to avoid it by telling them he didn't feel that he was worthy. He said that many at the University agree with the US position on Afghanistan. He had a copy of Solzhenitsyn in his cupboard, "The Oak and The Calf". I asked how he got asked to join the Party when he has a book that is banned and Americans in his home. "Obviously" he said, "they don't know."

And then I asked about the Jews. "Anti-Semitism is almost universal in Russia," he said. He told me it was very difficult for them, that they couldn't find jobs, that there was an unofficial 2% quota in the university, that most of the working class was anti-Semitic, and that even the intelligentsia was divided in its feelings about Jews.

We ate as we talked. Nadia served Georgian wine, tea, and a light supper of bread, cheese, lard, jelly, and candy. Everything was fine until I had to spread the lard on my bread and eat it. I had tried to refuse it, but they insisted. Only my fear of embarrassing myself and insulting them kept me from throwing up. Otherwise, it was a great evening, and I was happy to have had the opportunity to get inside a Soviet home, to meet people who were so friendly toward us.

Certainly Valery revealed a very different side of the USSR than I saw on the train when we were leaving the country, heading to Helsinki, Finland to catch our Finnair flight back to the States.

One member of our group who had hidden an illegally purchased antique icon in the ceiling of our compartment ran around the station at the last minute looking for things to buy, to spend all the rubles he had changed on the Black Market that were worthless outside of the USSR. He ended up buying a case of ice cream, so all of us were enjoying our treats as the train pulled out of the station around noon.

In the meantime, Veronica, my interpreter, was trying to quickly translate a letter given to us in Moscow.

To make contact with Galina's family, so that I could turn over the ring, I had gone to a telephone booth on the street, having heard that the hotel phones were all tapped. Luckily someone answered the first time I called, and I set up a time and place to secretly meet her brother-in-law. (Wanting to protect the contacts Natasha gave to us, those Russians who would risk getting into trouble for meeting with Americans, Veronica and I took care to list only their first names in our address books and to put their phone numbers in a code we devised.)

We met Galina's brother-in-law near the Hotel Cosmos, where he took the ring and gave us a letter for Galina in return. We knew, of course, that it was illegal to carry letters in or out of the country. Veronica had not had time since we left Moscow to read the letter, and knowing we had to go through customs when we got to the border between Russia and Finland, I advised her to memorize as much of it as she could, then flush it down the toilet.

When the senior customs official came, he asked to see the leader of the group. I identified myself and he then began pointing his finger and asking questions of all of us in the compartment.

"Whom did you contact in Moscow and Leningrad?"

"Who gave you something to take out of Russia?"

"Who gave you rubles?"

Interpreter Veronica Worth and the author

When we answered "no one" to each question, he came back with, "Lies, lies, everything you say is a lie!"

Next, he wanted to see my jewelry. When he saw that I didn't have the ring, he asked where it was. I said I had lost it. "No, you didn't," he replied coldly, getting angrier by the minute. Then he wanted to see any letters we might have, as well as a list of all our professional contacts.

While we were speaking with him, one young soldier went through my bags, stopping a long time to inspect my make-up kit. He would pull out something, examine it, then look at my face as if to determine how I used it. The soldier going through Veronica's bags, although also young, was less curious. He simply dumped everything out of her luggage. She was sweating. I suspected she was probably worrying about them finding the icon in the ceiling, or my old prayer book from Poland that I had carefully and creatively, I thought, hidden in my luggage inside my dirty underwear.

Suddenly the senior official directed her to go to a different compartment. While she was gone, we asked him why he was being so tough on her.

"Because she's made a bad mistake."

The owner of the icon said, "She's a young girl. All young girls make mistakes, you are upsetting her."

"She is nervous because she is guilty," the official explained.

When she came back, he barked that it was now my turn. She whispered to me that she had had a body search. Trying to joke with the angry official, I asked who was going to do my search. He pointed to a woman down the hall, and I replied, "Good, I was afraid you'd be doing it." That at least caused a momentary hint of a smile to cross his face.

Exchange Programs: 1980—Poland & Russia

My search wasn't bad. The uniformed woman patted me down and then in Russian asked if I had anything in my bra. Since I spoke not one word of the language, other than *please* and *thank you*, I thought she was asking if I were wearing a bra, so I kept saying "yes." Finally, I understood that she wanted to know if I had rubles hidden in my bra. I laughed and said "no." She did nothing else, but indicated that I should just stand there for a few minutes, presumably so it would look as if she had done a more thorough job.

When I got back to our compartment, they were still giving Veronica a hard time. The customs official demanded to see my journal. After he opened it, he stared down at me and exclaimed, "We have a letter in your writing." I emphatically said, "No, you don't". To which he replied, "We'll prove it to you."

He then showed me the letter for Galina and a piece of paper with names and phone numbers. I couldn't believe what I was seeing. The last I knew, Veronica had flushed the letter down the toilet, and here it was before me, dry. To say that I was impressed with the Soviet retrieval techniques was most definitely an understatement.

Before he could again say that I had written the list, Veronica admitted it was hers and that she had thrown it away. "And the letter?" he asked.

"I've never seen it before" she answered. Over and over, he said she was lying. Over and over, she denied it.

Then he turned and repeatedly accused me of lying when I said I had lost the ring. Finally, I looked him straight in the eye and acknowledged that he was right.

"Ah ha!" he exclaimed. And this time, a real smile crossed his face.

It disappeared quickly when I announced, "It was stolen from my hotel room, and since things are so tense between our two countries, I did not want to notify anyone about it and cause a problem. However, I would be happy to go with you right now to fill out any reports you think are necessary."

I knew at that moment from the hatred in his eyes that he probably wanted desperately to push me under the wheels of the train when it started moving, or worse. He gave me a long, hard Hollywood stare before he turned and stomped out of our compartment in disgust.

Veronica then told me that at the last minute, she had hidden the letter behind the pipes in the back of the sink in the bathroom because she felt she hadn't had time to really memorize it. Along with it, she had discarded her handwritten list of contacts. (There were no phone books in the USSR.) No wonder she had been so nervous. She was worried that they would take her off the train to interrogate her to find out where the letter came from. The letter was a bad one to be found. The writer said they were all disgusted with the USSR, that medical care was poor, there were food shortages, etc. I thought if the authorities did figure out who wrote the letter, if they were indeed following Galina's brother-in-law, things would not go well for the family.

However, with this distraction, the soldiers did not do a thorough search of the compartment or our luggage. The stashed icon and my old prayer book from Poland were successfully smuggled out of the country.

But I was very concerned that in the future, I would not be successful in any attempt to get a visa to return to Russia. I believed in the importance of these exchanges, believed that exchanges changed official stereotypes coming from both countries, believed that there was an urgent need to communicate, a need to understand that both countries had their own propaganda, a need most Soviet citizens understood. I also knew that many Americans were unaware that Russia had been our ally in WWII, unaware that the USSR had lost more than 20 million military and civilians during that war, while the US lost fewer than half a million, and unaware that Soviet citizens were as much afraid of confrontation with us as we were with them.

And we had had a very successful professional program—visits to several centers for the blind or deaf, and many meetings with people involved in the field. Nevertheless, I was very happy to be leaving, very ready to go home to my own bed, and very ready to breathe free air that wasn't tainted by the smell of diesel fuel.

Little did I know then how many times I would return to the country. How many times I would smuggle things out of the country. But no customs experience ever equaled that first one.

Shortly after that trip, I took another one to Canastota, New York, a weekend when it felt like I had come home. Where I soaked up the warmth and emotional generosity of the Setticases. Where MaryAnne and I went to the local bar, had some weed, laughed a lot, went to Sylvan Beach to play Skeeball, 3 in a Line, then to Eddie's Restaurant for ice cream.

Where the next night, Michael and I went to the beach. He told me I was precious to him, and that he had never stopped caring for me. For over an hour, we stood on the boulder in the sand, remembering, sharing, holding one another. And then we went to his house and made love.

I was struck by the fact that we had known one another for 17 years, and yet we didn't know who we were anymore. What we did know was that a love was still there.

Chapter 12
1982—Russia and Mongolia

*"The mighty force and charm of the taiga are not in its giant trees
or its mind-boggling silence, but in the fact that, perhaps,
some migratory birds alone know where it ends....."*
Anton Chekhov (1860–1904), Russian writer

RUSSIA

In 1982, Natasha was busy working with the New England Society of Newspaper Editors (NESNE) on an upcoming conference with Soviet journalists, but she took time out for an Audubon Society trip, organized through CEC in New York. She talked me into coming with her. She served as facilitator and interpreter and I served as the only non-birdwatcher in the group.

Again, packing was a challenge. Packages of tissues for my purse because there was rarely toilet paper in public bathrooms, soap that was often missing from hotel rooms, gifts, snacks, bags for purchases because none are provided, and Marlboros, the most desired American brand of cigarettes, for barter. All the *what ifs*. Especially medications, even extra shoelaces. And, things to remember: never jaywalk; take absolutely no photos of the military and always ask civilians for permission to take their picture, don't deal on the Black Market; always carry my hotel card and customs declaration with me. So my purse was always full—and heavy. One of my favorite things about the Soviet Union? The men carry the women's purses, at least they did then.

We were greeted at the Moscow Airport with the news that our luggage hadn't made the flight out of Finland. Hence, a five-hour wait in customs until it arrived. We were served a familiar dinner of unknown meat, carrots, greasy potatoes, and vanilla ice cream, made more interesting by vodka, and most unusual flower arrangements on the table—scraggly dandelions minus all their petals.

We had a decent night's sleep in the Hotel Rossiya, with accommodations for 6,000 guests. Because I was then working at the Massachusetts Eye and Ear Infirmary (MEEI), I was interested in seeing the Helmholtz Research Institute of Ophthalmology. Natasha took me for a private meeting and tour to the 250-bed facility before she headed off to be with the group. Even though I had written in advance, I was told it was not possible to allow me in. However, after showing sincere disappointment and my warmest smile, and simply not leaving, I was finally given the "not possible" tour by one of the physicians and shown all that I asked to see. The pediatric wards crammed seven children into tiny rooms with beds lined up three to a wall with no space between the foot of one and the head of the next. No space at all for visitors, hardly any space for the children. The operating rooms were very old, with white tile walls. The little old lady with a kerchief doing laundry in the sink in the hall outside didn't contribute much to making it all seem sanitary.

After the tour, Dr. Natalia Makarovskaya escorted me to her office, where she gave me things I hadn't asked for—three shots of cognac, two cups of tea, and several—definitely more than three—pieces of delicious dark chocolate. All of which I accepted, only to be polite, of course. We talked—some medicine, some hospital administration (500 doctors are affiliated with the Institute), some politics. We agreed that neither Reagan nor Brezhnev should qualify for "Man of the Year."

Back at the hotel, I chose to go for a walk. It was lilac time and the smell was carried by the breeze and the people on the street who held big bunches of the flowers in their hands. First, I photographed St. Basil's Cathedral from every conceivable angle, and couldn't imagine a time when I wouldn't find its onion-shaped domes enchanting. Then I strolled over to Lenin's Mausoleum, built in 1924 of wood, then rebuilt in 1930 of red granite and black labradorite. Lenin's name is over the portal, his body on view inside, and as always, his admirers and the curious were waiting hours to get in for a moment's glimpse. I was not one of them that day.

Outside the Square, I noticed a number of Red Bands—aspiring Party members who were a sort of unofficial, yet sanctioned, group of vigilantes who patrolled the parks and streets to keep order. They were often rough, demanded to search, and were known to beat up people, especially homosexuals or Jews. Apparently, they determined I wasn't of any interest.

(In spite of ongoing government denial that Russia had no prostitutes, no gays, no AIDS, in 2012 St. Petersburg passed a law to fine promotion of homosexual behavior. As a result, Canada issued a warning to gay travelers planning to visit the city.)

The next day, we boarded a bus to take us to Domodedova Airport. Along the way, we saw the summer home of Peter the Great, copses of birches whose leaves really do shimmer silver in the sunlight, and one old man, just barely walking with the help of a cane, clutching a bouquet of violets. When we got off the bus, we left the fresh air and flowers behind and walked into an atmosphere that reminded me of what Ellis Island must have been like during the height of the immigrations. Where all the flights arrived and departed to and from Siberia and Central Asia, and where there was no space not filled with crowds of people. There were swarthy men, many with the traditional Uzbek hats, but Western suits circa 1950s. Most of the women were round, many corpulent; all wore peds or knee-highs with their thick heels and babushkas. Little girls wore two huge ribbons in their hair.

A visit to the ladies' room contributed to the feeling of being in a time warp. At the entrance, there was a civil defense poster from the WWII era, with photos of people in gas masks, boots, different uniforms, with directions of what to do in case of an alert. In the 1950s, Americans were encouraged to create bomb shelters in their cellars, and when I was in grade school, we had those Civil Defense drills I mentioned earlier.

The American government eventually became more sophisticated and distributed evacuation plans for entire cities in the event of a nuclear attack. I thought of the little boys I used to know who played war with their toy guns, who expressed absolute delight with their pretend murders, and I saw the military and political leaders of the US and the USSR who still played war games, while the adults in their countries feared that they would turn fantasy into reality.

After a four-hour flight to Novosibirsk, a half-hour wait at the airport, then two more hours of flying, we arrived in Irkutsk, one of the oldest towns in Siberia. The sun was just coming up, turning the sky bright red. As we deplaned, we were enveloped by the sweet smell of the *taiga*, or boreal forest. (Russia has the most forests of any country in the world.) It smelled like Christmas with Siberian pine, scotch pine, spruce, and larch trees everywhere. There, instead of lilacs, people carried large bunches of pine branches. *En route* to our hotel, our bus took us down poplar-tree-lined streets named after Karl Marx, Lermontov, Gogol, and I saw my first wooden houses. One hundred to 130 years old, ornate fretwork adorned the porches, windows, shutters and cornices, and most were painted pastel shades of green, peach, and blue with white trim. All had lace curtains and plants in the windows and almost all were to be torn down soon because of the difficulty of heating them and the fire hazards that they posed. We were assured that some of the most beautiful would be preserved for historical value.

Even though we had not slept the previous night, Natasha and I decided to forego a nap and went immediately in search of her friend, Professor Stanislav Lipin.

We first stopped in a grocery story and compared products. Butter was the same price as it was for us at home; there were four big vats of different kinds of lard, also smelts, eels, tiny bagels, cakes, and fresh roses in a vase on the pastry counter. The shop was crowded with short ladies with their net shopping bags, wearing heavy stockings, black dresses, and scarves—all reminding me of my Bubbe. Even the little babies had little scarves wrapped around their little heads.

We found Lipin at the Institute of Epidemiology and Microbiology. A doctor of biological sciences, he often went on expeditions to the North, almost to the Arctic Circle, to Tiksi, to study the wildlife. He specifically studied parasites and animal diseases and how drastic changes to the environment affect the balance of nature. Slightly pigeon-toed, with red hair, a full beard, two gold teeth, and a potbelly that was

Stanislas Lipin, doctor of biological sciences (1932–2018)

somehow cute on him, I found him delightfully charming. He wore orange glasses, suspenders, a beret, and a pocket watch, and when he saw Natasha, his face lit up into a big smile. He gave her a great big bear hug and insisted that we come for dinner to his home that evening.

In the meantime, he accompanied us and our group on the 40-mile trip to Lake Baikal. We passed small villages and cows roaming freely and learned that it was winter there for six months a year, that while the average temperature was 25 degrees above zero, it sometimes fell to 75 below zero in the Irkutian Republic.

Twenty five million people endured this kind of weather in Siberia, comprising one tenth of the population of the USSR. The USSR covered one sixth of the inhabited globe, with 110 national strains, 12 seas, two million miles of rivers, one quarter of a million lakes. Of those lakes, Baikal is the deepest and holds 20 percent of the world's fresh water. At 25 to 30 million years old, it is the oldest lake on earth. I collected some stones from the lakebed and we all put our hands in the water to feel just how cold it was.

Unfortunately, two decades later, despite it being listed as a UNESCO World Heritage Site, the lake was polluted and facing even more threats from industrial waste, dams, climate change, agricultural run-off, all of which contribute to the huge growth of algae, which cuts off oxygen to plants and animals. The previously pristine water was no longer safe to drink.

At dinner, I met Stanislav's wife Lida and their fourteen-year-old son, Anton. Their home was immaculate, very warm and cozy. Books everywhere, pine bouquets, Oriental rugs, and hunting rifles and knives hanging from the walls. The house was modest, but dinner was anything but. An incredible meal, beginning with vodka and orange caviar,

1982—Russia, Mongolia

then sprats (fish from Latvia), *chermeska* (wild garlic with sour cream), *bolete* (pickled mushrooms with fresh dill), *pirogy* (small meat pies), and chicken with horseradish. Finally, tea from a silver electric samovar and chocolate cake.

The next day was our last in Irkutsk, in the taiga. The mosquitos were out, but not too annoying since we had all bathed in some sort of anti-bug spray or cream. In the morning, I joined the group in their search for the Siberian thrush, the oriental turtle-dove, gray wagtail, and the cuckoo, which I really enjoyed seeing and listening to. But sometimes I looked down, too, at the yellow violets, the wildflowers, and the wild garlic.

After a while, I strayed from the group and found a huge rock where I could sit alone to feel the gentle breeze and lift my face to the sun. A rooster crowed in the distance, dogs barked, butterflies flew by. There I was, enjoying my solitude in Siberia. Siberia! Where most Americans thought it was winter all the time, thought the sun never shined, thought there were prison camps around every bend.

After lunch that day, I spent time with Anton playing catch with a ball I had brought and different games on a magic slate. His English wasn't very good, but it was better than my Russian. When we played Hangman, he had to think of a word in English and I had to come up with one in Russian. As we spent more time together, he relaxed a little and smiled more. A nice boy, tall and lanky, blond, and shy. I sat with him on the bus on the way back to the hotel and at one point, when we stopped so the group could hurry out to look at another bird, he also went out—but not to look for birds. He returned with a tiny bouquet of forget-me-nots for me.

Today, in spite of the miles and the years between us, Anton, who now has three children, and I are Facebook friends. Stanislav and I corresponded once a year, every year, to send New Year's greetings, until he died from cancer in 2018 at the age of 86.

Anton and the author

Paths of Stones

> *"The view....is a never-ending desert...The endlessness gives a feeling of infinity.*
> *In infinity both death and life are suspended.*
> *It is a moment of freedom from both."*
> —Anais Nin, American writer
> (1903-1977)

MONGOLIA

Our Mongolian guide, Glegnem, met us at the airport in the capital city, Ulan Bator, (one of only four cities in the country, a country that is three times as large as France) and led us to our bus. Again, I couldn't stop looking out the window from behind the curtains. Like the child who wants to have all she sees in a candy store, I, too, wanted to capture everything I saw as we drove by, on film, and in my memory.

Most striking were the brilliant patches of color. The majority of the population still wore the traditional *del*, the double-breasted wool or satin brocade robes or tunics with high collars fastened by frogs on the right at the shoulder and under the arm. They were belted at the waist with bright sashes of yellow or tangerine, chosen deliberately to contrast with the magenta, copper, burgundy, blue, or green *del*s.

Although it was June, most of the men wore hats and heavy boots. The oldest sat at bus stops, leaning on their canes, or walked slowly, hampered by their years and a good many by extreme bowed legs. Women, some in their long traditional robes, others in Western dress with high, thick heels and thin socks, walked faster. In courtyards and between apartment buildings, children laughed and shouted and played in the same spirit children share throughout the world. Schoolgirls wore Soviet-style uniforms with

Natasha

The author

white pinafores and the wide bows in their hair, and whispered secrets in one another's ears. Most teenagers wore Western clothing, and a few proudly sported widely coveted jeans.

Russian soldiers, also in uniform, casually walked the streets, past red flags, posters, and huge billboards that extolled Lenin and the Soviet Union. Some middle-aged men, most likely officials, appeared in drab, old-fashioned Western suits.

We were to spend ten days in the Mongolian People's Republic, or Outer Mongolia, as it was still called by some. Our time was to be divided between various campsites in the Gobi Desert and the capital, Ulan Bator, which when translated means "Red Hero."

Mongolia had a dramatic, if not peaceful history. It was ruled by Huns until Genghis Khan appeared in 1206. Then his grandson, the great Kublai Khan, became emperor of China in 1271. At its peak, the Mongol Empire spread from Indochina to Tibet to the Persian Gulf and the Black Sea, until 1691, when the Manchus conquered it. Mongolia remained under harsh Manchu rule, sealed off from the rest of the world, until 1911, when it asserted its independence and became an autonomous republic within China. With Lenin's guidance and Soviet Red Army units, in 1921, Sukhe Bator, the National Hero, led the country in revolution. In 1924, the new order was established, and Mongolia was proclaimed an independent People's Republic.

Mongolia was important to the USSR as a buffer zone; there were Soviet artillery and soldiers stationed at the Chinese border. However, the Mongolians enthusiastically adopted Marxist-Lenin principles, and with the economic aid and influence of the USSR, during the next six decades, took a giant step from feudal state to modernity. It was easy to understand the Mongolian loyalty to the Soviet Union. Sixty years before, it was an illiterate country, languishing in the stranglehold of the Buddhist lamas and their celibacy; in 1981, a Mongolian orbited the earth. Jugdermedidiyn Gurragcha, the son of a herdsman, was on board the Russian Soyuz 39.

Thousands of Russians worked in Mongolia then, and the Russian language was compulsory from fourth-year elementary school. English was the second most popular language. It was only in 1921 that the first primary school was established, and in 1942, the Mongolian State University. The first national TV broadcasts didn't occur until 1967. The Mongolian People's Republic became a member of the United Nations in 1961, but refused diplomatic relations with the United States until 1987.

Our first stop was our hotel. Ulan Bator B. There were only two hotels in the city then; the other, as you might guess, was Ulan Bator A. We had mutton soup, an appetizer of liver, cherries, lard, butter and pickle, then the main course of beef and greasy potatoes. Dessert was a flaky pastry with raisins and fermented milk, called *aarts*.

Back on the bus, and three hours and 50 miles later, we arrived at Terelj, a yurt resort maintained by the Mongolian Tourist Organization. Forests of larch, birch, cedar, pine, asp, and elders, and creatures such as squirrels, chipmunks, wild boar, wolves, foxes, lynx, and sables surrounded the camp. The area was rich in edelweiss, which the Mongolians believe symbolizes eternity. It was thus used for kindling the first fire in the yurt of newlyweds.

We checked into our yurts, or *ger*s, as they are also called. These round dwellings with collapsible wooden lattice frames covered with felt and then canvas on top to protect from wind, dust, rain, and snow were to be our accommodations for the night. The outermost covering is white cotton, which is usually decorated. In the winter, there are many layers of felt. Our yurts were carpeted, had one naked light bulb, and a black, round iron stove with a pipe going through the open hole in the center of the umbrella-like ceiling. A felt flap, controlled by ropes, was there to be drawn across the vent to keep out light or the elements. Painted wooden spikes two inches wide extended from the top of the wall frames to that open space in the center and were decorated in bright reds, yellows, and blues, with floral, geometric, or paisley designs. Two poles stood on either side of the stove to support the roof. The wooden doors were red, lacquered, and always faced south, away from the cold winds blowing down from Siberia.

In addition to the four beds and dressers, there were also Parsons-type tables with four small stools, again elaborately designed, and a tray of bottled water and glasses. The American journalist John Reed described a yurt he lived in as "carpeted, comfortable, and cozy," adjectives also appropriate for ours.

Fifty percent of Mongolians still lived in yurts when I was there. Traditionally, there was a specific location for every piece of furniture and for every person who entered, depending upon his or her status. Goatskin sacks for *kumiss* (a fermented dairy product) and other dairy products were hung on the west side, trunks placed to the northwest, bed to the northeast, and the kitchen sideboard and utensils next to the stove to the north. Guests were granted seats near the door to enable them to keep a watchful eye out for enemies. Most nomads had a large yurt in a permanent place and simple undecorated portable yurts when they followed their camels. Each could be disassembled quickly and carried by one camel. The yurt has been the home of these Central Asian people since 2,500 to 3,000 B.C.

After we had settled in and then located the bathrooms and showers some distance away, we had a dinner of Mongolian vodka, trout, mushy (but not greasy) potatoes and strips of pork fat. Later, when most of the group had gone off to bed, a few of us talked to our guide Gleg. He told us that Mongolia was basically an agrarian society, with 20 to 25 head of livestock per person. While there were universities, too many of the young people couldn't go because they were needed to care for the animals.

One family could care for 1,000 sheep and recognized every one without marking them. At dawn, after five or six families took all their animals to wells for water, they could easily separate out their own. If an animal died or was lost, the family had to pay the state. The husbands followed the larger animals; the wives cared for the children and the younger animals that stayed in shelters or wandered just a short distance away. Each family belonged to a cooperative, but was allowed 75 head of livestock for personal use or profit.

After a cozy night of hearing nothing but the wood kindling crackling in the stove, Natasha and I stumbled into the dining room just in time for breakfast. Bread, tea, and two hot dogs to sustain us while our bus returned to Ulan Bator. (My father never allowed hot dogs in our house while I was growing up. "Absolute *drek*" (shit), he said.)

That afternoon, we walked through town. I got hot, thirsty, and really tired, so I planned my time so that I would get back to the hotel and have an hour or so to rest. However, Natasha and I had gotten separated and she had the key.

The front desk told me to find the woman assigned to my floor. She was nowhere to be found. One maid took sympathy and said she would try to find her. She returned breathless to tell me that there was a lady on the fourth floor with glasses and a key. I said thank you and raced down there. There was a lady, she was wearing glasses, and she did have a key. She should have; she was a tourist and the key was to her room. Back up to my floor. Slowly. Angrily. Near tears. The elevator wasn't working and I had already been up and down the seven flights of stairs twice.

Another woman came—with a key. Relief, for a moment. Until she put it into the lock and it didn't work. She then tried to tell me that the door was locked from the inside, where Natasha was. I explained patiently that Natasha was not inside. She insisted she was.

"Was not."

"Was."

"Was not."

I pounded on the door, to prove my point. She shrugged her shoulders and disappeared. I considered my alternatives: a temper tantrum, tears, a nap on the floor in the hall, none of the above. I was Lou Costello in an Abbot and Costello movie, wanting to jump up and down and scream and cry and bang my head against the wall.

The woman returned with 25 keys and we tried them all. Of course, it was the last one that finally worked. It had taken me an hour and a half to get into my room. Natasha returned seconds after I closed the door behind me, five minutes before dinner.

Dinner was fish, rice, tea, cakes with raisins again, and kefir (a non-alcoholic dairy drink, thicker than buttermilk, thinner than yogurt). I was disappointed to learn that we would not have the opportunity to sample the national drink, *kumiss*.

First mentioned in the 5th century BC by Heroditus, and popular in Central Asia and parts of Siberia, it is richly carbonated, fermented mare's milk. Considered beneficial for stomach and intestinal disorders, lung disease and hypertension, it was unfortunately available only in mid-summer, during the months that the mares have green grass to graze on. The mare's milk is hung in rawhide bags, left in the sun for several days, and stirred every few hours. A fresh supply is produced by constantly adding fresh milk to the starter. The highest quality of kumiss is believed to come from the milk of mares who are nursing their third and subsequent foals.

Traditionally, it was the custom all over Mongolia for the head woman of the family to offer milk to the gods every day. She would stand in front of the encampment with a basin of milk and a dipper, and with the dipper throw milk in every direction, turning first east, then north, west and south.

That evening, we were off to the circus, with the usual clowns, acrobats, and tightrope walkers. Performers wore bright costumes, often with gold boots, white leotards, and colorful sequins. There were also Soviet-style trained bears: one walked blindfolded across two narrow planks, another lay on its back and balanced a ball, and still others danced, rode bicycles, and jumped rope.

However, most incredible of all was the contortionist who put herself in such strange positions that some of our group were actually disturbed by her performance. She stood on her nose. She stood on one hand and rested her feet on her shoulders, then rested both feet on her head. Lying on her stomach, she rested her feet and her arms and her head on the floor in front of her.

The circus ended with the excitement of the horses, whose riders rode under them, or backwards leaning on their necks, or upside down, all to loud music, the cracking of the whip, and enthusiastic applause.

The next day was Sunday, and after the familiar breakfast, (again, the hot dogs), we went directly to the Gandan Lamasery, the only active Buddhist Temple in Mongolia.

Lamaism, the old religion of the Mongols, replaced shamanism in the 13th century, following Kublai Khan's adoption of Tibetan Buddhism. Before

1982—Russia, Mongolia

the revolution and the establishment of the Mongolian Peoples' Republic, there were 767 monasteries, 1,800 temples, and 100,000 celibate priests. The church controlled one half the wealth of the nation. Forty percent of the males were priests and 80 to 90 percent of Mongolians were illiterate. Since the revolution and the death of the holy emperor in 1924, the role of Buddhism was minor, more symbolic than anything else. It was tolerated by the government, but held no position of influence, and there were then only about 300 lamas.

As we entered the courtyard, my first impressions were again of the crowds and the colors. The temple buildings themselves were Ming style, with fluted roofs and painted eaves. Pigeons surrounded people praying. Some of the people held prayer beads and repeated mantras, some prostrated themselves on the inclined prayer boards near the temples' entrances, and yet others placed small scraps of paper on the prayer wheels. Each turn of the wheel symbolized one journey to heaven for the prayer.

Several lamas in their long, saffron robes walked through the courtyard shouldering ornate copper and brass buckets or supporting large, flat boards heaped with bread. Gleg had cautioned us that many of the people in the courtyard might take offense at having

People gathered outside the temple

Inside the temple, monks in saffron robes

1982—Russia, Mongolia

their photos taken, and that it was absolutely forbidden to take pictures inside the temple. I confess I was far too excited to comply and thus, with a zoom lens on one camera, 400-speed film in another, and with much subterfuge and just a little guilt, I was able to take many of the shots I so desperately wanted.

Once inside the larger of the two temples, I was simply overwhelmed. The ceiling was awash with the color of old silk tapestry hangings with lattice designs, dragon appliques, and frayed ribbons. Along the walls were glass cases filled with masks and hundreds of gilded Buddhas. Trays of short candles shed a soft, flickering light on the offerings—bowls of rice and raisins, coins, candy, and matches brought in by the devout.

And in the center, on heavy brocade cushions and long carpeted benches, was a sea of 100 or so round, bald heads—lamas in orange robes sitting in lotus position, holding open calligraphy scrolls, repeating the ancient prayers. They sat in two groups, facing one another, divided by an aisle that led to the offerings and the raised throne of the head lama. He had a vase of peacock feathers, which he waved at certain moments during the service. The guttural chanting, sometimes accompanied by delicate bells and cymbals, was unceasing, even when the conch horns were blown or the huge gongs struck. It had a tone and timing that didn't stop at one's ears, but traveled to the body's center, as if to make one a part of that repetitive rhythm.

After a while, Natasha and I proceeded slowly along the periphery of the room to the exit and then made our way next door to the smaller, simpler temple. There, the same as in the other temple, was the distinct, unpleasant odor of fatty mutton. Several lamas sat in individual open booths and spooned out measured packets of ground juniper incense. We hesitantly put out our hands and received ours without question.

All was peaceful at the monastery, and certainly spiritual, but another side of Mongolian Buddhism was depicted at the Religion Museum. Founded in 1941, it had previously functioned as a monastery. The works inside were of the 17th to the beginning of the 19th century and were from Tibet, Japan, India, and China. The cremated remains of the monastery's founder were incorporated into a paper maché figure, and another figure on a throne was his mummified teacher, who had died in 1909. Also on display was a small drum made of a human skull, and many ritual objects made of human bones. One, a horn covered in silver, was the femur bone of an 18-year-old girl who had died in giving birth to her first child.

On the ceilings of one of the temples were silk hangings and paintings depicting the evils of rejecting Buddhism—bloody hearts pulled out, decapitated heads hanging by pigtails. All around were masks with very mean faces. Some, the Darmapala gods, the keepers of the law, had 34 arms to crush their enemies, and 16 legs to crush the sinners. Each had five skulls on its head, representing anger, jealousy, lust, stupidity, and greed.

There were good gods, too, usually holding cups in their hands. Perhaps they contained one of the five liquids considered honorable: vodka, wine, honey, milk or kumiss, or maybe wheat. The early Mongolians believed that when there was wheat, the symbol of fertility, there was peace.

In the center of town, we saw a statue of Stalin, which of course one never found in the USSR. The Mongolians said that Stalin had been a friend to them, that he made his mistakes in the USSR, not Mongolia. And indeed, since the foundation of the Mongolian People's Republic, essentially a satellite state of the Soviet Union, there had been peace in the country.

Up at 5:00 am, breakfast of sour cream with sugar, and an hour-and-a-half plane ride to the desert. Since there was no runway, our plane, one of only two in Mongolian Airline's fleet, landed on gravel. Then we had a four-hour bus ride to our campsite in the Altai Mountains, in the Yol Valley, or the Valley of the Eagle.

Although the Gobi has all the typical features of a desert, it is not an uninhabitable wasteland. There is abundant wildlife, and many of the species are rare, such as the Przewalski horses, wild camels, mzalai (Gobi bear), mountain sheep, and snow leopards. Much of the ground is hard or sandy clay, or flat-flaked gravel that varies in color, even black in some places. There are more than 300 varieties of plants, spread across steppes, high mountains, springs, forests, plains, oases, and sand dunes. The sand dunes account for only 3 percent of the Gobi but the Gobi dessert itself comprises 30 percent of the country's land.

We had no idea what to expect in terms of accommodations. The supply truck had arrived before us and the cook was already busy preparing lunch. We soon found we did not have to worry about malfunctioning toilets—there simply were no toilets. No toilets, no showers, no running water except for that in the stream next to where we pitched our tents. We designated a ladies' hill and a men's hill and off we went with our pocket Kleenex in hand.

Nomad in the Gobi Desert

Lunch was served on a large tarp covering the ground, but we each had our own place setting and the food was a great surprise. Most memorable was the tasty soup with beef broth, flour, onions, and a touch of curry and the pineapple juice from Vietnam. Most unexpected was a rumble that sounded like either an avalanche or an earthquake. All heads turned to see hundreds of goats and

1982—Russia, Mongolia

sheep descend from behind our ladies' hill to water at the stream. Not ten yards away, they were accompanied by three Mongols on horseback who weaved quickly in and out of the herd, discouraging strays with the aid of *urgas*, the 15 foot birch poles with leather nooses at the end. A few minutes after they all left, a lone nomad on a camel with two other camels in tow came around the same bend. As he passed, he stared curiously at us, allowed photographs, but neither stopped, nor smiled.

When we finally finished lunch, we hiked for a few hours along the valley floor in search of birds. Purka, our Gobi guide there, told us of a recent unusual incident involving a snow leopard. Apparently one had entered a yurt by the vent in the roof. The man inside was barely able to rush out and close the door with the leopard locked in behind him. Because of this, Purka warned us not to stray from the group.

Of course, I ran off immediately.

I hoped to see one and didn't really believe I would, but imagined that an encounter with the rare, usually shy, snow leopard in the magnificent Mongolian mountains would certainly make an exciting story. It didn't occur to me that I might not live to tell it.

I didn't find the snow leopard, and I don't know what the group saw on their walk, but I was happy to discover bright pink and yellow wild flowers, horses grazing on the high slopes, and stones that I stashed in my pockets, stones of deep reds, light pastel greens, all so beautiful that I couldn't resist.

And then I came upon a snow and ice corridor that formed a hammock over the stream where the sun didn't reach, and at a point where one could walk no farther, six *khainag* stood side by side.

Odd-looking hybrids, they produce more milk and butter than either yak or cow parent. As I cautiously approached them, the group slowly stepped back. I stopped. I slowly retreated. They stepped forward. We repeated this desert dance several times until some of my group appeared and broke the rhythm.

Khainag—hybrid between yak and cow

I walked back to camp with Purka, whose real name was Purevdalai. He had an extremely thin, wiry body, straight, jet-black hair, and a charming smile. He told me that often he was a guide for solo hunters, many from America, who paid $16,500 for the privilege of killing and taking home the head and horns of one *argali* (mountain sheep) and one *ibex* (mountain goat). The round ram's horns were considered by some to be the ultimate hunter's trophy. They are more than five feet, curved, and weigh 70 to 90 pounds. Those of the ibex are also curved and range from two and one half to five feet in length.

A glorious, peaceful living creature becomes a trophy for a wall of a "brave" hunter.

We had some time before dinner, and I climbed the highest nearby hill. Natasha soon followed with her kite, a big dragon, and successfully flew it until it started to rain. We took refuge in our tents, and because of the shower, Purka brought dinner to us. This time, we had caviar, something resembling chow mein with thin sliced vegetables and meat, and butter cookies for dessert.

And it occurred to me how wonderful it was, among so many other wonderful things there, to wear only comfortable clothes and no makeup. But getting ready for bed while camping was another story, because it was so cold. I'm sure I was quite a vision in my long underwear, long men's flannel pajamas, sweater, knitted wool booties with tassel ties, a jacket, pink cashmere gloves with holes in the fingers and a wool hat with a dual function—to provide warmth for me and a barrier for any ticks looking for a place to land. All this, plus my down sleeping bag with a heavy wool blanket over it. And I was still cold.

After we ate, we lit a candle, brought out the Mongolian vodka, and listened to Tchaikovsky and Benjamin Britten. In the confines of our sleeping bags, Natasha and I talked, and the fabric of our friendship changed. We already knew much about one another, but that night in the Gobi, we came to know more.

About our parents in Russia. My father and his family chose to flee the anti-Semitism of the Tsar in 1910. Her father, one of the Tsar's artillery officers in the White Army that defended the Tsar's palace against the Bolsheviks, had been forced to flee with her mother in 1918, after the Revolution.

About our childhoods. Natasha, born in 1944, spent her first seven years in Leipzig, Germany, seven months of that time in a refugee camp before emigrating. In America, she was the little foreigner, struggling to learn English, always wishing she belonged.

While I was growing up, I always wished we lived in Paris, London, or New York City, a big city, an exciting city, any city where I could escape the repetitions and routines of the small city to which I belonged, the city I called Boring Binghamton.

1982—Russia, Mongolia

And we talked about the pain of our marriages gone wrong, of her children London and Sasha, and her dreams for them. Of my concern that someday I might regret having no children to dream for. That night, we talked until dawn, confiding so many memories, some almost forgotten, some unable to be forgotten.

At 6:00 the next morning, hot water from the cook's kettle provided water to brush my teeth, and when poured onto my face cloth, provided my morning "shower." After breakfast, we were off in search of the Altai Snowcock, native to Mongolia and Western Siberia. The heartiest of the group climbed to 8,000 feet. I reached the top second only to Purka and really enjoyed the climb. The air was clear and I liked the feel of the pull in my leg muscles, the decision of where to put my foot next, which way would be most efficient. The climb was a success; the group found the snowcock, and I found I wasn't squeamish over ticks after I calmly removed one crawling up my pant leg.

Actually, my fear was not of ticks, but of snakes. After reading an account of Roy Chapman Andrews scientific Gobi expeditions during the 1920s, my first purchase to prepare for this trip was a snakebite kit. While excavating on a promontory with steep, rocky sides, the Andrews group had unknowingly pitched camp on a nest of pit vipers, extremely poisonous snakes. When the temperature dropped to freezing one night, the snakes crawled up to get warm and invaded all the tents. They were everywhere—coiled around the legs of cots, in shoes, even in hats. All together, 47 of the vipers were killed that one night. (In 1930, the desert was closed to American paleontologists. On July 31, 1990, the *New York Times* reported that they were finally allowed back into the desert sixty years later.)

When we started our climb, yes, I was more than a little worried about snakes, but soon was able to concentrate on the beauty of the rocks, rather than on what might be wriggling around behind them.

As the group fanned out in search of more bird sightings, Natasha and I found a secluded place where we sat, topless, sunning ourselves and writing in our journals, and where we heard only the song of the cuckoo. Dozens of mountain peaks dotted the horizon below; above, the sky was a clear, cloudless blue, empty except for the occasional Lammergeyer (bearded vulture) in graceful flight, with its eight- to nine-foot wingspan.

Our next campsite in the Gobi was at Ulan Nur, or Red Lake. The landscape we saw *en route* changed often—from flat and empty to hills of sand, to saxual bush forest, to soil brown and then orange—and was host to camel herds, gazelles, lizards, dung pellets, and skeletons and bones bleached white.

On the bus, I chose to put on my earphones and a tape of Hoomi music. Gleg had told us that it takes a very long time to learn to do the Hoomi or throat singing. The source of this is supposedly a sacred waterfall high in the mountains of Mongolia, a waterfall that actually sings. Meditating there, men thus learned this singing from nature.

At the time, the Harmonic Arts Society in NY City stated:

> **"The Harmonic music is the source stream of essential human and musical facts relating the laws of vibration inside us and outside us. In Hoomi tradition, singers produce a fundamental tone in the base or baritone range, and then by extremely precise modulation of the abdominal muscles, chest and vocal apparatus—larynx, tongue, jaws, cheeks and lips—project simultaneously a higher tone or tones, related in frequency to the fundamental tone by simple whole number rations. Such high frequencies are called overtones or harmonic. Each fundamental tone has potentially infinite harmonics."**

I listened to the plaintive tones, so different from the melodies and harmonies we are used to, and for over an hour, I was separate from the group, my mind free to receive uncluttered impressions. Somehow, the primordial music and so much sand and sky and space awakened thoughts of both creation and obliteration. During those moments, I believe I may have at least come close to understanding infinity.

When we finally arrived at Ulan Nur, we discovered that not only was the red lake not red, it was not a lake either. No water. Only parched dirt and dry reeds where the lakebed used to be. Once again, we put up our tents and once again, there were no bathroom facilities. Only this time, there were no hills to label either. This time, each of us struck out in search of the tallest reeds.

We had a dinner of hot dogs (!), cucumbers, tomatoes, and tea, and an evening of conversation with some of the others from the group in our tent. Natasha and I had our bottle of vodka, which made us very popular.

I pulled a tick out of my scalp, a tick Purka said I must have brought along from the mountains, as there were none in this area. By this point in the trip, most of us had found at least one tick somewhere on our bodies, and like the grooming our primate relatives do for one another, each of us examined others for ticks as part of our daily routine.

One of the highlights of camping in the Gobi was walking the desert floor after dinner. Natasha insisted we leave behind our flashlights. I was reluctant (the snakes). But she apparently knew what Edward Abbey knew, as he wrote in his book, *Desert Solitude*, that "a flashlight tends to separate a man from the world around him".

1982—Russia, Mongolia

One moonless night, we wandered as far from our camp as we dared until we lost sight of it completely. We found ourselves in the middle of the vast space, where we couldn't see where the land met the sky, where we could see only stars and hear only silence. There we stood, needing to be quiet, needing not to move, very aware of our breathing until, at the same moment, we turned to each other and whispered "Do you hear it?" The sound, a low vibrating echo, was unlike anything we had ever heard. It not only surrounded us but also seemed to pass right through us. I don't know what it was we were listening to or how long we stood there. But during that time, there was no time —no beginning, no ending, no questions with no answers—only an exquisite sense of being and belonging.

"It's like being on another planet," Natasha murmured.

I slept well and woke up at 6:45 the next morning with a cold and my period. The group went on an excursion in search of the Henderson Ground Jay. They found it, and I found more rocks and bones and sandstone. Natasha excitedly showed me ancient pottery shards she had discovered. We broke camp after lunch. One woman encountered a tarantula on her sleeping bag, a female, carrying her young on her back. With several of us looking down at the mother as she scurried around trying to find cover, the tiny baby spiders dropped off her and scattered in every direction.

As the drivers and cooks packed the truck, the group dealt with the 105-degree heat and the punishing sun as best they could—which wasn't very well. All sat on or near the bus, in whatever patch of shade they could find, waiting, fanning themselves, swatting at bugs and bees. There was not even a hint of a breeze.

Natasha and I, as the youngest, became modern-day Gunga Dins (Rudyard Kipling's famous Indian water carrier) as we hauled water back and forth to the other members of our group. Most had placed wet towels or jackets of various shapes and colors over their heads; others had open umbrellas.

Finally, we were able to leave and our five-hour, very bumpy drive back across the desert to the yurt camp certainly satisfied my basic requirements for an adventure. We got lost, and then our bus got stuck in soft sand and had to be pulled out, twice, by the overheated truck. Next, a sudden sand storm.

In his journal, Roy Chapman Andrews also told of a time when the temperature dropped 30 degrees within ten minutes. When the storm hit, he couldn't see 20 feet ahead. The camp was uprooted and tents and equipment tumbled away. In order to breathe, he and his men had to lie flat on the ground and bury their faces in wet cloths. The storm lasted an hour and when it was over, the windshields of their automobiles were so badly sandblasted that they had to be removed.

In season, the storms can last up to four or five days. Ours lasted only 45 minutes, and while certainly not as severe as the one Andrews described, and in spite of our efforts to close up the bus quickly, everything and everyone was covered with gritty sand. It was in our nostrils, our ears, our mouths. All were relieved to finally reach camp intact, albeit with sandy bodies and sore bottoms. And in my case, with every pocket filled with used tissues, because of my cold.

For our last night in the Gobi, we had a special dinner of lamb dumplings, served in the ceremonial tent by our waiter, who wore a tuxedo. Once again, after everyone was asleep, Natasha and I took our walk into the night. All the yurts had stoves going, so the sky was lit by flying sparks escaping from the stovepipes, as if someone had collected thousands of lightning bugs and let them out all at once. And once again, we barely spoke.

After only a few hours of sleep, and after our usual breakfast of you-know-what, we went to a camel-breeding station so we could actually ride one. There were probably 200 of the animals, all sitting, facing the same direction, their backsides to the sun. Gobi camels are bactrian, or two-humped, and much more able to withstand the cold than the single-hump dromedary. Unlike other animals, whose fat is distributed throughout the body, the camels carry energy in the humps, which change in size according to their feedings. A solid hump indicates that the animal has just fed; a deflated hump means the camel has used up all that was stored. A fat layer also insulates against the sun. Because it sweats so little and loses so little water in its body functions, the camel can survive without water for up to three weeks. Also its dung has no odor and is an ideal fuel. The camels were comfortable to ride, and while none of them responded to us as a domestic pet would, they were not shy. Actually, they watched us, not warily, but with what appeared to be amused grins.

The smiles of the children there at the station were more obvious when Natasha blew several showers of Pustafex bubbles for them. Pure delight!

Back at camp, with a little less than two hours to wait for our flight to Ulan Bator, I examined the rocks I had collected, hoping to discard some of them to make my luggage lighter. I couldn't. They were souvenirs of some very special moments; stone symbols of a past so old I don't believe any of us can really comprehend it.

Until 1923, it was supposed that dinosaurs laid eggs, but there was no proof. The Andrews expedition found the first fossil dinosaur eggs. And in two of them, they found the skeletons of embryo dinosaurs, dinosaurs that had inhabited the Gobi 85 million years ago. (Actually, the French discovered dinosaur eggs in the mid 1800s, but didn't know at the time that they belonged to dinosaurs.)

1982—Russia, Mongolia

The world has extraordinary places, many breathtaking in their beauty, but I know of few like the Gobi that can evoke such a sense of wonder, of evolution, such a feeling that one is a part of all that has been and all that ever will be.

- **In 2011, the capitol Ulan Bator, also called Ulaanbaatar, was ranked the world's fifth worst city for air pollution, most of it coming from home heating systems and fuel used to keep warm in winter.**

- **In 2012, the last statue of Lenin, then viewed as a symbol of repression, was removed from Mongolia.**

BACK TO RUSSIA

> *"I believe in beauty. I believe in stones and water,*
> *air and soil, people and their future and their fate."*
> —Ansel Adams (1902–1984), American photographer

Back to Irkutsk and a visit to the Natural History Museum, founded in 1782 as a public library. From the New Stone Age, 4,000 to 5,000 years ago, there was a skeleton of a 27-year-old woman. She had died of a brain hemorrhage and it is believed she was probably murdered or hit at the back of the head. Because her features were different from her contemporaries, she was thought to have evil spirits and was thus buried face down so those spirits would go into the ground.

Also on display was a simple *uzba*, or hut, with an icon in the center, and benches along the wall. The master of the house always sat under the icon. Walls were never painted, and the floors were sawdust or branches and the stove was the focal point. People slept on top of the stove, cooked food inside, and kept fowl underneath the floor. So similar to what my father described in his home in Glubokoye.

After the museum, Natasha and I wandered a bit. Into a meat store, where rows of cases were filled with butter, lard and jam, but very little meat, and to a pharmacy, where there were no Tampax or sanitary pads available for women, only heavy gauze material. We stopped at Professor Lipin's home to tell them we were back, and after dinner, Anton and Stanislav came to our hotel and we had champagne and vodka in our room. Natasha gave Anton her dragon kite. At midnight, we said our goodbyes and departed for our flight to Khabarovsk, on the bank of the Amur River in the Russian Far East. We had to fly at night because the plane flew over restricted territory.

Not far from Khabarovsk is the Jewish Autonomous Oblast, formerly known as Birobidzhan, capital of the Jewish Autonomous Region there in Russia's Far East, 5,000 miles from Moscow, the actual first Jewish state. Established in 1928, it was given formal legal status and set aside by Lenin for Jewish colonization and by the mid 1930s, Yiddish culture was growing. However, in 1936, Stalin began his purges and persecution of the Jews there continued after WWII. According to the 2010 census, the region had a population of 176,558, with only 1,628 of them Jews, yet it remains to this day the only place outside of Israel that has autonomous status for Jews.

On her last visit to Khabarovsk, Natasha had met a woman named Galina Misjura. Galina joined us for dinner our first night in Khabarovsk. Fern salad, *pelmeni* (Siberian dumplings), and champagne. I decided not to join the group on their visit to a nature reserve the next morning even though it was the first time it was ever opened to Westerners, and instead spent the day with Galina, whom I had liked the moment I met her—she laughed a lot—who showed me around the city. She made it her mission to "find me a boy," and when Natasha and I showed up at her home for dinner, she did indeed have one waiting, and a nice looking one at that, with black hair, a good sense of humor, and a gentle nature. Sasha M., like Galina, taught English at the university.

Sasha M.

Because we had no hot water in our hotel, Galina told us we could take a shower or bath at her house before dinner. When I came out, clean, but with wet hair, Galina produced a heat lamp, which is used as a hair dryer, and Sasha patiently stood and held it for me. We all drank vodka with mango juice from India, wine, had krill with seaweed, Hungarian pate and fresh fruit and candy. We took a lot of photos, laughed a lot, and it was evident Sasha and I would have gotten along very well had we had more time to ourselves. As it was, I told him much about Mongolia, tried to explain what the Gobi was like, and why I was so captivated by its vast silence.

Galina came by the next morning, our last in Khabarovsk, and we went to visit Sasha on the roof of a cafe he was managing for the summer. I gave him the cassette tape I had made of the bells and the chanting at the temple in Ulan Bator. He took my hand, kissed it, and wished me much happiness.

Little did I know then that I would see Sasha again and again, and that Galina and Stanislav would continue to be in my life for many, many years to come. Or that Natasha would break my heart.

Back in Leningrad, I got to see Valery and Nadia once more. They had a new apartment, and Natasha and I had to climb six flights of stairs to reach them. Dinner was wonderful: fish and rice salad, fresh hake, krill with seaweed, lemon vodka with birch sap, and bread with lard. Well, wonderful except for, again, the lard. They said that butter had not been available in Leningrad for the past year.

When we left them at midnight, it was still very bright out. We were in the middle of the White Nights when there were only about three hours of darkness each day. Pushkin said of Leningrad during the White Nights of early summer: "One dawn hurries to change into another one."

The next day, I was able to go to the Russian Museum, and to wander around alone, for a long time, taking in the work of wonderful Russian artists from the 1800s—Briullov, Kramskoi, Surikov. I especially liked the expressive portrait of Tolstoy by Repin. Then, a return visit to the Dom Knigi, and an excursion to Petrohov, the palace of Peter the Great, located south of Leningrad on the coast of the Gulf of Finland. From the road, we saw field after field of Queen Anne's Lace, dandelions, and lilacs.

On our last morning, Natasha took several of us to the ornate Alexander Nevsky Cathedral for Sunday morning service, which was very crowded, mostly with old ladies in babushkas of every color and those wrinkled, heavy stockings, and many with canes. Surrounded by the shadows of the light of hundreds of tiny candles in brass holders representing prayers, they leaned up to the icons to kiss them, or kneeled on the floor in prayer, always crossing themselves. Throughout the cathedral, other elderly women polished the brass and the icons.

Most interesting was a pink satin casket with heavy silver handles, containing the body of a 75-year-old woman who had died some days earlier, whose name was Natalia Roba. There were flowers at her feet, brass candlesticks both at the foot and the head of the casket, and a photo of her namesake, Saint Natalia. In a woolen scarf hat with tiny pink embroidered flowers, she looked very peaceful in death. Her sister was one of the mourners, and told us that Natalia had never smoked, never married, but somehow became totally paralyzed. In her grief, the sister managed to advise us, "In life, friendship is the most important thing."

The atheist state, whose textbooks were anti-God, saying that religion was outdated and unscientific, allowed them to be there because they figured the believers would eventually die off. But the state also made it clear that it was not safe for younger people to attend church.

There were few men inside, many beggars outside. We were lucky enough to come out when the bell ringer was up in the cupola ringing the bells. Backlit by the clear sky, he cast a dramatic shadow.

After a difficult time for many of the group going through customs, thanks to my Polaroid, I sailed through quite easily with my five carry-on bags (in addition to the two bags I had checked), the most luggage of anyone in the group. The customs official who asked me to unlock my case was thrilled with the photo of himself that I took and gave to him, and he motioned me through customs without further notice. In the waiting room, I picked up several of the propaganda booklets available to everyone for free, including: *Lenin: The April Theses*; *Health is Public Wealth*; and *The Socialist Community in the World Today*. Each time I travelled to the USSR, I picked up more. *Who Profits from Telling Lies About the Soviet Union?* "*Do the Russians want a War? The Soviet Peace Philosophy.*" Most intriguing was the *Racist Essence of Zionist Ideology*, which stated that Israelis believe and behave as if all other nations and peoples are inferior and that "having been brainwashed ideologically and psychologically at school, an Israeli is ready material for becoming an Israeli army superman, emotionless and willing to follow any order."

En route to Helsinki for an overnight, I relaxed into my seat and thought about this and my first trip to the USSR. Of the images that recurred most often and left the most lasting impressions: cucumbers, cabbages, plants and flowers in windows framed by lace curtains, the wooden pastel buildings of Siberia, lilac bouquets, birch trees, big bows in little girls' hair, babushkas, high heels with no nylons—just peds or knee-highs—mesh shopping bags, red henna hair, red flags, Lenin.

Then, the international newspapers and a different kind of reality. The war in the Falklands was over, the war in Lebanon had begun, and the Dow Jones was the lowest it had been in 20 years. I calculated all the time we spent in the air, 47 hours. Add that to the time spent going to and from the airports, and waiting in lounges, and it totaled about four days of travel. No wonder I was tired.

Putting fatigue aside, I was still committed to the value of private exchange programs between the US and the USSR. Sasha M. had written in my journal "May our nations be friendly as we are."

Would that it were true.

* * *

Chapter Title

On a subsequent trip she took to the USSR shortly after our Mongolia trip, Natasha came back with a serious proposal for me. Seriously, a real proposal. While in Moscow, she had met Yuri Sherling, director and founder of the Jewish Drama and Music Theater that toured the country performing shows based on Jewish folklore. She told me he was a talented director, composer, and choreographer. She also told me she thought that I should marry Yuri, as a way to get him to the US. She showed me pictures he had given her of himself, of a few stage productions, and some theatre posters, as well as a June 1980 *Time* magazine profile, which identified him as being on a crusade, seeking "a renaissance of Yiddish culture."

I considered it. I really did. Seriously. So much so that I flew to New York to meet with the director of the New York Conference on Soviet Jewry to ask his advice.

"Absolutely not," he said. He had heard about Sherling and his desire to come to America, and then he explained what my considerable responsibilities and risks would be with this man I didn't even know. And thus, I turned down the proposal.

Yuri Sherling, director and founder of the Jewish Drama and Music Theater

In 1983, Sherling's theatre was closed down by another Yuri, Yuri Andropov, General Secretary of the Communist Party, who assumed power after the death of Leonid Brezhnev. And Sherling was imprisoned because of apparently false bribery charges made against him by the KGB. He was freed under Gorbachev in 1990 and the theatre was allowed to reopen, although he was no longer involved. As far as I know, he still lives in Moscow.

In February of 1981, Leonid Brezhnev, General Secretary of the Communist Party of the Soviet Union, President of the Presidium of the USSR Supreme Soviet, and leader of the USSR since 1964, said, "To try to prevail over the other side in the arms race or to count on victory in a nuclear war is dangerous madness."

On November 2, 1982 at 8:00 AM, Brezhnev died suddenly of a heart attack.

Chapter 13
1982 and The New England Society of Newspaper Editors (NESNE)

"In recent years the quality of American newspaper coverage of the Soviet Union has been as bad as I can remember. Too much of it is one-dimensional, distorted, and factually wrong."
—Stephen F. Cohen (1938–2020)
Professor of Soviet Politics and History at Princeton University,
Presentation in September 1984 to Harvard Russian Research Center/
Nieman Foundation

1982

When we returned home, Natasha resumed her work with NESNE, which had earlier in the year issued an invitation to journalists from the USSR to come to America to talk. NESNE, with 140 members, was at the time the only regional group of editors in the US. The Union of Soviet Journalists had 60,000 members. The role of the press in the USSR was to promote the government; the role of the press in the US was to serve as a watchdog of the government.

The idea for this program came from Catherine Menninger, a peace activist worried about nuclear war between the two countries. She contacted Tom Winship, the editor of the *Boston Globe* and he put things in motion.

NESNE agreed that dialogue between the media of both countries might help to lessen the threat, felt that "if we as professional communicators in the US and the USSR can't find ways to understand each other better as human beings, how can we ever realistically hope for the US and the Soviet Union to get along better as nations?"

The Soviets accepted the invitation and on August 30th of 1982, a delegation of Soviet journalists landed in Montreal, since President Carter banned all Aeroflot flights from landing in the US after the Soviet incursion into Afghanistan three years earlier. A donated corporate jet brought them to New England, to Colby Sawyer College in New London, NH, chosen because it was remote and thus the delegations were not likely to be disturbed.

Prior to this historic meeting, NESNE consulted with, among others, George Kennan, diplomat and Soviet expert at Princeton, Kevin Klose, reporter for the Washington Post, Marshall Goldman, Professor at Wellesley College and Associate Director of the Davis Center for Russian and Eurasian Studies at Harvard, and Roger Fisher, Professor at Harvard Law School who had worked with the Carter administration during the US-Iran hostage negotiations and was one of the authors of *Getting to Yes: Negotiating Agreement Without Giving In.* Fisher led two sessions during the Colby-Sawyer conference. NESNE also arranged for visits to newspapers, some sightseeing, and individual home stays, to provide an atmosphere more conducive to establishing personal relationships, and to avoid political discussions.

The New England delegation of 12 editors was led by Thomas Winship. The Soviet delegation of 11 was chaired by Yakov Lomko, editor of *Moscow News.* Natasha served as the conference coordinator. The conference had difficult moments, but was in general considered a success. And there were relaxing times. Pianist Frederick Moyer performed a concert at the college and one of the Soviets also played the piano and sang the *Battle Hymn of the Republic.* All the verses.

After the Soviets returned home on September 6, many articles about the meeting appeared in the Soviet press. And in December, a month after the death of Leonid Brezhnev, the Soviets invited an American delegation to visit the USSR the following year.

1983

I talked to my mother often on the phone. Or rather, she called me often, did most of the talking, repeated herself over and over. I also repeated myself, telling her she had to stop drinking, had to get help. To no avail.

She was living with a man named Tom, whom I liked. He also drank a lot, but didn't deteriorate like she did. I hated going to their apartment—it was dirty, dreary and reeked of cigarette smoke.

On June 1st, I got a call that she was in Our Lady of Lourdes Hospital because of an esophageal ulcer and gastrointestinal bleeding. They discharged her in seven days. Less than two weeks later, she was in again. This time, I got the message that it was really serious. She was in the ICU, disoriented, with pain in her liver, bleeding in her stomach, and vomiting four to five times a day. I sped to Binghamton and went immediately to the hospital. She was in a two-bed room and the staff let me sleep in the empty bed. She barely knew I was there. The doctor told me if she survived, there would be severe mental damage.

Around 12:30 in the morning of June 18th, the third night I was there, I talked to Michael on the phone. We had been in touch off and on and I wanted him to know about my mother. I was comforted by our conversation and was able to sleep after we hung up, in spite of my mother's very loud breathing and moaning.

A few hours later, what felt like a frigid gust of winter wind passed over my body. Shivering, I awoke suddenly and heard—silence. When I looked over at my mother, I knew she was gone. I immediately went out to the nurses' station to ask if they had checked on her recently. "Yes, not more than five minutes ago," they told me. "She was fine."

I hadn't been dreaming about being cold. So what was that icy chill?

I stayed at the hospital while the appropriate people came to first get her eyes, which she had donated through Upstate Medical Center in Syracuse, and then her body, which she also had donated to them.

Cause of death—an ulcer in her esophagus and bleeding in her stomach, both from alcoholic cirrhosis of the liver. She was 59 years old.

I couldn't cry for my mother, the mother who made me my very own little pies when I was a little girl. The mother, who was a warm person. A good mother. Until that mother got lost in her relationship with alcohol.

And I wouldn't be honest if I didn't admit that when she died, there was a sense of relief and release. Relief, because had she lived, she would have been facing a terrible future in a facility, where she probably wouldn't even have known where or who she was. Release, because I had no more obligation to the mother who had rejected my pleas for her to get help, who had become a stranger to me.

Renee, her second husband Ron Davis (nicknamed "Thumper"), their little daughter Tara, and Tambi came with me to the memorial service Tom and I had arranged for her. Tom and I met beforehand with the priest from St. James Catholic Church, a Monsignor Owens. My mother wasn't a churchgoer; he didn't know her.

"Speak of her generous nature," I said.

He spoke of Jesus and the Resurrection.

I was as alienated from the service as I had been from her for so many years. Her favorite song was *Broken-Hearted Melody* by Sarah Vaughn and I wish I had had it played then. There weren't many attending: a handful of men I assumed knew her from local bars, and a couple of well-dressed women who had been friends with her when they were teenagers and young adults.

One of them said to me, "You know, your mother was an entirely different person before she married your father."

"I know."

I felt sad, sad for that beautiful woman on her wedding day whose life turned out to be so tragic. She was the youngest of her siblings, yet the first to die. No, I didn't cry over losing her. I'd been mourning her loss for many years.

When do you actually grieve for an alcoholic, an addict, a person with Alzheimer's, a person you lose a little bit of every day?

Paths of Stones

* * *
"Drops of water erode the rock.
Drops of newspaper items fall on the human brain;
they influence thought. Everything depends on whether these drops
are clear or muddy and poisonous."
—Vikentiy Matveyev, political reviewer for *Izvestia* in the USSR

Also that summer, the first NESNE delegation visited the USSR for two weeks during the White Nights, from June 26 to July 7. When the 12 members arrived, the political stage was different than it was the year before. Brezhnev had died the previous November and was succeeded by Yuri Andropov, who had headed the KGB for 15 years.

And three months earlier, in March, President Reagan gave a speech to the National Association of Evangelicals in Orlando, Florida—his first recorded use of the phrase "evil empire."

Reagan said of the USSR: *"They preach the supremacy of the state, declare its omnipotence over individual man and predict its eventual domination of all peoples on the Earth. They are the focus of evil in the modern world...."*

Upon the delegation's arrival in Moscow, one of the first things they saw was an illuminated sign on a building, a quote by Lenin: "The newspaper is the most effective propagandist and educator, and we must bring the newspaper to every family." Elsewhere, another sign on another building had a picture of a rifle, stamped *Made in the USA*, pointed at a peasant woman with a dead child in her hands.

Their visit was indeed an eye-opening experience. The Americans learned that the subway stops looked like elegant ballrooms and the toilets were disgustingly dirty. Learned that they were an obvious mark for prostitutes, and that jeans were an extraordinarily valuable commodity. They heard from an old Jewish man in a synagogue in Leningrad that Jews weren't well liked in the USSR and that those who fought the system ended up in Siberia.

There were professional visits, the usual sightseeing, and in Moscow, they all saw an impressive exhibit of Lithuanian photography

In addition, our people were happy to spend time with a few of the delegates who had already come to New England, especially Albertas Laurinciukas and Sergei Vishnevsky. Albertas seemed the most interested in America, proud of his friendship with playwright Arthur Miller. (Before Albertas died on July 1, 2012 at the age of 84, he had also met the poet Pablo Neruda in Chile, the artist William Saroyan in the Philippines, and the artist David Siqueiros in Mexico.) Sergei, political observer for *Pravda* and their first Washington DC correspondent back in the 1960s, was by far the most colorful, outgoing, fun member of the mostly serious Soviet group.

1983—New England Society of Newspaper Editors (NESNE)

After their time in Moscow and Leningrad, the NESNE delegation was split into three groups, designated to go to three different republics: Georgia, Ukraine, and Lithuania. At the conclusion, the group met up in Tallinn, the capital of Estonia. It had been an extraordinary experience, one they would write about in great detail. There was relief that agreements were put in place for the exchanges of young working journalists, journalism students, and of newspaper articles, and enthusiasm for the return visit of the Soviets to America the following year.

Natasha had done a thorough and commendable job of preparing the delegation for this trip.

Chapter 14
1984—Natasha

*"....Like a white stone in the depths of a well,
One memory glimmers deep within my soul.
I can't, I don't want to fight its spell,
Joy and pain together make up its whole...."*
—Anna Akhmatova (1889–1966), Russian poet

And a year later, she was dead.

My dear friend Natasha died on July 14, 1984. She was 39 years old.

She had just returned from yet another trip to Mongolia, this time as an interpreter and editorial consultant to *National Geographic*. She came back excited, bringing wonderful stories and pride in a job well done. But she also returned with a cough and shortness of breath. We thought it was probably pneumonia. It was cancer, a metastasis of a melanoma she had treated five years earlier. In fact, two months before her trip, she and I celebrated her five-year anniversary of being cancer free.

After many tests and a decision to remove a lung, the doctors offered a little hope for a few more years. During surgery, they found they were unable to do even that; the cancer was already too aggressive. I saw Natasha that evening, just after surgery, just after the doctor had talked to her. As I took her hand, leaned over and touched her face, she opened her eyes, focused, stared deep into my eyes and said, slowly, "You know, don't you?"

I nodded.

"I know too," she whispered.

Fighting back tears, I thought, *Now we go about the task of living with dying.*

And I was reminded of a passage from Isaiah Berlin's *Russian Thinkers*, a quote by Alexander Herzen: "The death of a single human being is no less absurd and unintelligible than the death of the entire human race: it is a mystery we accept; merely to multiply it enormously and ask—Supposing millions of human beings die?—does not make it more mysterious or more frightening."

As I was leaving the hospital, five Black women sat bundled in coats and hats in the lobby, rocking, crying, singing and humming *Amazing Grace*.

The following four months weren't all bad. Natasha insisted that life continue as close to normal as possible. She had a man in her life, a man named John Murdoch, who lived with her and took care of the children when she was hospitalized. And during her illness, I met her ex-husband, Tim Leland. John was emotional, almost romanticizing her condition at times, but also visibly right on the edge. So much so that I found a family support group and recommended he attend. Tim, on the other hand, was constrained, trying to understand why this was affecting him as much as it was, tight with the effort of keeping his pain at bay. He paced a lot, like a pair of tweezers—open, closed, open, closed. At one point, he told me that Natasha had always told him that she knew she was going to die young.

The book she had worked so hard to translate, *A Field Guide to Birds of the USSR*, was published by Princeton Press and we celebrated in the hospital the day it arrived. It was a red-tablecloth occasion, with wine, St. Andre cheese, crackers, and fresh fruit. (The following July, I hand-carried the book's illustrations to the USSR, to return them to VAAP, the All-Union Agency on Copyrights in Moscow.)

Another day, John, an impresario who brought primarily classical music groups to Boston Symphony Hall and Worcester Mechanics Hall, had the Fitzwilliam Quartet come to her room to perform for her.

I tried to visit every day, whether she was at home or in the hospital. I got closer to her two children, Sasha and London. Natasha taught me how to plant petunias, how to prepare her lentil soup, and how to pretend behind a smile. On May 1st, I received 36 bright red carnations, and a note saying "Happy May Day, Fellow Traveler."

In late June, on my birthday, she gave me a large hand-painted wooden tray filled with dozens and dozens of dark, delicious chocolates, and a card saying "To my dearest friend, a very small token with all my love." (I also received a box of birthday chocolates all the way from Siberia, from Sasha.)

When I needed comfort, oddly enough, I found it at the Mt. Auburn Cemetery in Cambridge, diagonally across the street from where I lived. I often wandered among the headstones in the peaceful quiet, interrupted only by the croaking of the frogs or the quacking of the ducks. I read dates of births and deaths and calculated the ages. And some of the names on the gravestones were amusing: Sleeper, Bliss, Downward.

On one of my visits, when it was close to Easter, there were more flowers than usual. Potted tulips and lilies decorated many of the graves and since most of the lilac and crabapple trees weren't yet in bloom, the deep purple, light lavender, and bright yellow pansies bursting out to reach the light appeared even more vibrant.

My spot to read or reflect was on a bench by Willow Pond, under one of three stately weeping willow trees. Their hanging branches barely touched the water and shimmered as if they had an electric current running through them. And I thought ... *we are all as transient as the light reflected off those branches.*

Natasha

One of the things I admired in Natasha was her ability and desire to find and to create what was special in a situation, what was most moving, what was most memorable. That was evident one evening when I watched her put eight-year-old Londy to bed. Natasha's embrace of her daughter was warm and tender, loving and long, as if she wanted to somehow make an actual physical impression on Londy, one that would last forever after she was gone.

In May, Natasha and I had lunch outside on her deck and we had all afternoon to talk. She first asked, and then firmly persuaded me, as only Natasha could do, to take over as Coordinator for the NESNE Conference in August. I was worried that between my job at MEEI, teaching at Mass Association for the Blind, and seeing her almost daily, I wouldn't have time to do it properly. She succeeded in getting me to agree, then said she would talk about it to Frank Grundstrom, Vice President for Human Resources at the *Boston Globe*, and at the time president of NESNE.

She told me how awkward it was with some people who couldn't seem to cope with her situation. Fighting back tears, she said, "People treat you differently. I don't know if it is fear, or what. Their reaction is something I don't quite understand. They don't seem to know how to act. And I resent the illness for that, because it has a presence that takes away my personhood by creating a barrier and by preventing normal exchange."

I told her I thought she had to be the director, because we are never taught how to deal with death. It isn't addressed culturally.

The radiation and chemotherapy did give her some more time but it gave her severe nausea, too. The melanoma spread to her bones; tumors were visible on her head. Her calcium level increased, her vitality decreased, and she first needed a cane and then a walker to get around. The pain was constant, but "mostly manageable" she said.

It was her decision to die at home, surrounded by all that was familiar and precious to her. A hospital bed was brought in, a permanent IV was implanted and a nurse visited daily. Just before Natasha was unable to leave her room, she brought to it what she wanted and needed. She placed three Russian icons on one wall, several of Londy's drawings of trees and flowers and sunsets on another, and on the third, wall hangings she had carried back from Mongolia.

"Remember that sound we heard in the Gobi?" she asked me. "I think of that, of the beauty, the peace, the oneness we felt out there, and I'm not afraid to die. I know I will become a part of it all."

One evening, on what we didn't know would be her last lucid day, she weakly declared, "It will be soon." We embraced, and we cried. We said what was in our hearts —"Thank you, I love you, goodbye." Then I kissed her forehead, and took her warm hand. She squeezed my hand hard, and wouldn't let go. And thus we remained, silent, in the dark, for a long time. When it was time, I touched my fingers to my lips, then to hers. At the door, I turned to wave. "Sleep well," she said, as she blew me a kiss.

On a Saturday afternoon, July 14th, while her mother, her sister Tamara, and I were with her, after being barely conscious and unable to speak for five days, the warmth began to leave Natasha's hands, the cold to travel up her arms. She constantly fidgeted with her sheets, and then her breathing changed. I found myself breathing in rhythm with her, slower and slower, and silently talking to her, silently saying, "You can let go now, let go, let go, find your peace." Gradually, she did. One moment she was breathing, and then, she was no longer.

Tamara took off Natasha's nightgown, gave it to me to keep, and then the three of us bathed her with warm, soapy washcloths, brushed her teeth, put on a new nightgown and bedsheets, placed a white nicotiana from her garden in her hand, lit the candles, and called those who would want to come.

After all the visitors had left, Tamara put some of Natasha's perfume, Ivoire by Balmain, on her own, her mother's and my wrists, and we stood in a circle around her bed, holding hands, someone holding each of Natasha's hands. We quietly listened to Ravi Shankar while each of us said our final, silent goodbyes. And just before midnight, the hearse came. We followed the men who carried her to the vehicle, Hearse 821 MA, and we stood in the street as they gently put her in the back.

"Her last trip," Tamara said, unsuccessfully trying to smile through the blur of her tears as we watched the hearse take her from us.

The next afternoon, when I rang the bell at Seville Funeral Home in Arlington, the director led me through a viewing room and down to the basement. Natasha was laid out in a workroom: sink, closets and cupboards filled with hanging clothes, slips, hair rollers, make-up, all the tools of the undertaker's trade. Her hair had been washed and Tamara was blow-drying it.

We first put make-up on her, then the dress Tamara had sewn to Natasha's specifications. It was white silk, with royal-blue lily sleeves, and a blue yoke. Last, two beaded African necklaces Natasha had purchased in South Africa. Then we all helped to place Natasha in the box, which we had lined with white silk. We placed her head on her favorite antique pillow, beige with pastel, hand-painted, water-colored flowers. It took some doing to place her just right, to keep her head from rolling off to one side. We finally had to put empty bottles under one shoulder and one hand, and hid them in the folds of her dress.

The funeral director told us, "Not in 25 years has anyone come in and done what you people did for her."

When we were finished, we gathered up our things, walked through the coffin display room, up the stairs, and out into the sunlight.

Natasha

At the close of the wake, I scattered some juniper incense from Mongolia into Natasha's casket, incense that had come from the lamasery in Ulan Bator. She was cremated the next day, and her sister and her mother and I went, to be with her to the very end.

After a walk down a long corridor at the crematorium, we found ourselves in the room with the ovens. Three, I think, flush with the wall. One of the two men in uniform asked if we were ready, turned a knob, opened a door, put the box in, shut the door, turned another knob, then turned to tell us it would take about two and a half hours.

At that point, Tamara and her mother got into a fight, yelling in Russian and actually shoving one another.

Such disrespect for Natasha, I thought, keeping my distance, my mouth and eyes open wide. When I later talked to her mother about that, she had no real explanation, except to say that when the doors were opened and they saw the flames, the horror of it grabbed both her and Tamara.

It made no sense to me. Actually that was the way my cats behaved when a strange cat appeared at the back deck. Vodka and Grapefruit usually got nervous, agitated, then hissed and tried to get at the stranger through the glass slider. When that failed, they turned on one another and fought. A way of working out tension for some beings, I guess.

It rained for the memorial service the next day, held inside the chapel at Mt. Auburn Cemetery. The minister, a friend of Natasha's, spoke of her eclectic approach to faith, and read selections from Christian, Jewish, and Hindu prayers. Manny Borok, a violinist with the Boston Symphony Orchestra, played selections from Bach's *Partitas* and his wife sang a Russian folk song. Veronica read a poem she had translated from Russian, about fallen warriors who rose as cranes, *"cranes who in evening's dying glow fly quickly past in company, as once on horseback they would go."* John, Tim, and I spoke. I mentioned that Natasha's strong hugs and her magnificent smile were her very special gifts, gifts that made each of us feel very special.

Then, a soprano, a beautiful, heavy-bosomed Black woman sang *Amazing Grace*. A single bird at the chapel window chirped along with her.

Finally, the car procession to her plot, where half of her ashes would be. She asked that when he got older, her son Sasha take the other half to South Africa to be spread there, where he was born. A man in a yellow slicker unceremoniously put her in the ground, in her spot, a spot that happened to be about 20 feet from my bench at Willow Pond. We all put flowers in after her, Londy and Sasha first.

As we finished, the rain stopped. The sun broke through. And a duck and her ducklings paddled peacefully to shore.

* * *

"Are you Cynthia?"
"Yes."
"My name is Jonathan."

And there he stood, with her upturned nose, her radiant smile. The child Natasha had given up for adoption 36 years earlier, when she was only 16. The child, now an adult, after some searching learned who his birth mother was, but located her thirteen years after the melanoma found her. As he talked, I swallowed, hard and often, in an effort to beat back the tears that threatened to surface every time he smiled. He said he was one of the lucky ones, because most of those who have been adopted aren't so successful in finding their birth parents.

A voice ushered us to our seats. It was time for the wedding to begin, time for Natasha's younger sister Tamara to walk down the aisle to the music of Tchaikovsky's *Romeo and Juliet*.

Yuri Andropov, who replaced Leonid Brezhnev, served only 15 months before he died of renal failure in Feb 1984. He had vowed to rid the country of all dissent, in all its forms.

Chapter 15
1984, 1985—NESNE

"The press is the only weapon with whose aid the Party speaks every day."
—Josef Stalin (1878–1953), in *Pravda*, 1917

"There is nothing so fretting and vexatious, nothing so justly terrible to tyrants, and their tools and abettors, as a free press."
—Samuel Adams (1722–1803)
Founding Father of United States

1984

After my friend Dee (who had decided to go by her full name Delia) left her abusive husband Terry, she married a man named Eddie. Together they started a business, Optique du Monde, designer sunglasses, and were so successful that they bought a yacht. They lived in Cos Cob, Connecticut until that marriage failed. They sold the yacht to Revlon, and she shortly after married a high school boyfriend, John Skiffington, and they moved to Costa Rica, where they had two beautiful daughters, Olivia and Kimberley.

At the beginning of the year, I had visited Costa Rica and decided I wanted to move there. It was beautiful there, and I loved the thought of spending time with Delia. I even picked up an application to teach at their

Kimberley, Delia, Olivia Skiffington

English-speaking school. But then came Natasha's diagnosis, and I knew I wasn't going anywhere except to be with her.

After Natasha's urging back then, because she was so ill, I had an interview at the *Boston Globe* with Frank Grundstrom and soon after I took over her position as Coordinator of the NESNE Foreign Exchange Program. Shortly after, my title changed to Director of the program.

The 1984 NESNE Conference, to be held August 20th to 26th at both Brown and Boston universities, was the first thing I had to manage.

When our state department refused to provide a visa for one of the proposed delegates, Alexander Makarov, chief editor for the Soviet press agency Novosti, they stated that the denial was for "internal security reasons." Our appeal was denied and one of the NESNE editors was told by someone in a position to know that Makarov had KGB links. (This Makarov not to be confused with the 1982 delegate who did come, Evgeny Makarov).

But the August program went as planned and again, the delegation's Aeroflot flight, still refused entry into the US, landed first in Montreal, then caught another flight to JFK.

The first half of the program was held at Brown University. NESNE invited several speakers: Mark Garrison, director of Brown's Center for Foreign Policy Development; Anthony Austin, editor of the *NYT Magazine*, and US Senator Claiborne Pell of Rhode Island. The Soviets objected to discussing sensitive political issues. Tensions were bad between the US and the USSR. On February 9, Yuri Andropov had died, to be followed by his successor Konstantin Chernenko. Diplomacy between our countries was at a low due to arguments over missiles in Europe and nuclear arms. Pell addressed that fact when he said, "We have reached a point of compulsively belligerent rhetoric, where the arms-control process has become primarily a forum for propaganda, while real communication has slowed down to a trickle."

So, in an effort to achieve real communication, we took the delegates to see Liberace with his many outrageous costumes. I can say with absolute conviction that the Soviets were certainly bewildered, certainly not impressed, and certainly no closer to meaningful communication. That might have been one of the most bizarre attempts at diplomacy since the start of the Cold War. I think the lobsters we fed them and the volleyball game we engaged in on the sand at Narragansett Beach did a much better job of breaking the ice.

At Boston University, they met with university president John Silber, who had ran as a Democrat for governor of Massachusetts in 1990 and lost. (Because of my dislike of Silber, I voted for his opponent, William Weld, who did win and who to this day remains the only Republican I have ever voted for, for any office.)

Soviet delegates also met with female journalists from New England who wanted to discuss the role of female journalists in the USSR. For the most part, the Soviets comments were condescending, although it was clear they didn't see them that way.

There was discussion of the four programs that NESNE hoped to put in place: A student exchange, an article exchange, a photo exchange, and a working journalist exchange. Two Americans had already been chosen to go to the Soviet Union to work on papers there. Both were fluent in Russian. The Soviets stated that the probable reelection of Ronald Reagan would most likely result in postponement of this exchange. Bernard Redmont, dean of the Journalism School who gave the welcoming speech, was unhappy that it was taking so long to implement the agreed-upon exchanges.

However, Redmont thought that the Q and A with the journalism students went well. He wasn't sure the students were happy with many of the Soviets' answers, but he himself was pleased that such a meeting like that, during such difficult times between our two countries, took place.

At the close of the conference, each participant was given five minutes to share his or her feelings about its success. For the most part, the Soviets were positive and optimistic about the exchanges.

NESNE delegate and *Providence Journal* editor Larry Howard perhaps said it best when he stated that he hoped his Soviet colleagues "will tell their readers that the US does not want war with the same intensity that the Soviet people do not want war."

1985

"We don't hold the bombs in our hands,
but it is our duty as journalists to influence those who do."
Albertas Laurinciukas, chief editor of the newspaper *Tiesa* in Lithuania
(1928–2012)

July 3-11

If she were still alive, Natasha would have been on this exchange with the eight-member NESNE delegation, one of whom was Frank (Grundstrom), and our two interpreters. Instead, it was me.

We were met at the airport in Moscow by several members of the Union of Soviet Journalists, among them two old friends, Evgeny Makarov and Alexei Burmistenko. They ushered us through customs quickly and graciously insisted on carrying all my luggage and, of course, my purse.

It was an interesting time to be in Russia. Four months before our arrival, Mikhail Gorbachev had replaced General Secretary Konstantin Chernenko, in office only thirteen months before he died. We all looked forward to the newspapers for their commentary on Gromyko's new, largely honorary position as Chairman of the Presidium of the Supreme Soviet, the appointment of the new Foreign Minister from Soviet Republic of Georgia, Eduard Shevardnadze, and on the upcoming summit in November in Geneva between Gorbachev and Reagan. Also, beginning June 1st, Gorbachev's alcohol reform, which was really partial prohibition, went into effect. Prices were raised, fewer stores sold hard liquor, and had to be open for fewer hours. I wondered if our Russian counterparts would ignore the law or comply with it and serve us cognac or their usually warm, always sweet Russian champagne.

En route to the hotel, we stopped at the monument commemorating the halt of the Nazi advance on Moscow. We were also passed by a government motorcade for the President of Yugoslavia, accompanied by either Gorbachev or Gromyko.

Our first visit the next day was to the official voice of the Central Committee of the Communist Party, the newspaper *Pravda*, where we met with Viktor Afanasyev, Marxist philosopher and editor-in-chief, the most powerful journalist in the Soviet Union, perhaps in the world. He was also a member of that Committee of the Party, a member of the Academy of Sciences, and a deputy of the Supreme Soviet. I was immediately aware of being in the presence of a man of intellect and power. Lean, wiry, he appeared taller than his average height. He had high, Tartar cheekbones and his hair was streaked gray, straight with a long lock that often fell forward. He greeted each of us with a firm handshake and only one word, "Afanasyev."

Once we were seated at the table, which ran the length of the entire room, we were immediately served tea with lemon and sugar. He was immediately served, by either a secretary or perhaps a bodyguard, an ashtray and cigarettes. He used a cigarette holder, not large or flashy, simply adequate, which he held between his thumb and index finger.

Through an interpreter, he told us that *Pravda*, which meant (ironically) Truth, had been founded by Lenin in 1912.

"*Pravda* is a political paper," he said, "meant to spread the propaganda of Party policy and to create public opinion on decisions of the Party, to help the Party implement those decisions. With a circulation of 12 million, our main purpose is peace, reduction of arms, and the prevention of nuclear war.

"Today's issue carries a greeting to the American people, since today is July 4th, and the big news is of the upcoming Summit meeting between Gorbachev and Reagan. Gorbachev is young, energetic, and well-educated. I don't think there will be any revolutionary changes with him in office, but I think the style of the work of the Party has changed and the main goal is now economic progress.

"There is enthusiasm here for the Summit, and no doubt it will contribute to normalizing relations between our two countries. Lately, relations have been bad. We know we are behind the West in some fields and we are trying to catch up as soon as possible. But we are suspicious of the intentions and policies of your President. He talks about peace, arms reduction, but at the same time, there is an unprecedented military build-up taking place. The MX, submarines, Pershings in Europe, all are dangerous for the USSR. The ICBM can reach us from the US in one half hour, the Pershings in six minutes.

"Regarding the Strategic Defense Initiative, what you call *Star Wars*—it is not research and development as some claim. We Russians do not trust this. The 'research project' in Manhattan ended in Hiroshima and Nagasaki.

"First there will be research, then development, then experiments, and then the new weapons will be on the assembly lines. This new weaponry will cost 27 billion dollars, and where will it go? To the Military Industrial Complex in California, where Reagan is from!

"We believe that *Star Wars* is not a defense, but part of a strategy of first strike. First-strike strategy is an illusion because the retaliation would still come. Even American scientists agree about this. We don't know how the USSR will balance this situation, but 'to every poison, there is an antidote'.

Victor Afanasyev (1922–1994)

"I believe the best solution is to freeze the number and quality of weapons and stop all tests. Then reduce weapons. There are so many weapons now the world could be destroyed four times over. There are four tons of TNT for each person, but only 10 grams is needed to destroy life. Money should be directed to resolving social problems. The USSR is always trying to keep up with the US; first the Atomic Bomb, then nuclear subs. Let us stop," he shouted, as he pounded the table.

Throughout the meeting, the 62-year-old Afanasyev made eye contact. As he listened to questions, when he was not smoking, he rested his closed left hand in his right hand, at the wrist, in his lap. Whenever he stood up, his movements were quick, not nervous, but those of a highly charged, energetic individual.

I found myself wondering if the L shaped mark on his left cheek was a birthmark or a scar, and if it was a scar, what had so marked him.

Conversation was also devoted to possible joint programs between the Union of Journalists and NESNE. At the end of the meeting, he willingly, and quickly, autographed copies of the day's *PRAVDA* for each of us. And he told us we were the first American journalists he had met with that year. (The 100-year-old newspaper was banned by Boris Yeltsin in 1991, sold, then taken over again by the Communist Party's Central Committee in 1997.)

That evening, we went to Spaso House, built in 1914 and the residence of the American ambassadors since the establishment of diplomatic relations between the US and the USSR in 1933. We were surrounded by probably 1,000 other guests. The yellow and white building was even more colorful due to the blue and red balloons in the yards. Before we reached Ambassador Hartman's wife Donna, who received everyone, the line snaked up the drive, past the security people, past the coatroom with dozens of military hats from dozens of countries, up the stairs to the main hall. There was food in the first room, a New Orleans Jazz band featuring trombonist Freddie Longo, and a bar in the main hall, ice cream on a balcony, and hot dogs and hamburgers in the back garden.

But this was nothing compared to celebrations in the 1930s thrown by US Ambassador William C. Bullitt, who had "trained seals serving trays of champagne and on one memorable occasion, a menagerie of white roosters, free-flying finches, grumpy mountain goats, and a rambunctious bear." (David Remnick, *The New Yorker*, August 11 and 18, 2014.)

I had a gin and tonic and a hot dog! Yes, I ate one. And it was the worst hot dog I had ever eaten. Even worse than in Mongolia.

And speaking of Mongolia, coincidentally across the street from Spaso House was the Mongolian Embassy, where Natasha and I had gone in 1982 to pick up visas for the Audubon group.

The next day found us in the medieval village of Suzdal, since 1991 officially called again by its original name, Sergiev Posad, a complex of beautiful blue, white, and gold buildings where goats wandered and grazed freely. First mentioned in the year 1024, it was designated a museum city in the 1920s. There were over 100 monuments of secular and church architecture, many of wood, representing every century since the 11th. The town, which is actually the spiritual center of the Russian Orthodox Church, has been called "a great song in stone," a "stone chronicle," and a "fairy tale city." Writers better than I have described the beauty of its buildings. I can only say I was utterly enchanted by their exquisite simplicity.

The conference with Soviet journalists began with introductions and then a moment of silence for two people who had been instrumental in the establishment of this exchange: Natasha, and Soviet delegate Sergei Vishnevsky, from *Pravda*, who also had recently died.

But the talks did not go as well as we had hoped, in large part due to the head of the Soviet delegation, Ivan Zubkov, the Vice-Chairman of the Board of the Union of Journalists. Gruff, coarse, condescending, Zubkov was a stereotypical Party bureaucrat, and our impression was that he cared not at all about the conference or our exchange agreements.

There was much angry rhetoric between delegations and the dialogue deteriorated so much that I got angry and felt compelled to speak, to say that in the past, when relations were worse between our countries, there was a greater sense of cooperation, of mutual purpose. Now, on the eve of better relations between our countries, the delegates can only agree to argue. We left the conference depressed, feeling defeated by the seeming futility of it all.

The high point of the proceedings was Larry Howard's speech, in Russian, which he had prepared for during the previous year by studying Russian in night classes. This was Larry's second trip to the USSR. Editor of the *Providence Journal Bulletin*, Larry had been part of the first delegation to visit the USSR in 1983. The fact that he made such an effort to give this speech, putting aside his obvious shyness, demonstrated both what a dedicated journalist he was, and how much he himself was invested in this exchange program.

Larry Howard (died in 1985 at age 66)

> "Today, I want to speak to you in your own language.
> This year I have been studying Russian at home and at the university.
> I speak Russian poorly.
> I think Russian is a beautiful but very difficult language.
> I study. Study. Study. And I know nothing.
> But one thing I know.
> I am very glad to be here today.
> We want to see the USSR.
> We want to know the Soviet peoples.
> We want to understand the USSR.
> Also, we want you to see, to know and to understand the USA.
> Thank you for inviting us to your great country.
> You are very good hosts.
> It is important for Russians and Americans to talk together.
> That is why we are here.

We want to know you better.
Help us in this.
This will be useful to both sides.
I do not want to make a long speech.
I do not speak Russian well enough to do that.
And you would fall asleep, I know.
Therefore, I now finish my first speech in Russian.
Please forgive my mistakes.
Thank you. Thank you very much."

"*Horosho!"* the Russians shouted, *Good!*, as they enthusiastically applauded Larry.

The next day, we went to visit the town of Vladimir, one of the oldest Russian communities, did some sightseeing, and then, so that we could get to the airport in time, we had a speeding police escort to Moscow. The flight to Yerevan, the capitol of Armenia, wasn't bad and we were met at the airport by Armenian journalists who had red carnations "for the ladies."

The next morning, we were received by Babken Sarkisov, the President of the Supreme Soviet of the Armenia SSR, who proudly told us, among other things, that the Armenians are the most ancient people in the world. When that hour was over, we were taken to be welcomed by the Union of Armenian Journalists.

We were also taken on a city tour to see beautiful old architecture, whose most unique feature was the intricately carved stone that was the main decorative element. And to a cognac tasting at a cognac factory, (I really dislike cognac, maybe even more than hot dogs), to Lake Sevan, and then to the Children's Museum. I noticed at the museum that Larry sat down and looked very tired. He asked if I had any aspirin. When I found a small bottle and handed it to him, he was unable to open it. I took it from him, gave him two and someone got him some water. He looked very weak, was sweating, and two people helped him downstairs to an air-conditioned office. As soon as he sat down, he said he felt nauseated. Suddenly he gagged, choked, and turned chalk-white, while his head rolled to one side as he lost consciousness. Then he vomited. Nobody knew CPR, but Frank immediately began to pound on Larry's chest. It seemed to work because he came to and was extremely apologetic about having thrown up, although he didn't remember having done so. He said he felt better and that he most likely should not have mixed the cognac with wine and beer at lunch.

In the meantime, an ambulance arrived. The emergency technicians brought in a stretcher for him to rest on and did an EKG. They actually did two, and both indicated that Larry had suffered a heart attack. Although he protested, the doctors not only insisted that he go to the hospital, but told us that it had been a serious heart attack and that he would have to stay in the hospital for a minimum of three weeks. He reluctantly agreed and our interpreter Galina went with him. The rest of us, worried but knowing he was in good hands, continued with the planned program, a visit to a collective farm.

At the farm's field, we sampled juicy tomatoes right off the vine before we went to a private home in the town of Nalbandyan for an incredible outdoor meal and interminable toasts. So much food, too much food—veal, lamb, rice, scallions, fresh basil, peppers, olives, flat bread, rosewater mineral water, Czech beer, pineapple juice, and more cognac. And large bowls of fresh fruit—sweet yellow cherries, plump fresh figs, and watermelon. After eating, the chairman of the collective farm, our host and hostess, and Soviet and American delegates all danced to a tape I had brought of Bruce Springstein's music.

It was a lovely time, a joyful time, and we found ourselves singing on the bus on the way back to our hotel.

Until we saw Galina, ashen, waiting for us at the curb.

* * *

Larry was one of my favorites of the American journalists I worked with. He was intelligent, interested, involved. A gentle man, his eyes danced when he found something humorous. When I arrived at Kennedy airport to begin this trip, he simply smiled when he saw all my luggage. The speech he gave in Russian must have made him nervous, but I hope also proud. The night before, I had asked him to stand by the second floor window of our hotel and wait while I went down to the street to get what I thought would be a great photo of him. And it was. There he was, smiling in the shadows. (On July 11th, Senator Claiborne Pell read Larry's accomplishments into the Senate Congressional Record, and focused on his contributions to the NESNE exchange with the USSR.)

Larry Howard waving from the second-floor window

The next day was pretty low-key as plans were cancelled and people mourned and made calls home to tell what had happened. I spent some time talking to the guide provided to us by the Soviet journalists, a nice guy named

Oleg. We spoke about Larry, about the fact that he was only 66, about the fragility of life.

Then Oleg recited this poem, written by Swedish labor activist Joe Hill, who was a member and leading songwriter of the Wobblies, or the Industrial Workers of the World. In 1915, at age 36, Hill, convicted of murdering a grocer, was executed by a Utah firing squad. A book by William Adler, *The Man Who Never Died*, presents the theory that Hill was convicted primarily because of his radical ideas about labor.

Last Will

My will is easy to decide
For there is nothing to divide.
My kin don't need to fuss and moan,
Moss doesn't cling to a rolling stone.

My body? Oh if I could choose,
I would to ashes it reduce,
And let the merry breezes blow,
My dust to where some flowers grow.

Perhaps some fading flower then
Would come to life and bloom again.
This is my Last and Final will.
Luck to all of you.

The next day, before we departed, we made a quick visit to the Echmiadzin Cathedral, considered the oldest cathedral (not church) in the world, where we all lit a candle for Larry. Off to the airport, where the rest of the delegation would go to Moscow to meet their spouses, and I would go to the Caucasian coast of the Black Sea. I was looking forward to seeing Sasha, and had sent him a telegram from Yerevan telling him of my arrival date. We had been corresponding since we met in Siberia in 1982, and he said in every letter that he was looking forward to meeting me again.

Because I was a member of a delegation, I was assigned an Intourist escort to board the plane, which was already late. I settled in at a good seat and shortly after, everyone on the plane was told to get off. There had been a scuffle between two male passengers and apparently, by someone's reasoning, it made sense to empty the plane. Without the language, I had no idea what was happening, but I knew that it wasn't going to be fun in the airport without my escort and I certainly knew I would not understand any announcements about the flight.

So, I wouldn't leave my seat. For a half hour, the pilot and the steward, in Russian, and then with hand motions, repeatedly told me to disembark. I simply smiled as if they were issuing an invitation and not a request, shook my head, and stayed where I was. A half hour later, everyone re-boarded. I never learned exactly why all were told to leave the plane. I just kept smiling.

In Sochi, I was met by another Intourist guide, a woman named Albina, and a private car. My luggage arrived at the car seconds after I did, which was very impressive. "VIP treatment," Albina said. *I could get used to this*, I thought.

I was very pleased with my room at the Hotel Kamelia. A tall vase of hydrangeas had been placed on a table, the small refrigerator was stocked with champagne, vodka, mineral water, and chocolate, and there was a balcony overlooking a garden and two magnolia trees. It was clean and comfortable and welcoming.

At 7:00 PM, I went outside to wait for Sasha, as I had said I would in the telegram. And as I feared—he must not have gotten my telegram—he did not arrive. After a light dinner of simply an omelet and bread, I crawled into bed and tried, unsuccessfully, to stop thinking about Larry.

The next morning, Albina picked me up and we went first by cable car to the Botanical Gardens, then to meet with the Deputy Director of Intourist – at his request. He told me that since I was a journalist, he wanted to make sure that I wrote good things about Sochi. I dutifully, in VIP fashion, pen and pad in hand, took down the facts. Most interesting was that at 90 miles, Sochi is the longest town in the world, (San Francisco is second) and many refer to the area as the Russian Riviera. American tourists numbered 7,000 to 12,000 per year; on that day, not one hotel bed was available; Sochi is the northernmost subtropical zone in the world and the only place in the USSR where one can take a helicopter ride.

Which I did, that afternoon. We flew over the Caucasus, but were not allowed to take photos. Often the country was so frustrating. If there were sensitive sights, we would never have been allowed to fly over them. All I saw were mountains, more mountains, and many more mountains. With snow. While landing, the strong wind from the helicopter blades caused the nearby tall grass to ribbon and ripple, like thousands of snakes running to escape.

I never got a visit from Sasha, but what I did get was a terrible migraine. I don't know if I had it from the drastic change in the weather, too little sleep, or emotional exhaustion and let-down from Larry's death. In any event, I cancelled the day's plans, moved my pillow to the sofa, and as the pain lessened, played Luther Vandross, Gladys Knight and the Pips, and some classical music on my tape recorder, read, organized my papers, and wrote in my journal. By 5:00 PM, I was better and dressed and able to go with Albina to the outdoor festival hall, guests of the Deputy Director of Intourist and his wife, for a concert and fashion show. The designer, Zaitsev Vyacheslav, from

Prospect Mira in Moscow, came out on stage in a white suit and introduced his fashions, inspired by Russian folk art and nature. Most were black and white with an occasional accent of red, and many I would have loved to own. The men on the runway looked like they were straight out of a Raymond Chandler thriller, shoulders dropped, dark suits, hats worn low over their foreheads, hands in their pockets. After the models, a jazz band appeared and played swing-era songs and a tribute to Louis Armstrong. (In Zaitsev's 2001 collection, prices ranged from $2,000 to $3,000 for the cheapest clothes, and between $10,000 and $12,000 for the most expensive.)

When it was over, the four of us went back to my hotel for snacks and drinks. Few snacks, many, many drinks. And of course, we offered toasts. Not Albina, not the director's wife, just me, then him, then me, and on and on until I didn't care if I never in my entire life tasted the dreaded cognac again or lifted another glass to the beautiful Russian sunset.

The next morning, I again went to breakfast for hot cereal and pancakes, and to my assigned table in the dining room, adorned with a small American flag to announce to all where I was from. Apparently I was the only American in the hotel. It was the one year anniversary of Natasha's death.

Albina and I and our driver went first to the small town of Gagra, where we walked through the gardens by the sea, surrounded by peacocks, white pelicans, and black and white swans. Such a shame to be there, in the town where Sasha lived, and be unable to reach him because I didn't have a phone number for him.

Onto Lake Ritsa, a very scenic ride through the mountains, passing many interesting bridges, bee boxes, cows and pigs roaming the highway, and a few very old people, some of the women dressed all in black. Then to Pitsunda, where we walked down a wide boulevard lined by pitsunda pine trees and a small boxtree forest and stopped to eat at the Golden Fleece restaurant.

Over lunch, Albina and I talked about many issues, both political and social. Abortion, medicine, cultural approaches to death and illness, family structure, and she was very guarded. She asked a few questions, safe questions, and showed no willingness or desire to address any issue that might be "troublesome." Thus, I didn't push and the rest of the day was filled with small talk.

About a year earlier, Sasha sent me a postcard of the Pitsunda Cathedral, an 11th-century building where one can see 15th- and 16th- century frescoes on the ceilings. He went there to hear organ recitals. And when Albina and I arrived, a concert was in progress. We quietly slipped in and sat in the last row. Seat two for me. I smiled when I decided I would tell Sasha in a letter where I sat.

Soon after, I would learn that he had been in prison at the time I was there and that was why he didn't come to meet me. More about that later.

On the way back from Pitsunda, we passed citrus orchards, tobacco plantations, vineyards, and groves of eucalyptus trees. And all along the highway there were bus stops in very colorful, garish mosaics, all with a sea theme. Shells, fish, even one shaped like an octopus.

When we crossed over a bridge on the Psou River, we left Abkhazia, Georgia behind and put our watches back on Russian Federation time. Worthy of mention was Victor, the driver, whose personality could be glimpsed only in two ways. He spoke not at all, but on the shift inside the car was an elaborate wooden carved cobra, which he was clearly very proud of. And, he kept the radio on only to American music. After I heard Michael Jackson's *Billy Jean* and the theme from *Flashdance*, I started to think that things had really changed since Gorbachev took over. I decided I had better ask if it was indeed the radio, or perhaps a tape.

"No," he said, "it is the radio. Radio Turkey."

The day was pleasant and peaceful and entirely appropriate for a somber anniversary. That evening, Albina told me there was a movie in English in the hotel if I was interested. *Moscow Doesn't Believe in Tears*, which I had actually seen with Natasha and her father. I had dreamed of Natasha a few nights earlier. She was standing in a doorway, smiling, and I felt so happy and excited to see her. I chose not to go to the movie and to instead stay in my room and spend some quiet time on my balcony, thinking about my friend.

The next day started with a tour to a tea plantation, and then a visit to the Sanatorium Ordzhonikidze, where I toured the palatial, neoclassical facility. Built in 1936 by Stalin for workers, mainly miners initially, it was eventually named after Sergo Ordzhonikidze, one of Stalin's henchmen, who died under mysterious circumstances. It was thought by Nikita Khrushchev that Ordzhonikidze perhaps committed suicide because of Stalin's brutality. Other scholars believe that Stalin had him killed, or had him forced into suicide after he fell out of favor with Stalin because of his unhappiness with the course of events in the country.

The sanatorium, which had a pool and an outdoor cinema, was closed in 2010 for renovations. It opened briefly, but in 2016, it was closed to the public and designated a protected area, open for people to explore the grounds, but not allowed inside.

There I interviewed the assistant chief and unexpectedly, several of the patients. Most who went there suffered from cardiovascular problems, nervous conditions, and bone and joint diseases. Apparently the physicians of the sanitorium were in constant conflict with surgeons who preferred to operate or insert artificial joints, rather than try this natural method of healing. The heart of the treatment there was the *matsesta*, or sulfur bath, sometimes accompanied by physical therapy, inhalation therapy, massages and vitamin sprays.

Patients who smoked were asked to stop, and were prescribed things such as chewing gum with anti-nicotine to cause a negative reaction to a cigarette, or a liquid gargle with potassium and salt, which created an unbearable taste when one lit up a cigarette.

"Men have a more difficult time and less success in quitting than women do," the chief told me. "Women understand better and believe the doctors when they tell them that future children will suffer. As for the men, they are like children."

I didn't have an opportunity to take a sulfur bath, and of course have no way of judging the efficacy or success of the various prescribed treatments and of the almost holistic approach to healing, other than the glowing reports given by the patients I talked to. I can, however, offer first-hand comment on one of their therapies.

At day's end, I went to a beach hut outside my hotel for what I expected would be a glorious massage, with the soothing sound of the sea in the background. The room was lovely—wooden, newly painted, comforting in its simplicity, and the masseuse could not have been nicer. The massage itself—torture! She poked and prodded, pushed and pressed and pounded like someone overzealously kneading uncooperative bread dough, until I myself was ready to rise, right off the table. I tried to imagine myself somewhere else, a technique I suspect people being tortured or imprisoned used. It worked. I easily felt as if I were trapped in a clothes dryer or a punching bag at Gold's Gym. When my 45 minutes were up, I thanked her profusely—for not going one minute over the allotted time. Those poor people with joint problems!

When I emerged from the hut, which I then thought of as "the chamber," I decided I must at least put my feet in the Black Sea. It was warm and rocky, and I realized I was surrounded by thousands of potential finds for my suitcase. It wasn't the Gobi, but for a long time I was lost, head down, dazed and dizzied by the choices. With surprising restraint, I limited myself to only five stones—not small ones, however—which I lovingly wrapped in my beach towel to carry back to my room. A fitting finale to my Sochi sojourn.

The three-hour flight to Leningrad to meet back up with the NESNE group the next day was fine, and I was to be met at the airport by an Intourist person for the transfer to my hotel. I did wonder how that was going to happen. Would someone be standing with a sign with my name on it, or would I look so obviously American that they would know me immediately? Well, it was simple for Intourist; they simply did not meet me. I finally found my way to their office, presented my voucher, and patiently explained where I was going. In fact, I explained it several times because they called the hotel, the Pribaltiskaya, which apparently had no record of me or of the others, and finally, I just insisted they take me there and I would sort it out upon arrival.

The drive took an hour and at the end, I was tired, hungry, and somewhat cranky. Looking forward to a shower most of all. Reception told me that the group had not checked in. I told her that was impossible because they had arrived very early that morning. She kept shaking her head and staring at a piece of paper. After at least a half hour there, with my explaining the kind of group, the number of people, the Intourist Reference Number, I finally looked down at her paper, upside down yet, on which everything was written in Russian, and I immediately found our group—too aggravated to feel any sense of pride or triumph. At least my room was nice. It overlooked the Bay of Finland, and even better, had a wonderful bathroom, all too rare in Russia.

Galina Misjura

After my shower, that evening, I took a taxi to see Galina, from Khabarovsk, who was then working on her doctorate at the university. Her room was small and looked as if it would be very cold and drafty in winter. The common areas were dark and dreary. She served me some strawberries coated with sugar and showed me her things—a stereo, posters, books, and most unexpected, her white hamster, which was adorable. She let him out and with his nose constantly wiggling, he made the rounds of the room. Although somewhat shy, he did allow me to snuggle with him and to carry him on my arm.

The rest of the time in Leningrad was taken up with meetings at the Union of Journalists to discuss our exchange program, visits to Leningrad University, some shopping, some sightseeing. I tried to reach Valery S. in the hope of seeing him and his family again, but they were away at their *dacha* (cottage). I did meet Galina again for dinner, and she helped me mail a package to Sasha at the Central Post Office. She was also waiting at the curb when our bus pulled up at the train station for our departure to Helsinki. So nice of her to come to say goodbye.

Our customs experience this time was unexpectedly painless. With flashlights, they searched only the cabin itself—above the racks and under the beds and sinks. No questions about whether we had weapons or ammunition, drugs, antiques, or anti-Soviet printed matter. No search of any of our personal belongings. We all experienced a real lift after we crossed the border. And it was pure pleasure to use the public restroom—the very clean public restroom—at our first stop in Finland, where colorful flower pots hung from the roof of the station, and where the lawns were manicured and green, not gray gravel overgrown with dead weeds, as we had grown used to in Russia.

Time to decompress in Helsinki, easy to do without seeing armed soldiers around every corner, and a farewell dinner our last evening. Our last morning, I went to a Russian Orthodox church and stayed for part of the service. Then I again lit candles. One for Natasha. And this time, another one. For Larry.

Postscript: Getting Larry Home

The trip back home for the delegation was uneventful. Not so for Larry. One member of our delegation who worked with Larry at the *Providence Journal Bulletin*, Chuck Hauser, volunteered to stay behind in Russia to accompany Larry's body home.

The US Embassy provided no assistance. But the Armenian journalists in Yerevan could not have been more sympathetic, helpful or efficient. They cut through all the red tape and also paid for Larry to be shipped to Moscow in fewer than two days. Once in Moscow, the Special Services (Mortuary) Section of Intourist took over, with the gracious help of the Moscow Union of Journalists.

Then they lost Larry's body.

For four days, the whereabouts of his casket was unknown. Chuck was at a loss in terms of booking his flights to be with Larry, and was told the casket was most likely in Brussels. Or Amsterdam. Or still in Moscow. Maybe even in New York already, via Aeroflot, or Sabena, or KLM. Throughout this entire ordeal, from the day Larry died, the US Embassy was absolutely no help whatsoever.

Chuck did finally find a very helpful ticket agent behind the Sabena counter who, although he could find no trace of the casket, advised him to fly to New York and wait for it there. And indeed, when Chuck arrived in New York, he learned that the casket had arrived from Amsterdam a few hours earlier and been transferred to a hearse, which was waiting for Chuck to take them both back to Rhode Island.

It took a grueling, stressful, frustrating six days to get Larry home, much too long, we thought, until we later learned it normally took two to three weeks.

Five months later, NESNE received a letter from President Reagan. "To the extent that exchanges between American and Soviet professionals can be balanced, open, and mutually beneficial, I believe that they will prove extraordinarily valuable in lessening distrust and encouraging a more open dialogue. I think that you can take a good measure of satisfaction for being out front in this process which is so important to the future of freedom."

1984, 1985—NESNE

Konstantin Chernenko (General Secretary from Feb. 1984 to March 1985), died at age 73 of emphysema, congestive heart failure, and cirrhosis of the liver. President Reagan was said to have commented "How am I supposed to get anyplace with the Russians if they keep dying on me?"

Appointed General Secretary three hours after Chernenko's death, Mikhail Gorbachev, 54 years old at the time, was the youngest member of the Politburo. Unknown at the time, he would become the last leader of the USSR.

Chapter 16
1986—Sasha

*"Danger exists in the very amount of energy we use
that comes from sources other than solar.....
an increase in the planet's mean temperature of 4 – 5 degrees Celsius
would result in ecological disaster.
This is the line we cannot cross.
Technological progress brings more than blessings...."*
—Nikita Moiseyev (1917–2000), mathematician and
member of the Academy of Sciences of the USSR, warning in 1984

At a small dinner party with friends Judith Feher and Victor Gurewich at their home in Cambridge on June 23rd, I met Italian journalist Oriana Fallaci, fashionably dressed in shiny brown pants, clunky heels, a non-descript blouse, and a bright red scarf. "The color of anarchists," she told me. Her fingernails were red, too. She said that in Lebanon, she dressed as a soldier, helmet and all, and had her hands around her rifle.

"The Arabs never noticed the polish," she said.

I found her to be a little bird of a woman, intense, wide-eyed, animated, passionate, lonely and unhappy, nervous, talkative (non-stop), and a wonderful storyteller.

But also anti-Semitic.

"Religion is the worst thing that ever happened to mankind. They think they'll go to heaven, so they create hell here on earth."

"The Israelis are awful, the Jews of NY are awful; they all exploit the Holocaust. It's all economics. The Israelis are fanatics; the only good Jews are Italian Jews."

She wanted to interview Gorbachev. "If it works and I can set it up, I'll take you."

And I said, "And if I can arrange an interview, I'll call you." She then said, "And if we get arrested, shall I blame you or should you blame me?"

As far as I know, she never got that interview. I didn't either.

NESNE was not my only program. In April, I led a delegation of 42 members of the League of Women Voters on an American-Soviet Women in Politics program to meet with Soviet women of similar professions and backgrounds. Cities we visited were Moscow, Pyatigorsk, Ordzhonikidze, Tbilisi, Leningrad, and then Helsinki, where we picked up our Finnair flight home. My dear friend Debbie Grinnell had worked with me to organize the trip and I was thrilled that she was going to join me in a leadership role.

(A different experience than we had on the bar stools at Cambridge's Casablanca or Rialto with Debbie's niece Debbie Breen confiding Soviet-related work problems or pleasures, or on Plum Island, Newburyport, when Debbie G. and I decided to pitch a tent on the beach, when we got woken up at 3:00 AM by a policeman who was too embarrassed to tell two middle-aged women in flannel nightgowns with an empty champagne bottle turned upside down in the sand that what we were doing was illegal, or in Italy when we wouldn't leave the pool at the hotel in Tuscany when lightning was threatening, and our husbands and the hotel staff were yelling at us to get out. The lightning never came, but our smiles of stupid victory did.)

My Debbies: Debbie Grinnell on the left, Debbie Breen on the right

Two of my participants were interviewed by the FBI before the trip. After talking with them, we decided one was visited because she had a high-powered position in the defense industry, and the other because she was a left-wing activist. Both apparently "passed" the interviews, because they did join the group.

It was my third time staying at the Hotel Cosmos, which was much nicer than in 1980 or in 1982, when I was with Natasha. While my delegation went to Red Square and on a city tour, I went to the Union of Journalists to discuss the next NESNE conference in the fall. There appeared to be a lot of enthusiasm for what we had proposed: home visits and discussion of the responsibility of the press in each country in dealing with alcoholism, and the training of journalists. They were also optimistic about soon placing our young working journalists with a paper somewhere in the USSR. Good meeting!

I calculated that the group had spent 26 hours in transit, and I was tired, so I took some time for myself to wander the walkways and archways of GUM, across Red Square to the Beriozka (gift shop) at the Rossiya Hotel, and then back to the hotel to shower. Our evening program was a performance of the Bolshoi at the Kremlin Palace of Congresses. I was excited because it was my first time to see the Bolshoi perform in the USSR and not America (and it was impressive to learn that the company had been created in 1776, the same year as America!) The audience of 2,000 was seated in five tiers, surrounded by walls of deep red and gold. The company did several one-act pieces, all very creative and very enjoyable. I think. I fell asleep.

The next day, we were taken to School #56, where we toured the museum, the junior classes where the children shyly presented us with gifts and souvenirs, and then into the auditorium for a concert. On the back wall above the stage, a bust of Lenin and in large letters the slogan "The Communist ideal is for every Soviet person to actively participate in life."

The children sang *We Shall Overcome, Down by the Riverside, Blowin' in the Wind.* One recited Shakespeare. All wore blue uniforms. At the close of the performance, I was pleased to see that the students were encouraged to talk with us, which was not always the case.

I was not so pleased at our next meeting at the Soviet Women's Committee, because most of the dialogue was either routine or Party-dictated. There was an interesting exchange on birth control and the Soviet women emphatically stated that contraception was widely available. (Women's sanitary napkins or tampons were rarely available, let alone birth control.) So I asked, if contraception was widely available, why was there such a high rate of abortion? Vera Soboleva, the head of the International Department of the Committee, replied that there was no problem since vacuum aspiration had become available. I sat through the meeting, trying hard not to shake my head, wondering why we even bothered to schedule meetings like that, and decided that the only value was in introducing first-time travelers to the Soviet "way."

Because two Russian ophthalmologists had visited Massachusetts Eye and Ear Infirmary a few months prior, I was able with their help to arrange an afternoon at the Institute of Eye Microsurgery, whose director, Stanislav Fyodorov, developed the procedure known as "radial keratotomy" to correct near-sightedness.

After an orientation, we were taken to a changing room and given white scrubs to put over our own clothes, including papers shoes and hats and cloth masks. Our tour included examining rooms and surgery rooms, with operations in progress, and then the conveyer belt, where five doctors worked on one patient as he floated by on the assembly line, made in West Germany to Russian specifications. This system allowed them to do 25,000 cataract surgeries annually, compared to 9,000 or 10,000 in Boston.

(By 1989, Svyatoslav Fyodorov had 5,000 employees and opened a new facility in Moscow to add to the nine treatment centers he already had and to add to his $75-million dollar-a year business that grew 30 percent annually. *Fortune Magazine* May 8, 1989.)

The building itself was also impressive, very clean, new, with sparkling marble walls, colorful murals, and windows. Our group of white-clad ghosts laughed at our appearance and snapped photos at every turn. No one, Soviet or American, seemed to show any concern about patient rights. The hospital impressed me as a microcosm of the society at large where one constantly observed a blend of the obsolete and the innovative. There we saw shiny, new, revolutionary equipment, yet ladies in the hall sat in old wooden wheelchairs folding laundered gauze masks for reuse.

Once we had discarded our OR clothes, we were taken to a reception area, where the table was set with cucumber sandwiches, cold cuts, and cookies. Tea or coffee was poured and everyone of us was graciously handed a red carnation. Just a little more welcoming than the usual coffee in a Styrofoam cup that Americans provide guests during meetings in the US.

On our last evening in Moscow, four of us attempted a visit to the synagogue on Archipova Street that I had been to on my 1980 trip. Supposedly, according to Fodor's Travel Guide, there was a service every night at 10:00 PM. However, when we arrived, all was locked up tight. We went to the back of the building, where there was a light at the window, and found one man on the phone. We knocked on the window to get his attention, because we wanted to give some money. He came over to the window briefly, shook his head "no," and went back to the phone. In spite of our determination and repeated knocking, he refused to let us in. Afraid?

We had to get up at 4:15 AM, hurry up, and then wait at Domodedeva Airport until a heavy fog lifted. While the group was directed to sit in the lounge, I took a few people at a time on a tour through the real airport, the building adjoining our foreigners' waiting room, where thousands of people were in transit, also waiting. Babies and old men slept, soldiers and teenaged boys paced, and we lined up at a snack bar to buy some kefir. We were extraordinarily conspicuous because of our dress and our demeanor, and by the fact that we were clearly the only Americans in this part of the airport. There was no question that photos were out of the question, but what great faces!

After about a six-hour wait, our Intourist guide Tanya arranged for us to have lunch. We no sooner sat down to eat when they announced that we had to board; the fog had finally lifted enough for us to take off. As we stood in line, Tanya came up to me very distressed, stating that I had better come quickly and settle a dispute or the plane would leave without us. My American interpreters were in a heated argument with the women at the security gate regarding our cameras and film. The Soviets were insisting that our cameras had to go through the x-ray machines, which was known to damage film. I listened while Tanya translated for me, then I said, "Fine, our cameras go through, our film does not" and I went back through the line and told all of my group to take their film out of their cameras, and thus we were allowed to board.

Immediately upon our arrival in Piatigorsk, one of the oldest spa resorts in Russia (in the northern foothills of the Caucasus Mountains), we were taken to a sanatorium for a tour, tea, and talk. After a high priority visit to the ladies' room, we were ushered into an auditorium for a performance by the local English school. The children were spirited and seemingly very comfortable with their bodies as they danced. Most wore navy-blue pinafores with white shirts, some with red scarves, the girls with white knee-highs and the usual huge white bows in their hair, and all with assorted shoes. They danced a waltz, a cha-cha, acted a scene from *My Fair Lady* with Liza Doolittle, and sang *We Wish You Happiness* and *We Shall Overcome*, dedicated to Samantha Smith, the 10-year-old school girl who in November 1982, wrote to Soviet leader Yuri Andropov, expressing her concern about nuclear war between Russia and the US. Her letter was printed in *Pravda* and she was subsequently invited to and did visit Russia. But then in August of 1985, in one of life's sad twists, she died in a plane crash.

Once again, many of our group were brought to tears. When we left the building, all gathered outside to see us off. We were surrounded by their warmth, their smiles, their hugs, and as the bus pulled away, they all followed down the road, waving and shouting goodbye. We were overcome—excited, exhausted, and certainly emotional.

That evening after supper, a few of us were invited to the home of two members of the Academy of Science, Dariya and Ivan. We had met Dariya earlier at the sanatorium. With gray hair piled on top of her head, she was charming and her house was lovely. Books were stacked from the floor to the high ceiling. She served a delicious apple and nut cake she had baked, fresh apples, chocolate, and champagne. When I went to take photos, Ivan insisted on clearing away the champagne, stating that of course we knew there was a reform movement in the country to encourage people not to drink. We talked about problems between our countries, and how we could further the efforts toward peace.

Dariya told us she was a close personal friend of Raisa Gorbachev, whose home town was Pyatigorsk, and said that she felt that Raisa would be interested in coming to the US under the auspices of a women's group. If we wanted, Dariya told us that she would help secretly with the arrangements. We said we would work on it, then later, in private, expressed excitement about the possibility, remote as it was, and decided that the League of Women Voters would be the best organization to sponsor such a visit. I made a trip to Washington, DC to meet with the newly-elected National President of the League, Nancy Newman, to present a proposal that they invite a delegation of high-level Soviet women to include Raisa Gorbachev. The invitation was sent but unfortunately, for reasons unknown, that visit never came to pass.

Our last day in the area was in the lovely resort town of Kislovodsk, where roads were lined with forsythia and apple blossoms, with women hanging laundry, with old ladies wearing long black and blue coats and kerchiefs.

After lunch, I was interviewed by a young journalist who asked many questions about the group. *Whose idea was it to come? Who were we? What had we done there? Were any of our opinions about the USSR changed as a result of being there?* And then *"What did I think about the new Soviet slogan "The Sky is for the Birds"?* I answered that I thought "Peace for the World" would be better, trying to politely avoid discussion of our Star Wars program, even though I totally opposed it.

The next city was Tbilisi, in Soviet Georgia. *En route*, I wondered if Sasha would really be there to meet me this time, as his friend told me when I finally reached him in Moscow. And if so, how would he find me, how would we meet? When we arrived at our hotel, I scanned the parking lot, then the lobby. No Sasha. After some time inside, trying to get the group settled, I decided to go out again, under the pretense of helping some of the participants with their luggage. I saw someone who looked like him, then I got shy and wouldn't look in his direction again. Finally, inside the lobby, I saw him, cradling a huge bouquet of flowers—red roses and carnations, and one pink rose. I smiled, with a question mark, not really certain it was him, and then he smiled back. Of course, I wanted to give him a big hug, an appropriate greeting. It was, of course, impossible, as he immediately told me he had snuck into the lobby and must leave. We agreed to meet outside in an hour.

I admit I was excited. He looked wonderful in a tan safari jacket, plaid shirt, and a sweater. No moustache, more mature, and he smelled good. I couldn't wait to ask him a million questions. After showering and changing clothes, I tried to appear casual as I walked from the elevator to the front door. We took a cab to his hotel, and this time, I had to sneak into his lobby. Then to his room for a few minutes before we went upstairs to the restaurant to have some dinner—cucumber, fish, bread, cheese, and champagne.

After dinner, we went back to his room for Cognac and mango juice, which we had had the first time we met. He had flowers on the table, and candies arranged in a heart shape. Clearly he was prepared to turn his fantasy into a reality. However, much as I liked him, I had no intimate intentions. After much conversation, at 12:45 AM, I announced that it was time for me to return to my hotel. He announced in all seriousness that my hotel closed at midnight and I would have to stay with him. I was almost certain it wasn't true, but I had had just enough champagne to wonder, and I remembered that indeed I had been locked out of my hotel once, at midnight, in Jerusalem.

Anyway, I agreed to stay, but made it very clear that I was sleeping in one bed, he in the other. He promised to get up early because I had to be back at my hotel by 7:30 AM, and he was true to his word. At 6:30, I stumbled out of bed, kind of comatose, probably hung over, hardly able to move, much less talk. But we couldn't find a taxi, so walk I did, back to the hotel. The only clear thought I did have was that we had done a very stupid thing. What if he had gotten caught? At that point, I was more worried about him than me. He was worried that Debbie would have been concerned and told people I had not come back. I was worried about the KGB and their concerns.

Debbie was getting dressed when I arrived and I couldn't wait to tell her my story, but I had to wait, aware of the possibility of the room being bugged. On the bus for the city tour, I told her about my time with Sasha, all the while struggling to stay awake.

1986—Sasha

The only thing I remember of the tour was our guide saying that the five oldest languages in the world are Latin, Cyrillic, Armenian, Hebrew, and Georgian.

That night, after asking and learning that the hotel indeed did not close at midnight, I met Sasha in a nearby park. As we wandered looking for a café, I noticed that no matter what we were discussing, whenever soldiers passed us, we instinctively stopped talking. We spoke of Stalin, how horrible he was, how many people he killed, and how he was still sort of a hero in Georgia. Sasha told me he supported Reagan's build-up of weapons, saying " the only way to prevent war is to prepare for war."

We saw fireworks in celebration of the 25th anniversary of Yuri Gagarin's voyage into outer space. Gagarin was earth's first cosmonaut. On April 12, 1961, he became the first man to circle the earth in a manned space flight. Born in 1934, he died in 1968, having spent 108 minutes of his 34-year life in orbit.

We then ended up on a park bench, where I gave him some of the gifts I had brought for him: a Judy Garland tape and a small portable radio with headphones. He asked if I wanted to go to his hotel and I emphatically said no, because it was too risky. Plus, I told him as I smiled, I knew mine didn't close at midnight. We laughed about that and made plans for the next evening. After leaving and walking some distance, I turned to see him still standing there, staring after me. It struck me as sad.

The next day, after a visit to a kindergarten, my delegation went to the Georgian Friendship House, where I was again interviewed, this time by two journalists. They asked the usual questions, and then came out and wanted to know what I thought about the nuclear testing the US had just conducted. I exercised some restraint and good judgment and took the diplomatic middle road, neither casting stones nor adopting a defensive posture.

Early evening, I stole an hour of privacy as I walked around the city. I wandered in and out of bookstores, clothing stores, food stores, even bought a loaf of dark bread for 15 kopecks. When I got back to the room, Debbie was burrowed in on the balcony, writing postcards. We relaxed long enough to realize just how tired and harried we were, and then she came outside with me to meet Sasha. I wanted her to meet him, so that someone so important to me at home, one of my closest friends, could share this so tiny, yet so important, piece of my life far away.

It was a beautiful night and Sasha and I took the cable car up Mt. Mtatsminda to have dinner at a restaurant there. We first stood outside, overlooking the city and he said he would tell me the conclusion of his story once we were inside. Each day, I had been getting segments. I turned to him and said "Sasha, when did you get married?" He turned so red that I was sorry I had been so blunt, but I had been trying to save him the embarrassment of "confessing." And really, it didn't matter to me. I was getting involved with someone at home.

Inside, we had champagne, shashlik, a pear, and chocolate, and two glasses of vodka appeared, sent by a rather rowdy group of men at another table who made no effort to talk to us. We danced and laughed and in between, he told me the rest of his story.

When I first met Sasha in Khabarovsk, he was working on the roof of the Intourist Hotel, running the restaurant. He did not have any experience, and there were many shortages. He was fined—and fired. Before that time, he had taught English up in the northernmost parts of Siberia. He then went illegally to Gagra, where he managed to stay for a year without being detected. (Stalin had a *dacha* in Gagra and Krushchev was vacationing there when he learned he had been deposed.) As I understood it, Sasha used to steal oranges from a farmer and take them to the big cities to sell them. He says he never got caught because he dressed well, usually wore a white suit. However, on one of these trips, he was asked for his internal passport and when he was found not to have the proper stamps, he was jailed in a prison for "people with no identity," (which is why he hadn't been able to meet me the previous year in Sochi.) He nervously told me that he had not known of the existence of such prisons, nor did most Soviets. He was sentenced to one month in jail. His landlady, after driving all over Sochi, finally found him. She rolled up 50 rubles and surreptitiously gave them to the head of the jail, and thus managed to get him out after only a few days.

Conditions were awful there, he told me. "Once a day, we were given one cup of tea, soup, and a piece of bread. I fasted because I had already done that often, for good health."

He then returned to Khabarovsk. He stayed there for a while, where he legally belonged, but was very unhappy and went back to Gagra.

Sometime throughout this process, he started dating the landlady's daughter, who was married at the time. She got divorced and then she and Sasha got married and had a daughter they named Mary. He told me he married so that he could legally remain in the south. To change one's residence and get the proper stamp, one must have a job, buy property, or get married. So he stayed, and for work gave tours to English-speaking groups.

However, although he said he loved his daughter very much, he also said he was very unhappy with his wife, said she got crazy and violent. The more he talked, the more it sounded like PMS to me. I found myself counseling him to try to have patience, and to stay. He said he was pretty much trapped by the system "because if I don't stay married, I would have to leave the area. And worse, my mother-in-law is so powerful, she would arrange it so I could never see Mary again."

By the time he finished his story, we were outside on the park bench. I gave him another tape and the book, *The World's Family* by Ken Heyman and asked if there was anything else he could use. He told me a Polaroid camera would be very valuable to him, because he could charge his tour participants about $5 per photo, and thus make extra money. I had asked him earlier, since his English is so good, why he didn't work for Intourist.

"Two reasons—they don't pay well, and they watch you too much."

"Galina worked for Intourist, didn't she?"

"Yes, and she freely mingles with foreigners, so I don't trust her. I trust no one."

After talking for an hour or so on the bench, it was time to get back. I had been so engrossed in us, I was surprised to see that the restaurant was closed, all the lights were out, and we were pretty much alone up there. The cable car had stopped running, too.

Sasha suggested our best bet was to walk down the mountain. It took us an hour, one of the most memorable hours I have ever spent. For the first 20 minutes, we were unable to find the path and thus had to carefully shuffle along sideways. I wore his jacket, he carried my purse, and he held my hand.

Once on the path, we were surrounded by the smell of the forest, the site of the shimmering city below. For that time, the world was one of only quiet, of only trees, rocks, dirt, a wonderful moon—a devil moon, Sasha called it—the crisp air, and the two of us. Periodically we would stop to rest, say a few words, hug, then continue. Our goal was to get to the city; our desire was to remain on the mountain and under the moon as long as possible.

He picked me a flowering branch from a tree, a white flower he called *alicha*. We, of course, finally did reach the bottom, in an old neighborhood whose only sounds were our footsteps echoing on the cobblestone streets, the barking of a lone dog, and the noises cats make when, thinking they are alone, they are suddenly disturbed. We passed a home with a large black-framed photograph of a family of four hung above the door, the custom when people die. I peeked in the windows. The house was empty.

It was 2:00 AM when I arrived at the hotel. My shoes were so dirty and dusty and damaged that I was certain I had to throw them out because they could provide proof of where I had been. I found an apple on my pillow, a welcome snack from Debbie, who was sound asleep. I crept out to the desk in the hall, to leave a note for the *dezhurnaya*, the floor attendant, for an 8:00 AM wake-up. I heard a voice, looked up, and way at the other end of the hall, she was lying on a cot, asking what it was I wanted. I went over to her with the note and an apology for waking her. I, too, was tired, but it was the kind of fatigue one gets only under the most extraordinary circumstances, when your body screams for sleep and your brain fights to stay awake, to prolong and cherish the moment.

Sasha and I met after breakfast the next morning at the post office, so that he could help me mail a package to Stanislav and his wife in Siberia (from Natasha's mother). Then we went to a cafe, had tea with tangerine jam (in honor of his business dealings with oranges) and sweet cake. He brought me two glossy photographs of Stalin, probably available only in Georgia, one for me, one for a school project for my niece Tambi, and a beautiful black enamel carafe with six small cups. I told him about my family having come from Glubokoye, and about how funny my Aunt Ida was, and he said when he next travels to that region, he will try to go to the city to take some photos, ask the old people if they remember my grandparents. I thought he was so nice to think of that, to understand how much that would mean to me.

We walked back to the hotel and said goodbye in the pedestrian tunnel under the street, where we were least likely to be observed. I thanked him for coming, for my gifts, and wished him well. He kissed my hands, each finger individually. And then, there was nothing more to say.

I went up to my room, out on the balcony overlooking the small park that had become our meeting place. I was angry, at the Soviet system that wouldn't even allow me to write a thank-you letter to Sasha, telling him how much I valued our relationship. I would have to hint at all I wanted to say. And, I thought, how will I ever know if anything ever happens to him? As I stood there saying a silent goodbye, a red balloon slowly floated by. One of my participants had brought them to give away to children. She called them "peace balloons."

Once back in Leningrad, although we couldn't drink the contaminated faucet water there and the mineral water was horrible, I was grateful to be in the Hotel Pribaltiskaya, which, unlike our hotel in Georgia, was clean and had a decent shower. I threw out my black shoes, which had gotten ruined on the descent from the mountain. I was probably being too cautious, but had been reluctant to do so in Tbilisi.

Sasha had told me that the rumor was that the Soviet Union will pull out of Afghanistan. My interpreter heard that there was pressure on the government because mothers were being asked to identify their sons, decapitated by the Afghanistan freedom fighters who left behind only their heads.

And the latest rumor we heard was that the US had bombed Tripoli, the capital of Libya, lost three planes, and hit the French Embassy. How could that be possible? Why? There I was in Leningrad, which was already so familiar to me, and all it took was an incident like that, when one often cannot get international information, to feel so remote, so removed, so isolated.

The news the next day—the US had bombed Tripoli, with 40 to 50 planes. We did hit the French Embassy. We said we lost one plane; Khadafy said we lost three. An unknown number of lives were lost. Apparently the reason for the attack was some sort of explosion in West Berlin. Between our nuclear tests, and then that, it certainly was not an optimal time to be in the USSR. I was ready to leave. As much as I loved some people, I knew I wouldn't miss the smell of the diesel fuel or the awful-tasting mineral water.

1986—Sasha

On the bus to Helsinki, one of the participants passed out matzo she had been given at the temple in Leningrad, also cheese, salami, nuts, and chocolate. The chocolate made me feel better. And we sang "We Shall Overcome," "Blowin' in the Wind," and then "Amazing Grace." "Amazing Grace" reminded me of Natasha's funeral, of our trip together, and that brought tears.

Customs was not a bad experience. They made me and the bus driver go through first. They took the local papers, which I had been given because they reported on our visit. I explained why I had them; the officials explained that it is strictly and absolutely against the rules to take them out of the country for any reason. Five minutes later, they returned them to me. I remember thinking I would never understand the country.

The first thing we did when we arrived in Helsinki was buy their newspapers. It seemed that it was only England that supported the US against Libya, and that we killed Khadafy's daughter. Khadafy himself had disappeared. We were suddenly all a bit fearful of terrorist reprisals at US airports.

For dinner our last night, Debbie and I went to the Shashlik Restaurant for, what else, Russian food. Kebab, blini, crème de menthe and vodka crepes, and two bottles of wine. A Russian guitarist had moved to Helsinki after leaving the USSR four months earlier. He sang about Moscow, got tears in his eyes, and ended up making us cry. I guess it was an appropriate ending to the trip.

But those weren't the last of my tears.

April 23, 1986

Dear Sasha,

Our Soviet Women in Politics program came to a successful close and our participants carried home with them new impressions and warm memories of their first trip to the USSR. Many want to return, all felt excited and enriched by their experiences.

We had a very busy program and many valuable meetings with Soviet women who share common professions and concerns. In Moscow, we toured the city, saw the Bolshoi, visited a school, the Soviet Womens' Committee, a wedding palace, and the Fyodorov Eye Research Institute. In Pyatigorsk, we visited a vocational school, the Lermontov Museum, a carpet factory, and a sanitorium. We also went to Kislavodsk and very much enjoyed a walk through town and the opportunity to taste the various mineral waters.

Leningrad was beautiful, as ever, but cold in contrast to the south and difficult because we heard the very upsetting news about Tripoli. I took a day off from the group, for sleep, shopping, solitude. I even treated myself to a massage in the hotel. The next day, we went to a district court and witnessed three divorces. Some of the group went to the Hermitage, others to the Russian Museum, which is my favorite. I didn't see any old friends, but did see many new city sights. All the women were charmed by Leningrad.

But for me, the highpoint of the trip was Tbilisi with its roses, carnations, and alicha. The time there went by too quickly, as if I were waltzing through a wonderful dream. The city was warm, sometimes very warm, and the people very hospitable. I have special souvenirs, special memories. One night there were fireworks in honor of Yuri Gagarin, another night I rode the cable car to Mtatsminda and then walked down the mountain, under a devil moon, through the silent trees, over the rocks and grass, and finally along an old street. Our last morning, just before we left the hotel, I was able to steal a few minutes alone on the balcony. I looked out at the river, at the mountain, and at a small park with benches not far away. I was very sad to leave that which I had come to know, and to feel such deep affection for, wondering how long it would be before I would see it again.

This was my fourth trip to the USSR, and in many ways, the most valuable and most special. It was very fruitful, Intourist gave us an excellent program, we had no problems except a delay at Moscow airport due to fog, all my participants were happy and if it is possible, even more committed to work for peace between our countries.

But my sad news is that my 88-year-old Aunt Ida died. When I checked my phone messages after I arrived back in Boston, I had one from the police in Miami Beach, where she lived. Apparently she died in her sleep. The day we landed in Russia. With no pain, I hope.

I hope you are well and happy.

Always,
Cynthia

* * *

Five days after we landed back in the States, April 26th, at 1:23 AM, the Chernobyl nuclear power plant Reactor 4 had a catastrophic meltdown, with the power of 400 Hiroshima bombs and ten times the radioactivity. There was no official reaction from Russia to the international community until 65 hours after the explosion. And not until 36 hours after the explosion were residents of the nearby town of Pripyat told to evacuate and to leave their pets behind. All 26 of the first firefighters on the scene died soon after from radiation poisoning. The explosion displaced 400,000 people, spread radiation 1,100 square miles from the reactor—60 to 70 percent of the radioactive fallout went to Byelorussia—and thus Glubokoye was in the hardest hit area. It is still considered the worst nuclear plant disaster in history. (The USSR's nuclear power plants were built with prison labor. It can reasonably be concluded that the convicts lacked pride in their work, lacked any incentive to do a good job, or to be meticulous regarding safety issues.)

Today, the area abandoned by humans is teeming with wildlife that seems to be flourishing—horses, wolves, elk, bison, brown bears, and wild boar, and catfish up to 10 feet long living in the reactor's canals. Studies are being conducted to see how the radiation has affected them.

And there are returnees, primarily old Russian women who wanted to be "at home." In 2016, there were 180 residents. The explosion resulted in 16,000 permanently displaced people who were forced to abandon 1,600 square miles. It is estimated that the Chernobyl Exclusion Zone will not be safe to inhabit for 24,000 years.

In 2011, the Chernobyl Plant, the nearby ghost town of Pripyat, and other abandoned villages in the exclusion zone became tourist attractions. In 2018, there were more than 72,000 tourist visits, with that number growing higher each year.

The 1986 NESNE Conference, scheduled to be held at Middlebury College in Vermont that fall, was postponed because Nicholas Daniloff, Moscow correspondent for *US News and World Report*, was arrested at the very end of August and held by the KGB. The conference was to have taken place in mid September and NESNE, of course, had no idea then how long he would be kept in prison.

Consequently, we all met to discuss and debate whether the conference should happen. The vote to cancel was not unanimous. Those who dissented thought it was important to keep the dialogue going, especially when circumstances create tension, but the majority felt it was the right thing to do in solidarity with a fellow journalist.

However, Lithuanian photographer Zinas Kazenas visited Cape Cod in June, invited by Bill Breisky, editor of the *Cape Cod Times* and a NESNE delegate, to participate in a children's art exhibit. The two met by chance at an art gallery in Moscow in 1983. Also, we at OASES arranged for him to be part of a two-man show in Washington with American photographer Peter Costas and we also set up a reception and exhibit of his work at Harvard.

Several years later, I would meet Zinas again under the most exciting and unusual of circumstances.

This year, Yelena Bonner, activist and wife of Soviet nuclear physicist Andrei Sakharov, was permitted to visit the West for medical treatment.

Chapter 17
NESNE September 20 to 27, 1987
5th Annual Conference
and League of Women Voters "Women in Politics"
November 6 to 21, 1987
Breadloaf Campus, Middlebury, VT

"We want the working woman to be the equal of the working man, not only before the law, but in actual fact."
—Vladimir Lenin (1870 –1924), First leader of Soviet Russia
in a policy declaration February 1920

The eight Soviet delegates were welcomed by college president Olin Robison, expert in US-USSR relations and advisor to the Carter and Reagan administrations. Also there to greet the Soviets was Madeleine Kunin, Governor of Vermont, and Nicholas Daniloff, former Moscow correspondent for *US News and World Report*, angry about the 13 days he spent in Moscow in Lefortovo Prison, but still supportive of this exchange.

Over lunch, there was a joint presentation: "An American Covering Moscow: A Soviet Covering Washington. Rewards and Frustrations" by Andrew Rosenthal, *New York Times*, and a talk by Alexei Burmistenko, at the time the Washington DC correspondent for the newspaper *Trud*.

The historic exchange of young journalists, six years in the making, finally became a reality. Linda Feldman Roe from the *Christian Science Monitor* and Alan Cooperman, an AP reporter stationed in Moscow, returned from three months on the staff of *Moscow News*. Two Soviet journalists were to arrive in the US in December.

As usual, we found interesting ways to entertain our guests. We took them to the Shelbourne Museum, to a working dairy farm, to a clambake, and even square dancing.

During the conference discussions, both sides called for easing of press restrictions, and all delegates agreed this was the best conference yet regarding openness and productivity.

Perestroika (meaning in Russian: "restructuring") was a program instituted in the Soviet Union by Mikhail Gorbachev in 1986 to reorganize and thus modernize the Soviet economic and political policy. (It was only in early 1987 that the motto became a full-scale campaign and started yielding practical results.) Seeking to bring the Soviet Union up to economic par with capitalist countries such as Germany, Japan, and the United States, Gorbachev decentralized economic controls and encouraged enterprises to become self-financing. The economic bureaucracy, fearing the loss of its power and privileges, obstructed much of his program, however. Gorbachev also proposed reducing the direct involvement of the Communist Party leadership in the country's governance and increasing the local governments' authority. In 1988, a new parliament, the Soviet Congress of People's Deputies, was created. Similar congresses were established in each Soviet republic as well. For the first time, elections to these bodies presented voters with a choice of candidates, including non-Communists, though the Communist Party continued to dominate the system.

At the same time that Gorbachev instituted Perestroika, he also promoted *Glasnost*, or openness. One of our American delegates questioned just how much openness their Soviet counterparts then had, what kind of limits were placed on them. One of the Soviets replied, "Certainly you don't criticize Stalin. If you do, you won't do it for a very long time!" However, they subtly revealed that it wasn't clear to them what their limits or boundaries as journalists were, just how much criticism they could render, just how much light they could shine on prostitution, corruption, crime and drugs.

It was obvious that they still felt their function was to serve the Soviet system—as did the more than 8,500 newspapers and 5,000 magazines published annually.

November 6 to 21, 1987 Second League of Women Voters' "Women in Politics" Tour
Moscow, Sochi, Leningrad, Novgorod, Helsinki

> *"I am in Abkhazia. The nature is insanely and desperately wonderful."*
> —Anton Chekhov, Russian writer
> (1860–1904)

My group, which happily included my dear friend Debbie again, arrived in a Moscow far more colorful than usual because of the annual parade in Red Square on November 7, when the country shows off its military might and honors the October Revolution. We arrived too late to attend the parade, but when the group took their city tour the next day, Debbie and I, without the language, without a dictionary, without a map, took the metro to Red Square. It was still decorated with the flags and huge banners of Lenin from the festivities of the day before and it was remarkable to see how many Soviet families there were doing the same thing as we were, taking photos of one another, enjoying the grandness of it all.

The time in Moscow was productive. While the participants did the usual sightseeing, I did some NESNE business, delivered material to the US Embassy, and had a successful meeting with the Soviet Women's Committee.

Our next destination was Sochi. And Sasha. Flowers in hand, he was at our scheduled meeting place, the Hotel Kamelia. Again, I wanted to give him a big hug, and again, we very casually joined one another and walked along as if we barely knew one another.

Our dinner destination was the Caucasian Hut Restaurant, where the waiter put the flowers in a vase for us and then brought us caviar, vodka, tomatoes, beans, cheese, tongue, and a sour cream and meat dish. We ate, we danced to the songs "Lady in Red" and "Feelings," and then Sasha wanted to discuss politics. I asked him how strong *perestroika* and Gorbachev were and he said it didn't matter, that there was the era of Stalinism, now it is the era of Gorbachevism, and even if he were not in power for some reason, the movement was too strong to not make a difference. (If only he had been right.) However, he felt that Americans were too naïve about the USSR, that the only way the leadership would make changes in human rights would be by pressure and demands from the international community, especially America. He then offered a toast to President Reagan. I could not bring myself to join him, so I said I would drink to Mr. Gorbachev's success.

He told me to be careful and not let the waiter or any people in the restaurant see me handing him any of the gifts. I gave him two Nabokov books that I had sneaked through customs with no trouble, one of which was *Lolita*, still very much banned in the USSR, and a set of overall jeans for his toddler daughter.

When the restaurant prepared to close, the waiter packed up my flowers—red carnations and pink roses—and we started out down the long, dark, tree-lined road to the main road, about two miles away. As we walked, he carried my purse, as always, and started pulling presents for me out of his bag. First, a Georgian music box, black, which plays *Poloner Aginsky* by Shkatulka, a Polish composer of the 19th century, then a large Georgian bone horn, to drink wine out of, a gold chain and seven gold rings. Finally, a Stalin medal, given to distinguished people for their labor efforts. For Tambi, he said.

It started to rain a bit, but it was so still, so peaceful, that I was a bit sorry that a car came along and gave us a ride. The people in the car worked in the restaurant and had hot bread fresh out of the oven, which they shared with us as we drove along. Back at the hotel, I told him I had more gifts for him, too, and had to go upstairs to get them. Since he couldn't come into the lobby, we met alongside a brick building next to the hotel and I handed him the Panasonic dual tape boom box, extra batteries, and the *Billy Joel in Concert in Leningrad* tape that I had brought for him. He was thrilled and wanted to give me money. I wouldn't let him, of course.

While we hugged goodnight, a car suddenly pulled up and shone its lights on us. He said "KGB!" I, very calmly and without looking in their direction, asked him who would do the talking, me or him.

"Both of us" he replied. "We will say we were discussing cultural exchanges."

"Right," I said, "while we were hugging."

Luckily, after a few moments, the car left. I begged him to be very careful going home—he had to take a train to Gagra, which was about 50 miles away. I headed back to the hotel entrance, not knowing—and frankly not caring—if I was being watched.

The next day, the group took a bus to Sukhumi, the capital of Abkhazia, popular for its subtropical vegetation, its beautiful gardens and beaches. And one of the oldest towns in the world, said to be where Jason and the Argonauts went to search for the Golden Fleece. Most of the ride was along the Black Sea. We passed eucalyptus trees, persimmon trees, cypresses, bamboo, cedars, and palms. And donkeys, swans, and cranes. The same things writer Anton Chekhov saw when he was there in 1888.

After a visit to a 10th-century monastery and the caves of Novy Afon, the day ended with an exquisite sunset over the Black Sea. Upon our return to our hotel, Debbie and I had time for a hot shower, and an early night of quiet in our room. Our table was a still life of Sasha's red and pink flowers, a pedestal bowl with his green tangerines, and her candle that flickered yellow as it cast large, looming shadows on the walls.

The following day, after we all went to a kindergarten, Debbie came down with me to say hello again to Sasha. He had an enormous bag of gifts for me that we asked Debbie to take back to the room, and off we went to the Pectopan Melnitza, or the Miller's House Restaurant. Decorated in Ukrainian style, it had pretty red and white curtains, bright white walls, a fireplace, two cats, and a television around which all the employees sat and drank tea from a samovar. A table of four men sang as they dined. We had cognac, (I had about two sips) and dined on black caviar, delicious roast pork and potatoes.

And he told me more about his family. He had a brother who was a fisherman and who drank too much, and another who was a doctor. He didn't get along well with his father, who was a mining engineer, who didn't particularly like children, and was not close with his own. His parents were divorced.

Sasha refused to go into the Navy when he was drafted and consequently he was sent to a psychiatric hospital for four months. When I asked what it was like, he said that it was exactly as it was in the movie *One Flew Over the Cuckoo's Nest*.

He decided that the car lights the night before were the result of a crackdown on prostitution. There had just been a big scandal about the prevalence of it in Sochi, and he suspected they were watching for that, and then backed off when they realized that was not the case. Being arrested for prostitution would have been interesting!

After dinner, we went to a disco, ordered vodka and coke, and danced to the band that played American music. Then we walked, and walked, and walked—through town, along the water, out on a long pier where we watched a brightly lit boat disappear into the dark horizon. He said the next time I came there, he wanted to take me swimming at night in the sea.

In the car back from the restaurant, he took my hand and slipped a very pretty ring on my finger. He couldn't thank me enough for the video tape player, saying that if he chose to, he could sell it for $2,100. I think I paid $250 for it.

When it was time to say goodbye, I told him that our friendship was very important to me, and we made plans for our next meeting, on my next trip to Russia. In Leningrad, he would be in the park across the street from the Astoria Hotel, at 7:00 PM the first full day I am there. We of course had to arrange our meetings like this because it was too dangerous to put the details in a letter, so when I wrote, I simply talked about work, the kind of professional group I would bring, and the day we would arrive in the city.

When I got back to the room, Debbie was asleep and I quietly peeked into the large bag he had brought. Two cans of salmon roe, three cans of Georgian tea, and about four dozen tangerines, limes, and persimmons. I remember thinking that my suitcase and a mule would get me home with all that stuff.

At breakfast, I gave a tangerine to everyone, plus I put a persimmon on each table. In the time remaining after we had packed, Debbie and I walked again along the still water, losing ourselves in our search for nice rocks to use as paperweights back home, reluctant to leave when the time came.

That evening in Leningrad, I was able to finally get to the Kirov Theatre. Through the hotel's service bureau, I got excellent seats for Debbie and me to see *La Traviata*. The theater was small, with blue and green velveteen chairs, a wooden floor with a blue carpet down the center, and gold chandeliers hanging from the five levels of balcony seats. The stage curtains were aquamarine tapestries, with gold brocade tassels. I managed to stay awake, which means it was a good performance.

During the rest of our sightseeing time in Leningrad, we took a side trip to the city of Novgorod, first mentioned in the year 859, another visit to the Hermitage, to the Museum of Ethnography, to the Alexander Nevsky Cathedral, to the Poets Corner where Dostoevsky and Rimsky Korsakov are buried, and to the Peter Paul Fortress, where tsars are buried.

As for our professional program, we were received in School 185, which specialized in the study of English. We also had a meeting with the Soviet Women's Committee of Leningrad. There were 20 women, some with high positions such as the Deputy Mayor of the City, a Deputy to the Supreme Soviet, the Deputy Director of the Ministry of Health Care. After brief introductions, we broke off into small discussion groups and each American joined whichever group was of most interest to her: health care, environment, alcohol, social services, and economic issues.

I went into the group talking about economic issues. However, we had a very talkative Soviet woman there, the Deputy Chairman of the International Department of the Soviet Women's Committee, and she ended up lecturing for most of the time. She did tell us that women could not do work that would influence their ability to reproduce and thus become a future mother, that out-of-towners did the lower jobs in order to stay in the big cities, and that their young people were perhaps not as kind as the older generation was. Her committee was working to increase pensions, maternity leave, and sick leave.

We invited several of the Soviet women to join us for our farewell dinner, and five of them were able to do so. They were a motherly group who warmly embraced all of us. Debbie and I made friends with the youngest, a woman named Nina A., whose only son had died at 23 in a car accident two years earlier. Since then, she had been in and out of hospitals in an attempt to cope with her grief. She couldn't talk about it without crying. She and I exchanged addresses, and I had a feeling I would see Nina again.

We took the train to Helsinki, where we had our farewell dinner at the Troikka restaurant, and a debriefing session the last morning to answer the many questions the group had and to clarify any misunderstandings they might have had.

Were there any changes evident under *glasnost*? Not too much was different. The people seem to be a little better dressed, there were more pets and fewer banners extolling the virtues of the glory of the Communist Party. *Moscow News* was still the most radical of the newspapers, but also still hard to find. Journalists had more freedom, but were prohibited from covering such topics as the space program and environmental protection. People seemed to be more optimistic, more hopeful, although not unaware of the severity of the problems facing the country, and as they have been since the 1917 Revolution, ambivalent about political change.

And the fascination I had for Russia's history and culture, the affection for my friends there, and the determination to continue my exchange work? Stronger than ever.

* * *

The year was busy. In December, I did an interview on Buffalo, NY's public radio station WEBR, promoting the value of exchanges.

But that year wasn't all work. I took another trip to Canastota and stayed with Mary Anne's mother at their house alongside of the Erie Canal. Even my father liked Mary and visited her often. I loved to watch her stir the red sauce on the stove, to see her cute smile, to hear her old stories and to talk to her about my parents. Or watch her perform the Sicilian ritual to put the evil-eye curse on someone. Or hear her yell at me in the mornings when I had gone to bed too late and gotten up three hours later, "Get back to bed, Cynthia. You don't sleep, you'll make yourself sick." And one day, she whispered, with a devilish look on her face. "So what really did happen between you and Michael?"

Speaking of Michael. One night, he was tending bar at the White Elephant, the restaurant his family used to own. I stopped in for a drink at the bar and to say hello. While I was at the jukebox, Michael came up behind me, put his arms around me, gave me a big hug, and said, "I love you. I've always loved you. I think about you all the time. Let's get married and have children."

Oh, oh! I had fallen in love with Frank. More about that later.

The next day, Michael and I talked. He hugged me as if he were desperate and said I was the best thing that ever happened to him, said he was afraid he had lost me.

When he started talking about having a child, I cried, picturing a little baby, his baby, our baby, in my arms. But Michael was like an untrained puppy, a puppy that would make you laugh, lick you all over, shower you with affection, and then pee and poop on your just-polished floor. And I was never confident that behavior would change.

He told me he wasn't doing drugs so much, which I was of course happy to hear. I told him about Frank, which I suspect he wasn't happy to hear. We agreed that we couldn't get together, that it wouldn't work, but also that we would hold on to the deep feelings we had for one another, would never let them go away.

As we hugged, he told me, "You'd better live until at least 75, because I expect us to always be close. But I still can't watch you throw a baseball without laughing," he said as he smiled.

"I needed to see you," I confessed.

And I did, as I did every few years. For reasons I am not sure I understand even to this day, Michael always remained an important presence in my life.

After our talk, we went to the cemetery to see his father's grave, and I held him close as he sobbed. Then we drove through the green hills of Canastota, spotted with tall, deep purple loosestrife, and cheerful yellow patches of smaller flowers, and the sun was bright and finally warm. We found a park bench and talked some more.

"I've always compared the women in my life with you, and they never measured up, so I never committed to them, to having children with any of them."

"I love you, Michael, always have, always will. You'll take care of yourself, won't you," I whispered.

"Don't worry, I'll be here as long as you," he promised.

But I didn't believe him.

Beginning in 1987, the Soviets allowed a significant increase in Jewish emigration.

In February of 1987, dissident writer Lev Timofeyev was among the first 50 prisoners released by the Supreme Soviet.

On May 28th of that year, a German amateur pilot named Mathias Rust illegally landed a small aircraft in Red Square, embarrassing the Soviet military. Sentenced to four years in prison, he was pardoned after four months. Journalists described him as unstable and many of his actions since then seemed to fit their description.

In Washington, D.C, from December 7-10, Presidents Reagan and Gorbachev conducted a summit, where they signed a treaty on intermediate-range and shorter-range missiles. Besides arms control, they also discussed human rights. And they agreed on the importance of exchange programs between their people, and made a commitment to expand these contacts.

Chapter 18
1988, Uzbekistan

*"You can't make up anything anymore.
The world itself is a satire. All you're doing is recording it."*
—Art Buchwald (1925–2007)
humorist, newspaper columnist

Another busy year. In June, I sent a group of twelve on an Institutions and Lifestyles of the USSR tour, sponsored by OASES and Kentucky Wesleyan College and led by Margaret Britton, Associate Professor in Sociology at the college. They visited Moscow, Alma Ata in Central Asia, Leningrad, and Helsinki.

From November 9th to 20th, my third League of Women Voter's Soviet Women in Politics program took place in the USSR. Twelve participants and an interpreter/leader went to Moscow, Tallinn, and Leningrad.

I didn't accompany either of those groups, but did join the NESNE trip in June, from the 14th to the 23rd.

At our layover in Helsinki *en route* to Moscow, I heard my name called. When I turned, I spotted two people from the Kentucky Wesleyan College group that I had sent two weeks earlier. They were on their way home and by all accounts, their program went well.

In Moscow's Sheremyetova Airport, we saw three Hasidic Jews in line to get into the country—that was a switch! (Later, we saw a young Jew with a yarmulke at a demonstration in Pushkin Square protesting treatment of Jews, especially the refuseniks. That was definitely not the norm). Our delegation was met by three Soviet journalists who had participated in past programs. My favorite was Gennady Musalian, who greeted me with five fragrant, deep-pink peonies. My favorite flower. They got us through customs with no search, and we went directly to the Hotel Rossiya. Dinner was typical—greasy chicken cutlets, but preceded by orange and black caviar on eggs and concluded with creamy, sinfully fattening ice cream. We also had Georgian red wine—Stalin's favorite, we were told. (Was that information supposed to make us like it better?)

Our meeting at *Pravda* took place the next morning. I was disappointed we were not greeted again by Victor Afanasyev, but instead his deputy editor-in-chief, Evgeny

Grigoryev. He told us that *Pravda* had participated in *glasnost* and *perestroika*, which he said must succeed. The vast majority of people were in favor and there was no other option.

"But," he said, "you cannot feed people with words. The economic problems must be solved. And no economic goals can be achieved without further democratization."

When we asked his opinion on our presidential race, he replied that he personally liked Michael Dukakis.

On our way to our meeting at *Moscow News*, the huge Communist slogans and portraits of Lenin were noticeably absent along the roads. We arrived in time for an editorial board meeting, and then went on to the Union of Journalists, where we asked a Soviet journalist who specializes in judicial problems if *glasnost* was reversible.

"You can't be sure of anything," he said, "but I'm sure that even if Gorbachev were not in power, *glasnost* and *perestroika* would go on; there would be no return to any type of Stalinist regime, or even to the soft totalitarianism of Brezhnev." (He clearly didn't envision a Vladimir Putin.)

And yet another meeting, at the local militia HQ No 169 in Moscow district Krylatskoye. I had requested a visit to a police station as a way of making contacts to establish the police exchange I was planning. After I did that interview on Buffalo, NY public radio back in 1987, Bill Nye, an Aurora police officer, had called and asked about the possibility of a law enforcement exchange with the Soviet Union. I set about to make it happen.

I spoke privately with Lev Belyansky, Deputy Chief of the Main Directorate of the Bureau of the Ministry of Internal Affairs (Could their official titles be any longer?) to ask him about my proposed law enforcement program for the following year. I told him I would like to have scheduled visits to police training centers, police stations, courts, a duty station, time in patrol cars and visits to the drug enforcement department within the directorate. He thought all would be possible.

We toured the station, going first to the training room, which not only had a large photo of Lenin, but also one of Felix Dzerzhinsky, a Bolshevik revolutionary.

The detention rooms held five men, had toilets level with the red wood floor, and white stucco walls. Stealing was apparently the most common problem, from apartments and especially of car parts, but since the campaign against drinking began in 1985, crime rates had decreased.

After our tour, we were served cream puffs and eclairs with pink and green icing, decorated with silly faces and babies hats. Children's pastries in a police station?

When we left the building, one of our delegates noticed a healthy marijuana plant growing just outside the entrance. We spent a good amount of time discussing whether it was intentional or someone's idea of a joke that the police hadn't even noticed.

1988—Uzbekistan

A police escort with blinking red and blue lights on top of the car led us back to our hotel.

Our formal conference the next morning, which turned out to be more of a roundtable discussion, had as its subject "The Role of the Mass Media in American-Soviet Relations." The Soviets asked what kind of foreign policy was expected if Dukakis were elected. And what about the influence of Jesse Jackson? Then the most interesting questions.

"There was the Japan of Pearl Harbor and now there is Japan, the economic competitor. Which do you prefer?"

After we unanimously stated our preference for the economic competitor, they followed with this:

"Which USSR do you prefer? Should the US help us economically?"

We responded with a question of our own.

"Will or can Gorbachev remain in power?"

No definitive answer to that.

After lunch (more caviar, which I love), we went to the Danilov Monastery, where we waited outside shivering in the damp cold until the priest came. I had only a few minutes to look around there before I had to leave for my appointment at Gosteleradio, where I met with Valentin Yegorov from the North American desk about Bernard Redmont, retired Dean of the College of Communication at Boston University. I had agreed to help Bernie go to Russia and set up a program for him to do his research. Gosteleradio agreed to receive him in September and further help with his arrangements.

The day was cold and rainy and when I returned to my room, I quickly changed into my sweats and sneakers for the hour I could steal by myself. But then I was also happy to change clothes again to go out to an evening performance. Who would ever have guessed that it would be a rock opera? In the USSR?

The 38-year-old singer, Valery Leontiev, (the Russian equivalent of Michael Jackson) starred in the premiere of *Giordano*, based on the life of the Italian astronomer and monk, Giordano Bruno. At the beginning of the show, the audience was told not to storm the stage at any time. When Leontiev came out with his long hair and his sexy, tight, black leather pants, the reason for the announcement was clear. At the end, many, many women, although obviously excited, waited in an orderly line in front of the stage to go up one by one to present him with flowers. Apparently he had performed in Finland, India, Cuba, and Afghanistan, as well as throughout the Eastern Bloc. This opera was written just for him and I loved it!

The next day took us to Tashkent, the capital of Uzbekistan, where I could pretty much guarantee no one would be wearing tight leather pants. Neither the Islamic culture nor the heat and humidity would allow it. (The Jews were not the only ones to suffer oppression from the Soviet government, which tried to eradicate Islam, too, by destroying some 25,000 mosques and religious schools throughout the Soviet Muslim republics.)

Happily, our rooms in the Uzbekistan Hotel were air-conditioned, giving us a break from the temperatures, which were about 115 degrees every day.

The city tour guide told us that of the four republics in Soviet Central Asia, Uzbekistan, with its 100 nationalities, was the largest. Tashkent history began in the 1st century BC when Indo-Europeans settled there. Turks moved in in the 1st century AD and then the Arabs conquered and ruled for two and a half centuries. The 13th century brought Genghis Khan, who destroyed everything. The Russians moved into the area in 1865. During WWII, children were sent here from the north of Russia to be far away from the front. Families of Tashkent took in 200,000.

As we drove through the streets, learning about that fascinating history, the large propaganda billboards were still very much in evidence there, as they used to be in Moscow and Leningrad. But one exceptionally large one surprisingly stated "Our road to the future is through democratization and *glasnost*."

We stopped to take photos of a *madrassah*, a purely religious school at the time, although in prior years they also taught sciences there. I managed to get away for several minutes to wander on my own through the bazaar, taking pictures of the colorful fruits and vegetables. Fruits and vegetables that looked delicious, but which I knew I couldn't eat because even if they were washed, the water was unclean. Drinking water was the worst problem facing the country. Farming used most of the total water resources, resulting in agriculture chemicals and pesticides getting into the drinking water.

Our first official meeting was with Sayora Sultanova, the Deputy Chairman of the Council of Ministers of the Uzbek Republic, who oversaw higher education, culture, social services, radio, and TV. When we asked what was the most difficult aspect of *glasnost* and *perestroika* for her people to accept, she said they accepted the new policies, but did not yet know how to adapt to them.

At our next meeting, we asked Laziz Kayumov, the editor of the newspaper *Soviet Uzbekistony*, about the coverage of Afghanistan, since they were on the border. His reply was a typical safe answer.

"We have received no letters critical of the Soviet presence there, and our stories focus on the gratitude of the Afghan peoples to the Soviets for being there."

Our last meeting, unremarkable, was at the Uzbek Society for Friendship and Cultural Relations with Foreign Cultures. The Friendship Society, in our American waste-no-words parlance.

For some reason, the hotel air-conditioning had disappeared. My clothes, even my underwear, were soaking wet from the humidity, and my legs were always dripping perspiration. No wonder we were all so hot, fanning ourselves with whatever we could find. And I could not quench my thirst, no matter how much liquid I drank.

Up at 5:00 the next morning for a flight to Bukhara, the Central Asian rug capital. All along the grass between runways we saw scarecrows, some actually quite cute. And sensible, because we have since become aware of how dangerous birds can be to airplanes.

We checked into the air-conditioned Hotel Buchoro and rushed off to another city tour and a visit to a 10,000 acre collective farm with 1,700 cows. More statistics. More history. Bukhara, about 2,400 to 2,500 years old, was a Buddhist city first. In the 8th century, the Arabs brought Islam. It became part of the Tamerlane Empire in the 16th century, and there was slavery until the mid 19th century. This is probably not a surprise to anyone, but women were worth half the price of men. However, modern women there have value if they have many children. Ten or more children gave one the title of "Mother Hero."

Our last event of the day was a concert at a school for priests. We all sat on *topchans*, pieces of furniture that were used both to sleep on and to sit on during the day. Covered with thick silk pads, they were quite comfortable. Also comfortable was an unexpected breeze, accompanied by a bright pink sunset. Hundreds of swallows circled the stage, diving and shrieking, competing with the music. One instrument was particularly interesting, a *didjak*, which looked like a cross between a banjo and a violin.

Dick Stewart, a good friend of Frank's, shared a *topshan* with me. A very funny, old-school and respectful man, he had already told me he thought our group was boring. And in fact, although I liked everyone in it, the group as a whole was dull. Dick's sense of humor helped me deal with their lack of dynamism, as well as the heat and the thirst and the fatigue. While sitting there listening to the concert, Dick leaned over and said he couldn't wait to tell Frank that we were in bed together.

The next morning, while our luggage went on ahead to the airport, we went to the Forty Years of October embroidery factory. In the old days, only men were allowed to work with the gold that was used; it was believed that if women touch it, it would tarnish. (Who knows what they thought would happen to it if the women had their periods when they touched it!)

I walked up and down the air-conditioned aisles and watched hundreds of heads lowered over the multicolored silk threads, concentrating on their pieces. Most of the workers, about 98 percent, were women.

Our flight to Samarkand, land of Tamerlane's Tomb, was only forty minutes, but we had time for just an afternoon tour of the city.

First to the tomb of Tamerlane, vicious conqueror of Central Asia, built in 1403, under his order, only two years before he died. The dome is one of the most beautiful in the world. An inscription over one door read:

"Stranger, this is real paradise. You are quite welcome to come and stay forever."
Not me, it was too hot!
But there was an amusing quote at the entrance of the tomb itself:
"It is better to leave the world before people want you to go."

The grave was opened in 1941 and it was confirmed that it was indeed Tamerlane, with one leg shorter than the other, buried there. Also buried there was a man who had been beheaded. Although it is not confirmed, the tombstone said that Tamerlane belonged to Genghis Khan's family. During his reign, Samarkand was called the Pearl of the East, the Kingdom of the Universe.

Another inscription stated *"If I rise from the dead, the world will tremble."*

And yet another *"Those who haven't seen Tamerlane's tomb haven't seen the world."*

We learned that Samarkand's world had a population of 400,000, mainly Uzbeks. Women were emancipated—allowed to go without a veil—in 1920 and women were discouraged from wearing the hijab even in 2015, in an effort by the Uzbek government to ward off radical Islam.

Another mausoleum held the niece of Tamerlane. It is said that she, Shody-Muik-Aja, was as beautiful as the moon, as slender as a cypress, and as wise as Socrates.

Tamerlane's wife, who was a Chinese princess, is buried in the Mosque of Biba-Ka-Nom. Legend has it that when Tamerlane was away, she wanted to surprise him by building a beautiful mosque. She gave the architect all her money and jewels. There was a slowdown of construction and she called the architect in and demanded an explanation. He told her he had fallen in love with her and knew he would have to leave her when the mosque was completed. She offered him a beautiful girl. He refused, saying he only wanted to kiss her, that that would be enough, that a substitute would be like water in a wine cup. He kissed her cheek and went to complete the building. However, his kiss was so hot and so intense, it left a mark on her cheek. When Tamerlane saw it, he was furious and ordered the architect killed. Allah took pity and made wings for the architect to escape. Tamerlane then ordered all women to cover their faces.

After the city tour, I walked through the town with two of the delegates, then went to my room. I would have killed for ice cream that night, for anything really cold. But they don't believe cold drinks are good for you and little was refrigerated. They did serve dishes of ice at meals, but of course we couldn't have it because it was made from local water.

After a shower, I finished a Paul Auster book about solitude and began to read *Novel With Cocaine*, written by a little known Russian author, M. Ageyev, and described as a "Dostoevskian psychological novel of ideas...that explores the interaction between psychology, philosophy, and ideology." I had brought several copies of it to give away as gifts.

1988—Uzbekistan

The room, not air-conditioned like the one in Bukhara, was stifling. The curtain at the open window did not move at all. I stretched out on the bed, perspiring, but found that there was something almost romantic about the heat. For a bit, it felt as if I were connected to history as I imagined lying in a huge, silk-lined bedroom on a *topchan*, waiting for Genghis Khan or Tamerlane to come riding in with the hot wind.

We had to be in the lobby at 2:45 AM to catch our plane to Leningrad. Upon arrival, we checked into the Moskva Hotel and then departed for yet another city tour.

During the Great Patriotic War, as the Soviets called it, 640,000 residents of Leningrad starved to death. No food, no electricity, no running water. But hundreds and thousands of rats did survive, and were reported to have been seen running up and down the sidewalks. Living space was destroyed.

The war began in Russia June 22, 1941, when Germany invaded, and by August, the Leningrad region was occupied by German troops. The citizens built three defensive lines. The first, 120 km away, lasted only one month. The siege of the city began on September 8, 1941 and often 20,000 died in one day, although the average was 10,000. Only 636,000 people were able to be evacuated.

Two and a half million residents were left in the city, only one million of whom survived. The first winter was very severe—no heat, no transportation, yet no tree was ever used for wood. Instead, furniture was burned or wood was taken from burned out structures. The residents were starving, exhausted, weak, and had no strength to cut down trees.

Most who died starved the first year. They ate wallpaper, their family pets, leather belts, and books. Hunger drove people crazy, drove them to kill, drove them to eat those they murdered, or corpses found on the streets or in sheds and buildings where they had been stored. There was no decomposition because the winter was so cold, sometimes 20 degrees below zero.

Liberation didn't come until January 27, 1944.

I had years before read Harrison Salisbury's book, *900 Days: The Siege of Leningrad*, which was powerful on its own, but the longest siege in recorded history became so much more real when my feet raised dust there on the city's soil.

There are almost half a million unknown victims buried in Piskarovskoye Memorial Cemetery alone. At the mass graves:

"To you, our courageous defenders: Your memory will live unfading in grateful Leningrad, which eternally owes its life to you; the immortal glory of heroes shall in posterity's glory be multiplied."

On the graves of the military, there is a star on the plaque, while a hammer and sickle are used for the civilians. One half million roses are planted there, to equal the number buried. As we walked through, we heard music—Shastokovich's *Leningrad Symphony*, and we saw a copse of trees with red scarves tied to the trunks, put there by young Pioneers. (The Pioneers were youth groups for all children patterned after Boy Scouts but used by the Communist government primarily for indoctrination .)

And the inscription:

> "Here lie Leningrad's old men
> Children, women...
> All who come here remember that
> Remember that none are forgotten."

I had no idea then that I had relatives among those not forgotten.

The next night was my rendezvous with Sasha. I had, as usual, written to tell him when I would be in the city. His letter in reply had been vague, and although it sounded like he planned to come, one never knew. But there he was, in the park in front of the Hotel Astoria, (which had been turned into a hospital during the siege) with roses in hand and some perfume for me. He said he didn't really know if I would be there either.

We tried several restaurants on the Nevsky Prospekt. All had lines, and finally we went to my hotel's restaurant, where he had to pay off the waiter to get us in. We danced, and because my birthday was so near, he had the band play a birthday song, dedicated to "our guest from Boston," had them play "Feelings" again, as he had last year in Sochi. He really was such a romantic—which is of course why I liked him, even though I didn't feel that way toward him. For me, our time together didn't feel real; instead, it felt like I was the star in my own fantasy.

We had almost two bottles of champagne and a huge dish of black caviar. I wanted no more food, but Sasha did get dinner. And also, as usual, we talked.

Re *perestroika* and *glasnost*: "Only steam from a machine," he said.

Re human rights: "Only the USA can make things change. I don't want Dukakis to win because he is against the Strategic Defense Initiative (SDI), or Star Wars."

He gave me a silver ruble, dated 1844, for my niece Tambi. I confessed I didn't give her the last Stalin medal he gave me. He said he had been worried about me when he gave it to me, because it is illegal to take medals out of the country.

I told him I saw Valery Leontiev in concert in Moscow and he told me Leontiev was gay.

We left around 11:00 and walked toward my hotel, both of us weaving. He from too much champagne, me from too little sleep. It was so strange to be out so late and see the light so bright.

When I got back to the hotel, I learned that one of our delegates was in the hospital. The *dezhurnaya* heard him moaning and groaning in his room and called an ambulance. He was hospitalized with severe vomiting and dysentery. He drank much of the water in Central Asia, in spite of my repeated warnings to the group, saying that his doctor told him that his iodine pills would make the water okay. Right. They were no match for the water systems of Uzbekistan.

And no hot water for a shower the next morning, until I was all dressed and ready to go, and then of course it came on. Word came back that our ill delegate was feeling better and so the group went off to Petrodvorets by hydrofoil, and I hired a taxi for $10 per hour, to take me to various *beriozkas*, a poster shop, and the Dom Knigi bookstore so that I could do some shopping.

Then a meeting with one of the first Soviet journalists to be involved in our exchanges, Gennady Pankov, editor of *Leningradskaya Rabochy*, a workers' paper. He was much more open than he had been in the past. Over caviar, white wine, and borscht, he suggested that for the next Soviet delegation's visit to the States, we place them into the editorial offices of US papers so that in groups of two, they could follow the same editor and the same reporter during his work day.

When I finished, I went to the Hotel Evropeyskaya and waited for Nina A. to arrive. I was early, and happy to have a few minutes to myself, to sink down into the black leather sofa, to write, and to watch the city in motion. A breeze floated through the open window, gently blowing one of the potted plants, and I enjoyed the faint, peaceful tinkling of the crystal chandelier.

I was always too tired by the time I got to Leningrad, or too busy, to really enjoy the city, with its canals and colored buildings. But I did enjoy getting to know Nina, a professor of education at the Teacher's Training Institute in Leningrad. She told me that both her husbands had died, one from a stroke, the other from a heart attack, that both had been members of the Communist Party, but that she was not. She still grieves over her son. We exchanged gifts: she gave me a wonderful art book on the artist Surikov, I gave her some jewelry and told her I would be back in March. She invited me to her home then.

When I returned to the hotel, I learned that our sick delegate was still in the hospital and we were all a bit worried that they wouldn't let him out in time for him to leave with us the next day. Two of my other journalists were sick too, but not nearly as severely.

I met Sasha as planned, around the corner from my hotel, and we took a taxi to the Petrovsky Restaurant, a boat on the Neva River. This time he had a pink peony for me. We got a window table with a delightful breeze and a lovely view of the riverbank. The colors kept changing, first a bright pink, then a more muted one. Caviar again, both black and orange, some fish, then ice cream, and we danced to a live band, which was also quite good. After, we went for a walk along the river. Sunset was at 11:40 PM and it reflected the gold of the nearby Peter and Paul Fortress Tower, and across the river, off of St. Isaacs Cathedral. We found an empty bench along the narrow beach and sat quietly, listening to the sound of the small waves breaking along the shore. A few people in bathing suits ventured in and out of the water.

At midnight, we left. As we walked across the wooden bridge near the Fortress, the golden spire was still shining in the sun, and precisely at midnight, the bells began to ring.

In the taxi back to my hotel, Sasha slipped a ring on my finger, just as he had done the year before in Sochi. This one was gold with small emeralds and a small diamond. He also gave me an art book and a copy of Gogol's *Dead Souls*. I wished he wouldn't spend so much money.

He waited for me in a phone booth around the corner from my hotel and I went to my room to get the bag of gifts I had for him: a power converter, another cassette recorder, the *BAD* album by Michael Jackson, two books, magazines, and for his daughter, a little bathing suit, shirt, and a tiny jeans purse.

He was very nervous, and although he told me he would take a cab back to where he was staying, he practically ran to catch a bus that appeared. His fear was a stronger commentary on the system than all the rhetoric we got about *glasnost* and *perestroika*. I guess the issue was whether he would be afraid the next time, and the time after that.

Our departure was on June 23rd, the 11th anniversary of my father's death. When I am home on this date, I always light a *Jahrzeit* (anniversary) candle for him. In spite of how foolish he thought all religion was, I can't help but think he would like it that I do that.

But there was no candle that day because we were on the train leaving Russia. Customs gave us no trouble. It was all so familiar to me by then. At Vyborg, the first stop in Finland, I did exactly the same thing every time—changed money, went to the bathroom, and then got my usual egg and butter roll with an orange soda for a snack, and a *Time* magazine to find out what had been happening in the world while we were out of touch.

In Helsinki, we stayed at the Hotel Presidentti again. Our sick delegate did make it out with us, although he was weak and tired. He was given saline solution intravenously for dehydration in the hospital, plus many injections to make him sleep. He said they took blood many times. Luckily he spoke a smattering of Russian, because no one at the hospital spoke any English.

I was happy, after a great night's sleep, to spend the morning in my room with another good book, *The Master and the Margarita* by Mikhail Bulgakov. And Sasha's big bag of sweet, deep-red cherries, and his pink peony that I brought with me from Leningrad. By then, it looked like I felt, somewhat wilted, but hanging in there.

That afternoon, I took a taxi to the Kalastajatorppa, or Fisherman's Village Hotel, for a massage and sauna. The Finns do a sauna right: a mechanized table that actually moves forward and backward and up and down, and a private suite with a bathroom, a large shower, a large sauna, and a sitting room that overlooked the Gulf of Finland. I felt truly clean. A perfect ending for the trip.

Flying home, the group had mixed feelings about the USSR (and I had mixed feelings about the group). Many agreed with the columnist for the *Washington Post*, Art Buchwald, whom we met up with in Leningrad at breakfast one morning and who was coincidentally on our return flight.

"The country is a dump. It is the only country where you brush your teeth for two weeks with warm Pepsi Cola."

I was ready to go home, too. While I was happy to see Russian friends and was pleased about the work I got done, it had been a hard trip. I wanted safe water, my own shower, my own bed, a tuna fish sandwich, and an ice-cold popsicle! And most of all, Frank.

Three months later in September, (the 7th to the 17th), Frank was one of four past Presidents of NESNE who took a 10-day trip to Moscow and Irkutsk, invited in recognition of the roles they played in these exchanges. Their guide was a young guy named Valery Yelizov who worked at the Union of Journalists, (whom I met with on subsequent trips and who I am in touch with to this day.) The group visited the Angara River and Lake Baikal.

They had meetings with journalists, of course, and were told that the press was then able to denounce Stalin. One of their Russian colleagues, Stanislaw Kondrashov, wrote the following in *Moscow News*: "Authoritarian, bureaucratic socialism dreads American democracy like the devil dreads incense. The democratic socialism which we have started building finds much which is of use in America's democratic experience."

But the group's best meeting was one that was not scheduled and not professional. As they went for a walk on the outskirts of Irkutsk, past the charming *izbas*, traditional countryside homes, usually made of logs, and often painted in bright colors, a yellow school bus pulled up ahead of them and stopped to let three young children out. One of them, a beautiful blond girl with the usual ribbons in her hair, looked right at the three who were obviously American, gave them a wave and a big smile, and said "Fuck you," as she walked by.

The group got a good laugh and assumed, and hoped, that those were the only words in English she knew, and that she most likely did not know the real meaning.

Also in autumn of that year, Bernard Redmont travelled to Russia to spend two weeks researching Soviet TV. Gostelradio was true to its word and set him up with excellent interviews.

Redmont's first visit to Russia was in 1939, and from 1976 to 1979, he served in Moscow as CBS News Bureau Manager and Correspondent. While there he interviewed Soviet dissidents, including Andrei Sakharov and his wife Yelena Bonner.

Bernard Redmont
(1918–2017)

Bernie had a colorful career. As a foreign correspondent for 40 years, he also reported on the assassination of Leon Trotsky in 1940, the peace talks in Paris to end the Vietnam War, the Six-Day War in the Middle East.

By his accounts, the visit that I organized for him was a success in terms of who he met, what he learned about Russian television under Glasnost, and the fact that he lectured at the Journalism School of Moscow University—where in 2009 a statue of Walt Whitman was erected with the inscription:

"You Russians, and we, Americans!......so far apart from each other, so seemingly different, and yet....in ways that are most important, our countries are so alike."

Bernie and his wife Joan stayed in Moscow for five nights at the US Embassy Residence, Spasso House, guests of US Ambassador and Mrs. Jack Matlock. In Leningrad, they were guests of the US Consul General Richard Miles and his wife.

As part of the exchange, two Soviets came to the US, both from Gostelradio, Vitaly Sufan and Dmitri Puzikov. They visited and had meetings at TV stations in Boston and Washington, DC.

Bernie reported in *Television Quarterly* that the changes in Russian TV might possibly be the most dramatic changes Gorbachev made in the country, which claimed to have the "world's largest system of TV satellite broadcasting." Propaganda was much less prevalent, and reporting was much more honest. (It is unfortunate that that is not the case today, there or here!)

As I was doing research for this book, I googled Bernie to find out where he lived, because the last address I had for him was in Vermont. I was stunned to come across a July 17, 2009 article in *US News and World Report* stating that declassified Soviet and US intelligence documents declared that Bernard Redmont, codename MON, had been a Soviet spy with the Soviet Silvermaster group during WWII and had been for a time under technical surveillance by the FBI. Also, Harvard's *Neiman Report* in the fall of 2009 reported that he had been accused of being recruited by Elizabeth Bentley, operator of a KGB network. I dug deeper and found her December 20, 1945, two-page testimony that "Berny" was one of her operatives.

"In connection with the information that Redmont supplied to me ....it concerned principally information from cable intercepts and other such material concerning Latin America....this information was not of much real value."

The various reports I found present the case for and against his guilt. He vehemently denied that he was ever an informant and apparently he had to deny these accusations for decades. Some say that he was accused of being a Communist only after he was subpoenaed by the House Un-American Activities Committee and refused to testify and name William Remington, a Commerce Department official, a Communist. That cost Bernie his job at *US News* and he was on the McCarthy-era blacklist for a decade, unable to work for any American news outlet. During those years, he lived in France, where he spent years trying to get back his passport that the US government had impounded. There he worked for Agence France-Press and the Canadian Broadcasting Company. But his denials must have been believed by many because he did eventually go on to work for CBS News, and to hold several other high-level US positions before he became dean of Boston University's School of Communications.

Bernie died on January 23, 2017, when he was 98 years old, and his *New York Times* obituary mentioned all that I had learned doing my research. It shed no factual light on whether or not he had been a spy, but implied innocence when it stated that Redmont "made news himself when he was smeared during the anti-communist witch hunts of the 1950s."

This is a good example of how difficult it can be for the most well-meaning researchers or reporters to uncover the truth behind a story.

What I do know for certain is that many Soviets and Americans wondered if I was a spy. I kind of enjoyed the image of myself as a modern-day Mata Hari, but nothing could have been farther from the truth.

About the same time that I was sending Bernie to the USSR, I filed a FOIA (Freedom of Information Act) request to learn if there were any FBI files on my Soviet-related activities. After about six months, I got a response stating "a search of the indices to the central records system in the Boston office of the FBI discloses four instances where your name was briefly mentioned in, and indexed to, files pertaining to other subject matter. This material, consisting of five pages, is being withheld in its entirety in order to protect material exempt from disclosure...pertaining to the enforcement of criminal law ... and material specifically authorized under criteria established by an executive order to be kept secret in the interest of national defense or foreign policy ..."

I then appealed, waited another six months, and was told "you are not the subject of a Boston Field Office main file, but are alluded to briefly in three files, the subjects of which are other individuals or organizations. ... certain of the material pertaining to you is classified and ...your request is denied."

To this day, I have no idea who those individuals or organizations are.

That year, Shevardnadze made a speech to the United Nations General Assembly in which he said "faced with the threat of environmental catastrophe, the dividing lines of the bipolar ideological world are receding. The biosphere recognizes no division into blocs, alliances, or systems." (By 1979, 20 years of worldwide scientific research had revealed the severity of the threat of global warming. And yet today, the US is still unwilling to do what is necessary to successfully combat climate change.)

Chapter 19
1989, Marriage and More

"The time will come when we will make public toilets of gold."
Vladimir Lenin (1870–1924)
Russian Communist revolutionary

1989 was a busy year, both professionally and personally. I began the year with a hysterectomy in January.

In February, Frank and I went to Puerto Vallarta, where we stayed at a wonderful hotel, the Garza Blanca. One night we ate on the beach, under the stars, about 15 feet from where the surf pounded the shore. Candles in cups showed the way down the stairs to our table, the only one on the beach, where tall torches were set in the sand and red and orange hibiscus blossoms were scattered on our tabletop. Next to it, an antique walnut table with a white cloth and our wine, sharing its ice bucket with lush green leaves.

We made our decision there. On May 28, Frank and I got married at our home with only immediate family present. Mort walked me down the stairs to the music of "Sunrise, Sunset" from *Fiddler on the Roof*. During the ceremony, I saw tears in his eyes.

Frank and I honeymooned in Portugal! (One of the most interesting parts of our trip there—the angry graffiti on walls and garbage cans that commanded "Reagan Go Home".)

Initially, Frank and I were colleagues, then we became friends, and then I met his three children and really liked them. Gradually, we realized there was much more than friendship between us. And maybe most important for me, there was trust and respect. Now, all these years later, the friendship and love, the trust and the respect, they are still there. As is my belief that he is the most decent man I've ever known.

Four months after our wedding day, I was diagnosed with multiple sclerosis.

Frank and the author

March 3 to 18, 1989
Law Enforcement, Moscow, Tallinn, Pskov, Leningrad, Helsinki

In anticipation of the program, once I had participants signed up for the USA/USSR Law Enforcement Information Exchange, the first-ever meeting of its kind between Russian and American police, I contacted the FBI to tell them about the trip. I wanted everything to be above board. An agent in a dark suit and unmistakable FBI shoes came to my house, and we sat at our dining room table and talked. I told him all about the itinerary, my history with exchanges, and there appeared to be no problem. Until he got up to leave. The entire back of his suit was covered with cat hairs from my two cats, Vodka and Grapefruit. That I didn't reveal to him.

More troubling, after my initial conversation the previous year with Lev Belyansky, I never received any confirmation that we would be welcomed by the Ministry of Interior, or have any professional program. I took a big chance by promising the group a police program.

So it was me, who doesn't believe in the death penalty, and fifteen cops, one mayor, and two lawyers, all of whom I assumed did. And my friend Susan Sproviero.

Happily, I was the only one with anxiety; the group seemed like a good one, good-natured, always cracking jokes. Again, the Cosmos Hotel, but with one big change. Slot machines in the lobby. Is this what *perestroika* and *glasnost* had wrought? I wondered.

1989—Marriage & More

Susan Sproviero and
Captain John Damino,
1989 program participants

Each trip, I of course got to see something different. That time it was the Kremlin Armory, one of the oldest museums in Russia. In the Throne Room, Ivan the Terrible's throne of wood, delicately embroidered; Mikhail Romanov's golden throne, which took 13 kilos (or a little more than 26 and a half pounds) of gold to decorate; Peter the Great's father's throne, with its 1,000 diamonds, and finally, the double throne for young Peter the Great and his brother Ivan, with a secret hiding place behind Peter's throne for the mentors, who whispered instructions.

In the Carriage Hall, the 16th-century carriage of Tsar Boris Godunov, with battle scenes depicted between Moslems and Christians; Catherine the Great's carriage of beveled glass and red velvet and gold; and the small carriages for the children of Peter the Great, which were used with ponies and dwarfs for horsemen. We also saw the Russian National Costumes Hall, with caftans, coronation gowns with silver threads and long trains, and the Horse Hall, with saddles of precious stones and stirrups of gold and rubies.

After a full day of sightseeing, we all met in the bar after dinner, and I noticed that my guys kept disappearing and reappearing, a few at a time. I learned that they were going "shopping" under the road at the Metro entrance, paying $10 to $20 for fur military hats. They were also approached by prostitutes in the bar. The price I heard quoted was $100 for one guy, $400 for the group. So they were already doing everything I had told them not to. I remember thinking that this group was going to be very interesting!

I scheduled a visit to Fyodorov's Eye Institute for Eye Microsurgery for the next morning. I thought it would be very educational because it was so advanced, not at all what they would expect it to be, and also, to have something out of the ordinary in case the Ministry of the Interior didn't come through. I kept asking our Intourist guide, Oksana, about the rest of our program and she kept saying it would be available soon. In Soviet speak, that was not very reassuring.

Dr. Svyatoslav Fyodorov (1927–2000)

The Institute was very different from the last time I had seen it—new building, new equipment, and a new operating theatre from which we watched surgeries in progress below and on TV monitors above. Also, this time we were greeted by Svyatoslav Fyodorov himself, accompanied by his bodyguards.

He told us that there were eight centers, doing 18,000 procedures per month, and they had showed thirteen million dollars profit the year before. He also said he had plans for the future that would involve both a ship and a plane to do his surgeries. He was quite a showman. (In the year 2000, the 72-year-old Fyodorov died in the clinic's four-seater helicopter when it crashed. At the time of his death, he was working on something else new, laser eye surgery.)

That evening, my interpreter Paco Norall and I went to the home of the artist, Luis Ortega. We were served an ice cream sundae with peaches and nuts and some tea, but spent most of the time looking at his work. With his long hair, he fit a creative stereotype. Born in Spain, he was two years old in 1939 when his parents were killed in the Spanish Civil War. He was adopted and brought to Moscow.

I agreed to take—in reality, smuggle—some of his work out of Russia so that it could be sold in the US for him by a mutual friend of ours. I later bought one of his etchings for myself, of the poet Anna Akhmatova. (Luis died in Moscow in 2012 at age 74.)

The next day, finally, a meeting at the Ministry of the Interior. My guys were all dressed in their uniforms and we were met by three people very high up in the chain of command: Pyotr Bogdanov, Deputy Minister, General Bugayev, Deputy Head of the Political Department in Investigation, and General Lev Belyansky, whom I had spoken with the summer before about the possibility of this exchange. Under a 20-foot-high stained-glass window of Lenin, General Bogdanov, dressed in a stylishly tailored gray suit and suspenders, told us that this was the first meeting ever had with such a delegation, and that it would have been impossible just a few years ago. After he encouraged us to help ourselves to coffee, cookies, chocolate, and mineral water, he talked about crime and law enforcement in the USSR. It was informative, but we were overwhelmed with statistics.

Racketeering was rampant, but what I found especially interesting was what he told us about prostitution and drug problems in the country. Previously, it was always officially declared that there were no prostitutes, no drugs.

"This is, of course, not true," he said.

However, he told us it was under control. In the next breath, he warned our guys about the prostitutes at our hotel, saying "these beauties will give you no pleasure. They will add something to your drink, take you in a car, rob you, and kick you out of the car. Sometime there might be four or five men following in a second car."

He then jokingly suggested that my police and his could work together. One of the Americans should put lots of paper in his wallet to make it look thick, go with the prostitute, and the Soviet police would follow behind.

I still cannot confirm this, but I had heard that prostitutes were actually informants, paid by the state. I suppose that was possible. Certainly I knew then that I wouldn't have gotten an honest answer had I asked.

But the session went very well, there was a lot of laughing and talk, about our program, and about things that they had in common: low salaries, low prestige, long hours, danger, stress, and interference from lawyers. This quickly created a bond; probing questions and candid answers flew back and forth at every opportunity. We learned that women were not allowed to be officers but could only serve in secretarial capacities. Also, that the Soviets did not have handcuffs, but used leather straps to restrain a suspect. And that crime against foreigners was a growing problem. I guessed that my days of hitchhiking back to my hotel at all hours of the night and feeling safe about it were over.

It was clear that they had waited to get a look at our delegation before deciding whether a meeting was a good idea or not. The Soviets confessed they had been worried that we would be hostile. There was never any hostility on either side—not that day, not during the entire trip.

They gave us a tour of the Police Museum at the Ministry, (very difficult to gain admittance, apparently American reporters had been trying for years to see the inside) which had interesting cases profiled since 1917, and then took us to Militia Station # 99, Voroshilov District, where we were told some more statistics: the most typical crimes were thefts in flats, family conflicts, economic crimes such as stealing window glass and wiper blades from cars and videos from apartments. The biggest complaint of the Soviet officers was that they didn't have enough rights—that was a surprise. My delegates saw many instances of corruption among the Soviet cops, something they apparently relied on to supplement their low salaries. And we learned from private citizens that the police were generally held in contempt for being corrupt as well as incompetent.

Next, a number of the guys went out in blue and yellow patrol cars while the leader of the delegation, Bill Nye, and I were interviewed on Soviet TV about this exchange, "a first." CNN also covered our visit, as did *Pravda*. One of our guys helped break up a fight in a farmer's market. When one of the fighters tried to strike one of the Soviet officers, our delegate intervened and grabbed him. Stunned by seeing the American uniform, the fighter suddenly stopped all resistance.

I then met with some journalists over dinner to do NESNE business. The day ended in the bar, where my choice was warm champagne or Heineken beer. I don't like beer, but it was cold. When I finally got back to my room, it was 1:30 AM and I marveled at how I was functioning on so little sleep every night. Only 3½ hours the night before, very little more than that most nights while in the USSR. I don't know how I rallied, or where the energy came from. Adrenalin, I guess. Of course, often I wasn't thinking straight. Somehow, I hid that well.

The following day, after 45 minutes of standing in line, I finally got to see why a nation of people raised to honor and revere Lenin braved snow, wind, and rain to pay homage. He had died of a stroke in 1924, (although there are many scholars who believe Stalin had him poisoned) and his embalmed body, minus his brain—which had been removed to be studied for signs of genius, was still well preserved. He rested in a large red casket, surrounded by glass, and visitors were not allowed to stop as they walked by. His hands were placed on his chest in a most interesting fashion, his left with the fingers straight out, his right with the fingers slightly curled under. Somehow, just that position gave him character, made him more real.

Appropriately enough, afterwards we took a stroll past the Kremlin Cemetery and I was able to find the graves of four leaders of the USSR—General Secretaries Joseph Stalin (who had lain on display next to Lenin from 1953, the year he died, until 1961, when he was removed because of Khrushchev's revelations that he was a tyrant responsible for the deaths of millions of his own countrymen, not including the war dead), Leonid Brezhnev, Yuri Andropov, and Konstantin Chernenko. I looked for John Reed's grave, but our guide told me it was far back near the entrance to the tomb. The American Reed was author of *Ten Days that Shook the World*, an eyewitness account of the October Revolution. He died in Russia in 1920 and was buried at the Kremlin Wall because he was held in such high regard by the Soviets.

Our next city was Tallinn, in Estonia, the smallest republic in the USSR, and the Hotel Viru, which was a wonderful contrast to the Cosmos. The dining room was pleasant, the tablecloth clean, the food good. And we got a great professional program. My guys were very happy.

Also, we were met by Tiaa Hiie, an old contact of Natasha's. Tiaa took three of us to her home for a sauna—248 degrees Fahrenheit. We took three cold showers in between, then she fed us fruit, cake, tea, and liquor and we talked politics. She was quite optimistic that Estonia would achieve independence some day.

The next day, she accompanied me to the Estonian State Philharmonic, where I met with a man named Enno Mattisen to discuss a possible concert tour for Massachusetts pianist Frederick Moyer, who had made his Carnegie Hall Debut in 1982. I expected he would listen politely to my proposal and then agree to arrange a concert or two for Fred. Instead, he enthusiastically offered an official invitation for Fred to spend a week in Tallinn, all expenses paid, and suggested that he stay in the USSR for a month. Mattisen would arrange concerts in Moscow, Leningrad, Riga, and Vilnius. I wasn't used to things going that smoothly! As it turned out, there were no concerts held in Russia, but Mattisen did arrange for Fred to perform in Estonia and Latvia during the fall of 1990.

Every day ended in the bar. I had no idea what funny stories and experiences the police had. One told of his fear of and encounters with, while on duty, armadillos and cockroaches. (I didn't mention that I had seen cockroaches in every Soviet hotel I had stayed in.) But then, one of them shocked everyone into momentary silence with his statement that alligators chase dogs and "n…..s" because they both smell. It had been a long time since I had heard such blatant racism and several of the guys lit into him for that. I got up to let them settle it among themselves, went to the bar, and bought a bottle of champagne for the table, hoping that would calm things down. It did.

The next day, we met with Marko Tibar, the Estonian Minister of the Interior. He announced that he was a bit nervous because it was the first time he ever met with American colleagues. He told us that thefts had increased and the biggest problem was juvenile delinquency. Their drug problem wasn't as bad as ours in the US, but it had gotten worse when the policy against alcohol went into effect. Drugs came primarily from the southern Asian part of the USSR, although LSD was brought in through Leningrad and some addicts used things they could get from local pharmacies. Drug-sniffing dogs were stationed at airports and train stations. Prices were high, more addicts existed than were registered, and the greatest problem was trying to cure them because there were not enough beds in the hospitals to treat them.

Interesting, since our first priority in the US for those using too many drugs was then, as it still is now, to be punitive, to incarcerate them.

A militia colonel, Herman Simm, was assigned to us. He was in charge of the security system for all of Estonia and took Bill, Paco, and me to see the security system for the apartment complex where he lived. Then he took us to his home for what turned out to be a feast. His wife, who was a dentist, proudly served us canned salmon with tiny lemons on bread, Armenian cognac, Hungarian wine, pickled pumpkin, pelmeni with sour cream and coffee and chocolate. Best was their little white dog Silva, who won my heart.

Hermann told us that the ban against publishing crime statistics had only been lifted a month before. Perhaps that is why we were almost sinking under so many numbers. And then he gave us another: there were 500 prostitutes that they knew of in Tallinn.

He confessed that he had discreetly come to our hotel to have a look at us when we arrived. And when it came time for us to leave, his wife told me that not only were we the first American visitors in their home, we were the first Americans she had ever met. "It just wasn't allowed before," she said.

(Many years later, I learned that Herman was arrested in 2008. In 2009, he pleaded guilty to treason as one of Russia's highest-placed spies in NATO and was sentenced to 12½ years of prison, plus a fine. He was released early in 2019.)

As soon as I saw the fire trucks, I immediately jumped up into one and made someone take my picture. The fire station smelled of smoke and the trucks were old. We were received by both the Director and the Vice-Director of the Fire Service. The Vice-Director said he had worked for the department for thirty years and it was the first time he met colleagues from America.

While we were touring the truck area, an alarm went off and the Soviet firefighters shimmied down the pole, raced to their trucks, and went outside. It turned out to have been a demonstration for us, although the firemen apparently did not know that. Women did not fight fires, although they did work in the system in fire prevention.

That afternoon, to another militia station, where the lobby was graced with a four-foot statue of Felix Dzerzhinsky. The Chief of Police of Tallinn, Leo Tsupsman, greeted us. After yet more statistics, we were allowed to go into a cell with a prisoner, who had defecated all over the floor, seemingly intentionally, and they probably brought us to shame him. (Does disgusting sound about right?)

As we walked out of the cell, one of my guys said "I know, all prisoners say the same thing: *I don't know why I am here and I didn't do it.*" The chief laughed and they shook hands and bonded over a common problem. Exactly the kind of thing I hoped for in all my exchanges!

In another room, I tried on a heavy bulletproof vest that would stop an armor-piercing 30.06 rifle bullet (whatever that was). I had a hard time standing up straight!

There was time for questions and answers from both sides. They asked why all our uniforms were different, when the police could retire, and how much money would they get then, and what was the American public's attitude toward the police.

1989—Marriage & More

One of our guys told them that we were worried that our rooms would be bugged and that we would be followed. Their answer—an interesting "no comment."

Another American asked them if the quality of their lives had improved. The chief replied: "No, it hasn't, but the quality of our souls has become better."

We talked about them coming to visit us in the US and the chief laughed. We asked if permission would be a problem and he said it would be. It had become more and more clear that Moscow ruled everything and that there was an enormous amount of bad feeling and resentment toward Moscow, apparently felt at every level.

With sirens on and running red lights, a police escort took us next to the Tallinn Militia School. We saw the target practice range with blue lights and a siren turned on to simulate stress. Inside, in one of the hallways, Paco spotted a very anti-American poster and he and I stopped to read it. Several of the officers noticed and got embarrassed and a few minutes later we were told that it was very old and nobody paid any attention to it.

Each of us was given a militia hat and then we took a group photo. When we left, everyone there lined up on the street to wave goodbye. Hermann told us that they had all been worried that there would be hostile questions from us, and that he himself had a much more favorable view of us now than before he had met us. Another welcome validation of my work!

The next day, we had a most memorable bus ride to the town of Pskov (where in 2016, a bust of Stalin was installed in their War Museum). After a few hours, our driver stopped for us to go to the bathroom at a gas station across the street. The guys simply all ran into the woods. There were two outdoor public toilets which I knew from past experience would be revolting, so I talked my friend Sue into going into the woods too. I scouted around and found what I thought would be the perfect spot.

The only problem was that I started sliding down the little hill and was mortified to find that my perfect spot had apparently been the perfect spot for an army of people, because I really stepped in it. Both shoes, way up over the sides. Sue laughed and was not the least bit sympathetic. And I still had to go to the bathroom. She held her coat up for me, I pulled my pants down and circled, like a dog, trying to get somewhat comfortable on the uneven ground. On our way out of the woods, with me stopping at every tree to scrape off my shoes, I heard "Oh, no!" Sue stepped in it, too, but only with one shoe.

By the time we got out of the woods, we were doubled over laughing. Tears were rolling down my cheeks and I could hardly breathe. Of course the entire bus realized what happened. One of our guys was kind enough to take off our shoes, clean them as best he could and place them under the driver's seat as Sue and I slunk to our own seats.

We had lunch in the town of Pechory, at a drab restaurant where the toilets were, as expected, pretty awful—but at least we emerged with clean shoes—and then went to the Pechory Caves and Monastery. The best part of this site was that women were not allowed in the monastery while wearing pants. I promptly rolled my pants up above my knees and borrowed one of my guy's coats. I am sure I was a pitiful sight—shivering, with hairy, dry legs, black socks and black shoes, and coat buttoned crooked. Nothing to do but laugh some more.

We next had a short time to wander through the old city section of Pskov, and to go into a church during a service. I lit a candle for Natasha, as always.

The hotel was a dump and the bar gave new meaning to sleazy. Everyone appeared to be drunk—except us—because it took us at least an hour to get waited on. A fight broke out involving a very inebriated militia man, at which point we decided it would be best to go to our rooms. Several of us sat in the hall for a while, ill at ease because two drunks were walking the halls and trying all the doors. Probably they couldn't find their room, but we didn't go into ours until they disappeared.

We were all happy to leave Pskov the next morning. For me, most memorable was the local guide who first asked me my age, then wanted to know if I had had a facelift. I was only 42 at the time!

So, another long bus ride, another hundred or so potholes, with arrival in Leningrad at the Hotel Pribaltiskaya around 6:00 PM. After check in, I raced off to the Astoria to see if Sasha would be there in the park at 7:00 PM. He was. As I had hoped. With flowers. As always.

For dinner, we went to the Literary Café on Nevsky Prospekt, a restaurant I had always wanted to go to and which, by the end of our meal, had become my favorite restaurant in the city. Clean tablecloths, a piano and violin playing in the adjoining room, and a real feeling of "old Russia." After Sasha gave me a huge tin of caviar, we ordered some as part of our appetizer, along with champagne. Our entrée was very tasty meat with mushrooms, and for dessert, ice cream with pineapple and whipped cream. He insisted that I eat his dessert—he had apparently already learned the way to my heart.

After dinner, we went to the hostel where Sasha was staying. He had forged papers for me, stating that I, Svetlana Simonovna Rashnek, was from Riga, Latvia. I decided to pretend I was a deaf mute, so I wouldn't have to talk, but no one asked me anything as we entered. His room was not unlike other dorm rooms I have seen, and he had champagne for us, and that time dozens of walnuts set out on the table in the shape of a heart. He really was very sweet. And apparently without motive, because I had told him about Frank during my last visit and he made no overtures.

But there was a surprise. First, back in 1985, he had confessed to me that he had gotten married; this time, as we sipped our champagne, he told me he had gotten divorced. He got divorced so that he could buy a house, which he did, for 15,000 rubles and 1,000 rubles in bribes. His plan was to tear it down and pay that much again to build a new home. And his wife got remarried, so that she could move to Kiev. Her new husband was Jewish and expected to emigrate to the US. Meanwhile, she and Sasha were still living together and planned to do so for about another year. All for practical reasons. I didn't understand, but I didn't ask any more questions. In fact, we talked for less than an hour before I got a taxi back to the hotel.

The next morning, another first. At the Ministry of Internal Affairs, Anatoly Kurkov, Chief of Administration for Leningrad, told us that we were the first American police to ever visit their headquarters, which was the administrative center for Leningrad.

When asked by a Florida policeman what he would change if he could, Kurkov said he would advocate sterner punishment for criminals and he would pay more money to his police officers, who "deal in human garbage."

We then talked about a totally new situation in the USSR: demonstrations. The previous year, a special bill was passed that allowed demonstrations with permission. Permission was refused on two grounds: if a violation of the public order was expected or if the theme would instigate nationalistic feelings or hatred against a group or the state. There was a special force to deal with these demonstrations. Those police used rubber batons, helmets, shields, tear gas and they had superior skills. They were snipers, climbers, and knew judo.

He mentioned the group Pamyat, which I had planned to ask him about. Our US news had reported on their activities and their anti-Semitic ideology. He said that the mass media paid a lot of attention to them, that their stated purpose was to save the monuments of Russian culture. They stressed Russian culture, called themselves Russian patriots. But when they mentioned the offenses against the Russians, they blamed everything on the Jews, (even counting how many Jews were in the Soviet government), and the International Masons. (In 1993, Pamyat reprinted the *Protocols of the Elders of Zion*.)

"This, of course, cannot be tolerated," Kurkov said.

Paco then asked why, if this cannot be tolerated, were they given permission to demonstrate, since their agenda clearly violated the guidelines and incited hatred.

Kurkov said when they stated the subject of a proposed demonstration or meeting, it sounded innocent, something like the abolition of serfdom or the anniversary of the beginning of WWI. He also told us that it was only an extreme wing of the organization that was so full of hatred.

That's what he said. I wasn't so sure, based on what I had read about Pamyat and what I knew about Russian anti-Semitism.

After lunch, we went to a criminological laboratory-training center, whose main job was to provide technical background for solving crimes. The central body dealt with the most complicated cases. There were thirteen special labs, which handled fingerprints, bullet tracing, ballistics, chemical tests, food tests, fire, etc. The main task of the smaller divisions was to examine a crime scene and to make sure nothing was overlooked. This was the biggest department in the USSR in terms of volume. Yet their data bank was all paper, no computers.

We saw a counterfeit Soviet Certificate for Higher Education, and then fake money. We compared a counterfeit $100 bill with a real one. On the fake one, the paper was too yellow and too smooth, but the artwork was really good.

Then they showed us a photo of a woman's head whose skull had been found in a bucket. Forensic medicine reconstructed a portrait of the woman, which they also showed us, and which they had circulated all over Leningrad. They finally identified her and the portrait was very close to what she really looked like.

The inside view into Soviet law enforcement that we got during our time there was the first afforded any group from outside the USSR.

That evening, I went out to find the kids who were selling things by the bay. It was bitter cold, but I enjoyed the wind striking my face and the sound of the icy water lapping the shore. I found what I had gone looking for—the Paul McCartney Melodiya album "Back in the USSR," its cover printed in Russian and released only in the USSR. Cost: $5.00, American. (The ruble, which was worth $2.62 when I first went to the USSR in 1980, was, in 1989, worth 16 cents.)

Had I known then that the LP was selling for $100 to $250 a copy in the US (as much as $885.00 in London) and that Melodiya's licensing agreement with EMI, McCartney's British recording company, prohibited them from exporting the album, I probably would have bought many more.

* * *

Sasha came to the hotel first thing in the morning and we headed directly to the Nevsky Prospekt in search of a café. After a lot of walking, we found that the Nevsky Grill was open. By the time we got there, my hair was soaked from wet snow that melted on my bangs and dripped down my nose, so I really appreciated a hot cup of tea, some grapefruit juice from Cuba, and a bit of orange caviar with bread and a pastry.

After that, I was fortified and asked if we could go to the Museum of Religion and Atheism, opened in 1932 in the old Kazan Cathedral, where I had been trying to go literally for years because I agreed with what Lenin had said.

> **"Those who toil and live in want all their lives are taught by religion to be submissive and patient while here on earth, and to take comfort in the hope of a heavenly reward. But those who live by the labour of others are taught by religion to practice charity while on earth, thus offering them a very cheap way of justifying their entire existence as exploiters and selling them, at a moderate price, tickets to well-being in heaven. Religion is opium for**

the people (Marx). Religion is a sort of spiritual booze, in which the slaves of capital drown their human image, their demand for a life more or less worthy of man."

(Bolsheviks were atheists and no religion was officially allowed in all of Russia until 1991, although some churches were kept open for show and mostly attended by the elderly, who didn't have to worry that it would affect their jobs or their lives.)

It was great to be with Sasha because he translated and I trusted what he said. One section was devoted to Judaism and I mentioned to him that I was Jewish, although not religious. I didn't know if he was surprised or not, or if he harbored any anti-Semitism. If so, he hid it well. Another room was devoted to anti-religious sentiments and had another quote I liked, by Marx:

"What is given to God is taken away from the self."

In 1992, religious services once again were allowed there and in 1996, the state gave the cathedral back to the Russian Orthodox Church.

When we finished touring the museum, we said goodbye. I had no more free time on my schedule because the following morning, while the group was at the Hermitage, I wanted to get away to see Nina A.

I took a taxi to her flat and we had a very nice visit. She brought out wine, cabbage pie that her mother had made, pastries that she herself had made, and tea. She had a large apartment with three rooms and a kitchen and a bath, and a cute little dog named Micky. She said she would help me with the program for a group of women legislators I had scheduled to go to the USSR in June, and I told her I would invite her to come to the US sometime the following fall.

After a rare half hour to myself in my room, the group went to the residence of the American Consul General, where we were met by Dick Miles, the Consul General, and Joyce Marshall, the Chief of the Consular Section, who dealt with those who get in trouble with the police. They told us they don't generally receive groups unless they are very important or there is a personal connection.

Miles spoke briefly, told us of the Soviet efforts to democratize the society and the fact that it was a messy process since there was no history of it there. He believed they were sincerely trying. Was there staying power? Of course, no one knew, but he said the top leadership was committed to it.

I left the residence with Joyce Marshall to go to the Consulate so that I could issue an invitation for Nina A., a much simpler process in person than if I waited until I got home. All I had to do was fill out a form, sign it, put my right hand up and swear that what I had written was true, then pay $4.00. The next morning, Nina came to the hotel. I

Nina A. gave her the paperwork and explained what she had to fill out to complete the application process before she took it herself to the Consulate.

Sasha called to say goodbye, and then my group had another police escort to the airport. We waited in a long line there with all our luggage and with me somewhat nervous because of all the undocumented artwork of Luis Ortega that I had in my suitcase, and the 110 rubles I had hidden, probably not so cleverly, in the bottom of my purse, rubles I had changed illegally with my cab driver the day before, 6 to 1. It was the first time I had ever done that, and I had always warned my people not to do it. This group totally ignored me and some of them had gotten a 10 to 1 rate.

As it turned out, we were ushered through customs by Leningrad militia with no search, no questions, and no x-rays.

When we got to Helsinki, I searched out an International Herald Tribune for the first news in two weeks. The lead story was that the Mujahidin were expected to take over the city of Jalalabad soon, even though they failed in their first major attempt to overthrow the Soviet-backed government since the Soviet withdrawal a month before.

As I watched my group boarding our flight for home the next morning, I was struck by how fond of them I had become, both collectively and individually. They were terrific at every level—professional, flexible, funny, warm. And they did not complain about anything. I had had no idea what to expect, but sitting around in the bar most nights listening to their stories was very revealing, not to mention entertaining. Of course, I always wanted every group to have an incredible experience, but it was especially so with this group, and I did as much extra as I could to make it so.

Wayne Schmidt, Executive Director of Americans for Effective Law Enforcement in Chicago and a participant in this first exchange, was very much interested in being involved and expanding it beyond sending delegates to each country. We talked often about the best way to do this, and he wrote a letter to William Sessions, then Director of the FBI. Schmidt proposed that the FBI send an invitation for two English-speaking officers from the Ministry of Internal Affairs (MVD) that oversaw all law enforcement functions in the Soviet Union to visit the FBI so that cooperation could perhaps be established in areas such as world wide drug interdiction. Sessions replied that such an invitation was "inappropriate at this time."

It was another busy year professionally. Nina A. came to visit, and stayed in the US a month. I coordinated her visits from Boston to see friends she had met in Russia. To Washington, DC; Pittsburg, Pennsylvania; Des Moines, Iowa; Madison, Wisconsin; Bozeman, Montana; Pasadena, California; Kansas City, Kansas; Owensboro, Kentucky; Northampton, Massachusetts; and finally New York City, where she and I met up after her travels and had a delightful dinner at the Russian Tea Room. That was where she told me about her son, the truth about his death.

She had said when we first met that he died in a car accident. In reality, just as he was ready to leave military school, he was electrocuted on the campus. Officials there said it was his fault, but no one ever told her exactly what happened and that was part of her ever-present sadness.

* * *

On July 31, eight Soviet editors from Moscow, Leningrad, Yerevan, Tashkent, Kiev, and Noginsk came for the NESNE conference held at Connecticut College, New London, Connecticut. And for the first time, after our many requests, there was a woman among them.

They were given a tour of a police station (where they of course had donuts), took a ferry ride to Foster's Island, then visited the Nautilus Museum and the Coast Guard Academy.

Topics of discussion at their meetings were ethics in journalism, changes facing Soviet journalists due to *glasnost* and *perestroika*, and future directions for the eight-year-old exchange. They were pleased that two more young working journalists from each country were already chosen and scheduled to work in the other country.

NESNE was also pleased when they heard one of the *Izvestia* editors say "Now, when I travel abroad, I no longer have to lie."

In late September, three Soviet editors from the early conferences came to New England, the invitation extended in response to the four who went to the USSR the year before. As usual, they stayed at private homes. Frank and I happily hosted Albertas Laurinciukas, by then an old friend.

Also that September, I sent a group of women to Moscow, Tbilisi, and Leningrad for an American/Soviet Women's Policy Conference, sponsored by OASES and the Women's Peace Initiative.

Four-term Massachusetts State Rep from Amesbury, Barbara Hildt, led the delegation. In her press release, Representative Hildt said the group was composed of delegates "that included the former assistant to the President of the UAW International, the Women's Project Coordinator for the Committee for National Security, a former reporter for NBC News, and the Chancellor of the University of Michigan–Dearborn."

About half of the participants were current or former members of state legislatures. There were lawyers, lobbyists, and participant Debbie Stabenow, who went on to serve two terms as a US Congresswoman, and then in 2000, was elected US Senator from Michigan. Also Mildred Jeffrey, rewarded in 2000 with the Presidential Medal of Freedom by President Clinton for her life of activism. She was an organizer for the Amalgamated Clothing Workers of America in 1935, and a member of the NAACP, which she joined in the 1940s. She marched with Martin Luther King in the 1960s, helped found the National Women's Political Caucus, and helped Walter Reuther organize the autoworkers into the UAW and its work for social equality. And Cristina Caballero, who at the time of this writing is still President and CEO of Dialogue on Diversity, Inc., a non-profit educational organization that she founded after this trip, to promote discussions among women of varied ethnic traditions in the U.S. and around the world.

From the feedback after their return, I learned that the visit had been quite successful.

They went with an agenda to discuss common concerns, the roles of women in politics and government, in conflict resolution, and in securing human rights. But talks also included the environment, global security, public health, drug abuse, and the changing roles of men.

They learned that many Russian women have five to six abortions during their lifetime (the statistic I always heard was twelve) using abortion as birth control because of the unavailability of prophylactic methods. In the mid 1990s, abortion rates declined significantly in Russia.

They learned that homosexuality was a crime, with about the same level of severity as hooliganism, and that Soviet entrepreneurs and cooperatives were facing extortion and violence from mobsters.

They learned that alcoholism was not considered a disease and that it was a major factor contributing to the high divorce rate of about 80 percent.

And they learned that Russian women had free daycare, three years maternity leave, with eighteen months paid. And free education.

But, life was still difficult. There were no special services for seniors, who were mainly cared for by their families. Most Soviet women worked, were responsible for child-rearing and running the home, and because of shortages, often had to spend hours daily standing in line to buy food and other items such as soap and gasoline. And, as

1989—Marriage & More

mentioned earlier, very often they had to share housing with another family. But these women were hopeful about perestroika.

Besides the usual sightseeing, the delegation toured a museum in Tbilisi, where they saw a preserved crust of bread, saved from the rationing during the siege of Leningrad. And they also went to a grade school there where the children sang to them. Their song: "We are the World."

> **On October 19, Viktor Afanasyev was fired from his post as editor of Pravda by Mikhail Gorbachev. Circulation had dropped and the paper had been moderately critical of Gorbachev and very critical of Yeltsin and his drinking.**
>
> **Gorbachev was named *Time Magazine*'s Man of the Year.**
>
> **The Communist Party of Lithuania broke with Moscow.**
>
> **Between 1988 and 1989, the refuseniks were almost all released and many Jews were finally allowed to visit Israel as tourists. There was also movement toward making it legal to teach Hebrew in Russia and to open new synagogues. Approved by the Soviet government, a Jewish Cultural Center opened in Moscow in 1989, as did the first kosher bakery producing matzo for consumption by Jews throughout the Soviet Union.**

Chapter 20
1990, Lithuania Fights for Independence

*"Trust must be built up through experience in cooperation,
through knowing each other better, through solving common problems."*
Mikhail Gorbachev (1931–2022)
General Secretary of the Communist Party of the Soviet Union

The MS diagnosis, of course, had scared me; I made Frank promise not to tell anyone because I didn't want it to define me or any of my relationships. I tried not to worry about the future, not to think about Frank and what he must have been worrying about.

I decided I couldn't put off working out any longer. Luckily, the two neurological episodes I already had totally disappeared, so I joined the health club Le Pli in Harvard Square and was lucky again. I took aerobics classes with a tall, handsome, muscular, blond instructor named Robert Montague. Robert was a classically trained former professional dancer from the Boston Conservatory of Music. His classes were so much fun that I was inspired to go almost every day, and after awhile, I started personal training with him. Remember his name, because I will talk more about him later.

I submitted my father's name to be placed on the American Immigrant Wall of Honor at Ellis Island, unveiled that year (1990) Panel 112.

March 30 to April 14, 1990 Law Enforcement Tour
Moscow, train to Vilnius, Leningrad, Helsinki (16 participants)

We had full professional programs in both Moscow and Leningrad, but the highlight of this trip was the four days we spent in Vilnius. In fact, because of the recent unrest as Lithuania strived for its independence, I was certain that that leg of our trip would be canceled after foreigners had been ordered out by Moscow. Even the Lithuanian Minister of the Interior who received us was surprised that Moscow had allowed us to visit. (Ours was the first American police delegation the city and its militia had ever received.)

On April 7, the day that a big pro-independence demonstration was planned, our Lithuanian police hosts scheduled a meeting for us 64 miles away, in the town of Kaunas. They did their best to keep us there all day, finding excuse after excuse to delay our departure. I had told them that morning that I wanted to attend the demonstration and they, in good faith, I believe, didn't want us caught up in anything that might be dangerous or embarrassing. Finally, I told them that I was going to leave Kaunas alone and hitchhike if I had to. With that, they reluctantly returned us to Vilnius.

The Soviet Union barred foreign reporters from covering the estimated 200,000 to 300,000 demonstrators who chanted for their freedom and sang their national anthem, "Tautos Giesme," many with tears. They carried signs that expressed their fury:

"Communism equals Fascism!"

"Lithuaunia...Birth of Freedom – To be, To be...To be free!"

Another, addressed to the Soviet Military in Russia said: *"Occupiers: Your motherland is calling you. Go home."*

Lithuanian President Vytautas Landsbergis told the crowd there would be no backing away from their independence: "Iron will melt to wax and water will turn to stone before we will retreat."

At the same time, a noisy Soviet military helicopter dropped thousands of pamphlets into the crowd. Small children thought it was a game and ran around collecting them. Angry adults tore them up. The one-page sheets, printed poorly on one side in Russian and the other in Lithuanian, were an appeal from Mikhail Gorbachev:

"The situation in Lithuania is becoming critical!
Lithuania will remain a republic in the united family of the people of the USSR!
The people must immediately reject the decisions of the
Lithuanian Supreme Soviet!
Only common sense and calmness by the Lithuanian people
will save their native land from catastrophe!"

Amid a sea of flags from Lithuania, Latvia, Estonia, the Ukraine and Byelorussia, speakers addressed the crowd.

"We will never be Soviet again; we want to die in our own state. We will wait as long as it takes."

Fishas Grigoryus, lawyer, activist, adviser to parliament, spoke on behalf of Jews in Lithuania. His point was that a free Lithuania wouldn't be tainted by the ethnic strife besetting the Soviet Union.

"While there have been pogroms in Moscow," he said, "there is no discrimination towards Jews or any minority in Lithuania."

1990—Lithuania Fights for Independence

Zinas Kazenas, Lithuanian photographer, and the author

Lithuanian demonstration for Independence, Park Vingis, Vilnius

Few of my delegation were interested in the demonstration, so I found myself walking alone in the crowd in Park Vingis. About an hour into the march, I had that strange feeling that we sometimes get when it seems like someone is staring at us. I looked around and about twenty feet away was one of the only two people I knew in Lithuania: Zinas Kazenas, the Vilnius photographer who had four years earlier exhibited his work in Cape Cod.

We marched together and the next day, he took me to the Supreme Soviet of the Lithuanian Republic to see his photographic exhibit of Sajudis (the name of the Independence Movement, of which he was a member). He also arranged for me to interview Zigmas Vaisvila, a physicist, leader of the Green Party, and deputy of the Supreme Council of Lithuania, who told me he had just received word from Moscow that Foreign Minister Eduard Shevardnadze would be replaced.

I also got to see the other person I knew in Vilnius, friend and past NESNE delegate Albertas Laurinciukas, retired editor of Tiesa, the official Communist Party paper in Lithuania. He described himself as a moderate, but was also excited about the prospects of independence. Because of his past position and ties to Moscow, he had been asked to join the movement for independence, but he refused.

However, he went on to say, "There are no extremists here, just a people with national pride and ambition. Our independence would be good for Gorbachev. It would prove to his people that he is serious about his political reforms."

But many Lithuanians expressed a deep hatred and distrust of the Russians. Some thought that President Bush and Gorbachev made a secret pact—if Gorbachev would let Eastern Europe go, Bush would not interfere in his efforts to keep the Baltic Republics (Estonia, Latvia, and Lithuania) in the Soviet Union. Others felt that their freedom depended on Bush and the United States. They were hopeful. At demonstrations and in private they said, "We are waiting for America." What they feared was that Lithuania was just too small a country for Washington to risk upsetting its good relations with the USSR. Most seemed to agree with what was expressed on signs in Russian and Lithuanian, outside my hotel: "Lithuania without sovereignty is Lithuania without a future."

In private conversations I had later with Russian friends in Moscow and Leningrad, all were supportive of independence for Lithuania. A few were fearful only of how fast events were moving. A friend in Leningrad reminded me of Hitler's statement before he invaded the country—that the Soviet Union is a colossal giant on clay legs. "Today", my friend said, "one clay leg is Lithuania."

In Leningrad, crocus were just beginning to bloom.

After my return to the US, I wrote a report covering what I experienced in Lithuania. It was published in two Massachusetts papers, the *Patriot Ledger* and the *Cape Cod*

Times. Much of what I have written above of this trip to Lithuania was excerpted from those pieces.

Lithuania had officially declared independence on March 11, 1990, less than a month before this demonstration. It received international recognition and was admitted to the United Nations six months later on September 17th. However, Gorbachev did his best to keep Lithuania in the USSR. On January 13, 1991, around midnight, Soviet tanks and armored vehicles moved on its TV tower, killing 14 unarmed civilians. Stunned by the passion of the unarmed resistance there, and worldwide condemnation and recognition of Lithuania's independence, the troops backed off. Soviet troops remained in the country until the last of them departed on August 21, 1993.

NESNE-Union of Soviet Journalists
8th Conference
Moscow – Leningrad
June 5 to 15, 1990

It takes only a few moments in the Moscow airport and on the street to be assailed by very familiar, not-so-pleasant odors, odors that are so unmistakably Russian. A certain disinfectant, leather, ink, their awful cigarettes, and the choking smell of diesel fuel discharged in dark clouds of exhaust from the buses.

The Hotel Solut was large, the sheets were flowered and there were decorative blue tiles in the bathroom, but the rug was filthy and in general, it was pretty grim. I was anxious for sleep, but I forgot that being exhausted does not guarantee good sleep. I woke up in the middle of the night and read the Paul Bowles novel, *The Sheltering Sky*, until it was time for breakfast.

President Gorbachev returned to Moscow one day before we arrived, after his Summit with President Bush. Of course, both leaders called it a success, but there were still several unresolved issues: independence of Lithuania and the Baltics, reunification of Germany, and favored nation trade status, which we did not grant the USSR, although an expanded trade agreement was signed. I thought Gorbachev was a masterful politician. In spite of his troubles at home and increasing reports of his diminishing power, he appeared strong and in command. (I was wrong.)

Yet things were a mess in the USSR. There were ongoing large demonstrations in Moscow and throughout the country. Citizens demanded improved economic conditions. There were panic food lines, people were hoarding, buying everything they could find in anticipation of higher prices and/or more shortages and thus food shelves in the stores were empty. There were bad instances of anti-Semitism and ethnic unrest. Crime had increased, the Black Market was thriving and aggressive, and every day brought a new crises. Some were predicting the unraveling of the USSR itself.

And on Gorky Street, we saw a huge, flashing Coca-Cola sign and ads for Christian Dior.

However, our program went on as scheduled. Our delegation consisted of eight NESNE members, one interpreter, and me. The first morning, we had a meeting at the House of Journalists (the same building described by Bulgakov as the Writer's House in his novel, *The Master and the Margarita*), hosted by Vikenty Matveev, columnist for *Izvestia*, and Boris Fetisov, Deputy Head of the International Department of the Union of Journalists.

The Union was undergoing some changes and anticipated restructuring, but all seemed to believe that the exchange program was still a valuable one and should continue. They did tell us that money for the program was no longer so easily available.

In the afternoon, we walked past the traffic circle out front of the KGB with its imposing statue of Felix Dzerzhinsky, through oak doors into the KGB Headquarters—a well-kept, beautiful building, with wood-paneled walls and a red carpet on the shiny parquet floor. The marble stairs had wrought iron and brass handrails painted gold. In our conference room, we were surrounded by portraits of Lenin, Dzerzhinsky, and Gorbachev.

The Center for Social Contacts had just been created a month earlier to "inform layers of society of purposes, direction, and results of KGB activities, and to establish direct ties with the press and other institutions." And, we were told, "the activities of the KGB, founded in 1954, would be limited by the interests of society now under perestroika." In short, this was their Public Relations Department.

We were addressed by the Head of the Center, General Alexander Karbainov, who was actually their full-time public relations guy; a General Anatoly Grinenko, who was the Department Head of Central Archives and the individual in charge of rehabilitating those people condemned by Stalin during his Great Terror; Yuri Matsak, Head of the Organized Crime Department; and a Vladimir Vinogradov, Deputy Head of the KGB Central Archives.

In 2004, it was Vinogradov who, after a ten-year joint investigation by Swedes and Russians into the fate of Raoul Wallenberg - the Swedish diplomat who saved the lives of so many Jews during the Holocaust and was then arrested by the Soviets in 1945, never to be heard of again—announced the results of the study, saying "I am personally satisfied with the work of the commission. The official work is now closed, although there remain questions which have been recognized as requiring answers."

At some point, as with so many of the KGB, Vinogradov became a businessman. He owned several private security companies and was accused of launching criminal investigations against competitors or those whose assets he wanted to seize, thus victimizing small businessmen who took to calling themselves "Men of Vinogradov." He became very wealthy.

Of course, they said, Intelligence and Counter-Intelligence would not be the same if it operated in the open, and they resolved this dilemma by talking about activities, directions, results, but not about their methods to achieve goals. Their most important priority was still counter-intelligence. In the five years before, they said they discovered that some thirty of their own agents were also agents of foreign secret services.

The struggle against terrorism was always important, and they had a newer direction—the fight against the Mafia and organized crime. Organized crime was delaying perestroika and the criminal elements tied to the government threatened state security. Corrupt state officials were rarely prosecuted. In August of 1989, the Supreme Soviet passed a ruling that extended the battle against crime in general and organized crime in particular, stating that the KGB should increase its activity in that area. They were having a difficult time fighting the Mafia, who had better equipment, better technology, and faster cars. To effectively carry on the battle against organized crime, they needed laws, and the lawmakers were behind the problem. Thus, they said, the KGB's job was even more complex.

The Russian Mafia on the streets worked to get protection money from businessmen, and they were ruthless when they were refused. Business storefronts were machine-gunned, mysterious fires broke out. The Mafia members were racketeers, gangs, drug dealers, and they ran prostitution rings. They even disguised themselves as police. The streets were no longer safe after dark.

They also pointed out that the Russian Mafia was tied to the US Mafia. Their data showed that many former Soviet citizens who had criminal pasts had organized their own Russian Mafia in the US and America didn't know how to deal with them because these criminals were not afraid of prosecution—US prisons were comfortable. Plus, they specialized in activity a normal America criminal wouldn't even think of, such as watering down gasoline. Or running gas excise tax scams where they bought gas out of the country, sold it to independent US gas stations, collected excise tax from those retailers, and then never paid that tax money to the US government.

"The Russian Mafia in California does it beautifully and has earned millions," one of them said, smiling.

"Was this organized crime based on ethnic groups?" we asked.

The reply: "Jews are very smart and enterprising, so probably they are involved. It is not of an ethnic character, rather a commercial interest, which could be led by Jews and others."

Also, a priority was to work to overcome past KGB actions, to restore the good names of those unlawfully repressed during the Stalin purges of the 1930s, '40s and '50s, when he had established regional quotas for arrests, imprisonments and execution, when he encouraged people to name names, when he even urged children to tell on members of their families if they had said something negative about him.

More statistics. In 1988 and 1989, we were told that they reviewed 591,107 cases involving 856,580 people. Of those, 847,740 were rehabilitated and 21,333 were refused. The total didn't add up by my figuring, but who was I to interrogate the KGB?

As for the total they admitted were shot: 1.7 million during the purges. (Many American Sovietologists suspected it was many more.) Showing a bit of humanity, the KGB said that families of the rehabilitated were given items from the files of their loved ones who had been killed, items like family photographs, letters and anything else personal that had been saved.

I did inquire about the role of women in the KGB. Their reply, "We value women for what they can uniquely do, and some are indispensable for their accuracy, promptness and intuition." No mention of their intelligence.

Two guards saluted us when we entered and again when we left the building and our meeting with the Public Relations Department, but a visit to the restroom at the close of our meeting revealed no toilet seats, no toilet paper. Out front, a little old lady dressed in a standard gray-blue smock, white scarf, and green shoes swept the sidewalk with her old twig broom. I suspected that in spite of the new veneer, the KGB's methods had not changed any more than that old lady's.

Whoever created our program for that day had a sense of humor. Directly after the KGB, we went to the home of Lev Timofeyev, dissident writer, journalist, leader of the refuseniks, and editor and publisher of the publication *Referendum, A Magazine of Independent Opinion*, which was until recently *samizdat* (the mimeographed reproduction and secret circulation of censored publications of human rights appeals, political manifestos and self-published writing).

In 1983, the then 47-year-old Timofeyev published a book, *The Last Hope of Survival,* in which he was the first to use the term "stagnation" to refer to the Brezhnev years. In that book, he said he wrote about the economic crises in the country, the Afghanistan War, and the fact that the USSR was on the edge of war with other countries, on the edge of world war, in fact.

He created *Referendum* just after he was released from prison after having served two years of an eleven-year sentence of hard labor for anti-Soviet propaganda. His prosecution came after his 1985 book, *Technology of the Black Market, or the Peasants Art for Starvation*, highly critical of the Communist economic system, was published in France. He was released early under the free-speech leniency of glasnost and became active in the pro-democracy movement. He also served as Chairman of the watchdog Moscow Helsinki Committee for Human Rights.

Even though censorship rules were less strict, Timofeyev said that there was still government control through allocation of paper and printing facilities and the distribution system, and that system was only for those who had "correct" Party ideas.

"With or without censorship, the KGB still controls the country."

Timofeyev was himself critical of Gorbachev. He said that there was a danger in being General Secretary, that it was psychologically impossible to be democratic in that position; there was too much power. That power would break even a more moral person than Gorbachev, who, after all, was a Party child.

"And everything, both the government and the Russian Mafia, depends on the Black Market. Thus, any politician in Gorbachev's position would have had to institute reforms or face political suicide. But Gorbachev made his reforms too slowly, and he is moving too slowly now. He has lost the spiritual rise, the trust of the people.

"Today, the main thing is to give the Soviet people a clear understanding that Socialist ideals are simple political speculation, that's all. The fear today is of the KGB, not God, not Gorbachev, not Yeltsin. Of course, KGB repressions are much less now, but fear of the KGB is like a religion among the people."

At that point, his Siamese cat and his friend, Mikail Kukabaka, one of the last political prisoners in the country and Timofeyev's cellmate, entered the room. (I later learned from the Ukrainian weekly newspaper that Kukabaka was a Byelorussian dissident who was first sentenced in 1970 to seven years in the Sychovka Special Psychiatric Hospital for disseminating the text of the *Universal Declaration of Human Rights*, and was diagnosed "as suffering from a mania for reconstructing society." In 1979, he faced trial again for slandering the Soviet state and its social order; the prosecutor contended that Kukabaka's writing reached the West and was then used as anti-Soviet propaganda. Found guilty, he wasn't released from prison until 1988.)

We asked Timofeyev about anti-Semitism. He is half Jewish, on his father's side, but said that culturally he was Russian, not Jewish, and there were icons throughout his apartment. He wasn't too worried about anti-Semitism, although he thought that there were those who will still want to blame the Jews for their role in the Revolution.

Timofeyev, with a gray, unruly beard, wore blue jeans and sandals, and spoke with the kind of calm one notices in people who have undergone the greatest hardships. And he often used the expressions "not far ago" and "yes, surely," especially as he told us of his two visits to America, when he visited New York City, Cornell University, Boston, and Washington, DC.

His impressions of America?

"Good beer—and good lobster."

Timofeyev has since turned to writing novels: his 2006 book, *Negative* was nominated for a Booker Prize.

The next day, a meeting in the morning at the Faculty of Journalism at Moscow University with the Dean, Professor Yassen Zassoursky, who told us that William Colby, of CIA fame, had visited the school and spoken to the students.

Then, another meeting was arranged by Zinas Kazenas, who I had no idea was in Moscow and had surprised me at dinner the night before. Present at the meeting besides Zinas was the authorized diplomatic representative of the government of the Republic of Lithuania, Egidijus Bickauskas, who, as one of the members of the Supreme Council of the republic of Lithuania, (previously the Supreme Soviet of the Lithuanian SSR) had signed the Act for the Re-Establishment of the State of Lithuania the past March 11.

Bikasukas was very emotional as he talked about how important the Act was, told us that Lithuanians would not retract the independence proclamation, that they were in fact more determined than ever. He told us that Gorbachev would like to push aside the issue of the Baltics and Lithuania and that America must not let him do it. (During the coup attempt the following year, the US ambassador in Moscow invited Bickauskas to hide in the U.S. Embassy, but he refused, so sure was he of the victory of Lithuania and its Russian allies.)

Our group's next stop was inside the Kremlin walls, with press passes Valery Yelizov had obtained for us and which we had to show at every doorway, inside and out, to sit in on a session of the Supreme Soviet. Coincidentally, that day it voted on and approved a new press bill that was most likely influenced by our journalism exchange. The year before, one of NESNE's delegates gave a Leningrad journalist a copy of Connecticut's *Freedom of Information Law*. The Soviet passed it on to Anatoly Yezhelev, head of the Leningrad Union of Journalists and also a deputy in the Congress of the Russian Federation. He was said to have used Connecticut's law to help him and others create their own press bill.

On August 1, the first Soviet press law went into effect. According to the *Los Angeles Times*, the law stated that "the press and other mass media are free," and "censorship of the mass media is forbidden." You can imagine how happy NESNE was. And proud. We were eight years into the exchange program, the first in history. During those years, we worked hard to explain to the Russians how journalism worked in our country, how, without freedom of the press, we wouldn't have freedom in America.

We were able to get a quick interview in the hallway with famous dissident author Roy Medvedev, then a member of the Supreme Soviet, who had written for illegal protest publications and was in 1969 expelled from the Communist Party when he published his book, *Let History Judge*, in which he was very critical of Stalin.

His twin brother Zhores was also a dissident and was in May of 1970 arrested, declared insane, put in an asylum for 19 days, and stripped of his citizenship, which Gorbachev reinstated in 1990.

1990—Lithuania Fights for Independence

We asked how history would judge the current period and if a backlash was possible. He said that there were many different predictions for the future, but he felt that more reforms, more difficult reforms, must be enacted. He thought some conservative reaction was possible, for example, a victory of radicals could result in a short period of anarchy and a partial split of the USSR.

I asked what he thought of Yeltsin, who had been elected first President of the Russian Federated Republic on May 29th, and his response was exactly opposite that of Timofeyev's.

"I believe he is negative and destructive. Gorbachev is a world-scale politician. Of course, he has drawbacks, but Yeltsin is a populist in the worst sense—too ambitious, too little educated. I wish every success to Gorbachev and worry that Yeltsin will destroy him."

And speaking of Yeltsin, we next went to see him in action at the Russian Federation Council, although nothing exciting was being discussed. One of the council deputies told us that there was no real politics going on; it was simply negotiating for common sense.

"You know about the Kremlin's tsar bell, which is never rung?" he said. "Well, the reputation of the Parliament is that it never works."

It seems our two countries had more in common than many realized!

The next morning found us in Zagorsk, a town of about 100,000 people with beautiful churches. At the largest church, the Trinity Monastery of St. Sergiy, several old women with babushkas lined the benches outside on the grass. One of them was feeding pigeons and I asked her if I could photograph her. We then had a lovely talk. My Russian was so rudimentary that I didn't understand most of what she said, but I did manage to tell her where I lived, what I did for work, where my parents were from, and that I wasn't Catholic. She pulled out her cross from beneath her dress, nodded to the church behind her and asked if we had such beautiful churches in the US. I told her we did not. The entire time we spoke, the pigeons did not leave her alone—they alighted on her head and shoulders and constantly fluttered in anticipation of more food. If I had had more time, I would have asked her if I could feed them with her.

That evening after dinner, we went to the Arbat, the only pedestrian street in Moscow, where one could buy souvenirs: paintings and masks and Red Army hats and military uniforms and medals. Even kittens. Or watch the artists and street performers, the punks and the hippies, and listen to the musicians, poets, singers, and beggars.

We were there for a prearranged meeting with Mark Kotlyar, leader of the Kiev refuseniks. We ended up talking in the park in front of Spasso House, the residence of the US ambassador to the USSR. Kotlyar had just met with Margaret Thatcher and Mikhail Gorbachev that morning and had expressed his concern over Gorbachev's recent statement that Soviet Jews would not be allowed to immigrate to Israel if they were going to settle on the West Bank. In actuality, only one percent settled there. Thatcher told him, "We should press Israel about giving every nation the right to live. I understand Mr. Gorbachev because there is a lot of pressure from the Arabs, so I would do the same thing." He said he was impressed with his meeting with her, "… however, she is not the one who issues exit visas."

The Soviet Union could refuse to let Jews immigrate by stating that they held state secrets, an accusation that was always arbitrarily applied. Kotlyar began seeking to emigrate in 1977, but felt that eventually he would get permission to leave. In fact, I later learned that he and his wife and son eventually did receive their exit visas and went to join Kotlyar's brother in Los Angeles.

Our Moscow farewell dinner was held at the House of Journalists, hosted, as was our welcoming dinner, by Boris Fetisov and Vikenty Matveev. We were presented plates with filet mignon, floating in a ring of ketchup, and lingonberries with sugar for dessert. I received flowers, and Gennady Musaelian gave me an unframed oil painting by the Impressionist landscape artist Ivan Soshnikov. I had it framed and it has been in my living room ever since.

In Leningrad the next day, we had a meeting with several members of the Leningrad City Council, and we broke into small groups. An ecologist told us that there was more cancer in Leningrad than in any other city in the USSR because the pollution was so bad. The drinking water came from the Neva River, where industries all along the river dumped their hazardous waste out though underground pipes.

All council members said that they were working to obtain more rights for the people. But the Deputy Chairman for Law Enforcement made the biggest impression when he stated that only their children would live in a state governed by law.

As for the attitudes about the current state of affairs, perhaps the popular joke going around at the time said it best:

An American dog asked a Soviet dog, "How is all this glasnost and perestroika stuff shaping up?" The Soviet dog answered, "OK, I guess. They've made my chain two meters longer. Then they moved my food dish four meters farther away. But I can bark all I want."

The usual sightseeing—Pushkin, Pavlovsk and the Hermitage. At the Hermitage, a chance to see favorite things again: the DaVinci *Madonna with the Flower*, the 23 Rembrandts and the two Matisses that I love, *Music* and *Dance*, both done in 1910.

The next morning, I met Nina A. and Valery Monakhov, Vice Director of the new division of the Herzen Institute, to see if establishing a program there for adult Americans to study Russian language was feasible. They showed me the dorms, which were not great, but at least had private baths. At the time, I thought it was something to consider. Opened in 1918, the Herzen Pedagogical Institute was the first higher educational establishment of its kind organized by the Soviets to train teachers.

1990—Lithuania Fights for Independence

After, we went to Nina A's for lunch. Borscht, champagne, salmon salad, red, juicy ripe tomatoes, meat, potatoes, and a whole table full of desserts. Nina said she was able to get good meat because there was a butcher living below her and all the residents of the building saw him selling unofficially, so he took good care of them so that no one turned him in.

That evening, a stroll through the Summer Garden, past all its statues and tall trees, and then a two-hour boat cruise on the Neva River. The sun actually set just after 11:00 PM, painting the sky and the city below with its dazzling gold and pink light.

I did a lot of reflection the next day on the flight back to America. I was anxious to get home, but it was incredible to be a witness to the end of Communism, to a society in transition. Corrupt, insecure, full of hopes and dreams and fears. Erotica suddenly for sale near the subway entrances. A hurry-up attempt to imitate the West, to catch up on all the lost time. Yet these people had no knowledge of how to do it, no idea how business was supposed to work, or the democratic process. Yes, they used computers. They also still used the abacus.

As for me, I felt a little sad to see the McDonald's that had opened January 31st, with a waiting line over 500 yards long with 30,000 people, 27 cash registers, and 900 seats, the largest in the world. (By 2019, there were at least 750 McDonald's throughout Russia.) It was a bit sad also to walk into a *beriozka* full of Levi jeans, and to see the masses embracing religion. Some felt that the government was in such bad shape that it was encouraging religion, encouraging churches to become powerful. One good thing: for the first time ever, Soviets, almost all of whom smoked, left the room to light up when we were present, aware of American attitudes.

But I remember thinking that it was the old Russia, the heavy babushka-adorned women, men with burly hands and peasant features, the wooden houses, the traditional food, the music, even the smells—all of that is what felt so familiar to me, the familiarity coming not only from repeated visits, but from what seemed to be something that was and has always been a part of me.

* * *

In October, a Soviet delegation of ten flew into New York for an overnight, a luncheon with editors at the *New York Times*, and some sightseeing. It was the ninth NESNE conference with the Soviets in ten years. When they arrived in New England, they had home visits with their host editors and the conference, along with the farewell dinner, which was held at the *Boston Globe*. At the roundtable, most of the Soviets discussed their roles as journalists during the coup, the stresses, the difficulties, the fears.

And then, maybe the most important topic. The unknown. What next?

* * *

Massachusetts Governor William Weld greeting Russian police (1990)

1990 was another busy year. In May, the Soviet police came to the US, May 18-26. For their home visits, two went to Albany, NY, six to New Amsterdam, NY, one to Deland, FL, and one to Larkspur, CA. Their New York City program included visits to the Empire State Building, Rockefeller Center, Radio City Music Hall, Statue of Liberty, and the World Trade Center, Greenwich Village, Chinatown, and Little Italy.

While in Boston, they were received by the Massachusetts State Police Academy, where they were greeted by William McCabe, Commissioner of Public Safety for the Commonwealth of Massachusetts, and where they stayed one night in the dorms. They also went to the Massachusetts State Police Headquarters, where they met with Attorney General James Shannon. Then they toured the Massachusetts State House, where they were welcomed by Governor William Weld.

* * *

Also in May, I sent a group of 24 women on an Early Childhood Development program, led by Nancy Lauter-Klatell, Associate Professor of Early Childhood Education at Wheelock College. They spent two weeks visiting kindergartens, including pre-school and daycare centers in Moscow, Pyatigorsk, and Leningrad.

And in September, from the 10th to the 18th, another police exchange, this time to only Moscow and Helsinki.

Things in the USSR were even worse than in June. Poverty and crime were rising rapidly. The immediate crisis was the absence of bread in Moscow and Leningrad. The grain was produced, but had been left to rot either in the fields, *en route* on trains because of labor strikes, or in processing plants that couldn't handle the volume. The day before the 12 of us arrived, Bush and Gorbachev met in Helsinki to discuss the

1990—Lithuania Fights for Independence

Middle East crisis and both condemned Saddam Hussein's Kuwait incursion. In Moscow, Yeltsin was proposing a 500-day plan for total conversion to a market economy, saying that was all that would save the country.

At the same time, there was a rise of more political parties and nationalist groups, similar to Pamyat, that published and distributed anti-Semitic pamphlets. We learned of a Moscow group called Death to Kikes.

The police put our delegation up in a militia holiday home, the Berezovaja Rosha, or Birch Grove. And there was a wonderful grove just outside my room, which by Soviet standards was quite something: a two-room suite with a twin-bed bedroom and a sitting room, refrigerator, and a bath. I immediately went out to the balcony to get some fresh air and saw a man in sandals, black pants, jacket, and small hat, walking slowly as he was reading. I also noticed that all the Soviets who had met us at the airport were standing outside at the front of the building engaged in what appeared to be serious conversation. Discussing us?

Our first official event was a press briefing. All my people showed up in uniform and they looked great. The Soviets announced that they had just the past week arrested a Moscow mass murderer. They wouldn't give details about the suspect, but said that he had raped eight to twelve women, then slashed their throats.

Halfway through the briefing, my delegation was invited on stage to answer questions from the Soviet press. I would never have predicted the questions.

- Why are so many of you repeat visitors? Does that mean that only certain people are approved or allowed to come to the USSR?
- Tell us about the problems you have with Russian émigrés and the Russian Mafia in the United States.
- Do you ever interact with private investigators?
- Do you always carry a gun and how often do you shoot it?
- Can you be activists in environmental movements?

And my favorite:

- What do you think of the movie *Police Academy*?

Next, we went to 39 Petrovka Street, Police Headquarters, to meet with authorities of—and this one is really long—The Militia Headquarters and Officers of the Criminal Investigation Department and the Socialist Property Protection Department! We were greeted again by General Bugayev, Deputy Minister Lev Belyansky, and many other familiar faces.

General Bugayev began by saying that in order to improve communication with us, during this visit, they were going to tell us the entire truth about things.

OK. So over lunch, I asked one of the interpreters they provided, Oleg, about prostitution. "How is it that it is illegal, yet there are so many prostitutes in the hotels that someone is obviously looking the other way. Perhaps for money?"

He told me that in the old days, the official stance was that prostitution didn't exist in the USSR, so of course, there was no means to control it. But some of those in the bars were KGB and others paid bribes (standard was 10 rubles) to the doormen. When there was an arrest, if the woman was KGB, of course she was let go. If she wasn't KGB, she was fined 100 rubles and then let go, regardless of how many times she had been arrested. The only way to control the real prostitutes was to put them in the hospital for a week and test for AIDS and other diseases. There was a five-year prison sentence for knowingly spreading AIDS.

My next question was about the Black Market, because I wanted the real story on the risk for my participants. He said that when someone was caught changing money, it was very difficult to prove, and the tourist was never arrested. (I wish I had known that years earlier.)

Unknown tent occupant

After lunch, we toured Moscow. One of my people, Eugene O'Donnell, an assistant district attorney from Queens (who later became a professor at John Jay College of Criminal Justice and taught in both Europe and Africa), quickly became one of my favorite delegates because he made me laugh so often. While in the church we visited, as usual I lit my candle for Natasha. I told our Intourist guide that I did that for her on every trip, and she told me that I had placed the candle in the wrong place, that candles for the dead always go under the big Christ figure. Gene heard and asked, "Does that mean that you've always been getting busy signals?"

When we went to Lenin's Tomb, I decided to go inside again, thinking that his body might not be there in the not-too-distant future. Many people thought it was time for him to be removed. (He had been moved once before, sent to Siberia during the war to insure the safety of his corpse.) The line was shorter than usual that day. "Probably everyone is standing in line at McDonald's instead," Gene said.

Afterwards, we had free time in Red Square and Gene and I chose to leave the group and go to the Tent City that had sprung up during the summer in front of the Rossiya Hotel. It was difficult to estimate how many people had established makeshift cardboard shelters there, maybe 50 to 75. Each had put up big posters stating their grievances.

The signs were, of course, in Russian, but we managed to stumble upon one person who spoke broken English and he was only too happy to explain to us why he was there.

Genrikh Vasilyevitch Kozhemyaka, a man of 52, with white, bushy hair, told us that he was in Moscow for two reasons. In 1976, he said he was wronged by being put unlawfully into a psychiatric hospital. He wasn't there long, but when he was let out, it was under the constant supervision of a psychiatrist. Then, his mother died recently at home under strange circumstances and Genrikh felt that maybe the cause was unnatural and that somehow his neighbors were involved, that they influenced the doctor to stop attending to his mother because they wanted him out of town.

When the authorities would pay no attention to his suspicions, he did leave town. He went on a hunger strike in Pushkin Square in May, and then in August, with no money and 900 rubles of debt, he set up in this park. He said he didn't sleep there every night, that he sometimes went to the railroad station. He was circulating a petition for a prompt and an unbiased investigation into his case.

He spoke slowly and it was thus difficult to determine if the inconsistencies or holes in his story were due to fabrication or to his poor language skills. Was he legitimate, or just another poor, pathetic, paranoid soul? Anywhere else, his story would sound unbelievable, but in the Soviet Union?

And I, (supposedly a normal person), could not stop staring at the piece of string-like lint, most likely from a handkerchief, hanging from that poor man's nose and blowing back and forth with the breeze. Or at all the wax build-up so very visible in his ears. When we left, I gave Genrikh 25 rubles, about $5 for me, a lot for him. Gene and I decided that he sounded sane, but of course, we couldn't be sure.

Six months later, a Moscow prosecutor, under instructions from the Moscow City Council's executive committee, ordered the protest site, home to 200 to 300 people at its height, to be razed with trucks and bulldozers. It took less than an hour. The occupants were taken to undisclosed locations.

We stopped at the Rossiya Hotel, dashed into the Baskin Robbins there for some Mandarin Orange ice cream, then ran to catch the bus, which next took the group to the Arbat, where other members of the militia were awaiting us. We actually had bodyguards, members of Spetsnaz, their elite Special Operations forces controlled by Military Intelligence. We went off in small groups and for fun, some of us tried discreetly to lose our "tail." No luck. And I couldn't even buy anything because the Soviets knew we hadn't yet changed money into rubles. What they didn't know was that I had over 500 rubles with me, which I had smuggled out the previous June. The question we all had later about this outing was, "Who was it that they didn't trust? Us or their own citizens?"

Members of both delegations did a lot of drinking in their rooms after dinner, and the next morning, our bus had to stop *en route* to the Moscow Militia Training Center so that one of my guys, Scott Lowenthal, could get out to throw up. No Americans are a match for the Soviets when it comes to vodka! Especially a Jewish guy not used to drinking. There was one other person on the bus that day, the only other Jewish person, who barely managed not to throw up because of the hangover. Me.

Scott was able to keep up with the group. When we were shown around the Center, I was pleased to see in the computer training room the *NY State Police Basic Officers Training Manual* that had been given to them by one of my police a year ago.

We next went outside to observe the trainees run the obstacle course, which they had to complete in three to five minutes. This woke us all up and even cured our hangovers. While instructors shot rifle blanks, the trainees had to negotiate trenches with fire, climb ropes, and engage in hand-to-hand combat with assailants with real knives. Never mind my adrenalin; I couldn't imagine what it did to the guys running it. My group said that this was much tougher than their training had been.

That afternoon, in groups of two, we all went out on patrol with the Soviet police. Again, Gene and I paired up and a lot happened in the hour and a half that we were with two very young militiamen who we were assigned to from Kuntuskaya District Police Station #169. They answered a call to the top floor of an apartment building. While Gene and I stood off to the side of the door, for our own safety, our two young Soviets stood directly in front of the door, knocking politely. When a woman opened it and saw who it was, she slammed the door shut in their faces and locked it. Her neighbor was just arriving home and she started shouting at the police, complaining about that woman, saying she had no right to be there in that apartment because she was constantly bringing in men. Suddenly the slammed door was flung open and a fat woman in her fifties or sixties, obviously drunk, flew out and attacked the returning neighbor. The cops separated them, took the drunk woman into her apartment and motioned for us to follow.

Surrounded by tall piles of dust, overflowing ashtrays, and plates heaped with moldy food, her son was slumped in a kitchen chair, glassy eyed and barely conscious, leaning on the stove, which held several large knives. The first thing the police did was ask to see their identity papers. Gene and I looked at each other and read one another's minds. The first thing we would have done was remove those knives!

Meanwhile, the woman, wearing a dirty orange print dress, with brassy, dyed-red hair and swollen bare feet, continued to yell.

Their dog was so scared it crouched under the table, tail between its legs. Then, when the woman's yelling became screaming, the dog went out on the balcony and paced nervously. When it turned to come back in, the curtains framed its face and it just

1990—Lithuania Fights for Independence

stood there looking as if it were wearing an enormous scarf. But it was obvious by its posture and the fear in its face that it was used to violence and to being hit.

The police had been called because the neighbors had heard the mother and her son fighting. At one point, while the police were talking to her, the woman grabbed a photo, held it in front of her face as she rocked back and forth on the sofa, and kept yelling "my son, my son." We later found out that her husband was in jail for the murder. Apparently husband and wife had together killed their youngest son with a knife, motive unknown, although the husband alone confessed.

Gene and I decided to leave the apartment, sensing that our presence was aggravating the situation. Soon, more police came and arrested both mother and son. Outside, as the two were being put in the car, I worried about what would happen to the dog.

That evening, another banquet-type dinner—too long, too many toasts, too much food. A couple of my guys got very drunk, one was so bad that on the bus, he put paper rubles in his mouth and tried to light them with a match. Then, from a seated position, he fell on the floor. At the time, I realized that the entire group was getting edgy. There was too much regimentation and confinement, too little alone time. We were with the Soviets every minute, unlike all past programs, and I wasn't sure why.

The next morning, a visit to a model juvenile facility, where the kids stayed from three to six days, depending on how quickly someone could be located to do something for them. The director and her staff were in uniforms, all had on high heels, every hair was in place, and each had manicured nails and good makeup.

As we toured, the smell of disinfectant was strong. Each room had flowers, some with dark pink dahlias, others with healthy jade plants. Each room also had at least one display of the US and Soviet flag standing together. In the gymnasium, all the boys lined up for our inspection. We were told that 90 percent of them were juvenile delinquents, the remaining 10 percent orphans. For the most part, the boys looked pathetic and some of them actually cowered, not unlike the dog of the day before. One boy cried as he stood at attention and when we asked why, we were told, perhaps truthfully, perhaps not, that he didn't want his mother to see him on television.

A classroom with teenage girls was startling in its contrast. The girls were alert, curious, some almost sassy. They were not at all shy about asking questions, or staring at our clothes and makeup. A room for the youngest children was full of bright lights and toys, and each child looked well cared for.

Our visit was covered by a cameraman and a female journalist, both Soviets. I spoke briefly to the cameraman and found out that he had become a member of Hare Krishna in 1986, when they first appeared in the USSR to proselytize. The journalist pulled Scott aside and said, "The children's clothes and uniforms are usually torn and tattered. These were all issued this morning. The girls were warned that if they told you the truth, they would be punished." It apparently wasn't her first visit to the place, now apparently a "showplace facility."

That afternoon, we were all given different experiences. I was invited for lunch to the home of a Soviet we all liked and whom we had nicknamed "Big Sasha." He first gave me a tour of his apartment. He himself had built the kitchen cabinets and a jungle gym for his kids' room, which he had also wallpapered with cartoon characters. His daughter Nadia was an adorable blond; his son Dima wore thick glasses and a Mickey Mouse shirt. At one point, he shyly approached me to give me three of his drawings.

The meal was exquisite. First the *zakuski* (appetizers): egg with cheese salad, fish, marinated mushrooms, vodka. And the vodka was my favorite, the o*khotnichya* or Hunter's flavored vodka, made with cloves, ginger, anise, lemon peel, coffee, and other herbs. The main course was chicken with red, ripe, juicy tomatoes and Fanta orange soda. Finally, tea around the samovar, with strawberry compote and a jam made from small green berries, and pastry his wife Vera had made. She also had sewn the dress Nadia was wearing, as well as her own skirt and blouse. Vera's mother was there to help out, and took the children for a walk for a while. When they returned, the children presented me with a bouquet of red and orange leaves. "Their own idea," their grandmother said.

And there were more gifts. A book on Brueghel from one cabinet, a coffee grinder from another, then a vase, and a cup and saucer from Zagorsk, and two spoons. I genuinely hated to say goodbye. The afternoon had been fun, the atmosphere warm and open, and they were such a nice family. Sasha was a big man with a big heart. I had a hard time picturing him as a policeman, never mind possibly KGB.

After dinner at our place, we all went to my room to discuss the day and share experiences. The common theme was that we were fed too much food, too much alcohol, and all that while there were breadlines in the country. Three of the guys were told that we were under constant surveillance, that people watched and followed us even when we were with the Soviet cops, let alone when we were alone, which was all too rare. The reason? The general had told his people, "If so much as one hair on one head ..."

One of our guys, John Damino, a captain from Albany, NY, on his second trip with me, was taken to a bathhouse, or *bagna*, where he had no idea what was happening, especially when they told him to get naked. The chief of the Moscow Metro personally led him through the experience. As was the custom, the chief slapped John with birch twigs, then sent him to a whirlpool. Finally, he had John put soap all over himself, then the chief took hold of some sort of a pipe, got under the water, and personally began to "vacuum" him. In between all these steps, they ate and drank, and then drank and ate some more.

1990—Lithuania Fights for Independence

Three other guys also had a special *bagna*. They had the birch twigs, too, a cold pool, food, liquor, and then an unimaginable surprise. A big bear, muzzled, was brought in from a nearby circus. The bear stood on a chair, which made him very tall, and saluted them.

Those same guys also said that they were told that one of the Soviet majors we knew from the past exchange, a guy we called "Little Sasha," was KGB. For all we knew, they were all KGB, although they led us to believe that they were not administratively connected. Anyway, lots of laughs and stories until almost 3:00 AM.

Another impressive display the next morning, at the Training Center for Spetsnaz, the same men who served as our bodyguards as we roamed the Arbat. In camouflage uniforms of green and black, trainees ran an obstacle course surrounded by smelly smoke and loud shot blanks. We walked the path right beside them or sometimes just in front of them. Suddenly, they would be there, supposedly chasing one another, but definitely scaring us as we scrambled to get out of their way. When the chase was over, they gave a demonstration of martial arts and hand-to-hand combat. The knives were fake, but they broke bottles over one another's heads and shattered bricks with their hands. They also jumped over burning fire fences and descended from the roof of a building to climb inside through a window. Finally, in their white helmets, as they held shields and batons, they marched in a straight line while their trainers threw objects at them.

Throughout, there were sounds of deep breathing, grunting and groaning, all part of a simulation intended to help them visualize themselves making contact before it actually happened. When the demonstration was over, they lined up in a row and we shook all of their hands, except for one who had cut his and refused to offer it because he didn't want to get blood on us.

In reality, "Spetsnaz forces were trained to fight without rules or weapons, to use anything that would help them destroy the enemy, from hammers, spades, guitar strings for strangulation to noiseless crossbows, poisons, chemicals, rocket launchers and land mines." (*Spetsnaz: The Inside Story of the Soviet Special Forces*, by Viktor Suvorov, 1987, by W.W. Norton and Co, Inc.)

But the instructor explained that there were rules regarding the firing of weapons. It was the same as we had heard from someone else, that first a policeman must say "stop or I'll shoot," then must shoot up in the air, and only after that could a person be shot at, and only in defense of the policeman himself or of other people.

We next went to a police dog training facility. I was particularly anxious to go there because I was considering an exchange for police canine handlers. But the facility seemed pretty pathetic to me, and I don't know which looked worse, the trainers or the dogs. We saw only a few of the 500 dogs for whom there was room there. First, a demonstration with a cocker spaniel that was trained to sniff out drugs, which she did twice, very quickly and very nervously. Some of my guys suspected that she had been intentionally hooked on drugs herself to better train her. In another room, a different dog successfully chose which suitcase of many had drugs inside. At the end of this site visit, one of the Soviet militia, a rather young detective with prematurely gray hair, took one of my people aside and told him that this, and everything else we had seen had "all been a façade." So much for General Bugayev's comment at our first meeting that they would tell us the entire truth!

At our farewell dinner, we were presented with our gifts. Seventy-five pounds (each!) of Soviet porcelain, with a delicate, pink peony design. (I can only imagine who came up with this gift idea, or the circumstances under which they got the dishes.) In addition, a special toast from Valery Bobryashov to me, the woman who was responsible for the relationship between US and Soviet police. Probably a dubious distinction, but it made me feel good to be praised for being competent instead of being a "lovely woman."

My macho police delegation made it to Helsinki on Aeroflot with their ladylike dishes in big, unwieldy boxes, strapped into empty seats. That, of course, was not allowed with Finnair. After some negotiation, Finnair graciously distributed boxes that would fit in the overhead compartments and we quickly repacked. When I say we made a mess of their boarding area, I'm not exaggerating. I can only imagine how that scenario would play out with any airline these days.

> **After centuries of Russian and Polish rule, in 1918 Lithuania declared its independence and two years later joined the League of Nations, only to be seized by Stalin in 1940. On March 11, Lithuania again declared its independence.**
>
> **On July 15, Gorbachev issued a decree that gave access to the airways to all political groups, thus ending the Communist Party's monopoly of state-run TV and radio.**
>
> **On December 10th, Mikhail Gorbachev was awarded the Nobel Peace Prize.**
>
> **On December 14, Andrei Sakharov died of a heart attack, 12 days after he led a protest against a move to amend the Constitution to grant the Communist Party more power.**
>
> **On December 20th, Eduard Shevardnadze resigned as Prime Minister of Russia, predicting that a hardline dictatorship was coming. While he served under Gorbachev, he was considered the more progressive reformer.**

Part Four

Chapter 21
Family

*"Every book is a quotation; and every house is a quotation
out of all forests, and mines, and stone quarries; and ....
every man is a quotation from all his ancestors."*
Ralph Waldo Emerson (1803–1882)
American essayist and philosopher

The year 1990 had something else planned for me, something big.

"Is Dickstein your married name or your maiden name?" he asked when I handed him my business card.

Mark Segal was visiting Cambridge, MA, not a mile from my home on Harvard Street. I met with him at the Quality Inn on Mass Ave to pick up a letter he had brought from my friend Nina A., and to discuss a possible program with Valery Monohav, Director of the Herzen Institute in Leningrad, where Segal was director of the Foreign Languages Department. Monohav and I had initially talked about this when I was in St. Petersburg.

"Maiden name. Why?"

"Because my mother's maiden name was Dickstein. Do you have family in Russia?"

No," I replied, remembering what my father told me. "They all left by 1910."

But then I asked politely, "Where was your mother from?"

"Glubokoye," he replied.

"That's where my father was born!!!"

We sat down, discussed family, and I took him home with me immediately, made coffee, showed him photos. We had enough information that went beyond coincidence to know we were related, but not enough to figure out how.

He asked me for permission to smoke in the house, telling me he was simply too excited. Lucky for me, he was smoking Dunhill and not those awful Soviet things. And he asked me if I had any books on Yiddish humor because he collects them. I presented him with the *Encyclopedia of Jewish Humor*, which he took in both hands and held up to his face. Then, he kissed it.

Mark and I had first determined that both his mother and my father were from the tiny town of Glubokoye, and then he said he knew he had relatives who had gone to America, to Scranton, Pennsylvania. "My mother used to get letters from Scranton back in the 1920s, and she told me that was where her cousin went."

And Scranton was, of course, where so many of my family were.

We thought that maybe my grandfather and his mother were cousins, but couldn't be sure.

And then, another surprise. "You have family here in Boston."

He called his niece, Alla Makarovskaya, who had arrived in the US only eight months before, and within an hour, I met her and her son Leonid, who himself had come to Boston just ten days earlier.

Alla had been a chemist in Moscow for 25 years, in Moscow at the Organoelement Compound Institute, part of the Academy of Sciences, but when she came to this country, her English wasn't good enough for her to get a job in her field, so she relied on her sewing skills and became a seamstress. She worked for six months at a shop in Wellesley, and then opened her own tailoring shop in 1991 in Lexington, MA. (Three years later, in 1993, her mother Sofya immigrated to America.)

We met at the Boston University Bookstore in Kenmore Square. Alla was standing under her son's umbrella, we exchanged hugs and kisses and she showed me a photo of her mother and her grandmother, who was a sister to Mark's mother. All were Dicksteins.

Mark invited me to Leningrad to spend a year, six months, however long I could—to learn Russian, to lecture at the university, whatever I wanted. When I told him that I was going to go to Minsk and Glubokoye the following year, he said he would meet me in Minsk and we could go together to Glubokoye. I had thought it would be exciting to finally visit my

Alla Makarovskaya
and her son Leonid

Family

father's birthplace, but the possibility of going with a Russian relative, one I never imagined existed?

No wonder I couldn't sleep that night. And I kept thinking, what if I had taken Frank's last name instead of going back to my maiden name? Mark and I would have talked and never known we were related.

There was no question that I would do all I could to determine our relationship. It took two years, a few trips to Russia and a trip to Israel for me to learn how closely we were related, to learn that I did have family in Russia, to learn the fates of those members of that family who lived natural lives, and of those whose lives were taken from them.

I had spent so many years trying to decide what kind of work I wanted to do, work to which I could passionately dedicate myself. I was very happy with what I was doing, it gave me so much that was important to me—just enough excitement, just enough adventure, just enough time away from home, and more than enough professional gratification. And then it gave me family.

In time, I discovered that Mark and my father were indeed first cousins, my grandfather Chaim Lazar was his uncle, making Mark and me first cousins once removed. His mother, Yelizabeta, was the sister of Chaim Lazar.

Mark subsequently came to the States often, sometimes with an invitation from me via OASES. He came to celebrate his 80th birthday with a party at St. Petersburg Café in Brookline, Massachusets on Sept, 23, 2001. I learned more each time I saw him.

Mark had been born June 22, 1921 in Kublichi, Belarus, in the Vitebsk District. His older brother Abram was born there too, as well as his younger brother Zalmon. Sadly, both died during the war. Abram at the Battle of Stalingrad, where over half a million people died, mostly soldiers, some civilians, more than the US lost in the entire war, and Zalmon in 1942, one of the 800,000 who starved to death during the 900-day siege of Leningrad.

Mark remembered that his mother told her children about her youth in Glubokoye, but unfortunately couldn't remember what she said or what year his parents were born.

He shared a great anecdote. Mark Chagall (born Moishe Segal) was a remote relative on his father's side. Mark met the artist in Budapest at an exhibition of his work. He went up to Chagall and told him that he was a distant relative and the newly famous Chagall replied, "During recent times it seems many relatives of mine have appeared."

Mark told me he and Dina were not religious but they treated religions and religious people with respect. In Israel, they visited each place related to Jesus Christ and in the US, they attended services in both synagogues and churches.

"And where were you during the war?" I asked.

"I was there from bell to bell, beginning to end. When the war started, I was in the Western part of the Ukraine, in Shtetovka, almost at the Romanian border. We were the first who in that part of the country saw the aircraft with the German crosses on the wings, flying very low toward Kiev. I was on the 2nd and 3rd fronts, Voronish and Central. I served by recording the enemy aircraft coming, and immediately informing how many planes there were and where they were flying, what direction, what objects could be their targets of bombardment.

"Once, there was a festival and a professional actor was scheduled to give a performance for the army. I was chosen to be the toastmaster. And, can you imagine, it turned out that the actor was my cousin Abram!

"The war ended for me on May 8, 1945, when I was in Prague. I was decorated five or six times and received fifteen medals, including those from the government of Mongolia and Czechoslovakia. My superior during the war sent in an application for me to get the highest orders of the Soviet Union, but because I was a Jew, I was rejected. The war years were the toughest of my life.

"I don't remember everything from the war. However," and then he smiled, "I do remember the girls."

"What about your career?" I asked, also smiling.

"I became a member of the Communist Party in 1943, for four years during the war. Membership in the Party gave me a chance to help three Jewish students to continue as students, when the Institute wanted to remove them.

"Besides my work at the university, I gave classes on TV and taught English for adults, lectured in Hungary and Yugoslavia in the 1960s and 1970s. I taught at the university for 60 years, was a full professor, and was honored with medals for being accomplished in higher education."

When Mark retired, he donated 1,200 books to the university—on methodology, some fiction, and about 100 dictionaries.

Alla Vainberg Makarovskaya

It was a thrill to have found that I had Russian relatives after all, and how extraordinary that some lived in Boston. Alla, my second cousin, and I became close immediately. We got manicures together once a week, at Yelena Sirotin's home, a friend of hers who later became a very close friend of mine and had come here from Minsk. Alla and I worked out together at Robert's gym. He had left Le Pli and opened his own private training facility on Commonwealth Avenue. Alla and I went to parties together, and whenever Russian family came to visit her, I got to meet them, too.

At the time, she was married to a man named Yakov, her son Leonid's father. They were together from 1964 until 1978, but he did not treat her well at all and she divorced him. Yakov came to America and worked as a chemist at MIT. They remarried in 1989, Alla came to America, and again the marriage didn't work.

In December of 1995, she called to tell me that Yakov had beaten her a few days earlier, on a Saturday when they got into a fight over the card that lets them into the garage of their apartment building. She ran out in the hall, started screaming, then managed to call the police, who came immediately. When they arrived, Yakov was on the ground, pretending to have a heart attack (he had had a small one a few months earlier). The police asked if Alla wanted him taken to the hospital or to jail. She told them to take him to the hospital, but to a psychiatrist because it was his head that was the problem. They took her to a different hospital because she was bruised and her lip was cut and bleeding.

On Monday, she appeared in court and the judge explained her rights and asked if she wanted a restraining order. She said yes.

"One year or six months?"

"Six months", she replied.

Then they brought Yakov into the courtroom in handcuffs and she said he looked pathetic and she felt sorry for him because she knew he had no place to go. Of course, she knew, as did I, that he had all kinds of money squirreled away because he was very frugal. So she said he could come home if he promised not to abuse her physically, emotionally, or psychologically again. He promised.

Once home, he was nice to her, no doubt grateful that she didn't put him out on the street. I remember telling her that I didn't want to burst her bubble, but that it wouldn't last and that she should try to find an apartment, because by the time she does, she'll need it. She told me that he had even hit her when she was pregnant. I had been telling her to leave him for about a year. She worried she wouldn't have enough money to leave, to live on. I worried that she had no expectation or hope that she could have a better life. Her mother didn't do too much to make her feel special or worthy. In fact, Sofya was a true Dickstein in one respect. She periodically went months without talking to Alla, same as my father used to do to my mother and me. The silence ended only when an apology was given to my father or Sofya, regardless of who was at fault.

Alla finally got up the courage to leave Yakov for good, and their divorce became final in 2001. Yakov, born March 5, 1935, died on March 3, 2016.

Of her childhood, Alla told me that her first memories were in Saratov, of the war, of the bombings, and of her grandparents grabbing the kids to go into a basement or air-raid shelter. Also during the war, there was nothing to cook. Only cabbage soup, served first to her grandparents, then to her Aunt Cecelia, to the kids last. She said that once she was so hungry, even before her Aunt Evgenia started serving, Alla asked if there would be second helpings.

The apartment in Saratov was big, as was the dining table. Alla remembers one day when her Aunt Cecelia came home from work, the entire family was passed out on the floor. The stoves were running and emitting carbon monoxide because they had run out of wood and were using sunflower seed shells. Cecelia was able to drag everyone outside to save them.

During the evenings, Evgenia crocheted. Once she lost her needle and Alla still remembers how proud she felt because she was the one who found it.

Alla felt some anti-Semitism as a child, when other kids called her "Bomb." She doesn't know where that came from except maybe they couldn't think of anything worse to call her. When she was older, she knew people didn't like Jews, but she also knew that the people where she worked liked her.

I asked about her father. When her family was living in Moscow and she was sixteen, she had to apply for a passport. *En route* to the government building, her mother told her that her father wasn't her biological father, although he was the father of her brother David. Shocked and angry, for several months she wouldn't talk to her mother. It was too painful, she said, that her mother hadn't told her the truth earlier.

Around that time, a young boy came to her apartment and gave her gifts. He said he was her brother. She had no idea she had a brother from her biological father. Sometime later, a friend invited her to go cross-country skiing. The girl then asked Alla if she had a brother or sister, because she had a friend named Weinberg. It turned out that he was the girl's boyfriend, and he was indeed Alla's brother. Alla liked him right away. She thought he was cute and they had a good time together. Eventually he and her girlfriend got married.

During her graduation ceremony from high school, a man sat down next to her, started talking and asked to see her diploma. She didn't know who it was, but later her teacher told her that it was her father. Her father called her shortly before her brother's wedding to ask her to meet him. She was nervous first, then disappointed because he didn't ask her anything about herself, only asked all about the girl his son was going to marry. Alla thought that meeting was one of the major moments in her life. After that, she never saw him again.

Her father's brother called a week before she married Yakov and asked her not to change her last name. She ignored the request.

Yet Alla thinks she would have been proud of her father. She met a woman in Boston named Clara who knew him and said he was a wonderful man and she admired him very much, said he helped people, especially his students.

After Alla came to America, she found her half-sister and brother on the Internet, in Israel. She knew her father had already died, but she had never met her sister. Her father had told the sister about Alla, that she was cute. Alla said they talk about once a

Family

month and that the sister, Nazira Golda Vainberg, lives in Kiryat Arba in Israel and never got married, loves only her cats and dogs. Alla's brother is Alexander Vainberg, also of Israel. Both are mathematicians.

As for Alla, in 1997 in Boston she met a Russian man named Julius Frumin.

They fell in love, moved in together, and finally got married in 2018.

Chapter 22
1991, The Coup and After

*"We have won! By 'we' I mean the people, democracy.
We have witnessed an historical victory of the nonviolence of unarmed people
over the extreme violence of the military and secret police."*
—Igor, 28-year-old activist in Moscow

"Dear Cynthia, As you know, we are free!"
Letter from Zinas Kazenas, Vilnius, December 20, 1991

Police visit US from June 11-18, 1991

In June, ten Soviet police arrived in New York for their part of that year's exchange visit, led by Major General Yuri Tomashev from the Ministry of the Interior.

Two went to the annual meeting of the State Association of Chiefs of Police (SACOP) in Salt Lake City, Utah, where they gave an hour-long presentation on Soviet policing, and addressed issues such as narcotics, youth gangs, organized crime, and their perception of the future of law enforcement in the USSR.

The others were sponsored in New York by Metro North Railroad Police and New York City Transit Police. We attended a one-day conference at John Jay College for Criminal Justice, hosted by college President Gerald Lynch, where they discussed common problems such as substance abuse and white-collar crime. And we saw all aspects of law enforcement and training in New York City. We also met with Chief of New York City's Transit Police, William Bratton, who went on to become New York's police commissioner from 1994 to 1996 and then again from 2014 to 2016. From 2002 to 2009, he was chief of the Los Angeles Police Department.

At the police academy on E. 20th Street in Manhattan, the visitors got to hold and point a tommy gun used by gangster Al Capone. They witnessed an arrest of a fare beater in the subway, who was stunned to suddenly be surrounded by Soviet cops. They went to a baseball game at Shea Stadium and out on patrol with our officers.

And they also got something totally unplanned, unexpected and unprofessional. When six of the Soviets (the others and I were with Metro North Police) and their interpreter went to be received by Transit Department Chief George Latimer, they found him drunk, very drunk. He insisted that they watch Triple X porn movies on his office

Far left, Chief William Bratton; Gerald W. Lynch, president of the John Jay College of Criminal Justice; John Phillips, interpreter; and Major General Yuri Tomashev, USSR Ministry of the Interior

TV. A subsequent investigation of his behavior made the news but as far as I can tell, he received only a reprimand for this. He was, however, although second in command, passed over to be chief when Bratton left. The third in command was appointed to take Bratton's place.

Also in June, Attorney Genrikh Padva, Deputy Chief of the Union of Attorneys for the USSR and Vice President of the International Union of Attorneys, was hosted in Boston by the Quincy District Court at the Kennedy Library for a Soviet/American Symposium on Alcoholism. I attended the reception and was pleased to meet Attorney Padva and talk to him about the work I was doing.

(In 2004, Padva was lead defense attorney for oil tycoon Mikhail Khodorkovsky, the richest man in Russia the year before. Putin, who became president of Russia in 2000, accused him of fraud, tax evasion and embezzlement and he was sentenced to nine years in prison. Putin pardoned him a year early and he immediately left the country to reside in Switzerland, taking his many millions with him. His supporters say he was initially targeted by the government because of his vocal political opposition to Putin.)

July 17– 24
Trucking

One of the wonderful things about my work was that I never knew what new projects might appear, projects outside my experience or imagination. One of those was a request from a Massachusetts tank truck company that wanted to host Russians. The Executive Vice-President read that transportation difficulties was one of the main problems within the Soviet economy and offered a site visit to Certus, parent company of Petroleum Carriers.

The Coup & After

In a month, I arranged for four Soviet visitors from Glavmosavtotrans, the main administration of Motor Transportation, Moscow, the appropriate counterpart for this meeting.

Besides Certus, the four individuals visited Exxon/Shell Oil Company in Everett, Massachusetts, and several other suitable sites. There was, of course, sightseeing and even a typical American cookout.

August and the Communist Coup

In June, Soviet police arrived in the US for their part of the exchange; the Americans were scheduled to visit Russia in September. The two weeks before the American visit were tense, to say the least. On August 19th, Hurricane Bob hit New England and we lost our power. The coup hit the USSR and Gorbachev lost his power. For three days, he was detained and placed under house arrest at his dacha in the Crimea, under orders from eight high-ranking members of his own government, military and police forces. The next day, the plotters issued a statement saying their actions would save the country from a "national catastrophe."

According to the *NY Times*, the plotters had drawn up a list of those to be arrested after the takeover and they emptied Lefortovo prison to make room for them. And, in anticipation, they ordered 250,000 pairs of handcuffs from a factory in Pskov.

During the attempt, state-run airways aired nothing but hours and hours of *Swan Lake*. (I think there is some irony to this, because for the plotters, the coup's failure represented their swan song.)

On August 20, 1991, a letter was sent to International and National Bar Associations from Attorney Genrikh Padva and Peter Barenboim, member of the Board, Union of Soviet Advocates, both of whom were in New York at the time of the coup:

> "Dear Colleagues:
> In this difficult hour of extreme danger for our country and all humanity, we, representatives of the Union of Advocates of the USSR, appeal to you with a call to raise your voices in protest against the illegal attempt by the military-party junta to seize power and destroy the developing constitutional-democratic system. Your immediate and decisive declaration that it is not now and never will be possible to recognize the legality of this seizure of power or accept the authority of the junta may strengthen the resolve of the Soviet people as they face the tanks and rifles now on their streets. Your declaration will help consolidate the opposition of Western governments in the face of this junta. All the same, we hope that this may be averted.

In a few days, since we consider it essential to be there, we will return to Moscow and may perhaps lose for a long time the ability to contact you. For this reason, we are using this final opportunity to turn to you, our colleagues, with a call to support – with whatever means available – the struggle against the reactionary dictatorship which now threatens our country."

During that time period, while the world was holding its breath to see what would happen in Moscow, I got a phone call from there, from Valery, the NESNE interpreter who had become my friend. He wanted to discuss programs scheduled to take place in the fall.

"Never mind that. What about the coup?" I shouted into the phone.

He seemed remarkable calm, not very optimistic for the coup's success, and he told me that the tanks were right outside the Union of Journalists building. Every so often, he would go down to the street, give the soldiers cigarettes and the latest news. The soldiers told him that they were following orders to be there, but that they would not fire on any citizens under any circumstances.

By August 23rd, when it was obvious that the coup had failed, Boris Yeltsin emerged the hero by successfully defending the Russian Parliament building while standing atop a tank. Just as the Bolsheviks had shut down hostile bourgeois newspapers when they seized power, Yeltsin, then President of Russia, the only Russian leader ever to be freely elected, decreed that *Pravda* and other Communist Party newspapers be shut down. Editors of "democratic" papers, several of whom had been NESNE delegates, protested that the suspension of the papers was a violation of press freedom.

Gorbachev returned to Moscow and retained his position as President of the USSR, although he was significantly weakened politically. And many Soviets, with their historic propensity to believe in conspiracies, were convinced that Gorbachev orchestrated the entire thing in an effort to strengthen his position.

Subsequently, with the failure of the coup, the Communist Party also lost its power, perhaps forever. By the end of August, eleven Republics declared their independence.

September 4th to 12th, Police Exchange

The day we arrived, the Soviet paper *Literaturnaya Gazeta* reported that the widow of one of the leaders of the coup, Boris Pugo, died of self-inflicted gunshot wounds. Thirteen days earlier, her husband put a bullet through his head when he learned that officials were coming to arrest him the day after the coup failed. Reports differ on whether he shot his wife first and then himself, or whether she shot herself moments after her husband put the gun to his mouth. Both left suicide notes. She was hospitalized until she died.

Far left, the author. Third from left, Eric Adams

I was convinced that my September law enforcement visit would be cancelled, but I received the visas for the ten police and me, which had been mailed from the Soviet Embassy right during the middle of the coup. I was stunned, and remember thinking that perhaps they figured if we were being hosted by the Ministry of the Interior, we would be in safe hands no matter how the events played out.

I called my delegates, some of whom were quite nervous about going, to assure them that all would be fine. (One of the delegates, Eric Adams, officer with New York City Transit Police, ran as a Democrat for mayor of New York City in 2021 and won.)

I, too, was nervous, but for a different reason. Every day, I worried that something would happen in the USSR that would cause the Soviets to cancel our visas. I didn't care about any chaos while we were there. In fact, I would have given anything to have been in Moscow during the coup, to have witnessed Dzerzhinsky's statue being pulled down from KGB headquarters. If we did end up going, I planned to take my shortwave radio. I knew the Ministry of Interior wouldn't tell us if anything was going on because they knew from past experience that I, at least, would want to witness it.

And regarding the Ministry of Interior, I wondered what changes had been made. Every day, the news carried reports of the dismantling of the KGB. After communicating directly with Deputy Minister Lev Belyansky since 1989, the most recent fax I got which outlined the upcoming program came from someone else, a name I didn't recognize.

We did leave as scheduled on September 4th. And again our accommodations were at the secluded Birch Grove. The City Tour took us first to Lenin Hills, where, for a fee, life-size cardboard figures of Gorbachev and Yeltsin were available to stand beside for a photo. When our bus took us past the KGB, we saw the base of what had been the Felix Dzerzhinsky statue, covered with graffiti, and the old Russian Tsarist red, white, and blue flag flying from where Felix had dominated the landscape (and the country) for so long. The most interesting graffiti at its base said SEX & REVOLUTION. Elsewhere, a statue of Karl Marx, though left intact, was similarly defaced. (A few months later, Warsaw, Poland toppled its statue of Dzerzhinsky in the city square named after him.)

We drove past a demonstration calling for the resignation of the chief of the Moscow police, who supposedly did not denounce the coup, although he did follow the orders of the Moscow mayor who supported Yeltsin. The parade of protesters carried the Tsarist flag, which became the official flag of Russia after the coup attempt.

When we got to Red Square, my group left the bus and I stayed behind to talk to our police interpreter, Alexei. While the soldiers in their blue uniforms were stiffly goose-stepping for the changing of the guard at Lenin's Tomb, he pointed out that there were now two flags flying in the Kremlin, the Russian one for Yeltsin and the Soviet one for Gorbachev. He also said that hours before, Russia had officially become a state, and it was also the last day of the Supreme Soviet. An interim government was created to adopt a process for the election of new Deputies.

I, of course, asked him about the coup.

"It was a very dangerous situation in Moscow those days. There were seven divisions of tanks, 70,000 soldiers. Many Afghanistan vets formed rings to protect the White House (Russian Parliament), although they were unarmed. And ten tanks left to go over to Yeltsin's side. The tension was greatest the first night and into the next day, when it was expected that the KGB would attack. Those special KGB forces later said that they had refused to do it because of the bad feelings that were generated by the violence they had perpetrated in Vilnius, but many suspect that they knew they had no chance of reaching Yeltsin on the third floor. Others say that an air assault had been planned, but possibly the weather was too bad for the Bell 206 helicopters to fly in."

"And why had the architects of the coup not arrested Yeltsin before the takeover?" I asked.

Alexei told me that they had moved to arrest him at his *dacha*, but they had arrived twenty minutes too late. Yeltsin had received word of what was happening and had rushed back to the White House, taking care to follow a different route than usual.

"And what about my police friend, Lev Belyansky?" I inquired, smiling slightly. "What was his role in the coup?"

Alexei smiled back, and told me that Belyansky had gone on vacation the first day of the coup. He was apparently still with the Interior Ministry, but for how long, no one knew.

He pointed outside to the broken pavement in the road and said that was a result of the tanks.

The Coup & After

Finally, he told me that the group of Soviet police who had come to America the past June were paying for 50 percent of the cost of hosting us; the budget for the Ministry had not been revised and did not take into account inflated prices.

The next day, we headed first to 38 Petrovka, where the bust of Dzerzhinsky was also missing. Apparently, there had been some demonstrations after the mayor's order to take him down came from KGB headquarters. The big guys at Petrovka Street police headquarters saw to it that their statue of Dzerzhinsky "went quietly into the night."

I was happy to see Big Sasha, our "keeper" from last year. In the brief welcoming reception, we naturally asked about the role of the police during the coup. They said they had no political role, that their main task was the security of the citizens, and that Mayor Popov later thanked them for their work during those days.

And then, we went to a funeral of one of their police who had been killed on duty. Four police had been sent with warrants to arrest some people known to have weapons. A grenade was thrown. Two officers were hospitalized, one went missing, and the fourth, Captain Mikhail Samoilov, was killed. The captain had only months earlier been appointed to the Criminal Department, and he left behind a wife and two daughters, two and six years old.

Roses, carnations, and evergreens were strewn everywhere and surrounded the open casket. Samoilov's sobbing wife sat beside him and the Moscow police, all in uniform, filed by to pay their respects. We did as well, and then moved off to the side. The walls were draped in red and black, the casket was covered with red cloth, and there was an honor guard. His six-year-old daughter sat near her father, in her grandmother's lap, a hanky in her hand. Between tears and a look of disbelief, she repeatedly pushed aside one lock of hair that kept falling over her eyes.

The highest-ranking members of the department took turns standing at the head of the casket, until General Bugayev said a few words. Anatoly Yegorov, Colonel and Chief of the Moscow Criminal Investigation Department, the leader of my first Soviet law enforcement delegation to the US in 1990, also spoke, as did the victim's father. The general thanked his American colleagues for being there, and Captain Al Kenwood, the head of our delegation, went up to the family to express our sympathy.

At the close of the ceremony, we went outside. A regular bus was waiting to carry the body and a band was waiting to play. Also outside was old friend and suspected spy Little Sasha, Alexander Bouzykin, Major in the Criminal Investigation Department who took part in our first police visit to the USSR. He clearly had been drinking. I would have liked to have gone to the cemetery to witness the entire ceremony, but we were ushered off to eat. No matter what we were doing or wanted to do instead, we always had to eat!

After lunch, a visit to the Metro Police, where we were greeted by a Colonel Valdayev, Deputy Minister of the Interior. A tour of the Metro stations before they hosted us for a very good dinner at the Praga Restaurant. Vodka, caviar, and octopus (a first for me in the USSR), then fish and potatoes, then ice cream. Followed by many, many toasts. Finally, the Soviets began to sing. We could not respond in kind, until, desperate, we came up with "99 Bottles of Beer on the Wall" and a very weak version of "When the Saints Come Marching In."

During the singing, three of my guys decided to sneak out to go dancing in one of the restaurant's other rooms. One of them was spotted leaving with a young girl. Suddenly, there was a mass exodus from our room. Our guy was led in, flanked on all sides by Soviet police. Valdayev handled it very well, I thought. He slapped his American friend on the back, laughed with him, but clearly gave the message that he was to stay with the group. In an attempt to keep us happy, but more importantly, keep us in the room, someone brought in an accordion player so that we could dance a little. I suspect we would have done the same had the situation been reversed, but somehow there it seemed as if we were under "friendly" arrest.

When we finally got back to our hotel, Big Sasha was waiting for us and several of us got together with him for a drink. He told me that Belyansky would most likely be out of power because he had been KGB and very active in the Communist Party. Bogdanov, part of the "old guard," had already "retired" a few months earlier.

The next morning, I went off by myself to the Rossiya Hotel to meet Attorney Genrikh Padva. After our meeting in Boston, he contacted me to express his interest in an exchange of criminal lawyers. He brought with him two other lawyers (both Jewish) and we discussed his proposal, which I thought was a good one. He was quite well-known and was in fact defending one of the suspected coup plotters, Anatoly Ivanovich Lukyanov, the past chairman of the Soviet Parliament.

"Lukyanov is sitting in prison writing poetry these days," Genrikh said.

According to Masha Gessen in her 2012 book, *The Man Without a Face, The Unlikely Rise of Vladimir Putin*, Genrikh Padva was "possibly the country's (Russia's) most famous defense lawyer." He was quoted in *Newsweek* on May 11th: "Our legal system was in place for more than 70 years. To make it democratic overnight is not possible."

After our meeting, I went off to the Arbat to do some shopping. I bought two creative political nesting dolls, one with a rat (which symbolized Communism) held in various states of health by each leader. Another one of Gorbachev holding both the Soviet and the American flag. I purchased both in dollars, violating Law #88. The kid from whom I bought them made me walk far away from his stand, and then he approached me with a bag. I had him put it at my feet, spoke a few words with him, then shook his hand, at which time I passed him the $75. I thought we were so nonchalant.

The Coup & After

Just like on TV. But I suspect all the undercover cops there witnessed the whole thing and had a good laugh at our expense.

While I was going about my business in the city that day, Gorbachev declared the independence of the Baltics. And Leningrad voted to once again be St. Petersburg.

The city had been founded in 1703 as Saint Petersburg. It became Petrograd in 1914, Leningrad in 1924, which it remained until the fall of the Soviet Union.

From *Democracy, A Journal of Ideas, Spring 2012, No 24 Book Review of "Moscow, December 25, 1991: The Last Day of the Soviet Union* by Conor O'Clery, the following:

> **According to Michael Dobbs, author and former Moscow bureau chief for The Washington Post, Gorbachev's election coincided with a collapse in international oil prices and a sharp decline in Soviet oil production that was itself the result of grossly inefficient extraction methods. The fact is that Gorbachev had very little choice when he decided to launch perestroika. If anything, he was acting far too late. ……Gorbachev's economic blunders did more to hasten the end of the evil empire than anything Ronald Reagan could possibly have devised.**
>
> **Even years earlier, in a review in buzzflash.com of "After the Empire" by Emmanuel Todd, written in 1976, Thom Hartman validated Todd's prediction that the USSR would fall and said "the USSR rotted from within. Hindsight tells us that Reagan and Bush had nothing whatever to do with the fall of the USSR. In 1979, Todd had written "The Final Fall, On the Decomposition of the Soviet Sphere", where he predicted the downfall of the USSR based on, among many things, demographic studies, living standards and infant mortality.)**

As before, Big Sasha invited me to his home for dinner. All looked the same, although Vera seemed to have lost a little weight. No surprise, because by the summer of 1991, food was in very short supply, which made this dinner invitation even more special. The children were blowing bubbles with bubblegum and kept tapping me on the elbow each time they blew a particularly big one. Then Nadia proudly showed me a Barbie doll, which she had named Cynthia. You can only imagine how I felt at that moment.

But the next morning, I turned on my TV and saw something that angered me—the inane preaching of American Pentecostal televangelist, Jimmy Swaggert. Looking, no doubt, to see how many people he could mislead in this country and get to donate their hard-earned money to him and his scandal-ridden ministry.

Then, I met Valery and he took me to the Barricades of the White House. I took photos, and even got a big stone piece of the barricade to take home, where it serves as a paperweight in a prominent place on my desk, as a reminder not only of that day, but of all my days in Russia.

Nearby, red spots in the road marked where the three young men killed by troops in armored personnel carriers during the coup had fallen in an underpass near the US Embassy. Graffiti on a wall, written in white, said "August 1991 Eternal gratitude to you boys." I learned that one of those boys was an artist and was Jewish, and that the funerals were religious, in a church and in a synagogue.

Valery told me that when the coup began, since there was no regular programming on all state radio and TV stations, many found out about the coup by watching CNN or listening to *Voice of America*. Valery's wife was scared, and didn't want him to leave their apartment. She cried, demanded that all letters from foreign friends be destroyed, along with business cards and a videotape recorded when he addressed a Rotary Club in Defiance, Ohio. He had told the audience about the difficulties in getting food in Russia and how so much is rationed by the government.

"Get rid of all of them if you love me and our son. You know how these people act. I do not want you to end your life in a camp."

He didn't destroy them, but bundled them up and hid them.

Valery told me that he thought Gorbachev had grown a bit in stature since the coup, that people respected him a little more

Next, across from Gorky Park, we went to the House of Artists, just below the very elegant hotel of the Central Committee of the Communist Party. It was there that all the mutilated and dismantled statues were thrown. Solitary and almost surrealistic sat the bronze head of Gorky. Farther away, placed together on the grass in no specific order or design were Stalin, Dzerzhinsky, Kirov, and Sverdlov. Dzerzhinsky had a red carnation sticking out of his nose, which someone quickly pulled away as I went to photograph him. Stalin and Dzerzhinsky had been vandalized, spit upon, defaced with paint. I found the vandalism troubling, and even Valery was uncomfortable with it. After all, he said, "It is history." I agreed, but then neither of us directly lived through what those men had wrought.

* * *

But in 1991, the city of Moscow fixed up the damaged sculptures, put them back on pedestals, fenced in the area previously known as the Park of the Fallen Heroes or the Fallen Monument Park, and proceeded to create a sculpture garden, which was officially named the Muzeon Park of the Arts. It now has over 700 sculptures. And no visible signs anymore of the people's anger.

However, almost half of Russians want the statue of Felix Dzerzhinsky returned to its former home on Lubyanka Square, in front of former KGB Headquarters, now headquarters of the Border Guard Service of Russia. Located there since 1990, instead of Dzerzhinsky, is the Solovetsky Stone, a monument to the victims of Soviet political oppression.

Valery dropped me off at the Rossiya and at 5:00 PM, as previously arranged, I met David, Alla's brother, who was with Mark (Segal), the cousin I met last fall. They took me directly to Alla's mother's apartment. Mark's wife Dina, David's wife Natasha, and a cousin Bronya were also there. We ate, drank, laughed, exchanged gifts. And in typical Dickstein fashion, everybody talked at once. I clearly was with family and I loved every minute of it.

The next morning, I heard on the BBC, on my shortwave radio, that China had recognized the independence of the Baltics.

I then left to meet with N. Brushlinsky, director of the Fire Safety Foundation in Moscow, which had approached me a year earlier with a request for an exchange of

David Khilkevitch, Alla's half-brother

firefighters. There were ten men waiting outside the building when I pulled up, with the standard bouquet of flowers. We ironed out details of their visit to the States to take place the following month.

And the day after, we became the first US police to ever be hosted by the Moscow Railroad Police, and they gave us a very special day, beginning with peach gladiolas, then a tour of the newly renovated Paveletskaya Station, and ending with, of course, dinner. We were met inside the dining room with the traditional hospitality of bread and salt, watched over by the portrait eyes of Lenin and Gorbachev. The RR Chief, Major General Anatoly Romanov, took me aside and proposed that we expand the police exchanges to establish one with the railroad police.

Because I had to leave early for another meeting with Valery at the Union of Journalists, I missed a private concert by the Red Army Choir, which I later heard was wonderful. Besides the choir, there was a solo balalaika, and other soloists sang with simply piano accompaniment. All was in Russian until the choir ended the performance with "God Bless America" in English.

I gave Valery some money in appreciation for all the help he had given me over the years, not only for NESNE, but for OASES also. He in turn asked if I wanted a large dry point of Lenin that had hung for years in the Union of Journalists offices. I was thrilled with it and because I always brought a mailing tube with me to the USSR, I wasn't worried about it getting damaged on the way home. I wish it were signed so I would know the artist, but I framed it, and it has hung in my office ever since.

Even as I write now, Lenin is looking over my shoulder.

Then, smiling, Valery told me that someone in Moscow had told him that I was with the CIA. We both had a good laugh! I had no idea then that in the not-too-distant future, I would have an experience with the US government, an experience that didn't make me laugh at all.

When I got back to my room, it was only 7:30 PM. I was happy to have the time to wash and set my hair, to spread all my work out on the bed, and to get myself organized a bit. Around 10:00

Portrait of Vladimir Lenin
(1870–1924)

PM, there was a knock at my door. And there was Big Sasha, with a gift for me, a beautiful book on the Soviet Union, in English. I had to invite him in and there we sat in my tiny room, he not so tiny and I in my huge rollers and flannel nightgown. Finally, I suggested he go to the lobby so that I could get dressed and I would keep him company while we waited for my group to return. There went my early night.

But, it was worth it. My guys returned carrying all the colorful samovars, which were our gifts from the railroad police, and I found a tiny tiger kitty wandering around the lobby. She settled right into my arms, went with me when we all settled in one of the guy's rooms for a nightcap, then happily with me to my room, where she looked around and without hesitation jumped up on my bed and curled up for the night.

Newly found kitten

That cute little girl slept with me all night. Every time I moved, she moved with me so she could cuddle, and her little paw would inch up over my arm. In the morning, I turned on the TV and coincidentally, there was a show on cats and we both sat on the edge of the bed watching it. I put her in my blue canvas bag and took her to breakfast with me and told my guys I desperately wanted to bring her home. After imagining all possible scenarios, and listening to them strongly advising me against it, common sense won out and she and I said our goodbyes. I was probably more upset than she; her main concern at that moment seemed to be to find a place to go to the bathroom.

The morning's excursion was to the ten-year-old MVD (Ministry of Internal Affairs) Museum, where at the time there were 640 names on the walls of police who had died fighting crime, two of whom are buried in the Kremlin. The police department was established on November 10, 1918, and one room had old photos of their first days in different regions of the country. Other rooms had stories of spectacular or especially lurid crimes, or profiles on dogs or fire departments, old uniforms and weapons. One of my guys, Bob Matusick, gave the curator a plaque from Florida's Volusia County Sheriff's Department, which she said she would place in the display case with the police patches and memorabilia from other countries.

As I got dressed for dinner that night, I got to thinking that this visit wasn't as much fun as the last one. The group of Soviets was too straight, maybe too preoccupied with politics, or perhaps it was the deaths in their department. They had lost five that week. One of the officers, who had been in the hospital from the grenade attack that killed Samoilov, died and they found the missing man from that attack buried in the woods. As if that wasn't enough, a traffic officer died in a car accident and yet another was killed in a fire.

At the farewell dinner, Little Sasha came in and was drunk. Again. Apparently he was having a difficult time with the deaths, since they were his men. For some reason, I was happy to see him, and I felt bad for him. Plus, he and Big Sasha were our only two old Soviet friends there. Little Sasha sat down, but kept falling into the person next to him. One of my guys and I walked him out to his car. It took both of us to hold him up. We were happy to see that he had a chauffeur for his white BMW. The year before, he had a Mercedes. As best I could tell, he had escaped any fallout from the coup.

Back inside, we passed out our group gifts, the Sony Walkmans and batteries that I had purchased, and our hosts hastily left, saying they knew we had to pack and get up early. I got the strong feeling that we were an obligation, unlike past times when we couldn't get them to leave until it was the middle of the night and the vodka was gone. Of course, my group wasn't that amusing either. Everyone was fine, but the group dynamics just didn't translate to fun. No bonding, no solidarity, no one to make us laugh.

I looked for my little kitty, but couldn't find her, so I slept alone.

At the airport, my cousin David and his wife Natasha were there to see me off. So nice of them. Customs was no problem, and then we all went to the bar for a beer. (Only in Russia would I drink beer, which I hate when it is cold, let alone warm, at 10 o'clock in the morning!)

Surprisingly, the Aeroflot flight to Helsinki was comfortable. I sat next to Scott Lowenthal and we discussed a possible exchange program for training purposes, to give the Soviets some help in protecting themselves. One statistic I heard was that the US lost about 20 police on the job per year. The Soviets lost about 300.

So, what had obviously changed? There was food everywhere I went, but of course I didn't visit poor people. I did, however, see many people begging on the Arbat. One of the Soviet police told me that the gypsies went to orphanages or hospitals, bribed the caretakers, and took babies for a day so that they could use them to elicit sympathy. They could make up to 150 rubles a day doing that.

And the signs of capitalism were ever more present. Pizza Hut and McDonalds of course, the gambling casinos, people selling their own artwork. Some healthy signs, some not so wonderful. I thought that I almost would rather see pictures of Lenin and Communist slogans on the billboards than all the advertising I saw on the way to the airport. Hyundai, Goldstar Audio and Video, Korean Air, *Business Week, Reader's Digest, Economist Magazine, Sunkyong* (a Korean newspaper), and more. And I wondered how long before Moscow had its own tacky Route 1.

Many people were very insecure about their jobs, certainly those who had been Party members. It was almost like a witch-hunt, reminiscent of our own McCarthy era, and everyone was busy proving that he was on the correct side during the coup and pointing fingers at those who might not have been.

There was no sense of euphoria over the victory of democracy, only worry about the future. Russians have traditionally had a desire for benign authority, probably because of their fear of chaos and anarchy. And crime was still increasing rapidly— organized crime, criminal gangs, drug trafficking, illegal currency transactions, racketeering, robbery, theft and fraud. Guns and bodyguards were commonplace. People were afraid to walk their dogs at night.

And I think back of how often over the years I hitchhiked and took rides in the middle of the night back to my hotel!

* * *

The biggest question, of course, was "where would all this lead?"

The *NY Times* reported that organized crime was demanding protection payments from 70 to 80 percent of private businesses. Organized crime had better communications equipment than law enforcement. An economist, part of President Yeltsin's administration, recommended the establishment of an elite anti-crime unit, with no one hired who had worked in the old Interior Ministry, including our Law Enforcement Program host, because of his past involvement in illegal activities. And Paul Goble, a member of the State Department, was quoted in the June 1994 issue of *Atlantic*

Monthly, where he said, "We're going to see the rebirth of a Russian state that will be highly authoritarian, and will use organized crime as an excuse."

As we now know, former Communist officials allied with organized crime made millions of dollars for themselves, much of it from selling former state property for huge profits. Most of the power of organized crime came from its connections to the government and the Party. And then came Putin, former KGB, who began his looting from the country long before he took office.

Democracy in Russia never had a chance.

First Firemen Exchange Program, to New York, Nebraska, and Boston, Oct 18 – 25

General Rubtsov headed up the delegation. Four of the twelve Russian delegates were ranking Soviet officials with the command staff at Chernobyl. They went to New York City and Boston fire department headquarters, and two visited the Central Florida Fire Academy in Orlando. While in Boston, they saw the National Fire Protection Agency in Quincy and had a site visit to the firefighting facilities, with demonstration, at Logan Airport.

Funding was provided by equipment manufacturers and vendors, and Fire Captain Paul Calderwood from Everett, Massachusetts. Paul had from the beginning expressed a keen interest in the exchanges. I appointed him OASES Fire Service Consultant, and worked closely with him as he gave generously of his time and money to ensure that successful exchanges were able to take place. He went on to become Deputy Fire Chief in Everett as well as a national and international lecturer on fire and life safety issues.

NESNE, October 15 – 29

The ten Russian delegates flew into New York City for the ninth conference since 1982. They had a meeting and lunch at the *New York Times* the next day, as well as some sightseeing. And then the usual visits to host newspapers in New England.

At the conference in the dining room of the *Boston Globe*, NESNE was told that Soviet editors who had supported the coup were excluded from the Union of Soviet Journalists. This had the effect of breaking up the Communist Party's control of the press.

There were a lot of questions about the coup and how it affected Russian journalists. They replied that censorship was lifted and that there was optimism about the possibility of a free press in Russia. One editor felt that the coup failed because the younger journalists were not so fearful, didn't have as much anxiety as the older ones.

Another said that NESNE and this exchange had already influenced their history. Later, as they talked among themselves, NESNE delegates expressed their opinions about the influences of the exchanges. Several thought that they laid the groundwork for glasnost; others disagreed. While I didn't think our program was causative, I did believe the exchange helped glasnost establish itself in the country. And the exchange and the subsequent relationships that were established between delegates certainly assisted our papers in their coverage of Russia, which became more personal and much better informed.

At the close of the conference, the delegates asked themselves "What next?" Should the exchanges continue? Their visit ended with a question mark.

OASES Journalism Tour, November 4-13

It was November 6, 1991, less than three months after the attempted coup in Moscow to bring down the Soviet Union's President Mikhail Gorbachev. The group leader was Steve Riley, from the *Portland Press Herald*, and one of the participants was Alabama newspaper publisher, Terry Everett.

And the calm, thoughtful man I was interviewing was Eduard Shevardnadze, who had been Gorbachev's Minister for Foreign Affairs of the USSR and who, after leaving that position, had founded a Movement for Democratic Reform. In an ironic interview, he recognized the importance of a people believing in their leader.

Eduard Shevardnadze and the author

That November, and during that interview, I had no way of knowing that in less than two months, President Gorbachev would resign, that in four months, Shevardnadze would leave Moscow to participate in the political arena of his native Georgia, one of the USSR's former republics, that in four years, almost to the day, Shevardnadze would be elected President of the country, and that on November 23, 2003, twelve years after my interview with him, Eduard Shevardnadze would be forced to resign as President of Georgia.

That day, I was at a round table with Mr. Shevardnadze, who had granted an interview to my small group of ten visiting American journalists. Seated beside me in a gray suit with a vest, a blue silk tie and black ankle-high boots, no wedding ring, no gold teeth, the 63-year-old Shevardnadze's most striking feature was his thick, white hair, (which earned him the nickname "Silver Fox") and his most striking characteristic was the slow, measured, somehow reassuring manner in which he responded to questions.

I asked the first question. "Was President Gorbachev in any way involved in the coup?"

"Just at the time of the coup, I declared to the press that if President Gorbachev had sanctioned the coup, he was a criminal like the other plotters. If he was unaware of the coup, it is unclear to me why he was not allowed to talk, even if he was sick. And actually, I had some suspicions right afterward that he was mixed up in the plot.

"But I met with the President often after his return to Moscow after the coup, and I came to the conclusion that he was not mixed up in the plot. However, he had many dire warnings that the coup was inevitable. As president, he could have prevented it. I criticize him now and will continue to criticize him for this miscalculation."

My next question: "How would you predict Mr. Gorbachev's political future?"

"It depends upon the destiny of the USSR. If we preserve the Union, he probably has a future; if the USSR disintegrates, the only thing left is for him to write his memoirs."

Others in the group also had things to ask.

"What is your opinion of Yeltsin?"

Shevardnadze: "Yeltsin has enormous standing as a political leader today. He is courageous, a man of principal, you can trust him, and you can deal with him. And most people in Russia believe in Yeltsin and that is very important for a leader."

"Do you have any interest in becoming part of the new Russian government?"

Shevardnadze: "I give advice to the President, so if I have deep and clever thoughts, I can realize them. And my work now is very important. We are trying to set up a new democratic reform movement. Life will show that all honest people here have a responsibility for the country and the people and must work to prevent civil war."

And finally, "Do you anticipate that the Movement for Democratic Reform will become a political party?"

Shevardnadze: "Probably in several years, we may register as a party. For now, we prefer this type of organization of the movement. The attitude of all Soviets toward all parties is very skeptical after the collapse of the Communist Party. The status of our movement allows us to build good relations with other democratic movements in the Republics. This is very important. Our final purpose is the creation of unilateral democratic space in the USSR, meaning that all Republics of the Soviet Union will be ruled by democratic parties and governments."

After collaborating with other democratic organizations, the Movement for Democratic Reform lost several elections, and subsequently the party disappeared a few years later in 1995.

* * *

It had only been two months since my previous visit to Russia. The sun was out and the day was not too cold when we arrived in Moscow, but it was all downhill after that. And we initially had no idea that an audience with Mr. Shevardnadze was on our itinerary; it was listed only as a "surprise visit." Had I known we had a scheduled meeting with him, I might have been more tolerant of the fact that we had to carry our own luggage a long distance to the entrance of the Journalists Resort home where we were staying, and it took a long time to get our room assignments straightened out.

After a quick mid-day dinner, we all were anxious to get to our rooms to nap. I took a shower first, down the hall, and thought I was out of hot water until I realized the red knob was cold and the blue was hot. It was hot, but it was also smelly. When I emerged from the shower, I discovered that my room was locked. There was no lock on the door, but the handle and latch had somehow jammed and as I stood there in my flannel nightgown, shivering, soap and underwear in hand, two repair men tried to fix it. They succeeded after about ten minutes. When I finally did get to take my nap, I was so cold that I wore my coat to bed, and even with two blankets, I froze. I dressed for supper with long underwear under my dress. But there was one wonderful moment. Bob Marley's "Buffalo Soldier" came on the radio and I danced as I put on my makeup. One of the last songs I'd expected to hear in Russia.

I think all of us were so tired we were on automatic pilot. But I later found many blankets in my room, with a little note saying they were for whoever was cold in Room 214. That was nice. And the cold one, of course, was me.

We had many meetings with many officials during our ten days in Russia, and opinions were split regarding the coup, who was behind it, who supported it. Were Gorbachev and/or Yeltsin involved? The role of the KGB then and now? But one thing was clear; there was anger at Gorbachev. Food lines were longer, the economy poorer, life harder.

Again, I found myself and the group meeting with the KGB. Again, our host was Major General Karbainov. We asked a lot of questions and we got a lot of answers. How many of them were true was anyone's guess. If he didn't want to answer a question, he'd begin by saying, "That is difficult to know. Or "That is a difficult question". But when asked what the KGB was doing to protect domestic dissent, that apparently was not a tough question because he immediately and emphatically said "The priority of the organization is to provide and protect human rights." He went on to say that before the introduction of democracy, the state was most important, followed by society and then at the bottom was man, totally dependent upon the state. Democracy turned everything upside down and now man was at the top, society second, and the state at the bottom."

How could he possibly believe that we believed that?

That night, while listening to a ferocious wind batter my windows, after I learned there was no hot water for my shower and that the elevators were ridiculously slow, after repeated attempts to use the phone seven floors down, after I killed a cockroach headed for my bed, I chose to have dinner from my suitcase. Peanut butter crackers, honey-roasted cashew nuts and V8 juice.

The high point of the next day was a big, bright colorful billboard on a major street advertising M&Ms! And, I bought another *matryoshka* nesting doll, the likes of which I never expected to see. A Boston Red Sox one, with different uniforms for the years 1908, 1921, 1931, 1939, 1977, 1992. Perfect gift for Frank.

However, I had an excellent dinner the following night at Big Sasha's home, as always when I went to Moscow. While eating, we discussed Yeltsin's decree regarding price increases. I almost cried as Sasha talked about his concern about providing for the children and the difficulties and fears that he and Vera had.

Author visiting Big Sasha and his family

He also told me all the gossip regarding the Ministry of the Interior. Almost all our old pals from the various police exchanges were gone, or demoted, or pending demotion, including Belyansky. The new chief was someone named Mirashov and the second in command was none other than Anatoly Yegorov, who had been involved in these exchanges since the beginning.

And I had a wonderful visit one day with General Rubtsov at his office. He was so pleased to show me two big display cases, the first with the OASES logo and photos from my firefighter's delegations' recent visit to Moscow, and in the second case, my name and photos from my visit to this office in September. I, too, was pleased, to see the photos, and especially the OASES logo displayed so prominently.

He offered cake and when I politely declined, he insisted, stating that it was made by the same baker who provided pastry for Reagan's visit to Moscow. Of course, I gave in, not that I ever need an enormous amount of persuasion to eat sweets, and it was very good.

He told me repeatedly how much the Russian delegation enjoyed their time in the US. A few of them were hosted by the Central Florida Fire Academy and were present in Orlando, Florida the day the city demolished its government building, footage of which was used in the filming of the movie, *Lethal Weapon 3*. Since then, I have had a photo hanging in my office of two of the Russian firemen standing with Mel Gibson (whom I used to like until he started to talk).

The general also told me how much they were looking forward to our next visit in May. As if to prove it, he handed me the official invitation for the delegation, along with a preliminary program for the week and a very big smile, while clearly looking for my approval. He was a very sweet man and unlike many of the higher brass, he didn't hide behind his rank; he expressed pleasure over small things, and in fact seemed to be very genuine.

Then, it was November 7th, the first time in all the trips since my first in 1980 that I had managed to be in Moscow on that day, and the first time since 1941 that there were no displays of military might in Red Square during the annual parade. Not much happened in the Square, but there was a very large demonstration in front of the KGB at Lubyanka Square (no longer called Dzerzhinsky Square). We heard loud speakers and musicians, saw Russian flags and women holding candles. A member of the City Council spoke in memory of those who died during the years of repression. Another blamed all problems on the fact that the Bolsheviks had turned their face from God. Candles flickered as people repeatedly crossed themselves.

During all the condemnations of the KGB, Bolsheviks, Soviets, etc. a woman was selling 1992 calendars with Lenin's picture. The crowd was very rough with her and made her leave. Obviously the concept of free speech wasn't fully understood yet.

In between meetings, I got to go to the Bolshoi again, for a performance of *Tosca*, and to see Alla's brother David again. I thought he was coming to the hotel only, but he took me to his apartment. Natasha served a big lunch. I was already fond of David, but I fell in love with their little white twelve-year-old dog. Somehow, with David's little bit of English and my tortured Russian, we managed to communicate. On the drive back to the hotel, he volunteered that he had been a member of the Communist Party, which was the only way to succeed in one's job, and that he had quit two years earlier.

Minutes after David dropped me off at the hotel, Larissa N., a woman I had met on one of my women's programs a few years earlier, came wearing jeans and white boots and took me to her apartment, which was right on the Moscow River, just up the street from the Russian Government's White House. Her apartment was very impressive, probably the nicest I'd been in in the USSR—two large rooms, kitchen and bath, and modern because she had spent many months remodeling it before she moved in. The walls of one of the rooms, her library, were adorned with icons and for the first time, I noticed that she was wearing a cross very visibly around her neck. She also insisted on feeding me and serving tea and vodka.

She wasn't happy with the situation in the country, believed that Gorbachev was involved in the coup, and said that Shevardnadze was lying when he said he believed otherwise, since in his book he had indicated Gorbachev's involvement. She had no confidence in Gorbachev or Yeltsin.

One thing of great concern to her was the fact that there were no medicines in the hospitals, no food there, not even sheets. In addition, she told me people had figured out a way to take the medicine from the ampules and replace it with distilled water in a way that no one could tell. So when a person was sick, the doctor prescribed an injection, then waited hopefully for a response from the patient to learn whether there was actually medication in the vial.

She was also discouraged about the morality of the people. "Even during the worst times during WWII, there were no children on the street. Now you see many abandoned children and animals."

Then, out of nowhere, she volunteered that she had never been a Communist, that she rose to her position because of her work as a lawyer and senior criminologist. I wish she hadn't said that, for two reasons. Because frankly, I didn't believe her and because I didn't care if she had been a Communist. Probably most of the people I knew in the country were Communists, and I understood why. Her saying that was a betrayal of trust somehow, was somehow a statement that we were not good enough friends to be really honest. Of course, I didn't know for sure that she was lying, but I seemed to remember that when we met, she said that she was a loyal Party member. It didn't matter to me which was the lie; it mattered only that there was a lie.

I remember thinking that maybe I should be more forgiving, more understanding of the current situation, and more cognizant of the fact that she might not exactly trust me, might wonder who I really was. After all, I had been going to the country at that point for eleven years. But my experience up to then was that nobody trusted anyone, and when there, you end up thinking like they think, questioning everyone's motives. And it has been like that since the tsars, so one can't blame it exclusively on the Bolsheviks or the Communists. My father and his siblings didn't trust anyone either.

When Larissa learned I soon had a scheduled meeting with Genrikh Padva, the attorney, she told me about the three organizations of attorneys in Russia before she drove me to the appointment. The Association of Soviet Lawyers was the oldest and hated by all. Newly organized three to four years earlier was the Union of All Soviet Legal Professionals, headed by an ex-member of the Central Committee, also hated by all. Finally, there was Padva's organization, the Union of Soviet Advocates, separate from the other two, made up of only Jews, and active with the American Bar Association. Larissa said that this group was the most aggressive and because of their personalities, they also were not liked at all.

I frankly thought I detected a bit of anti-Semitism in her statements, then wondered if I was simply exhibiting the same signs of paranoia the Russians had. I didn't know if she knew I was Jewish.

Genrikh was waiting for me out in the street, since his apartment, located in the oldest district of Moscow, was difficult to find. Padva's home was impressive, too, but in a totally different way from Larissa's. It was clearly the home of an intellectual, full of tables piled high with books and great artwork on the walls. I was immediately drawn to contemporary paintings by Natalia Nesterova, to her allegorical symbolism of trust and mistrust. Genrikh told me he was related to her through marriage.

Of course, I had to eat yet again. Tea, coffee, brandy, vodka, candy, cookies, pastry, all served on beautiful old porcelain dishes, some of them from Tsarist Russia days. During my visit with him and the two young attorneys he wanted to send to the US, I brought them up to date on what progress I had made with the exchange (which wasn't much actually; I was still waiting for responses to my letters), and I mentioned Larissa N. and who she was. The three were guarded in their comments about her and I did detect a raised eyebrow or two.

Well, as Galileo said, "All truths are easy to understand once they are discovered; the point is to discover them."

* * *

The train ride to St. Petersburg was fine, and in each compartment, the usual activity for these rides—a lot of eating, drinking, talking about other participants, and then, with luck, a little sleep.

We stayed at the Hotel Leningrad, in the city that was now called once again St. Petersburg, after the recent name change. Our first visitor was Dmitri, whom I called "my tee-shirt guy." He met all my groups and designed the tees-shirts to reflect the program, took orders for sizes and quantity, then returned with them a day or two later to sell them for $5.00 each. One of my participants asked him how he got the shirts to print the designs on.

"Better you don't know," he answered.

Then he laughed and revealed that he pays someone at a factory to designate a quantity as flawed or damaged, and then he gets them. Business as usual! But if all the new entrepreneurs were as creative and charming as Dmitri, I wouldn't worry a bit about this country's capitalist future.

Our first meeting for the group was with the Leningrad City Council for Ecological Problems, where I learned that the major problem was cleaning the industrial wastewater and the drinking water. I already knew that, since all visitors to the city are always told they cannot even brush their teeth with Leningrad water, but I didn't know that the equipment for drinking water was installed in 1894! Other problems were the processing of the toxic industrial water, radiation security, keeping the city clean of mercury, keeping the city free from oil and oil products, and waste from autos.

We then had another meeting with the St. Petersburg City Council of People's Deputies and its chairman, Alexander Belyaev, one of those who defended against the coup. He discussed at some length the economic problems and then said that while the situation with medicine was not critical, it was not up to standards. Meanwhile, Larissa had also told me that there was not even aspirin available for a simple headache, let alone more important medications.

(But, there were Hare Krishnas in the usual orange garb chanting in the street. First time I'd seen them there. And by April of 1991, the Jehovah's Witnesses were registered in Russia.)

Belyaev told us that the coup hadn't really caused any unrest in Leningrad and that the municipal authorities actually found out from the radio what was happening in Moscow.

Again I asked the question "Was Gorbachev behind the coup?"

He replied that they never accuse anyone here before investigating, but "I greatly doubt that he was involved in any way in organizing the coup. His political stand and his position and attitude to the right could have contributed to their activity, to create the illusion that the President would help in case of their victory."

I made my rendezvous with Sasha that evening right on time, 7:00 PM, the Astoria Hotel Park, as usual. Opened in 1912, the hotel was a jewel of the city. But its history was more impressive than its beauty. After the Russian Revolution, it housed members of the Communist Party. In 1919, Lenin spoke from the balcony. It served as a hospital during the Siege of Leningrad and was featured in the James Bond movie *Golden Eye*. And Hitler had planned to have his victory dinner at the hotel when the city fell, which of course never happened. I liked it that with our meetings there in the Astoria Park, Sasha and I created our own bit of history, a secret history that belonged to only us.

Sasha had three red carnations for me and we went immediately to the Balkan Restaurant on the Nevsky Prospekt. Over dinner, he told me he thought Gorbachev was definitely behind the coup, and that all people expect Yeltsin to be the next leader.

We met a few more times. At the Literary Café, I asked to be seated in the room with the violinist and pianist. There, looking out the window we could see umbrellas bobbing by, and looking up, the huge chandelier with bronze leaves and glass birds that represented the restaurant's old world charm. It moved ever so slightly when someone walked under it. Where else but Russia would one have vodka, caviar, mushroom soup, and tea for lunch?

And one evening we attended a performance of *The Nutcracker* ballet at the Bolshoi, before we went to the Hotel Astoria for dinner. Finns had renovated the hotel, and sadly, the grand staircase in the lobby was gone, replaced by a generic square space, totally without any resemblance to Russian design. The dining room was without warmth or charm, the food just mediocre. However, the three shots of vodka we each had went a long way toward making us not care.

And toward making him open up more about himself. His father drank, used to hit his mother, and Sasha had little luck when he tried to make him stop.

I asked him to tell me again the story of when he was in jail, because I wasn't sure I got all the details the first time. I remember when he told me the story before; he was very anxious and made me swear not to tell anyone, since he was clearly still afraid then of the authorities. This time, it was just a story.

Relaxed, we parted at the Union of Journalists, remembering past goodbyes when we were both nervous about his being seen with me, when it was dangerous to be in the company of foreigners.

I also had a lovely time with Nina A. this visit. Her mother had made a pastry just for me. She was 84 and I asked Nina if I could adopt her as my grandmother. I had fun playing with their dog, Micky, too. Nina wanted an invitation to the US ("it's a secret," she said) to meet a man who likes her, a veterinarian named Warren from the Midwest.

The next day, we went to the Consulate together, so that I could drop off her invitation. Hanging there were, of course, large portraits of President Bush and Vice President Quayle, grinning down at everyone,

Nina and I had time for coffee and caviar in a nearby cafe, and as we sat, something prompted her to tell me the story of her childhood, a story she said she had told no one else. She stressed how much she has had to lie.

"My father had been an engineer who travelled often to Germany for his work, which aroused suspicion. During WWII, he was arrested and accused of treason and within a short time, my mother was told he had been executed.

"She remarried a man with a daughter four years older than me. During the Siege of Leningrad, when returning home from school one day, I saw our home bombed. My stepsister was shot and killed. Among about 1.3 million evacuees, mostly women and children, I was evacuated across Lake Ladoga's Road of Life, the only way in or out of Leningrad.

"Because my family had ties to nobility, which would make me a less desirable citizen to the Bolsheviks, and because of the political nature of my father's death, when we returned to Leningrad, my mother decided that I should assume the identity of my dead stepsister, which I did. After doing so, I was again evacuated, this time to the south with most of the Leningrad children. With all the chaos that the war brought, no one knew about the identity switch.

"Some years later, my father turned up alive and married. When my stepfather died, my father said he would divorce his present wife to remarry my mother, but she said no. I never told my first husband or even my son about having switched identities with my killed stepsister.

"I believe that because I kept this secret, I have lived under a curse, which has prevented me from finding happiness."

She did express the hope for some happy moments, such as during her proposed trip to the US to see Warren.

When I met Nina, she was very active in the Leningrad Regions Women's Council and a professor of Education at the Teacher's Training Institute in Leningrad. She had also taught for 15 years in subarctic Murmansk. She wrote and published poetry, and served for a time as the head of the Russian Federation of University Women.

Once, while walking on the Nevsky Prospekt, she spoke about a woman I knew from past professional meetings in Leningrad. Of her, Nina said, "She loves only herself, and then only once a year." I actually had to stop walking because I was bent over laughing. It must be one of those Old Russian sayings, because it sounded so much like something my Aunt Ida would have said.

I was fortunate to have time for another private evening with my cousin Mark. I didn't realize it was going to be a party of sorts, with his wife Dina, his son Leonid, Valery Monokhav from the Herzen Institute, Alla's mother Sofya and our cousin Bronya, and two of their friends from Purdue University. I politely passed on the fresh eel, but joined in with all the toasts, and then surprised everyone, including myself, by being able to speak a bit in Russian with Sofya and Bronya. I looked around, still not quite believing that five of those faces belonged to my family.

Finally, after all those years, I got my passport stamped leaving the country, something they never did. I was almost ashamed of how I did it, giving the guy what I hoped was a coy look and a big smile when I asked. He was nice. It worked!

Uncharacteristically, the Finnair people were less nice and the man who checked me in insisted that I check one of my two carry-ons. It wasn't locked and things were stolen: my cassette recorder, brandy Sasha had given me, and a few souvenirs. Luckily I had taken out my film. Theft was becoming a big problem, but that was actually the first time I had anything taken in Russia.

Shortly after I returned home, a few events.

Nina A. did come to the US to see Warren. I met her in NY, in front of Carnegie Hall, and she arrived beautiful as ever with her wonderful, wrinkle-free creamy skin and her unique bushy eyebrows, in a silver fox hat with a matching collar on her coat. Over lunch at the Trattoria Dell'Arte, she told me of her time with Warren, told me he was a little stingy, a little messy, but sexually, very much a man.

"I was enriched. I fell a bit in love," she said.

Some years later, within several months, Nina's mother died at 96 in 2004, Warren died, and her cute dog Micky was hit by a car and died. In a long letter to me, she wrote of her despair, said she now had no one. She turned to her friends—and her poetry.

* * *

I heard Pulitzer Prize-winning journalist Harrison Salisbury, the first *New York Times* regular bureau chief stationed in Moscow after WWII, speak at a NESNE conference, and he expressed a fearful prediction of a return to fascism in Russia.

On December 25th, having lost his power and influence to Boris Yeltsin, Gorbachev resigned. Gorbachev, who thought he was helping the Communist Party. Who wanted a socialist state that worked for the people. Who allowed unprecedented freedom of speech and the press to report on corruption. Who freed Andrei Sakharov from exile. Who ended the war in Afghanistan. Who ended up dismantling the totalitarian empire. Who launched the beginning of a free-market democracy and became the darling of the West.

On December 25th, the Soviet flag was lowered for the last time, replaced by the Russian flag.

There was no more USSR.

The thought never crossed my mind that I would ever write those words. I watched Mikhail Gorbachev's farewell speech on TV at Renee's house in Binghamton, watched as he gave up his power and his position as president.

> "We are now living in a new world. An end has been put to the Cold War and to the arms race, as well as to the mad militarization of the country, which has crippled our economy, our public attitudes, and our morals. The threat of nuclear war has been removed......We opened ourselves to the rest of the world....I am positive that sooner or later, someday our common efforts will bear fruit and our nations will live in a prosperous democratic society. I wish everyone all the best.......I consider it vitally important to preserve the democratic achievements which have been attained in the past few years....."

Chapter Title

We witnessed a peaceful transition of power, rare for a nation.

Many to this day, both Americans and Russians, give Ronald Reagan and his Star Wars program credit for the demise of the Soviet Union.

If I may, that is much too simplistic.

Back in 1945, in *Foreign Affairs Magazine*, American diplomat George Kennan predicted that the USSR would lose power, because it bears within it the seed of its own decay…..and should the Communist Party give way to infighting…..the chaos and weakness of Russian society would be revealed in forms beyond description.

In November of 1982, American intelligence analyst Herbert Meyer stated: "The Soviet Union … is comprised of more than 100 nationality groups and dominated by the Russians. There is not one major nationality group that is content with the present, Russian-controlled arrangement; not one that does not yearn for its political and economic freedom. It's hard to imagine how the world's last empire can survive into the 21st century except under highly favorable conditions of economics and demographics – conditions that do not, and will not, exist."

> **January 7, 1991, first time since 1917 that Orthodox Christmas was celebrated as an official holiday, with a Christmas tree lit in Red Square.**
>
> **Boris Yeltsin banned *Pravda*, but it published under different ownership until 1997 when it was taken over by the Russian Communist Party's Central Committee.**
>
> **Eduard Shevardnadze became Foreign Minister again.**
>
> **It was widely reported that there had been two top-secret government orders issued after the Chernobyl disaster: All information on the extent of the radiation contamination was to be kept secret and there were to be no medical diagnoses connecting illness with radiation exposure.**
>
> **It was revealed that on the night of August 23-24, the statue of Felix Dzerzinsky was toppled by five heavy-duty cranes, accompanied by the cheering crowd. It certainly symbolized the end of an era.**
>
> **During the August Coup attempt, carried out by hardline Communist officials, the KGB, and the military, Vladimir Putin was still a KGB officer.**
>
> **On December 1, in the filled-to-capacity conference hall of the Kremlin Palace of Congresses, Moscow Jews celebrated Hanukkah.**

Chapter 23
1992—Glubokoye

*"When we illuminate the road back to our ancestors,
they have a way of reaching out, of manifesting themselves...
sometimes even physically."*
—Raquel Cepeda (1973–)
American journalist
From *Bird of Paradise: How I Became Latina*

May 18th to 26th, 1992 Second Part of the Firefighters' Exchange, US to USSR
Moscow, Tallinn and Leningrad

Chuck Ramsey, a physicist and fire safety specialist with the US Department of Energy, went to Russia as a delegate on this program. Because in the planning stages, the Russians had asked questions about nuclear safety, and accidents caused by fire and explosion and their prevention, I had contacted DOE and asked them if they wanted to send a representative for this important exchange visit. During that visit, Ramsey got an invitation to visit the nuclear power plant in St. Petersburg. He also heard from Russian officials that they "would be willing to discuss our use of their orbiting space station."

I had planned to go for this first meeting, but couldn't because I got a sinus infection. Ramsey reported back to me and DOE that although each country's fire departments were similar, the 60-year-old Moscow Scientific Research Institute of Fire Protection had no peer, in the US or elsewhere. "More than in the US, firefighting in Russia is viewed as a courageous and honorable profession with broad public safety responsibilities, including nuclear safety when accidents occur."

Other delegates reported seeing no fire hydrants, and no fire poles to slide down to get to the trucks. Just the stairs. There were no women firefighters, although they were allowed to be dispatchers. But most interesting to hear about was the night that two members of my delegation actually responded to a fire. They smelled smoke in their Leningrad Hotel room around 4:00 AM, looked out their window, and saw a fire in a garage across the street. They raced to the desk clerk and made sure he called the Fire Service, then ran to the site, where one climbed a 10-foot wall with barbed wire so they could warn and evacuate all the residents of an adjoining building threatened by the fire. All this 15 minutes before the Russian firefighters arrived, earning my guys a Russian Fire Service Medal of Valor.

July 6th to 20th, 1992—Combined Fire and Police USSR Visit Moscow, Minsk, St. Petersburg, Helsinki

Our group was small. Four police and nine firefighters, with two repeats from my police trip of 1990. But this group include one extra-special someone, my grand-niece Tambi. The trip was my high school graduation gift to her.

I wasn't sure if Tambi was excited or nervous in anticipation, but she got a taste of Russia immediately when we checked into our hotel, the Leningradskaya. It was one I actually liked very much, very Gothic, with much more character than the average Moscow hotel. When we got to our room, Tambi sat on the bed. It immediately broke and she dropped with it to the floor. Once we stopped laughing, we got our room changed. Perfect introduction to Russia. I had always told my people to be flexible and to expect the unexpected.

Good hot cereal for breakfast the next morning and then a visit to the Kremlin for a tour of the three cathedrals. There weren't as many tourists as usual and not nearly the military presence in the city as I had always seen in the past. Most impressive for me in the churches were the jasper floors and the coffins of the tsars, the oldest from the 1300s.

While we shopped at the Arbat, we came across a young girl playing the violin, with a small dog in a hat sitting in her violin case. Having played the violin for so many years, I of course wanted to give her some money, but I wanted it to be in dollars, so I shook her hand and passed it to her that way. She accepted it very graciously. We also ran into a woman begging. When we ignored her, she became angry and swore at us. Then she spit at us. Charming! Luckily she missed.

Two months earlier, a sex shop had opened in Moscow, the first of its kind, with sex toys—some battery-operated. Sexy lingerie, condoms, and ointments lined its shelves. I didn't take Tambi there.

That afternoon, we had our first professional visit to the Fire Technical Institute, where a Professor Brushlinsky waited outside to greet us. The Institute is the oldest fire school in the world, established in 1906. After WWII, it became a part of the Ministry of the Interior, currently turning out only officers.

We toured their museum and I was particularly moved by one exhibit behind glass, displaying an old helmet and a nozzle used during WWII at the Hermitage. Alongside it, in memory of the one-third of the school's faculty killed in the war, stood red carnations, a red star, and the inscription "No One is Forgotten."

1992—Glubokoye

That evening, Big Sasha came for Tambi and me in a new militia car, to take us to his home. He had become a major and was quite proud that he, unlike those of lower rank, could thus carry his gun with him while off-duty. Once again, it was a great evening. Vera's dinner was delicious. My favorite part, of course, was the dessert—coffee mousse cake with cherries. I was disappointed that Tambi didn't get to meet Nadia and Dima because they were away at camp.

The next day, Tambi and I first went to the National Aerobics School to meet with Olga Ivanova, founder and director, to discuss my upcoming fitness exchange, then to the Union of Journalists so I could talk about OASES programs. When we caught up with the group, we went to the Fire Research Institute, and then to a fire and rescue station. General Rubtsov met us, presented me with roses, and while the group toured the station, he and I had a short meeting.

After a few hours of rest time for the group back at the hotel, General Rubtsov sent his car for me, along with more flowers. We had tea, I met his wife and we talked further about the exchange. They invited Tambi and me to live in their house all summer, any summer, so that we could learn Russian. They would move into their *dacha*, they said. Lovely, lovely people.

More tea and pastries at the Praga Café, where we met Natasha's daughter, London, who was visiting Russia. Tambi had met Londy eight years earlier, the year Natasha died, and they hadn't seen one another since. Tambi and I then did some of the usual sightseeing before we promptly arrived at Manezh Square to wait for Big Sasha.

We heard the buzzing of the helicopter before we saw it and when it landed in the square, everyone in the streets watched as we ran toward it and got in. It was new, blue and white, one of two 7-seat US Bell 206 helicopters the Ministry of the Interior had recently obtained. It was quite impressive and we felt quite important. It was Big Sasha's idea to give us a tour from the air; it was a beautiful day and fantastic to see the rooftops of the Kremlin.

Unfortunately, Tambi, who faced backwards in her seat, started to feel sick and was afraid she would throw up, so we landed after only a half hour. Once on the ground, she felt better and we went for yet more tea, to the Paradise Restaurant, part of the Hotel Moskva. Unfortunately, that tea was expensive because I left my Armani prescription sunglasses there.

I met again with Genrik Padva to further discuss the proposed exchange program for criminal lawyers. Padva said it was on hold until he could find the money to fund it. He was very interested to learn that I had family in Russia (probably also interested to learn that I was Jewish, since he was as well). I asked again how the defense of the oligarch Lukyanov was progressing and he simply stated that it was a lot of work and going slowly. (Anatoly Lukyanov, considered by some to be the leader of the coup, was never convicted.)

The next day, Sofya, David, and Natasha visited us at the hotel and we were able to spend some time with them before we went with the delegation to the cemetery where the Chernobyl heroes were buried and where we knelt and gently placed flowers at their graves.

Three of my firemen spent the night at a fire station and rode with Russian firemen, the first time that had ever happened in Russia. That made the Moscow nightly news.

While in Moscow, we learned that anti-Semitic violence had increased during the spring. Jewish cemeteries were desecrated. A synagogue had been set on fire. Also, with the Soviet welfare system collapsing, childcare was being dismantled, making it more difficult for women to work.

The next leg of our journey was to Minsk, via train. Minsk, where Lee Harvey Oswald lived from 1960 to 1962 and worked in an electronics factory before he immigrated to Texas. The following year, he appeared in Dallas on that fateful day when he assassinated President John F. Kennedy. The Russians who knew him said that he was so incompetent he could never have planned and executed the act alone. There are many other theories about what happened that day. Maybe we will learn the truth when all the documents are someday released. Or maybe the truth is already out there. Or maybe we will never truly know for sure.

I relaxed, knowing that I had done most of the groundwork for my upcoming programs. And I was very excited to be in Belarus, because we were about to embark on a very special excursion—for me, the highpoint of this time in Russia.

Mark came from St. Petersburg to take Tambi and me to Glubokoye. Unfortunately, it took us four hours to drive there, instead of the normal two, because the President of Romania was making a visit to Khatyn, the memorial to the 2,230,000 Belarusians who were killed during WWII, to the 186 Byelorussian villages completely destroyed, never to be restored, and to those that were burned and later rebuilt. Consequently, all traffic had to be rerouted and then pulled over to the side so that his caravan could pass by.

We waited in a parking lot for the vehicles to pass, and ended up talking to some Byelorussian men from Glubokoye. When I mentioned that my father had come from there, they were a little more friendly, and when it was time to get back on the road, one of them kissed my hand. I thought immediately of my father's story of having to kiss the hand of the wealthy landowner of his childhood every time he met him. One generation later, and my hand was being kissed.

When we finally reached Glubokoye, we noticed hammer-and-sickle signs hanging from light posts. Mark stopped to ask two military lieutenants where the old Jewish cemetery was. One answered sarcastically, "Only the Jewish cemetery?" Mark told them that there were Americans in the car who had come to pay respect to their ancestors, and the soldiers immediately became polite and helpful. One, whose shirt had

1992—Glubokoye

come undone, revealing his big belly and its big belly button popping out, came over to the car window and asked if we wanted to meet a very old Jew.

He directed us to Yakov Rabinovitch Pelkin, who fortunately was at home.

Yakov was not what I would call very old, only 67, his hair graying, but he was the oldest Jew in Glubokoye. With a population then of 20,000, he told us that before WWII, there were about 11,000 residents, half Jewish, almost half Polish, and the remainder White Russians and others. When the Germans came to the ghetto, armed Jews fought them. Consequently, the Nazis set the ghetto on fire, killing 5,000.

But he said even the poor enjoyed life in the town back then, before the war. There was a gymnasium (high school), a Jewish private school, and several religious schools. He himself went to the Hebrew school when he was a child. In 1921, Glubokoye became a part of Poland and then in 1939, it was annexed to Soviet Belarus.

Yakov Pelkin and his wife Frieda at their home in Glubokoye

Yakov began speaking with Mark in Russian, but soon switched to what Mark said was wonderful Yiddish. We sat at the table with him and his wife Frieda, next to a refrigerator with a black transistor radio on top, and a light green sewing machine under a window with lace curtains. And they told us about Glubokoye.

Only about 500 of the town's Jews survived the war and their descendants lived in the US, Israel, or Argentina. (According to the *Encyclopedia Judaica*, only 100 Jews of Glubokoye survived the Holocaust.) Only fifteen Jews were living in Glubokoye when we were there, and Yakov was the only one who had been born there. He remembered no one named Dickstein.

It was our good luck that he was the keeper of the over-100-year-old Jewish cemetery, which we walked to from his house. The cemetery, surrounded by a strong wrought-iron gate paid for by a wealthy Jew from Glubokoye, who then lived in Dusseldorf, sits on a hill above Lake Berezvetsher. Yakov unlocked the gate and we were able to walk around inside and to see pieces of the destroyed tombstones, some more than 150 years old, with their faded Hebrew inscriptions, surrounded by overgrown, knee-high grasses. Before the war, he said there were beautiful pine, fir, and birch trees, all destroyed when the Nazi soldiers forced the Jews to cut them down. They first made the Jews break down the fence with their own hands, then to tear up and break the tombstones. With those tombstones, the Germans paved sidewalks and built a theatre in Glubokoye.

There was a market just across the street. I wondered if it was the market my father always went to, and was the cemetery the one that frightened him so much as a child?

As we walked a different route back to Yakov's house we passed the Russian cemetery, so striking in its contrast to the Jewish one. Well-maintained, ornate, full of plants and flowers. I preferred the Jewish one, in spite of its disrepair. Peaceful, it stood in quiet condemnation of the past.

Along the road, slow and squeaky horse-drawn wagons and small, squat automobiles shared the streets with dogs and cats, and ducks parading in a straight line. Old wells with dirty brown water and old women with floral scarves and gold teeth lined those streets. In the distance, fishermen in boats sat in solitude, lining the shore of the lake.

Yakov asked us to stay for tea and coffee. Maybe we wanted dinner, and then we could all watch TV together? Unfortunately we couldn't stay longer because we had to get the car back.

"*Zey gazunt*, Be healthy," he said as we left.

I would have loved to have had an entire day to wander through the town, but was of course grateful for the few hours we did have.

The twilight moon was full when we left, and beautiful, as was the countryside surrounding Glubokoye. The field grasses were waves of green and red, and sheep, cows, and goats dotted the landscape. Since my father had told me they had lived about a mile from the center of town, I began to wonder about those old wooden houses we passed on the outskirts. Could any of them have been his old home? I smiled, because I pictured him as a child, in front of each one, playing.

The next day, our excursion was to the Khatyn Memorial. The word *powerful* doesn't do it justice. In March of 1943, a German division entered the village and punished people for the actions of partisans. They ordered all residents, including women and children, to come out of their homes. Placed them all in one big barn. Set fire to the barn. People tried to break down the doors and a few did get out, but they were shot immediately. Only five children survived, one because his mother fell on top of him when she was shot. The rest were able to hide or escape. The youngest child to die there was two weeks old.

A very tall, very imposing monument was erected in the late 1960s in memory of a blacksmith, a Josef Kaminsky, who, with half his body burned, found his eleven-year-old son alive and raised him in his arms. However, the boy didn't survive.

1992—Glubokoye

Twenty-six homes were memorialized, with only a chimney and a bell at every one. A bell rang every 30 seconds. A sculptured Tree of Life had engraved on it every village in Belarus—433 of them—that was burned during the war and then rebuilt. Some were burned and rebuilt five or six times.

For those 186 villages that were not rebuilt, there was a separate section, a sort of cemetery of villages, where the name of each destroyed town was listed. Alongside the names, a container of soil in a black urn, one from each place, rested on a square red platform.

The following day, we went to another memorial, the only Jewish monument in the city of Minsk, unique because it was engraved in both Russian and Yiddish. It was dedicated to the 5,000 Jews who were killed in Minsk on March 2, 1942. I insisted we go there, and our guide had some difficulty finding it, so clearly it wasn't a popular tourist spot.

After that, a professional meeting, where my group said that fire prevention was more advanced in Minsk than in the States. Some shopping, time to wander a bit, to take a cab to a church so that I could light the candle for Natasha, then dinner.

On the overnight train to St. Petersburg, Tambi and I joined Mark in his private compartment. We ate, drank, laughed, and he taught us dirty words and curses in Russian. I remember them still.

I also remember the trains with fondness—the familiar smell of coal lighting the samovar, the diesel fuel, the noise of the wheels on the tracks. When I could, I stuck my head out the windows, like a dog in a car, to feel the wind gusting against my face, to get a whiff of freshly cut grass and hay, to see the life of rural Russia roll by with its swimming holes, gardens, and campfires beside fishing spots. That night, there was even the bright orange of a distant forest fire, a problem that summer throughout the former USSR.

After we said goodnight to Mark, Tambi went to play poker with some of the guys in the group. And she won!

Upon arrival, a city tour. Of course. I remember thinking that some day I should read through all my journals to see if the info on each tour was consistent and correct. That day, the guide told us that:

- Five million people had lived in St. Petersburg before the war.
- 640,000 starved to death during the war.
- There were 365 bridges in the city.
- Twenty-two drawbridges were up between 2:00 and 5:00 AM.
- And there were over three million exhibits in the Hermitage Museum.

Paths of Stones

When a country undergoes the kind of upheaval Russia has, there are good changes and bad changes, important changes and less important changes. For the first time in Russia, I found M&Ms to buy! An important change for me.

The St. Petersburg Fire Department showed us a video of the fire at the Leningrad Hotel in February of 1991. There were 700 guests who got out, 230 of whom were rescued by the fire service, and two who survived a jump from the seventh floor. But there was a backdraft and flashover, which resulted in the deaths of nine firefighters, seven hotel guests, and one policeman. Sadly, the firemen did not have high enough ladders to reach the upper level floors.

A month before our visit, *Pravda* reported on June 16:

> "Last year, more than 7,500 people in Russia died a fiery death and about 65,000 suffered burns and other injuries. Every year, more than a million of our fellow citizens lose their housing as a result of fires…..In the Ministry of Internal Affairs system, fire protection has always been financially and materially neglected."

We also went out on patrol with police from St. Petersburg. After asking for my permission, our car took Tambi and me to the River Neva, where a body had been fished out of the water. The police thought it had been floating about a week and that it was probably a drug-related murder, since the male torso had no arms, legs, head, or genitals. Not the usual experience an aunt provides for her niece.

On a happier note, she and I later went to the Astoria Hotel for my 7:00 PM rendezvous with Sasha. He was there, soaking wet since it was raining quite hard. He immediately got a cab for us to go to the Nevsky Prospekt and the Polyarny Restaurant. We warmed up with champagne and brandy, listened to a pianist who played "Hava Nagila," and talked politics. Sasha was especially worried about the fascist leader Zhirinovski, from Crimea, who ran against Yeltsin and got 1½ million votes, and who advocated a return to the Russian Empire. There was fear in the Ukraine that its 20 to 30 million Russian residents would want to join Russia. Some were even worried about nuclear war between Russia and the Ukraine. (In 2014, Putin invaded and occupied part of Ukraine and annexed Crimea. In 2020, Russia again attacked Ukraine. By 2023, Putin was still on the attack, targeting civilians' homes, schools, and hospitals.)

After dinner, we took the Metro to Kolpino, close to Pushkin, where Sasha was staying with his sister-in-law. It was farther than we expected, but when we arrived, we were greeted with more vodka, champagne and food, gifts, and her grandson who had suspicious-looking bumps all over his face. They looked a lot like chicken pox, which Tambi had never had, but they assured us the bumps were mosquito bites. We left around 1:00 AM in a private car that Sasha hired to take us back to the hotel. (When we got back to the States, not only did Tambi have wonderful gifts and exceptional memories, she also brought back a unique souvenir: chicken pox.)

The next evening, Sasha met us again at the hotel, but this time with a serious hangover from the night before. He took us to the Kirov, called then the Marinsky Theatre. The first part of the program was classical, the second choreographed by Judith Jamison. One short ballet was based on a Chagall painting of Russian village life, but my favorite was the five sequences based on Rodin sculptures, the same ones we had just seen at the Hermitage during the city tour. After the performance, we had dinner at the Literary Café.

I wish I had known then that it would be the last time I would ever see Sasha. In years to come, he would struggle to get settled. When I met him, he had already graduated from the Institute of Foreign Languages and spoke not only English, but also Swedish and German. He taught English for two years in the north of Siberia to local kids. Since then, he spent time in Gagra as a tour guide based in St. Petersburg and eventually ended up working with a timber company in the town of Tikhvin, 120 miles east of St. Petersburg. His letters didn't usually reveal much, a lot of weather reports and kind wishes for my well-being and happiness. He did tell me that his younger brother, a 28-year-old doctor, married with a daughter, died of a disorder of the spine. And he told me of reading a lot of Carlos Castaneda.

But in a letter of July 1996, he wrote to share what had been happening with and to him.

> *Dear Cynthia,*
>
> *At long last your letter with the article about me in the* Cape Cod Times *reached me here in Priozersk, and I really enjoyed it. Thank you! Now I must tell you about an adventure.*
>
> *It was nearly one year ago that I decided to visit Gagra in the summer. There was an invitation to work as an interpreter for the UN Mission. As soon as I arrived, I applied to them at their headquarters near Pitsunda, at the Samshitovoya Rotscha Sanitarium. After filling out the questionnaire, I was told I would be contacted. While waiting for the new job, I used to dive for mussels, catch fish. I led a rather idle life.*
>
> *My house was all right, the weather was fine, the sea was warm, but what was unusual was the lack of people everywhere: empty beaches, empty streets, empty houses. Many people, mostly the youth, perished in battles, the majority had left before the military operations to go to Russia or Ukraine, etc. One could meet rare persons in the afternoon, bearded, with a strange look in the eyes, often armed with automatic guns, and drunk.*

Paths of Stones

Compared to Sukhumi, Gagra was not damaged except for broken windows after bombing attacks. Christ's words came to mind: "The divided Kingdom is to be left and devastated." Once a tourist paradise, Abkhazia turned into hell. Paradise without love becomes hell. The King of Hatred reigns there – hatred toward the Georgians.

During the war, I also was recruited to the Abkhazian army, though I managed to avoid it by leaving for Kiev. Later the Abkhazians let me know that I was like a traitor. So one day, I was asked by a gang of those patriots, when they found me on the pier, to "come into the car." They drove me to a remote desolate place along the shore, took me down to the basement of the water-supply building, where I saw a gallows waiting for me. When the rope was tight, they loosened it a little and put a pen into my tight hand. They told me to write down what they dictated, which was approximately the following:

That I had no right to live in Abkhazia since I had not fought for its liberation, and had not helped financially. Moreover, and I do not remember this exactly, I was either a debtor to someone or committed burglary.

So I promised verbally to return all the debts, and by talking, I weakened their vigilance and escaped. My first direction was the mountains. Three days and nights I went towards the Russian border. It took me so much time because I chose the wild in the mountains. One night I spent near the border, the river Psou, when some heavy beast made much noise around midnight. Like Tarzan, I whistled, clapped my hands, and the animal went away.

What made me nervous while crossing the border was the latest news of military outposts along the border with Abkhazia to defend against the Chechen rebels, who penetrated there from Chechnya, then crossed the frontier back to Russia to go on fighting. The roaring river would make it impossible to hear anybody cry out or shoot.

But also there was luck because I crossed the river in the daytime at the broadest place. My friends in Sochi were glad to see me safe and sound, and after a week of recovery, I left for Kiev. This ordeal is very important for people like me, careless in this life. So now you know in short, straight from the horse's mouth, the story of one of many refugees now in Russia.

I now live in Priozersk, near Lake Ladoga, about three hours ride from St. Petersburg. I work doing translations for a Swedish timber firm and teach English at the local secondary school. I moved to Russia, leaving behind my small house in Gagra, Georgia, in order to get Russian citizenship. In Ukraine, as a citizen of the former USSR, I would have had to wait up to five years. Here I will get it in a week. Also I will receive about $2,000 in rubles as an interest-free loan for ten years, eligible because I am now a refugee.

1992—Glubokoye

I am well now, and only wish that I could go visit my daughter Mary in Kiev in July. I rent a room, enjoy jogging in the morning, swimming in Lake Ladoga. Now it is the time of the White Nights. Last night, I could not close my eyes, it was very light (or maybe it was because of strong tea?). It is now also midnight and I write to you sitting by the window, with only the outside light.

Thank you for thinking about me. I hope someday I will be able to see you and return my debt in person. I wish you health, beauty, happiness, and success with your writing.

Happy Birthday, many happy returns of the day.
Yours,
Sasha

In other letters, he spoke about how difficult it was during the war in Abkhazia. (In 2008, after bombings in June in Sukhumi and Gagra, as well as other places, in July Abkhazia closed its border with Georgia and in August, it became a sovereign nation, recognized by Russia, but few in other nations).

He wrote how bad the Russian government was even under Gorbachev. About corruption, red tape, and bribery required to do construction on his modest home, and how hard it was to find work. About the devaluation of the ruble, but the smell of big money in Moscow. In his opinion, "Russia for me is like a sinking Titanic."

My last letter from Sasha came in the autumn of 2002. He had written regularly until then, never forgetting my birthday, never forgetting to enclose that small dried flower in the envelope, often a Lily of the Valley, and always encouraging me to write a book about my Russian experiences. Since then, nothing.

When I learned his email address in 2019, I emailed him several times. Received one brief reply, saying there is nothing new to report and then, three years later a photo of him with no text. Every year, I send a brief greeting at New Year's and on his January birthday. Still no real response. I know he is ok, because we have a mutual friend who is in touch with him. And so I am left to wonder. What happened?

* * *

Mark picked Tambi and me up the next morning after breakfast, to drive us to his *dacha* in the town of Systroyvets, about thirty kilometers from St. Petersburg. Along the way, we first stopped at a market, and then a train station to use the bathroom. We were faced with stalls with no doors, and with a porcelain bowl in the floor with metal feet beside it, all the better to help you squat. We did what we had to do, barely breathing, and got out of there quickly. I think it is a bit of an understatement to say that Tambi was mortified.

Mark got stopped for speeding twice, but escaped trouble by telling the policemen who I was and that I was in the country as the leader of a police exchange.

The *dacha* was impressive and located in what looked to be a wealthy area. Mark had designed it and built it himself, with some help. Dina made a delicious dinner, and Mark and I went through our family trees, compared what we knew of one another's families. And I was happy to see his son Leonid again, to walk around the neighborhood with him, and to meet his white angora cat who was roaming freely and seemed to be enjoying the outdoors.

Back at the hotel, Tambi and I played gin rummy and ate more M&Ms and cashews. I took a shower at midnight, since there was hot water then. There hadn't been any in the morning for several days.

Dinner the next night was with Nina A. Nina had a boy, the son of a friend, who she kept trying to fix Tambi up with. Tambi had refused already, but when Nina asked if she could have him join us, Tambi graciously, and I could tell, reluctantly, said "Of course." She was worried about what they would talk about, but they managed quite well and it was mainly Tambi's voice I heard during their conversation.

Our ride back with a private citizen we hailed on the street was 50 rubles, or the equivalent of 33 cents. If I had paid in dollars, the rate would have been at least $3.00.

After some shopping the next day, the group had an excellent guide for the Russian Museum. I took Tambi to the Grand Europe Hotel, formerly the Evropayskaya Hotel, for our farewell dinner. It was the only five-star hotel in Russia, a joint venture with the Swedes. The building had served as a hospital during the war, and then had become a desperate, dilapidated place to be. In time, though, with renovations, it regained its elegance.

Tambi and the author in Moscow

* * *

To bed late because of mosquitos, or what I thought were mosquitos. I learned the next morning that what I felt dive-bombing my head, what I tried to swat away repeatedly, was

1992—Glubokoye

Tambi and the author in Moscow

Tambi impersonating a mosquito. No wonder she was laughing so hard before we fell asleep.

The movie on the flight back was *Backdraft*, about firefighters in Chicago. How appropriate! I anxiously read, as always, the newspapers and *Time* magazine. The dissident Lev Timofeyev was quoted in an article about the loss to emigration of Russian's most intelligent people. An article in *Time* stated that Moscow had 8,000 registered unemployed; by winter they expected to have 60,000.

As always, I wondered when I would return next to Russia, how many more trips would I make, and what further events would unfold there. Each trip was interesting and exciting, but having Tambi with me, taking her to Glubokoye, made this one extraordinary.

That was the last of my four years of law enforcement exchanges. I was unable to get funding for the Russians' return visit in 1993, primarily because of the ongoing investigation of Transit Police Chief Latimer's behavior with the last delegation of Russian police. Also, with the breakup of the Soviet Union and the introduction of reforms, Americans' desire to go to Russia wasn't as strong. It was seen as less of an adventure.

I have to say I truly enjoyed getting to know not just the Soviet police, but the American delegates. John Damino, one of the delegates from Albany, invited me to his precinct, where not only did I go out on patrol, I also participated in an interactive training exercise where I was faced with a video situation that may or may not require me to shoot. I was judged by the appropriateness of my decision, how quickly I responded, and how accurately. It gave me much insight into the difficult situations police are so often put into, the split second decisions they have to make.

And travelling with them was fun. They had amusing and astounding stories. I was, however, correct in my initial assumption—only one of them didn't believe in the death penalty.

* * *

From June 4th to the 10th, two Russian police did come to the US to participate in the Durham, NH SACOP (US State Associations of Chiefs of Police) conference. When I went to Russia the following month, I took two bulletproof vests for them, made to their measurements, gifts from their American counterparts.

Journalism Program, August 23rd to 31st

As I mentioned earlier, one of the delegates in my journalism program in Russia in 1991 was a newspaper publisher from Alabama. Terry Everett wanted to return to the USSR as a leader of a journalism group, so I worked with him to create a program. He took 13 people he knew for a nine-day visit to Moscow and St. Petersburg, which I did not accompany. That fall, he ran as a Republican against Democrat George Wallace, Jr. and won a seat in the US House of Representatives, a position he held until 2009, during which time he served as the Republican head of a House Veteran's Affairs Subcommittee.

September 16th to 20th
Aerobics Exchange
Sunday, September 13th

I thought it might be fun to do something less serious in Russia. I asked my personal trainer, Robert Montague, if he would be interested in conducting classes there. He was. The original plan was for him to go by himself, but when Reebok responded positively to my request for their sponsorship of the Aerobics Exchange, I decided this was a program that could grow and thus I should accompany Robert.

Frank and I picked up Robert *en route* to the airport. The Finnair flight was comfortable, and Helsinki was fun. The day was beautiful; there was time enough for a quick walk and a very nice lunch at a restaurant called Kronig. During lunch, Robert asked me how it felt to know that I was with him the first time he was ever out of America.

Back to the day room at the Hotel Vakkuna for a nap and shower before we had to return to the airport. The Aeroflot flight to Moscow was fine; we had a very easy time through customs. Olga Ivanova and entourage were waiting with flowers for both Robert and me. They put us up at the 1984 Olympic Village because they had 280 people signed up for Robert's classes, not only from all over Russia, but from all over the former USSR, all excited to take classes from an American.

Our rooms were just ok, and actually, my bathroom was quite pathetic. Not clean, the worst I had ever seen in Russia, but complaining was not an option.

Tuesday

With the help of one of Robert's strong muscle relaxer pills that he took for his back, I got a decent night's sleep. But the next morning, I had no hot water, so I padded down to his room to shower there. Before breakfast, he and I took a short walk around the track just outside our building, and after breakfast, we got a quick tour of the facility, which was pretty run down. At least the room in which Robert was to teach was more than adequate—big, and with lots of light.

After lunch, we went to the Kremlin and Red Square, did a little shopping at the Lenin Hills, went to a food *beriozka* to get bottled water, and were back in time for dinner with Olga and her friend and business partner at the National Aerobics School of Moscow. Then it was off to the gym to meet with the Reebok people who sponsored Robert, a drink in Robert's room and finally, some quiet time and a chance to get a real good night's sleep.

Wednesday

His teaching began the next day. Russian TV and print journalists came to cover the classes. Robert's funk aerobics class was a big success, as I knew it would be. He lectured in the afternoon and then Olga taught Robert and me Russian words, for body

Robert Montague (bottom left) and the Reebok Fitness group (author, bottom right)

parts. He put in a lot of effort planning his classes, tried to learn as many Russian words as possible, and was easy and charming with everybody.

The next day went by very quickly. Classes, then lecture and practice groups. Robert continued to be superb, and presented a wide range of information about dance, Laban movement, rhythm combinations, and spatial movement, as well as the weight training, funk aerobics, and relaxation.

At one moment I had, as I did often with different projects, the recognition that I was experiencing my professional reward. I looked around at all those expectant, enthusiastic faces, people anxious to learn all that Robert had to teach them, anxious just to have his autograph, enjoying the dancing. There were 225 students, all women except for six or seven men. He would bring pleasure to their lives for five days, and enrichment, for, I hoped, many years.

Each morning, I put my head outside my window to see if the little orange kitty who wandered the grounds was still there. She didn't disappoint.

Strange, sometimes in the dreariest moments in Russia, I was struck with how much I loved the country. The people reminded me of the little flowers that somehow manage to grow up between the cracks in the sidewalk, with so little room and so little nourishment, yet the spirit peeks through.

Americans asked me always what I thought would happen there. I told them honestly that I didn't know. But I did know Russia's history, and I was very afraid it would repeat itself—maybe not Communism, but a strong dictator could certainly emerge and even be welcomed by a good number of citizens.

The five days went by fast. Six hours of classes and intensive workshops each day and one night at the Olympic Village Concert Hall for a performance by the Bolshoi and others; Strauss *Electra* and Glazunov *Raimonda*.

3:20 AM Sunday. Now, this felt normal for me in Russia, not the eight or nine hours sleep I had been getting. We had gone to the Disco Lisa in the Lenin Stadium complex the night before. There were many armed police with walkie-talkies, both outside and inside, and Robert, along with all the men, was given a brief pat down as we entered, and had a metal detector waved over his body, but he got an apology when they realized he was American. We all danced a lot, but Robert was the center of things and got everybody going.

En route, we had a crazy taxi driver who went so fast that we had to hang on to anything we could reach in the car. Most interesting along the way was passing the KGB building and the base of the Dzerzhinsky statue, which was empty since the coup, and still empty when I was there two months ago. However, that night, a big wooden cross stood on top of it.

I worried I was catching cold, or maybe it was an allergy to mold. Every time I took a shower, the water went out into the entryway of my room onto the carpet. I was terrified to lift the carpet for fear of a full-scale attack by whatever creatures were taking refuge underneath. The cockroaches weren't afraid to be visible.

And when I opened the door to my room, I was assailed by a noxious smell. At least once I was inside a while, I got used to it. I was afraid to open my windows for fresh air because Robert kept telling me he was getting bitten by mosquitoes.

But I kept sneezing, my nose kept running, and any moment I expected to get sick. I was not looking forward to getting yet another tough Russian cold.

Russian TV came again to interview Robert and film his classes on the next-to-last day. We spotted one newspaper with the headline "Montague Comes to Us." All participants seemed happy. I was happy, too. I knew he would be great, and he was even better than I had expected. They loved him, they worked hard for him, he made them feel good about the work that they did. He learned a lot of Russian and they loved it when he spoke it. No one could have done it better. And I myself loved the opportunity to work out five days in a row—to do funk aerobics, muscle classes, and relaxation every day.

Our last night was maybe one of the best evenings I'd yet spent in Russia. First, dinner. Then, with some of the women from the Aerobics School, we went to dance. When Robert went to bed, Olga invited anyone not tired to her room. Vodka, champagne, lots of talk about life in Russia, about men. I could have stayed up all night. I remember thinking that night that my life was so rich, and that experiences like that were a reminder of just how lucky I was.

The next morning, after stops at two *beriozkas* so that Robert and I could get water, we headed out for Zagorsk. The original name was Sergiev Posad and it was changed back to that in 1991, but most people still referred to it as Zagorsk. Driving through Moscow, Robert noticed things that I had grown to take for granted—buildings with missing windows and doors, façades with the paint chipped and masonry removed.

"Derelict," he called the city.

The sun was shining, the temperature comfortable. The highlight was the Troitse-Sergiyevsky Monastery, the medieval complex of white, blue, and gold buildings, the spiritual center of the Russian Orthodox Church. (At the time, we didn't know that on September 28, 1986, the Troitse-Sergiyevsky Monastery had a fire in which five seminary students had died.)

We also got some excellent shopping done, with especially good prices at the Zagorsk Hotel, where we had lunch. I lit my candle for Natasha at a nearby church, and had a moment, staring at the flicker of all the lit candles, of profoundly missing her.

Robert and I had a good conversation in the car, our first intimate conversation, and I got to peek behind the façade. I told him I thought he created distance, built a wall by talking so much and saying and asking so little that is personal. As he responded, I sensed the emotional scars from his abuse as a child. As I wrote in my journal then:

> *"This is someone who lets no one in for fear of being hurt, a scared child at heart, but a master of manipulation, a person who will push away anyone who gets too close. It is sad, because Robert has so many wonderful qualities, he could have a full and rewarding life. I believe he will achieve a lot, but will carry with him always an empty space, a desolate area. I think that lighthearted veneer that he presents to the world is of a man whose exceptional mind is engaged in a push-pull struggle with the defenses that he erected as a child to protect himself from the pain of his life, defenses which now threaten to prevent him from experiencing the joy that he appears so effortlessly to embody."*

I was 43 years old when I wrote those words, seven years older than Robert, old enough to have some wisdom, I thought, old enough to believe that having insight into another person's vulnerabilities would protect me from my own. That turned out not to be the case.

After I wrote and gathered up my things for the next day, there was a quiet knock at the door. Robert. We had sort of feigned fatigue to get rid of our interpreter, who clearly had a thing for Robert, so it was a bit uncomfortable for him. (I doubt even one of the many women who took his classes suspected he was gay.) We were tired of partying, so we sat with a glass of vodka and talked quietly. I remember thinking then that maybe we could be real friends after all, instead of casual ones.

Another nice day! Breakfast again in Robert's room, then the car from General Rubtsov picked us up. Robert enjoyed the meeting a lot and was actually very funny. Rubtsov invited me in December or January to come and to go hunting. I asked if he meant with a rifle and he said of course. At that point, Robert made us all laugh when he told me I should tell the general I only go hunting with my knife. Robert also embarrassed the general when he took a photo of him and me, saying we had to get a picture of his handsome face. The general turned bright red.

Next, to the Olympic Stadium where Robert taught his last class. I had no energy, but muddled through it somehow. But it was nice to see how many of the students wanted their picture taken with Robert, how many gave him gifts, how many of them cried when they had to say goodbye to him. Every day, people had swarmed him for his autograph and one guy even asked him to sign his socks.

A light lunch, then to a meeting at the Reebok office in the Kiev Hotel, which was a pretty dreary spot. But we got them to sponsor Olga's ticket to America for that part of the exchange, which made her very happy.

1992—Glubokoye

We had a very good dinner at the House of Journalists, sponsored by Sofia Timofeyeva, who had worked with me on several of my programs. We enjoyed caviar, wine, chicken Kiev, strawberry ice cream with lingonberries. She surprised me by inviting Russ Kendall, the photojournalist whom I had placed in Suzdal with a family who had a nine-year-old daughter and a ten-year-old son. He was there for three months so he could write another children's book for Scholastic Press. After his experience, he wrote the book, *Russian Girl: Life in an Old Russian Town*, published in 1994 by Scholastic for first through third graders.

Robert and Olga were happy, so this exchange was clearly a success. (And Olga was able to come to Boston later in October. She taught several classes in Boston and Cambridge, at Le Pli and The Squash Club, then Robert and I took her to see New York City.)

Our last day was lovely. After breakfast in Robert's room—the usual bread, cheese, and tomatoes—we went to the new Tretyakov Museum (the old one, my favorite, was still under renovation). Sad, the art there was pretty poor, but it was a relaxing time and Russ Kendall joined us. Robert was understandably calmer, so much easier to talk to. Coffee and pastry break, then across the street to Gorky Park, where we rode the Ferris wheel. Except Robert, who was afraid of heights, mistrusted Russian repair and maintenance work, and only half joking said he thought it was best to stay on the ground in case he was needed to contact my living relatives.

At 4:00 PM, we met Olga and others at a restaurant and had much vodka and more lessons with dirty words. Wouldn't you know, that evening at the Bolshoi, Robert was approached by a gay Russian man, earring in ear, the moment I left him alone in the lobby when I went to the ladies' room. Robert told me that in the public toilet outside the Kremlin, he had seen old men cruising the room.

Anyway, Robert loved the ballet, as did I, and we had a nice talk during intermission. At one point, he got teary-eyed talking about a friend who had died from AIDS, who had said he was just beginning to understand what life was all about when it was soon to be over.

Back at the hotel, the girls were waiting with food, champagne and vodka, and we had our farewell party. We danced, played music, and exchanged gifts until close to 3:00 AM.

Robert was quiet the next day, subdued, and I liked that side of him, too. He was very happy at the Bolshoi, and thanked me for this experience.

Happily, I hadn't caught a cold. We drank a lot of sparkling wine on the flight home, and I think Robert enjoyed the trip. I definitely enjoyed getting to know him better, and I couldn't have been happier with his teaching and professionalism. We made it home, exhausted, with all our luggage, our memories, and our bedbug bites (not mosquitos after all).

> The first Ben and Jerry's Ice Cream store opened in Russia this year, in the town of Petrozavodsk, northeast of St. Petersburg.
>
> *Izvestia*, Feb 19   Russia's criminal code decriminalized drug addicts.
>
> *Izvestia*, March 24, Street prostitutes in Moscow are mostly concentrated at the Kosmos, Rossia and Intourist hotels, laying their snares for foreigners.
>
> September and October, the Institute for Soviet American Relations reported that 40 cars were stolen every day in Moscow.
>
> According to *Komsomolskaya Pravda* on October 10, 1992, there was a surge of child pornography and it was estimated that more than 1,000 girls under age 18, some as young as seven or eight years old, were working as prostitutes in Moscow.
>
> Almost 30 years after Gorbachev's anti-alcohol campaign, according to the *World Population Review*, in 2020 Russia was sixth in per capita alcohol consumption, Belarus was #1. The US ranked 25th.

Part Five

Chapter 24
Sofya's Life

*"This creature softened my heart of stone.
She died and with her did my last warm feelings for humanity."*
Joseph Stalin (1878–1953)
Revolutionary and Soviet dictator

Sofya Kaplan (1915–2020)
One Hundred Plus Years of a Life, 78 of them lived in Russia

In Her Own Words

In 1993, at age 78, Alla's mother Sofya, my father's first cousin, came to America. She was living in Moscow during World War II when the Germans launched a surprise invasion of Russia, called Operation Barbarosa, on June 22, 1941. In November, the Germans marched on Moscow and they were halted by the Russians less than 20 miles from the Kremlin, the seat of government. Sofya's life history embodies much of the story of Russia in the 20th century, from the pogroms, to the Revolution, Lenin and Stalin, and of course the world wars. Her compelling narrative is in her own words, as told to me over several meetings, with the help of translators.

Childhood

"I don't know if I was born at home or in a hospital. I was the seventh child. In 1921, my oldest and favorite sister, who was born in 1900, died from typhoid. At the time, she was married and four to six months pregnant. Everyone in the family got sick but she was the only one who didn't survive. My parents had thirteen children in all. The six oldest all died, at different times from different causes, most at birth or in infancy.

"My mother (Sara Leah Dickstein Kaplan) was born in 1878, I think, and my father (Gavril Kaplan) about seven years earlier. My parents were from Kublichi, which is about 26 miles from Glubokoye. Because of the pogroms, in 1915 when my mother was pregnant with me, we moved to Saratov, a beautiful city on the Volga River, a good city, a liberal Jewish city. It is the city of my childhood and youth, my favorite city.

"Regarding my father, in 1921, there was starvation in Russia. I don't know what he had done for work, he couldn't read Russian, but when the famine began, he and his friend opened a butcher shop and made good money. He was one of the leaders of the Jewish community in town. He wasn't faithful to my mother. She knew it, but couldn't do much about it. In fact, when he was around 80 years old, he was caught by a teenager in town making love to a *goyim* (non Jewish) woman.

"For the rest of my life I will remember the package from America that came in '21—the taste of condensed milk, the first time I had ever had it. I also remember a photograph of four boys from America. They were the ones who sent the package … your father and his three brothers, my mother's nephews. But by the 1930s, it became dangerous to get packages and they stopped communicating with family in America; they said it was too unsafe and we shouldn't even tell anyone that we had relatives in the US.

"I was afraid of my mother, who was very strict. I don't have a favorite memory of her. I don't remember her ever laughing. She probably was witty in Yiddish, but I didn't understand Yiddish. But I know she was very smart, very wise, and Jewish ladies would come to her for advice. She was a good cook, so good that in 1924, she opened up a little restaurant in the house, mainly for Jews who came on business. About 70 percent of my neighborhood was Jewish, but not orthodox.

"I did have a happy childhood. Those were good years. I took ballet lessons, then piano, and I appeared in shows. When there were school parties, I played the piano and was in the chorus. I took part in all the productions.

"Our home on Kirovskaya Street, the central street of Saratov, was a four-story house. The building used to be a stable for horses. Wallpaper had been removed and the stone walls were then painted gray. My mother hung copies of paintings I loved—one of a forest by Shishkin and another a seascape by Aivazovsky.

"I remember a large dining room table, a piano, sofas, chair, and cabinet. There was also a black cast-iron Dutch stove, from floor to ceiling, which burned wood. We played ping-pong in the dining room.

"I played mostly out on the street. There was a sort of gym in the backyard of the Armenian family who lived nearby. We did acrobatics, handstands, we danced and sang. When I was about 10 or 12 years old, this was my favorite song:

Mom and Papa are not at home
There is nobody to be afraid of!
Come to my house
So that we may kiss!

Мамы, папы дома нет
Некого бояться!

*Приходи ко мне домой
Будем целоваться!"*

Then she laughed. "I never taught this song to Alla, so she never got to kiss a lot of boys!"

"Before the famine, I used to love *taighleh*—pastry rolled, cut, and fried with honey and nuts. I also loved *lakekh* or honey pie. After the famine, I don't remember any foods.

"My father went to synagogue every morning, but my mother went only on holidays.

"I was first a Young Pioneer in the youth division of the Communist Party and then, when older, a member of the Komsomol or the All-Union Leninist Young Communist League. I didn't join the party when I was an adult.

"My mother passed on the responsibility of educating and taking care of me to my oldest sister Cecilia, who was a taskmaster.

"When my mother opened the Jewish restaurant in the dining room, a guy from Moscow came and had dinner. He saw my sister Yelena and liked her, wanted to make a match between her and his son. The son came to town, they went on a walk and then after one date, he asked for her hand. They got married in Saratov under a *huppah* [the traditional Jewish wedding canopy]. At some point, Lena fell into a ditch and damaged her eye and had to have an operation for it.

"Everyone in the family was tall except Lena, who was petite and chubby. All were well dressed. The family had its own tailor and we studied music. My brother Abram went to college in Leningrad, played the violin and sang. And as I said, I played the piano.

"We had a dog, a fluffy white Spitz named Pushok. Also, a gray cat named Murka, because she purred all the time.

"I remember that in 1936-37, there was a farmer's market in Saratov, considered the best in Europe. It was a very long, two-story-tall enclosed building. One Sunday, there was an explosion there and many people died. It had been packed with shoppers. I was already living with my husband, but when I heard about it, I ran home because my mother went to the market every morning."

Until they came to America, Sofya's life was clearly very different from my father's and his immediate family.

Marriage to Ivan

"During high school years, I went to the Saratov Ballet Studio. There I studied in two departments, drama and ballet, and I graduated from there.

"At 19 years old, I married Ivan Khomenko, 25 years old, a Russian, not a Jew, and my parents were not happy about the marriage. My mother was so angry that she laid down across the doorway and said, "You will marry him over my dead body." I stepped over her and went to be with Ivan.

"Ivan, whom I called Vanya, and I took a vacation on a steamship. The boat went to Astrakan, at the delta of the Caspian, and on the way back, it dropped anchor in large cities. When it stopped in Kazan, Vanya and I were walking around downtown and it started raining. We entered a building to wait till the rain stopped and we were curious what kind of a building it was. Turned out it was a wedding palace and he said, "See, God brought us here. Let's get married."

"On the boat, we didn't have our own compartment, but we did have a wedding night."

She smiled. She didn't volunteer and I didn't ask for details.

"When we landed, we had to decide where to live, and we ended up with his family. But first, I went home alone and didn't immediately tell anyone about the marriage. My brother Naum was home, and my mother. When I eventually told them I had gotten married, Naum slapped me.

"Vanya and I had dated two years before we married but we lived together only one half year, in Saratov. One September evening—it was in 1937—we were sitting in bed, under a cover of embroidered lace, beige or off-white with two pillows that were also covered in lace. It was about 1:00 AM and we were still up talking. Suddenly there was a knock at the door. Three men in uniform, from Stalin's NKVD, [Secret Police] with only their rank on their collars, no epaulets, entered. They had a search warrant and an arrest warrant for Ivan. They were very polite."

She paused.

"I was pregnant. I was in shock. I couldn't believe what was happening. I changed from my nightclothes and we all walked a short distance to headquarters, probably three to four blocks, to where he was to be detained. We were immediately separated. No hug, no kiss, no chance to say goodbye.

"They then interrogated me, repeatedly asked what I knew about Ivan. I actually didn't know much about his past, except that sometime in 1933 or 1934, he had come to

Saratov from Harbin, Manchuria, where he was a sailing champion and head of some department of the Siberian-Ural Railroad.

Harbin was a Russian enclave, mostly of refugees from Communism during and after the Revolution. All those refugees who came back from Harbin and resettled in many Russian cities were thus considered spies.

"The police let me go after about a half hour or forty minutes. Then, no correspondence, no communication from or about Ivan. I got word months later that he had been executed. To this day, I don't know where he was sent or where he was shot.

"I have no photos, not a single one. They took everything when they arrested him. I remember he had an athletic build, gray eyes, and soft hands. He was blond. I was a brunette. Everyone said we were a great couple. He was very well educated, had a good sense of humor and was looking forward to being a father. And he was very attentive to me, didn't want me to lift anything heavy. Very protective, yet not jealous.

"Shortly after I learned he had been killed by Stalin, I miscarried and had to stay in the hospital for three months because of complications.

"He had an older sister, Zinaida, who, along with her husband Vladimir, was arrested six months after Ivan. They weren't immediately shot, but were exiled to the Gulag, to separate places. I have no idea what happened to them next.

"Before Vanya and I got married, Zinaida visited my parents to advocate for the marriage. As I said, my mother was very much opposed. My father, in spite of being so religious, was less vocal about it, because he really loved me. In fact, he later loved Alla more than all his other grandchildren. But after Ivan died, my parents insisted I get an official divorce from him. My whole family was still unhappy about the marriage.

"After I immigrated to America, whenever I went back to Russia, I went to government offices to try to find archival material about Ivan. I had no luck."

Second Marriage

"In 1939, a young man originally from Saratov travelled from Moscow and through a matchmaker, was paired with my sister Evgenia. I had three sisters and the whole family was in Saratov except Yelena, who had gone to Moscow. Whenever young suitors came to the house, my parents didn't want them to see me because I was too pretty, so they made me hide. When this man came, he invited Evgenia to go to a concert. When they left for the concert, I was able to come out of the room.

"However, a girlfriend of mine had invited me to the same concert. During intermission, when we were promenading in the foyer, I saw my sister and this man. My sister didn't know my parents made me hide, so she introduced me to Mordechai Veinberg, a well-known professor and mathematician. He came to my house again and said he wanted to marry me and not Evgenia. He stayed in town only a few days and I refused to marry him. All my relatives tried to talk me into marrying Mordechai and moving to Moscow.

"In the autumn of that year, about a year or two after Ivan's death, I gave in, moved to Moscow and married him. I don't know why.

"My degree was as a building engineer and my sister Yelena's husband found a job advertised in the newspaper in Moscow. So, I went to work at the KGB First Building Construction Trust, their construction arm. I did the finances, the budget.

"Mordechai was insanely jealous, wouldn't allow me to visit even my own sister, didn't want me to work. He would deliberately change clocks to make me late for work, which was dangerous because you could be arrested and fired from your job. He would also show up at work to see who I worked with, young men or old. But my managers then treated me well because they knew how jealous he was and thus they didn't take punitive measures if I was late.

"We lived together only six months before I left him and I was officially divorced in 1940, just before Alla was born. He didn't want us to divorce, but I said I preferred to live in awful conditions rather than with him. He had two rooms in a different place, very small, to live and study. He gave me the study, which was four to five square yards, with no heat, no kitchen, and in a one-story wooden house, where the owners also lived. The room had simply a table and a bed.

"The walls, which were boards, were covered with ice. I had only a burner to cook, lantern-shaped with no glass. In winter, I never took off my coat or boots, never uncovered Alla and we slept with all that clothing on, in -27 degree temperatures.

"Mornings, I got up at 4:00 AM to dress Alla and then later, to take her to the nursery. Once she was late because during the winter of 1941, it was very cold, there was no subway, no heat in the streetcars, so on our way, I would get off the streetcar to go into a store to warm us, then we'd get back on the tram. That made me late for work too.

"Another time when I was late, the nursery wouldn't take Alla, and I took her to my workplace and put her on the desk in front of the chief and said, "I can't live anymore at that place because my baby will die."

Sofya started to cry then and had to pause for a moment.

"After that, I got a new room, arranged for by the chief, one yard more than before, but with a huge radiator along the wall. Then, it was too hot, about 90 to 100 degrees. Before going out, I put on my own winter clothes first so that I was the one getting hot, then dressed Alla. We were healthy when we lived in the cold, but when we had the hot room, we were always sick.

"Alla's father repeatedly asked me to return to him. My answer was always no."

After Ivan and Mordechai: The War

"My sister Yevgenia had a dacha in Saratov and a month before the war started, I took Alla there to spend the summer with her and my parents and I returned to Moscow. At that time, Yevgenia hadn't had children yet.

"When the war started, everyone was building bomb shelters. I saw planes drop incendiary bombs, saw buildings go up in flames. But most of the battles took place on the outskirts of Moscow, so I wasn't really afraid. I heard the bombings, but no rifles. A plane was shot down on the KGB construction site where I worked with probably two in it.

"At work, they showed us how to extinguish gas bombs. Large wooden boxes were placed on the roof filled with sand and we were taught to toss the bomb into the boxes to snuff them out. When the troops were approaching Moscow, my co-workers and I were sent to build trenches west of Moscow. In October, word came that my place of work would evacuate all to Kuibyshev, on the Volga, but I wanted to go to Saratov.

"When it was time to depart, we were put into freight trains. Most of what I took with me was for Alla. In this freight car, there were no berths and we had to lie on the floor. I hoped the train would go through Saratov on the way to Kuibyshev and then I could drop off the clothes for Alla, who didn't have warm clothes with her. When I had taken her during the summer, we didn't know the war was coming and that she would be staying there. It took thirteen days and besides the train, we were put in horse-driven carts, trucks, and then a boat. Normally, it would take an overnight by train from Moscow to get to Saratov.

"On the steamship to Kuibyshev, we were told there would be no stop in Saratov. I approached the captain and explained why we had to stop in Saratov, lied and told him that my manager had given me permission to disembark and stay in Saratov. I got on my knees and begged the captain, crying that I had to give winter clothes for my child. All my colleagues also asked the captain to stop for me, and he finally agreed, but only at a distance from the pier. I kissed him! We stopped at an island, "the Green Island," and he provided a rowboat and two sailors to take me to the pier.

"My joy was indescribable.

"Alla didn't recognize me.

"I stayed in Saratov and looked for a job. Alla and I and my parents lived with my sister Yevgenia, who worked in a tank/tractor factory where tanks were brought to be repaired. She found a job for me there in my profession, as a building engineer.

"Yevgenia was Chief of the Planning Department and was, among all us children, the only member of the Communist Party. When the suburbs of Saratov were bombed, a lot of petroleum reserves were there and it was dangerous. There was a big fire and when they started bombing the plant, Yevgenia came back to gather and disarm the as-yet-unexploded bombs. She was very brave. She wasn't afraid of bombs, but she was afraid of blood and would faint when she saw it.

"I worked at the same plant in Saratov until 1944. There were battles, air raids, but no infantry. At night there were raids and we would all gather at the factory. A group of my fellow workers and I volunteered to help wounded in hospitals and Yevgenia and I both were blood donors. Yevgenia was weak and always had a hard time after giving blood. I am Type O, the universal type.

"Before the war began, I was dating a man named Grigory Khilkevitch, Grisha for short. He was Jewish and we met at work. He was a pilot in the Reserve and was sent first to Ukraine and then to Kazan for his training. I found out where the regimen was in Kazan and by myself, for fun, I went there. I was told the guys, all of them, were in the baths. When they came out, they lined up and started marching to the barracks. I spotted Grisha, who was stunned to see me, but he had to continue in formation. Later, he got permission to come see me in Saratov at the end of 1941, and we got married then because he said if he died, I'd get his pension. He couldn't read or write in Russian, but he did read Hebrew and Yiddish. I really didn't want to marry him, I was disappointed in men in general and didn't want to marry again. He gave me presents, gold bracelets, but it didn't matter. However, my family wanted me to marry him and again, I gave in.

"When I left Saratov to return to Moscow in 1944, I couldn't take Alla with me. But when I was leaving, Alla, who was by then four or five years old, grabbed my knees to stop me; she was afraid I would never come back. She cried, she was hysterical. Actually, when she was a baby, she loved me 100 times more than she does now," Sofya joked.

"My whole Moscow apartment was gone. I got a very small room in an area where prisoners worked outside, not a place I would want to leave Alla. In this new place, I was robbed twice. The prisoners or inmates were working on construction, building a Highway Construction College and prison on Leningradsky Prospekt and mostly it was food they stole. The second time, they caught a 16- or 17-year-old Jewish boy stealing from me and the guards beat him. I felt sorry for him.

"During the war, Grisha was sent to the Baltic Front, where he was wounded and was still there even a year after the war, on active duty, based outside Riga in Latvia. He worked with nuclear power and was a foreman in a KGB construction branch. I went to the Minister of KGB Construction and petitioned that my husband be able to return to Moscow to his wife and daughter. It worked.

"When Alla was six, my mother brought her to me in Moscow.

"I couldn't keep Alla in my room all week, so I put her into kindergarten for five days, where she lived and came home on weekends.

"My son David was born November 25, 1948. He became a Project Engineer Manager and went to work for Gipromost, or All State Bridge Design.

"Grisha and I lived together in Moscow 45 years.

"The firm where he worked had an infirmary and offered a total medical work-up for two to three days if you wanted one. So he went for a check-up, not because anything was wrong, he was feeling fine, but because we were going on a vacation. He did say he was short of breath during the check-up. The following day, before I was supposed to go to work, the infirmary called. 'Sofya Gavrilovna, we have sad news for you. Your husband passed away.' It was in 1986, just before his 75th birthday. They said he had an aneurysm and instead of giving him a blood thinner, they gave him something else.

"I turned numb. I had spoken with him at 10:00 PM the night before and at 7:00 AM, they called me.

"It was Mark who told Alla her father had died."

Sofya's Relatives During the War

"My brother Naom, born in 1908, was killed during the first days of fighting, without knowing he had a daughter. He and his wife lived together only six or seven months. Vera was born the day the family received notice that he had died. Before the battle, he had sent a card saying he was in the trenches and that they were going to attack the Germans. Naom was an economist who graduated from the Institute of Finance and Economics in Saratov and worked about two to three months before he was drafted at the beginning of the war. We didn't tell my mother of his death till after the war was over. He was tall, with wavy hair, very kind-hearted, very family oriented. He loved our parents and they never got angry with him; he never gave them a reason to. He was kind of serious, quiet and rarely laughed. He never told jokes or anecdotes.

"My handsome brother Abram, my favorite sibling, was an actor first in the Bolshoi Dramatic Theater, then after the war, in the Pushkin Theater in Leningrad. It was unusual for young Jewish people to take up this profession because acting was considered an insult to religion. Abram loved women, was a ladies man, a self-made man. Very talented not only as an actor, but as a painter and a violinist. His first wife was a beautiful Jewish woman named Kseniya, but the marriage lasted only a little over two years. He then married Valentina, a tiny Russian woman who was a ballerina and music hall dancer. They had no children but were married about 40 years and lived a good part of that time in Gomel, in Belarus. She was very clever and he loved her dearly.

"Abram volunteered for the army and played the part of Stalin in the Russian theater in the Crimea, in Savrastopol. He also played Tevye in *Fiddler on the Roof* and he said that Tevye's destiny reminded him of mine and my fate. Abram suffered six years from esophageal cancer, couldn't swallow, could only eat soft food and lots of water, but never complained. He was born in 1910 and died from that cancer on April 11,1977 at 6:00 AM

"My sister Yelena lived in Moscow from 1927 on. While I was living with Ivan and his mother and brother in Saratov, Yelena used to come to visit and try to talk me into leaving him, to come back to the family. She married a clever man, a chemical engineer who didn't like the Soviet government. We observed all religious holidays at their house. Yelena wasn't so religious, but her husband was.

"They had one child, Raya, born in 1927. Her parents dressed her well. She graduated from two institutions of higher education, the Institute of Foreign Languages in Moscow and the Petroleum Engineer Institute, where she became a geologist. She also worked as an English interpreter.

"I was with Yelena when she died in the hospital, but she was unconscious and didn't know I was there.

"My sister Cecelia, born in 1904, was commander-in-chief of the family even when my parents were alive. She eventually married and her husband, Alexander Zilberman, made everyone laugh. He would tell a story about an armored train with a canon and he would do the sound effects.

"But, I also remember that in 1936, four years after her son Simon was born, Cecelia found she was pregnant and she went to get an abortion. Her husband came and pulled her off the table at the hospital.

"That baby girl was named Bronya.

"Cecelia's husband, who was a Bolshevik Red Partisan, was still sent into exile and then, on January 23, 1938, when he was 42, he was executed by Stalin's firing squad. He was buried in a mass grave where there is a monument placed there by a Memorial Society of people who suffered during the repressed years. Alla has a copy of his death certificate. He was Party Secretary of an oil company and was a member of the Party. His boss went on a business trip to the US, so both he and his boss were arrested, Alexander simply for being negligent for allowing the boss to travel to a capitalist country. The sad thing was that Alexander was an honest man, a man who truly believed in Communism.

"In 1941 Cecelia, who had been living in Kublichi, was sent with her children Bronya and Simon to the gulag near Stalingrad, to the small village of Achtuba, in what was called "family exile." She worked as a pharmacist in a small hospital. After a few months, the hospital was bombed and the director asked Cecelia to hide the children underground there. She said no, 'If we die, we die together,' and she took the children home with her while she prepared medications. One day, after she had prepared the medicines, she took the children with her to the hospital to deliver them. That day, their house was bombed and a cabinet fell down on the kids' beds. And then, a bomb did fall on the hospital, killing people. Cecelia tried to take the train to leave the area, but it was bombed too, so in 1942, she and her children walked 186 miles back to Saratov, eating what they could find in the fields, mostly seeds.

"I remember all this as if it were yesterday. It was 1942. When they arrived in Saratov, Cecelia's son Simon, who was 10 or 11 years old then, came on foot a long distance to tell my parents that his mom and little sister were waiting at the train station, where we hurried to meet them.

"When Simon was 13, he jumped from a roof during play. They took him to hospitals in Moscow and Leningrad because the leg was so swollen. The doctors examined his leg, said he had sarcoma and then they amputated it because of the cancer. In spite of that, he biked, played basketball and volleyball. He wore his artificial leg only when he went out on a date.

"Six years later, he graduated from medical school first in his class.

"Then he died.

"One day he said he didn't feel well; he had been bleeding from his mouth and people thought maybe it was the flu. Several hours later, he was gone. An autopsy was performed and while the doctors found no cause of death, they did say he had not had sarcoma and that there had been no need for the amputation.

"My mother, Sara Leah, was at the time sick in the hospital with cancer of the esophagus. For 1½ months, no one told her that her grandson had died. After she came home from the hospital, every day she asked where Simon was, saying, "If I see him, I know I will survive." Cecelia first told her that he had gone on vacation after his exams, then said he was in the hospital. One day, Cecelia wanted to go to the grave but told her mother she was going to visit Simon in the hospital. Her mother made her take chicken soup, which Cecelia threw out at the grave.

"But I need to tell you something about Cecelia. She was born in 1905, 12 years before me, and as I said, she was a pharmacist. Each time I got pregnant with Vanya, she gave me pills. Each time, I miscarried. The doctor asked what I had been taking to make me lose my babies. It took me awhile to figure out that my sister wanted me to lose them, the entire family did, because they didn't want us to remain together, to be connected by children.

"Cecelia and I were never very close, and I never discussed this with her. She died at age 83.

Bronya Zilberman
(1936–2006)

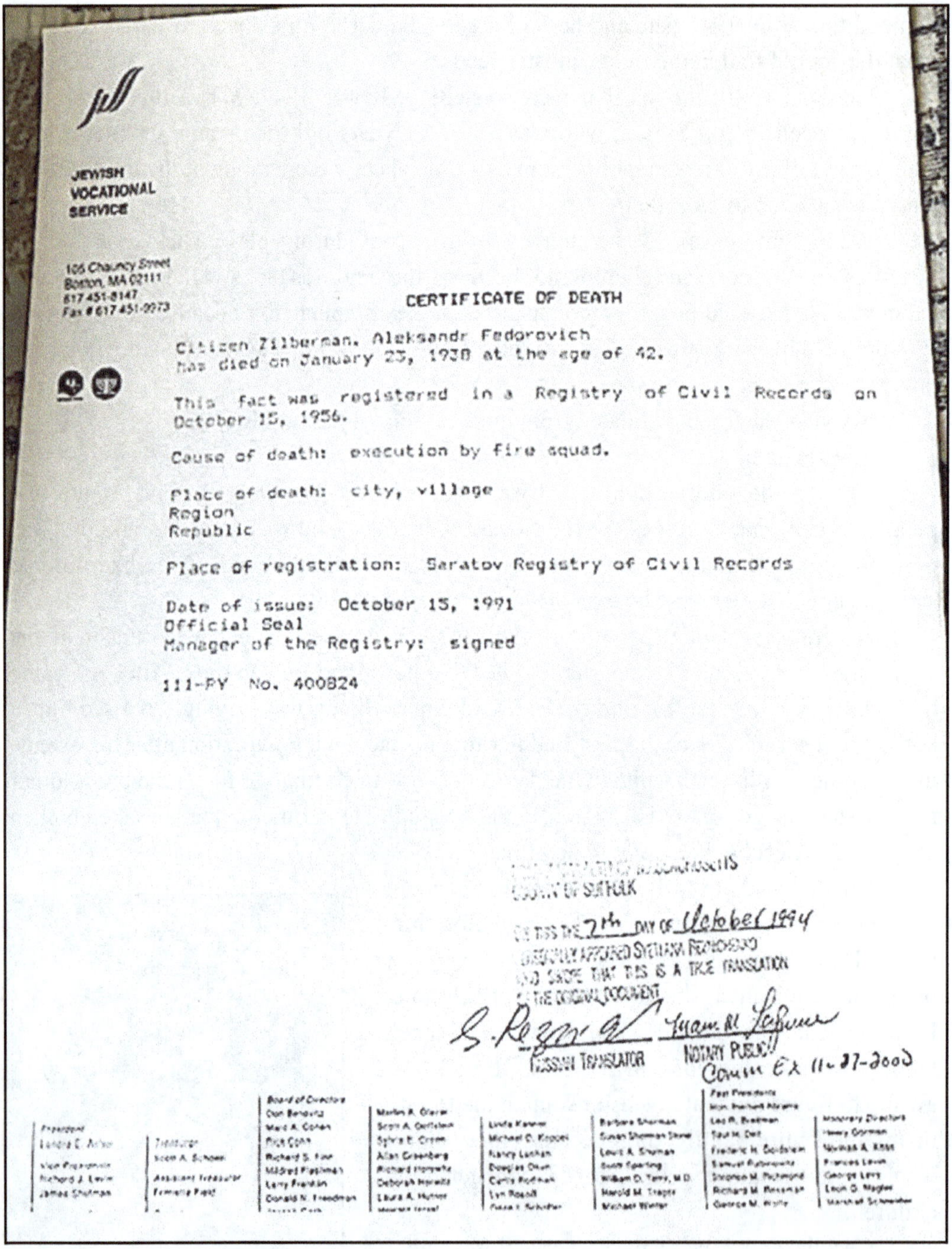

CERTIFICATE OF DEATH

Citizen Zilberman, Aleksandr Fedorovich
has died on January 23, 1938 at the age of 42.

This fact was registered in a Registry of Civil Records on October 15, 1956.

Cause of death: execution by fire squad.

Place of death: city, village
Region
Republic

Place of registration: Saratov Registry of Civil Records

Date of issue: October 15, 1991
Official Seal
Manager of the Registry: signed

III-РУ No. 400824

JEWISH VOCATIONAL SERVICE

105 Chauncy Street
Boston MA 02111
617 451-8147
Fax # 617 451-9973

MINISTRY OF SECURITY OF RUSSIAN FEDERATION
SARATOV REGION HEADQUARTERS
City of Saratov

Saratov city
Saratov,
ul. Dzerjin.,
20. 8.95

Zilberman B.A.

17.06.95   No. 10-z/1094

Dear Bronislava Aleksandrovna!

Your father, Zilberman Aleksandr Fedorovich, born in 1895 in city of Mogilev, was arrested on September 16, 1937. B form has arrest list recided in city of Saratov, and worked as a Head of supplies department of regional off-se "Glavneft".

On January 25, 1938 Military Board of Supreme Court of USSR in city of Saratov has sentenced him to execution by fire squad due to accusation of participation in anti-soviet, terrorist and sabotage organization. The sentence was executed on January 25, 1938 in city of Saratov.

As you know your father was rehabilitated by Military Board of Supreme Court of USSR on March 31, 1956.

Saratov Region Headquarter of Ministry of Security of Russian Federation does not have any photos or personal documents of your father.

Chief of Headquarter   V.P. Shevchenko /signature/

JEWISH VOCATIONAL SERVICE

105 Chauncy Street
Boston, MA 02111
617 451-8147
Fax # 617 451-9973

ATTORNEY GENERAL OFFICE
RUSSIAN FEDERATION

Attorney General Office
Saratov's Region

410002, city of Saratov
Ulitsa Revolutsionnay, 33/39

03.31.94

Certificate of
acknowledgement as a victim of political repression

Citizen Zilberman, Bronislava Aleksandrovna
Year and place of birth: 1936, city of Saratov

According to Public Notary Certified copy of Birth Certificate No. 21683, issued by city of Saratov Registry of Civil Records the person named above is a daughter of Zilberman Aleksandr Fedorovich, born in 1885, who by decision of Military Board of Supreme Court on January 23, 1938 and according to articles 58-8, 58-9, 58-11 of Criminal Code of Russian Federation of USSR was sentenced to be executed by fire squad. This sentence was executed on January 23, 1938. By the decision of Military Board of Supreme Court of USSR on March 31, 1954 he was exonerated.

According to part 3 of article 2 of Russian Federation Law "Exoneration of victims of political repression" from October 13, 1991 Zilberman Bronislava Aleksandrovna is acknowledged as a victim of political repression.

Assistant Attorney General of
Saratov's Region : signed G.I. Zadkov

COMMONWEALTH OF MASSACHUSETTS
COUNTY OF SUFFOLK

ON THIS THE 7th DAY OF October 1994
PERSONALLY APPEARED SVETLANA REZNICHENKO
AND SWORE THAT THIS IS A TRUE TRANSLATION
OF THE ORIGINAL DOCUMENT

RUSSIAN TRANSLATOR   NOTARY PUBLIC   Comm EX 11-17-00

"As an adult, Bronya went to the KGB to see if she could see her father's files. An officer told Bronya it would be too upsetting, so he read them to her. "Your father supported the West and policies of foreign countries. Your father had been interrogated using torture so that he would implicate other people." The officer also told her that the KGB got their confessions by beating the prisoners, taking off their fingernails, or burning the soles of their feet. Bronya didn't learn if her father confessed anything.

"Fifty-six years after his execution, Bronya received a letter from the Russian Federation's Ministry of Security, stating that her father had been accused of participating in anti-Soviet, terrorist organizations, but was exonerated on March 31, 1956. The exoneration came a little over a month after Soviet leader Nikita Khrushchev stunned the USSR and the world when he attacked Stalin's memory and denounced Stalin's crimes.

"My sister Yevgenia married a man named Simon, who had been wounded and was recuperating in a military hospital. When he was discharged, a Jewish family took him in. That family knew my family, introduced him to Genia, and shortly after they married. But he never told her that he was already married and had a son. There had been no divorce; both the wife and son were living in Kiev. They had been partisans and in fact, a book had been written by a Medvedev, about their partisan group, *This Happened near Rovno*,

"Simon, this new husband, was handsome, but dishonest. After he and Genia married, they had a daughter, Nina. They lived with my parents; he stole money from them and ration cards suddenly disappeared, leaving the whole family without any food. Genia was ironing his slacks one day and discovered a bank book, along with a good amount of money in his pocket. Then someone saw this Simon in a store selling ration cards, so the family figured it out and tossed him out of the house. Nina never saw her father again.

"The other relatives I saw most often were my aunt Yelizaveta (Liza) and her three boys, Abram (1914), Zalmon (1917) and Mark (1921), all born in Kublichi, who came to live in Saratov in 1924. Before the war, Abram had lived in Leningrad with his wife, a Russian girl from Siberia who was uneducated and an alcoholic. He was a photographer who went on expeditions to the mountains with a research institution to photograph nature.

"Before Liza was evacuated from Leningrad to Novosibirsk and after Abram was drafted, she left during the blockade to go to Novosibirsk to see him. She arrived one evening only to learn that he had been mobilized that morning. She was treated very poorly there—there was much anti-Semitism—so she left and went to Saratov.

"Liza never got to see Abram again. He had sent a card to the family saying he would be coming through Saratov via train *en route* to Stalingrad, but they didn't get the card until after the train had come through and was already at the outskirts of Stalingrad.

Abram died right before the Stalingrad Battle when a German airplane bombed his plane. He was somewhere between 28 to 30 years old. He had a daughter, Luba, born 1940 and a son Oleg, born in 1942, but I don't think he ever saw his son.

"Liza's son Zalmon graduated from some kind of technical college. He was exempt from the army because he had very bad eyesight. He had been a hooligan and had played with explosives. When one exploded, his vision was severely damaged, so he avoided the draft. Zalmon loved dancing. Never married. He worked in a factory to earn a bigger ration than he would normally get. However, he died of starvation during the Siege of Leningrad when he was 25 or 26 years old."

Mark, of course, survived the war, and was always my favorite cousin.

Thoughts

"My mother died from cancer in 1952 when she was 72. But she had all her teeth. My father died 13 years later, in his 90s. After my mother's death, he wanted to remarry, but Cecelia wouldn't allow it.

"I was on the streetcar in Moscow, March 5, 1953, when I learned that Stalin had died. And I cried. People believed in Stalin. I believed in Stalin. We said that if Stalin only knew, these horrible things would not have happened. I didn't even blame him then for Ivan's death.

"The most difficult time in my life was during the period when Alla was a newborn and we lived in that room without heat. I felt like committing suicide. My sister Yelena even wrote to my mother to say I was on the verge of doing something crazy. I was nursing Alla and my mother came to Moscow to talk me out of it.

"Alla is not religious but believes in God. God has no role in my life. God crosses my mind, but always with a question mark.

"My son David married a woman Natasha. They never had children.

Natasha was killed in a car accident, hit by a truck on June 23, 2016. Only after a few years was Sofya told of her death, only after she saw that David was happy with a new woman in his life.)

"I never really experienced anti-Semitism, probably because my patronymic was Gavrilovna, which is a Russian name. Prior to WW II, people didn't really experience too much anti-Semitism.

"My happiest moment. When I married Vanya, and while we were dating.

"My saddest time, his arrest and death. He was the love of my life, and he has been with me my whole life. I respected Grisha, but didn't feel passion for him. But I think I was everything to him.

Sofya's Life

The bright red dress—Sofya's gift

"When was I most afraid? After losing Vanya, I was afraid of losing anyone I loved.

"Dearest to me now are my children. When Alla married Yakov, I didn't like him. But I knew from my personal experience, so I agreed.

"Even now, I'm afraid of my reminiscences, because they don't give me peace."

* * *

I called to wish Sofya happy birthday when she turned 105 in 2020. She was still living alone without help in her apartment in Arlington, Massachusetts, the last living member of her generation, the last of Abram and Chiena Dickstein's grandchildren.

On one of my birthdays, Sofya got me a gift, a bright red dress I would never have bought myself. Surprisingly, it fit. I wore it only once, at a party at my house when she was there. The smile on her face expressed her delight.

After I met Mark and Alla, I met Bronya in Russia and she also visited Boston a few times. I thus got to know another Russian cousin. Alla became a US citizen in 1995, and then tried repeatedly to do what was legally necessary for Bronya to move to the States. Unfortunately, Bronya was always refused permission to emigrate and ended up living in Goslar, Germany, 145 miles south of Hamburg. In 2006, she had a stroke, and she was in a facility, in a coma, until she died 11 years later, on February 25, 2017. She was found on the floor, and thus the police were called to investigate what happened since she was immobile. There were no findings.

Up to this point, I had met Mark and Sofya and their families, and Bronya. Three out of six branches of my great-grandparents' children's descendants. Four if you count my father and siblings. There were two more branches to get to know.

Number of victims of Stalin's Repression: It is impossible to know exactly but it is estimated that from 1929 through 1953, 21.5 million were murdered.

Stalin's secret police, the NKVD, employed more Jews than most Soviet institutions.

According to the NY Times on March 13, 2013, the American Holocaust Museum released the following figures:

There were 42,500 Nazi ghettos and camps all over Europe, including:
- 30,000 Slave labor camps
- 1150 Jewish ghettos
- 980 concentration camps (later info showed more)
- And 500 brothels filled with sex slaves.

More than two million Jews were killed in German-occupied Soviet territories.

Chapter 25
1993—Second Visit to Glubokoye

"Unless we remember, we cannot understand."
—Edward M. Forster (1879–1970)
English novelist

Aerobics Tour
Moscow, St. Petersburg, Minsk, Helsinki
September 17th to October 7th, 1993

Finally, after weeks of preparation, some of it frantic, Robert and I were again in Moscow, this time with a group of six Americans who wanted to do aerobics. Our Hotel Minsk was pretty shabby, but no one complained.

After we unpacked and had lunch, our group took the city tour with a guide named Katya. The first stop was Novodevichy Cemetery—to Khrushchev's tomb, to that of Stalin's wife, and then to the burial place of renowned Russian writer Nikolai Gogol, who starved himself to death when he was 42 years old, due to bipolar affective personality disorder and torturous medical treatments.

Our bus driver was nice; icons and pictures of Christ and the Virgin Mary adorned his vehicle. The city had changed in a year. Robert pointed out that there were far more American cars—Lincolns and Cadillacs—as well as Mercedes, Volvos, and BMWs. People flaunted their newfound wealth. Also, there seemed to be a lot of renovating going on, and I saw Baskin Robbins kiosks, a *New York Times* kiosk, the three McDonalds, a Rosie O'Grady Restaurant, fresh fruit for sale on the street, horses available to rent for short rides, and a bunch of brightly colored balloons and parrots for purchase at Lenin Hills. And Korean Evangelists.

A newspaper feature story in *Argumenti and Facti* reported on Michael Jackson's concert three days earlier. Tickets sold for $100 and sales were so slow they ended up giving away tickets so that the stadium wouldn't look empty. And for the first time, I saw color in a newspaper. *Sovesednik*, a weekly illustrated, featured a color photo of Jackson on the front page, with an inset photo of a babushka in the corner, hands up to her face in shock.

Speaking of old women, our nice bus driver tried to sell us a Khokloma painted pot, and when we looked inside, there was a bunch of hair. "It is dog hair, it's common for babushkas to use it to knit scarves." We chose not to purchase it.

At the contest at the National Aerobics School the next morning, the Russian National Aerobics Champion for 1993 led the warm-up and Robert gave a great demonstration for TV. Robert and Olga were both judges for the contest, which included about 100 competitors.

After lunch, we went on a metro tour and then to the Pushkin Museum. My favorite piece there, the "Charioteer of Delphi." I had gotten goose bumps when I saw it 28 years before in Delphi, and again that day when I saw the museum's replica. His eyes!

The metro was fun for the group, and I noticed that there were many lovers being affectionate with one another, even two men—another first for me to see there. That evening, a short TV segment from the morning when Robert and Olga were interviewed, with a longer program to be aired the beginning of October.

The news the next day (unlike past years when I was isolated from the real story of world events) was dramatic.

- John Demyanuk, convicted of Nazi war crimes while a concentration camp guard, was freed and would leave Israel in a few days.
- Shevardnadze, parliamentary chairman in Georgia, appealed to Russia and the West for help against the rebels attack on Sukhumi after a seven-week ceasefire fell on September 15th.
- Protesters were refused permission to march that day on Pushkin Square to demonstrate a desire for a rebirth of the Soviet Union. Denied because it would "disrupt traffic."
- Moscow metro drivers targeted a date for a strike for pay raises and better working conditions.

After morning classes, we headed to the Kremlin for a tour with a most informative guide who was very cute. Well, not really cute, but appealing in a funny, old-maid sort of way.

Afterwards, Robert and I took a walk down Tverskaya Street (previously Gorky St.), stopped at the McDonalds to look inside, then headed for a Pizza Hut, which was unexpectedly closed. By accident, we found a Mexican restaurant and discovered that the waitress was a Boston University student from Springfield, Massachusetts, and the bartender was also from Boston. I had an enchilada, Robert a chicken fajita, and we had several margaritas.

Later, back in the room after two shots of vodka, we had a very personal conversation. He opened up and talked a lot about his fear of intimacy, his relationship with his parents, his partner Neil. I offered whatever insights I had and was pleased that he felt comfortable enough to confide in me.

Big Sasha was out of town, but his wife Vera met us at the train station just before our departure to St. Petersburg. Unfortunately, it was too late for the children to come. I had really wanted Robert to meet them. We had a brief talk and an exchange of gifts, and along with a tablecloth, she gave me my pair of Armani sunglasses, which I thought I had lost in a restaurant last year, but had actually left behind in the helicopter when Big Sasha had taken Tambi and me for the flight.

I actually slept about five hours on the train, a lot for me that trip, and a lot considering I was worried about theft, having heard so many stories about break-ins on this train. Eight hours, 400 miles to St. Petersburg. Thieves were reported to even use gas. But Robert had brought a bicycle chain, and he secured the door handle with it so that it would be very difficult to get in without bolt cutters.

I awoke with a cold. And laryngitis, which perhaps delighted Robert. But, I felt all right most of the day. The Hotel Russ was better than the Hotel Minsk, and I was happy to be able to unpack everything because we'd be there for a while.

City tour that morning and after lunch, we went to the gymnasium where they had a huge banner saying "Welcome Robert." He did great, as usual.

I easily reached Nina A. She told me that Yeltsin had disbanded Parliament and that members had barricaded themselves in the White House, but no one was attacking them. Yeltsin had called for elections in December and received support from President Clinton. There we were in Russia and we knew nothing about it. I couldn't wait to hear the radio and get hold of an English-language newspaper.

One night with our group, we enjoyed a lovely dinner on the Nevsky Prospekt almost directly across from the Literary Cafe at a restaurant called Druzba, with a disco. We had our vegetarian meals, we danced, and then we realized one of our group participants, Craig, was practically passed out, so Robert and I took him back to the hotel in a taxi. He was drunk. Really drunk. I fished his room key out of his pocket and we got him to his room and undressed him (only after Robert helped him pee in the sink, after he had tried to do it at the elevator door) and got him in bed with pillows propped between him and the wall so that he wouldn't roll over on his back and possibly throw up. I put his room key in my purse and about one hour later, I went back to check on him. He was ok and I covered him up with another blanket.

Craig was a great addition to the group, a sweet guy, and during funk or swing classes, he encouraged all the women by yelling "You go, girl!" He had confided in Robert that he was HIV positive. He looked good, but not too long after the trip, we were sad to learn that he had died.

Another first. The hotel was covered with notes advertising the services of women escorts and listing a phone number to call. Those cards were above our doors, on the stairs, the sofas, everywhere!

I was pleased with the fitness program. Robert did a lot of his teaching in Russian and my group was happy. Their departure from the airport, though, left me less than pleased. It was a madhouse, and I had to run interference. Since everyone waiting to go through security was pushing and shoving, I had to actually place my body in front of the line, arms straight out to the side, and grab and pull my people through one at a time. That had never happened before. Robert and I stayed behind so he could teach in Minsk, which we hadn't included in the group program.

Mark picked us up later and we spent a wonderful afternoon and early evening at his home with him and Dina, Sofya and Bronya and some other friends of his—an English student and a professor from Israel. And, it was Yom Kippur. The Israeli came in saying "*gut yontif*" and I think Mark and I were the only ones who knew that it meant "good holiday."

Dinner was delicious. Champagne, vodka, fish salad, mushrooms, meat and chicken, meringue dessert and more. And of course, lots of toasts. So many that Mark ran out of vodka, so Robert and I went out to the street and were able to buy a big bottle from Germany for $3. It was called Rasputin. I never heard of it. There was something bizarre about being in the vodka capital of the world, drinking German vodka, named after the Russian Mad Monk.

Abram, the professor from Israel who was born in Russia, speaking in Yiddish, gave a toast and told about the only other time he had broken the fast, when he was in the Israeli army fighting the Arab-Israeli War of 1948, and they, all starving, entered Jerusalem. He was a colonel, and by the time he and his troops reached the city, several of his men had actually died of starvation. Although it was Yom Kippur, they ate and drank a little bit, for strength, all the while crying because they were supposed to be fasting. Those memories were reflected on his face as he spoke. Mark translated for us.

The next day, we learned that there was a constitutional crisis, a political standoff between President Yeltsin and the Parliament. There were 3,000 people in Moscow demonstrating opposition to Yeltsin and support for Parliament and its leader Ruslan Khasbulatov, but more than 30,000 on Tverskaya Street to support Yeltsin in his efforts to dissolve Parliament.

We went to Nina A's for a great dinner that evening. Her mother was still endearing, 85, losing her memory a bit, and wearing the same sweater I always saw her in. Nina was clearly in love with Warren, the man from Paulina, Iowa, whom she had been seeing for some time. He was with her for a month the past summer; they rented a cabin for a week in Kizhi (an island on Russia's Lake Onega) together and she was sad, not only that he was gone, but that they had no way to be together. She certainly couldn't move to America and I didn't think he was going to move to Russia.

Another breakfast of two hot dogs and peas and cabbage soup. We packed up, paid an extra $10 to have one room for the afternoon so we could leave our luggage and have someplace to return to later to rest before our train to Minsk. Then we went off to meet Marina Alexeyeva, head of the Union of Journalists, St. Petersburg, to discuss NESNE. She first gave us a tour, proudly pointing out the dental clinic they had. We covertly cringed at the sight of the thick needles and the outdated equipment.

Later, when we were out on the Nevsky Prospekt to do some food shopping for the train to Minsk, I heard a high-pitched voice call "Cynthia." It was Mark's wife Dina, who took us to a bakery, cut in front of everyone in line, insisted on buying us two loaves of bread, then sent us on our way because she knew we were in a hurry.

To the hotel to pack up our last few things. I showered while Robert napped. I went out to talk to the maid, to ask if we could buy two glasses, (which we needed on the train for our vodka!) and I suddenly had a terrible coughing spell. Tears came, nose ran, couldn't stop, couldn't get a voice to talk to her. Finally I thought I made myself understood and she indicated I should wait. What she really thought I was asking for was hot water, steaming, so I could breathe, and that is exactly what she brought me. It was a complete surprise, and actually wonderful. I sat down with it for about ten minutes and it did help. Then, of course, I had to ask her again for the glasses. She brought me two dirty ones, and I gave her $2.00. Robert slept through it all.

The station was horrible. We had to wait for the train, which arrived a half hour later than we had been told, and my feet got very cold, so I put on a pair of Robert's socks. A "fashion disaster," Robert declared. Back at the hotel before we had left, one of the ladies who worked there saw me leaving without nylons or socks and admonished me. I should have listened to her.

Predictably, Robert slept like a baby on the train, and I had a tough time falling asleep. I lay there for about two hours, worried again about someone breaking in in spite of the bicycle chain, probably because the train station, a different one than we usually went to, had been so sleazy. I'm not sure I can provide an accurate picture of just how disgusting it was. It smelled of body odor and there were big gobs of spit everywhere on the sidewalk (and not just at the station, just more of it there) and the people, the men, were in horribly mismatched, dirty, ill-fitting clothes, smoking, and looking as if they had not bathed in a month and didn't care if it was another month before they did. Worst of all was the expression in their eyes. If not glazed from too much alcohol, or maybe even drugs, they were shifty, wary, appraising, sizing us up like an animal does before it attacks its intended prey. Just a glance from one of them made me want to run for the shower.

Long digression, but I finally fell asleep after midnight. I woke up often, the train seemed noisier and bumpier than usual, and then I heard Robert whispering ever so quietly "Cynthia, are you awake?" It was 8:30. We had our breakfast, which was last night's supper of fresh bread and cheese, minus the vodka.

Natalia Novozhilov, owner and director of the Minsk fitness club Bagira (Black Panther) and her interpreter Natasha V. met us right at our compartment and with their two cars, took us to our hotel. She had faxed me that we would have a flat, but plans changed and we were in sort of a hotel suite with a living room and a refrigerator. We hurried to shower, happy that we had hot water, unpacked, then raced off to lunch at Natalia's house. Delicious. Then to the gym for classes. I shouldn't have been surprised to find that both the gym and the hotel were not heated.

After classes, back to her house for dinner. We had requested just soup and vegetables, but she served a tasty meal of chicken soup, mashed potatoes, coleslaw, and a compote drink of boiled apples and water. Also some wine and vodka. Then, as we discussed business and our program, she made me inhale some eucalyptus out of a funny pipe-like contraption, while her 8-year-old son Viktor raced around the living room.

When Robert and I returned to our suite, we unpacked some more, tried to get organized, and especially tried to get warm. The heat didn't get turned on until October 1st, state regulations, regardless of the temperature. I dressed for bed in socks, long underwear and sweats. Still cold, I woke up later to add the wool sweater Natalia had given me, then had to take two Tylenol PM to get back to sleep. The hotel had given us a space heater, but it helped only if we were within three feet of it.

Our interpreter, Natasha V, arrived early the next morning, bearing a wool scarf for me to use. I was thrilled. Until I smelled it. Permeated with horrible, heavy perfume. I thanked her, then gave it back to her, telling her I was allergic to it. We walked to Natalia's for a breakfast of cereal, eggs, bread, tea, and more of the wonderful honey she gave me for my throat. She also insisted on giving us $50 in Byelorussian money for us to buy souvenirs.

The gym, which had the faint smell of smoke from a recent fire, wasn't heated either. The only sign of comfort was a colorful samovar where we could get tea. I was not in my best mood of the trip, annoyed that I had a cold, annoyed that I had to wear so many clothes in a futile effort to get warm. Happily, Robert was in a good mood. He never complained. Wearing his one-piece bodysuit with a full-size human figure with bones and muscles drawn on it, he lectured on range of motion. Thirty to forty faces stared up at him with something close to adoration, although they were shivering too.

At least when we walked outside after classes ended, the sun was shining. But our interpreter Natasha V was driving Robert and me crazy. There was something about her that was very off-putting; she was pushy and didn't stop talking.

1993—2nd Visit to Glubokoye

We went immediately to the World War II Museum, and then Robert and I chose to walk back to our hotel. In the stores we saw Avon for sale, Camay and Old Spice, and a window sign for an FTD florist! Herbalife was a strong seller there and Robert made sure to tell the group that he considered it a scam.

We quickly changed for dinner again at Natalia's—borscht and blintzes. (That day, I took my first bite of a blintz since my father and I got ptomaine poisoning from Lindy's blueberry blintzes in New York City when I was five years old.)

We took a pile of dirty clothes with us to Natalia's for her housekeeper to wash. Natalia and her husband Viktor were interesting. They were a two-car family, she wore very fine jewelry, she had a maid, and she was a professional woman. They handed me $1,100, cash to pay for all the workout clothes I had brought for them to sell. But I remember wondering: Who in Russia had that kind of money back then? Was Viktor paid that well as President of the Olympian Sports Club and of the Waterski Federation of Belarus?

As for the next day, and the day after that, that hot water we were so grateful for? Yup, it was gone. Somehow, we managed to keep a sense of humor.

We settled into a routine. Classes during the day, dinners at Natalia's, and performances in the evenings. And then sleep. Within minutes of walking in the door, Robert was in his bed. Maybe I had my coat off by then. Within another five minutes, he was asleep. Then I undressed, brushed my teeth, washed my face, got out my clothes for the next day, earrings too, wrote in my journal, read, and maybe an hour later crawled into my bed and turned out the light. Occasionally the routine varied a little—for example, one night, I killed a cockroach.

One evening we saw the ballet, *Corsair*, the same one we saw the previous year at the Bolshoi. Another night to the light opera. First, Strauss's *Night in Venice*, and then two dances, one of Adam and Eve and the other about a water nymph. The performances were impressive on their own but our private box seats with champagne and chocolate just for us certainly enhanced our enjoyment.

The best part of one day was the *banya*, with champagne and watermelon, purple and green grapes. I went in and out of the sauna and shower several times. I washed my hair. Shaved. Stayed in the shower as long as was decent. Then stared at the fire in the fireplace in the outer room. Just as the afternoon was about to end, I sneaked back into the sauna, to steal a few moments of peace. I took off my bathing suit, lay back, closed my eyes, took in a deep breath, started thinking Minsk wasn't so bad after all.

Then, the door banged open, Natasha V burst in, and immediately started talking. And talking. And talking. I could have cried. As the saying goes, she meant well. But I really couldn't tolerate her; she had the most annoying mannerisms and I seriously wanted to strangle her. Robert wanted to help me.

Paths of Stones

Every day that Robert taught, we had been interviewed by radio, TV or newspapers. Some of the students said they saw us on the Moscow Sports TV channel. On his last day, he did all the dance work, Funk, Country/Western, Swing and Latin, but no real floor work or muscle conditioning because it was so cold there. At the close of the classes, a surprise for us. A presentation. They made us go on stage and from the netting in the ceiling swung down two large, adorable, handmade cloth Byelorussian dolls, one for each of us.

After our last dinner at Natalia's, we watched the video of that morning's classes in her living room, with candles, Amaretto and tea. Little Viktor was up to his usual antics. Natasha called him a little devil and her older son Alex called him a terrorist. Meanwhile, he was my favorite person there.

Then, off to the evening festivities at Natalia's club Bagira. Some wine, tea, fruit and pastries, some aerobic dance performances, some circle folk dances, and Natasha played the guitar and sang. We all danced, too. Viktor was on the dance floor all night. People were happy, expressing gratitude, pleased to be called up to be presented with their certificates by Robert and me. On the way home, little Viktor sat on my lap in the car and his father showed us the piles of stone from the first building in Minsk, over 900 years ago.

But the highpoint up to then? Our hotel's hot water came back! And then, even a little heat came on.

When I was planning our itinerary, I asked Natalia if she could arrange for Robert and me to go to Glubokoye. I didn't tell her I had already been the year before. She honored that request and her husband Viktor drove us. The original plan was for Natasha V to accompany us to interpret. Robert and I insisted that it absolutely was not necessary for her to come. Of course, it was absolutely necessary for us to have an interpreter because Viktor's English wasn't very good. But we could not have tolerated her presence for five minutes, let alone an entire day.

There were not many cars on the road, since there was a shortage of gasoline. I had actually heard about it before we left the US and worried we might not even be able to get to Glubokoye, but Viktor and Natalia seemed well connected, with access to the essentials.

We stopped at a roadside memorial to a village called Shunevka, which the Nazis had destroyed. The stone foundations of some homes were still visible, and a metal sculpture had been erected, representing flames at the houses that the Nazis burned, with the etched names of the people who had died inside. But most chilling was the small well with its wood frame, the well where the Nazis had thrown fourteen children to their death. The young ones' names were carved into a piece of iron resting on top of the well. Robert stood there for a long time, his fingers tracing those names over and over again as he silently stared down into the dark space below.

1993—2nd Visit to Glubokoye

(When we got back to Boston, he wrote a piece about that place. It appeared in the *Boston Globe*, and in it he talked not only about the cruelty to those children, but about "feelings of abandonment and hopelessness" that he experienced in his own childhood as a result of an extremely cruel and abusive father, and a silent mother. "The autumn leaves that gathered at the corners of the well appeared to huddle hopelessly together for warmth at this chilling monument and tomb for the death of innocence.")

A stone outside of Glubokoye marked the grave of prisoners of the ghetto.

> *"Let the world not forget about the spilled blood because the memory of the people is not subject to age."*

After we reached the town center, and after Viktor filled the tank with gas he carried in his trunk, we set about to find Yakov (whom I had visited the previous year). We asked a woman with a mouthful of gold teeth and she knew him well. We found him at home, repairing his customers' shoes. His wife Frieda was in bed with a broken leg; she had just the day before come home from the hospital after two months. She was more than happy to have Robert film her as she pulled off the covers and showed us her sad little leg, in its flesh-colored full cast.

Yakov did not remember meeting me, so when I gave him the photos of him and his wife, he was surprised.

He consented to show us Glubokoye. In his long brown leather coat and a cap, shoulders slumped, hands in his pockets, he led the way. First to the cemetery, which had a new monument with inscriptions, and then down stone paths to show us several other burial sights hidden away in the woods. He told us that one of them had 2,000 people buried there, and in 1946, "bad people robbed the graves of gold teeth, jewelry, etc."

Another site had plaques in Hebrew, Russian, and Yiddish, which read:

> *"This ground is hallowed by the spilled blood of those who had all possible kinds of tortuous death."*

At the last site, where 53 of his family were buried, Yakov told us that he and his son provided the marble pieces covering the path and the granite for the monument, which had a Star of David carved on top and mentioned the Jewish massacre by "the German Fascist Occupiers, 1942–1943." It also had statistics about who was buried there. Yakov said that kind of memorial had never been possible before.

Cemetery monument where the author placed her father's tie clip

A black ribbon was draped around that monument. A plaque read, *"Here is the grave of 4,500 peaceful Jewish citizens of Glubokoye and suburbs who were killed by the German Fascist occupiers in 1942-1943. We will not forget."*

When I saw that, I knew that that was where I would leave my father's tie clip, the one he had worn so often, the one I remember so well from my childhood. The Greek masks of tragedy and comedy, side by side, symbolizing to me both the hardships and the happiness in his life.

I fastened the clip to the black ribbon and felt good about leaving something of his in Glubokoye, 93 years after his birth there. I had brought it to do just that. I also picked up a piece of marble from the path, and a few small stones and some flowers, tiny pansies that I planned to dry, so that I could take back a bit of Glubokoye with me.

I still wonder what happened to the clip. Did it perhaps drop during a strong wind to be aimlessly carried along the ground of Glubokoye, only to eventually be buried there? If that happened, will someone find it 50 or 100 years from now and wonder whose it was and what story it could tell? Or did a resident of Glubokoye see it on the ribbon, perhaps take it as his own and wear it? Or did a visitor to the town take it away, so that once again my father left his Russian home?

Next stop, a Russian Orthodox church, where I lit my candle for Natasha. So nice to do that in Glubokoye. She would have been pleased. When we came out, after some conversation we gathered that Yakov, who had waited outside, wanted to go home. I suspected he was annoyed that we went to a church. So we said our goodbyes, walked past his garden lush with apple trees, and left the town, stopping at a public well to take some photos.

After pulling off the road several times in search of the perfect place, Viktor did find a pretty spot for us. He spread out some blankets and we had a picnic in the woods. Tomatoes, red peppers, hard-boiled eggs, bread and cheese, blinchiki, boullion and tea—all delicious. And it was so nice to eat outdoors, in spite of the cold. The sun was out, we were surrounded by forest. A memorable ending to a memorable day.

However, as it turned out, there was one more memorable event. Viktor's driving, not so bad *en route*, was scary returning home. I was in the front seat and at one point, the car speeded up and we were heading off the road toward a group of people standing on the sidewalk at a bus stop. I shouted, "Where are you going?" and when he didn't answer, I grabbed the wheel, turned it hard, and got us back on the road. He looked at me, didn't acknowledge that he had fallen asleep, and acted so peculiar that Robert and I later wondered if he had a *petit mal* seizure. I asked him repeatedly if he was tired and he said, "No, not at all."

But when we stopped at a sports ski training center and he turned in so we could watch the kids jumping, he went right up over a high concrete curb. When we finally got back to Minsk and were getting out of the car, Robert turned to me and, *sotto voce*, announced, "Never again, Cynthia. Never again will I get in a car with you in Russia."

But Viktor was a dear man. In spite of his limited English, we really enjoyed the day, and were grateful that he took us. We were also grateful, very grateful, that Natasha V did not come with us!

Viktor, who then seemed fine, took me to the store to do some shopping so that Robert and I would have food for the train. Viktor insisted on paying for our food, so I finally agreed because I handed back to him the rubles Natalia had given us when we arrived. Unfortunately there was nothing to spend them on. Anyway, he was unbelievable as we roamed the aisles. If I said I wanted one of something, he got four of it. I ended up with champagne, chocolate, bread (three loaves), cheese (enough to feed a village), juice (four cartons), even dried apricot sheets. Then he insisted on buying an ice cream cone for me. I was still full from our picnic, so I ate it slowly and gave what was left to Robert when I got back to the hotel.

Finally, we, after eight days and with our eight pieces of luggage, plus two overflowing bags of food, were on the train back to St. Petersburg. Same car, same woman steward as when we came. A bottle of champagne and one hour later, Robert was asleep. I lit my candle, put his country music tape on my player, and again, as I watched the countryside rolling by with the familiar birches, goats, cows, horse-drawn wagons, people walking, drunks stumbling, it was easy to imagine we were visitors in a past century.

Meanwhile, Moscow was in the middle of another coup attempt. Apparently the latest round of violence started the day before. We watched some of it on TV that morning. Parliament continued to hole up in the White House, which was on fire. CNN reported an unconfirmed 500 dead. Khasbulatov and the Vice President Alexander Rutskoy were still trying to wrest power from Yeltsin, who finally gave the order to the troops and tanks to fight. I wanted to be there! I did write out a fax for Viktor to send to Frank, so that he and Neil wouldn't worry.

Olga and her husband met us at the train station, took us to the hotel so we could drop off our luggage, and then we went directly to their home for a luncheon feast. Tomatoes in sour cream, orange and black caviar on bread, blini with caviar or fruit compote, champagne, cookies.

Later, Mark met us in the lobby of our hotel and walked us to his house for vodka and caviar. The best part of that time was that he kept calling Dina "Catsella." I've never heard anyone use that expression except my father.

Robert and I had dinner alone—our choice—at the Literary Cafe. I had gone in earlier to make the reservation and we got a chance to relax and enjoy our last evening in Russia with more champagne, blini and caviar, and pelmeni. A violinist and pianist in the background provided the relaxing atmosphere, and I thought of all the different times I had been there.

We got up at 4:30 AM; Olga picked us up at 5:30 and took us to the station. And then we were on the train again. First class. The bathroom was clean—it even had soap and toilet paper! I laughed during those three weeks how I went nowhere without my roll of toilet paper that I had brought from home, as always, and how nonchalant I was in pulling it out to blow my nose or take it to a restroom.

Some firsts on that ride: first time first class; first time a dog came into our compartment and sniffed for drugs; and first time we kept our visas. I couldn't figure out why they did not take them. Whatever the reason, they were a great souvenir, with a stamp from every hotel we stayed in and the dates there. The only visa I still have.

It didn't feel like we had been traveling for three weeks, although this trip was the longest since I went with Natasha to Mongolia and Siberia in 1982.

As usual I picked up a *Time Magazine* at our first stop in Finland. Shevardnadze was in trouble in Georgia. He had been holed up in Sukhumi, vowing to keep his nation whole or die trying!

We went crazy over the bathrooms at the Hotel Hesperia in Helsinki—bidet, deep bathtub, spotless. I took a long bath and as I do at home, I lit my candle, put on a tape, poured Neutrogena oil into the water, and I was one happy lady, so happy in fact that tears came. Then, down to the saunas. I could have cried there, too. Superlatives aren't

1993—2nd Visit to Glubokoye

enough. I was actually there for two hours. The first hour Robert and I were in and out of the sauna, then he went for his massage and I stayed on for another hour. I don't think I can find the words to express how good it felt to wash away every bit of the grime from Russia, to feel clean, really clean, for the first time in three weeks.

After Robert, I had my massage, strong, deep, the perfect way to end the trip. When I managed to waddle up to the room (the vodka we had smuggled into the sauna didn't help my gait any), we got ready and went to dinner at the Plaza Hotel and Restaurant. It felt so good to put on the one outfit I had not worn. I always brought one clean change of clothes to save for Helsinki, or the last day of any trip. It really made a difference.

After a bottle of champagne and a six-course meal for about $230, we went to a disco called Finnea, danced a few good dances, than stood back and watched the Finns having fun.

Helsinki, as always, was pristine. No spit gobs all over the sidewalks, no pot holes big enough to trip an elephant, no dirt, no smelly or brown water, no absence of water or heat, no bad breath or body odor, no dirty fingernails, no meals swimming in grease, no warm champagne.

The return flight was fine. And we learned that the crisis in Russia seemed to be over. Reports were that 137 were dead and 600 were wounded. Rutskoi and Khasbulatov were in prison, the White House was being called the Black House because of the fires, and for the first time since 1924, no armed soldiers goose-stepping and guarding Lenin's Tomb. Who would have imagined two weeks prior, when we saw them there, that they would be gone so soon?

Olga came to the US in October, and among other places already mentioned, she and Robert gave a class at Buckingham, Browne & Nichols, a private school in Cambridge, Massachusetts.

Chapter 26
1993—Health Update

"We must not confuse dissent with disloyalty.
When the loyal opposition dies, I think the soul of America dies with it."
—Edward R. Murrow (1908–1965)
American broadcast journalist and war correspondent

In June, OASES again changed its name. Since the Soviet Union was no longer, it was clear that we didn't want to reference Soviet exchanges in the organization's name. We became International Professional Exchanges, Inc. (IPEX). I was still president and my good friend Armen Dedekian was vice president. I had a few years earlier independently established Cynthia Dickstein, Inc., so that I could keep finances from my initiated programs separate from the organization's, and my personal funds safe should liability ever become an issue.

In April, my Russian firefighters were invited to attend the 5th Annual Fire and Emergency Services Dinner in Washington, DC. Vice President Al Gore gave the keynote address. While there, we met with representatives Steny Hoyer and Curt Weldon.

We also visited FEMA (Federal Emergency Management Association) Headquarters in DC, the Congressional Fires Services Institute, the National Emergency Training Center in Emmitsburg, MD, and the University of Maryland's Fire and Rescue Institute.

On May 4th, the *Boston Globe* published an op-ed I wrote about Sasha. In that piece, I focused on the fighting in Abkhazia, when Georgian troops and tanks occupied the capital, Sukhumi, in an attempt to overcome the Abkhazian separatists.

Sasha had moved there in 1984, to the Black Sea town of Gagra, where he built a home. I worried about him because Gagra wasn't far from Sukhumi. But I finally received a letter from him reassuring me he was safe.

"In Gagra I survived the bombing from helicopter, bombs, and rockets. Many dead were found in the streets when the city was liberated by Abkhazian forces. And now there is heavy fighting near Sukhumi and the army needs more and more recruits."

Olga, who had moved to Kuwait, where she was a personal trainer to the royal family, also came to Boston to teach in early August. Again she stayed with Frank and me and when it was time for her to leave, she told me she wanted to take some (forbidden) vodka to Kuwait. I emptied two bottles, one with shampoo and another with suntan lotion, washed them thoroughly, and filled them with 100-proof Stolichnaya. She didn't get caught!

At the end of the month, another aerobics group of 10 came to Boston from Russia.

And in mid-September, six American delegates went to Moscow, St. Petersburg and Helsinki in the last program of the fire exchange. Evgeny Karpov, previously a firefighter in Mongolia, and one of the April delegates, said, "Firefighters are the same all over the world. Only people with a kind soul can do this job."

Journalist Anna Politkovskaya reported that the year before was a record year—10,267 Russians died in fires, almost 3,000 more than the prior year—due to run down and unsafe buildings. She stated that victims got no support from the state.

Then, a Russian law enforcement delegation visited the US, headed by the Chief of Moscow Metro Police Colonel Alexander Veldayev. I again arranged for a reception to be held at John Jay College of Criminal Justice in New York City, where we were once again greeted by Gerald W. Lynch, President of the College, and also William Bratton, then Police Commissioner of NYC.

*　*　*

By the fall of 1993, I had had five MS episodes since 1989. Two demyelinating ones, when my entire body tingled and felt like pins and needles were piercing my skin, and three of optic neuritis, where my color perception was off and I saw blurry images, as if I were looking through dark smoke or thunderclouds. But I was lucky; none of the flares left me with any lasting physical impairments.

Back in 1989, I became a patient of neurologist Dr. Lou Caplan, who had initially been pretty upbeat about my prognosis and told me that episodes like mine could be caused by things other than MS, such as viral infections. But four years later, when my eyes were affected, I saw neuro-ophthalmologist Dr. Simmons Lessell at the Massachusetts Eye and Ear Infirmary. After he looked at my MRI and into my eyes, he said, "In fact, you have a rather mild episode of optic neuritis, even though it may not seem so mild to you. However, that, along with your MRI, shows that you definitely have MS." What I had been trying to deny became a reality that day.

Dr. Lessell went on to tell me that 17 percent of all people who died from trauma who were autopsied had MS and didn't know it. And that I may never have another episode or could have another one soon.

It was an unusual doctor visit. I certainly wasn't happy with my diagnosis. But prior to the appointment, while I was in the waiting room, I smiled at a picture on the wall identical to one Frank had in his office. A print of a watercolor of stones at the seashore. Then, as I was leafing through an old March issue of *Lear's* magazine, I was totally surprised to see myself, full-page photo, in color, running on the treadmill in the

1993—Health Update

Trotter ad. I had been asked to model for the Trotter Treadmill brochure and they used one of the photos for ads. Besides *Lear's*, one other publication I knew of that ran the ad was the *Wall Street Journal*. The irony—I got no pleasure from using a treadmill. But I did get paid nicely.

I looked like a picture of health.

In the fall, Boris Yeltsin, the only leader in Russian history to be freely elected, who was expected to continue to expand democracy, disbanded an elected parliament in 1993, enabling Putin's rise to power.

Yeltsin did eliminate the section of the Russian Criminal Code that applied a penalty for homosexual relations.

And on October 6th, with no announcement and for the first time since WWII, no honor guard was posted at Lenin's Tomb.

American Demographer Murray Feshbach, from Georgetown University, estimated that there were then 2,000 – 5,000 full-blown AIDS cases in Russia and 10,000-20,000 people who were infected with HIV.

There were more homeless who slept in railroad stations, and more babies who were kidnapped from homeless mothers than ever before. There were more drug and alcohol problems, more runaways and homeless youth. The number of murders increased, more than 1/3 the year before, and juvenile crime was growing 15 times faster than adult crime.

We got word from Russia that they wanted to continue the journalism exchange so they could learn how to operate in a for-profit environment.

Pravda **had become a capitalist enterprise.**

Part Six

Chapter 27
Israel

"You don't know me from the wind
you never will, you never did
I'm the little Jew who wrote the Bible.
I've seen the nations rise and fall
I've heard their stories, heard them all
but love's the only engine of survival."
—Leonard Cohen (1934–2016)
Canadian poet and singer-songwriter,
from "The Future"

1971

Hebron Boys

It was Hebron, 1971, and the city, the oldest Jewish community in the world, was under Israeli military rule. When Israel was created in 1948, the Jordanians captured the city and it remained under Arab control until 1967, when Israel took it back during the Six-Day War. (In January of 1997, 80 percent of the city was transferred to Palestinian authority, with the remaining 20 percent still remaining under Israeli rule.)

I spent almost two months in Israel then, going freely to Hebron and the towns of the West Bank. My visit there was bookended by war—the Six-Day War in 1967 and the Yom Kippur War in 1973. Obviously, the Israelis didn't know what was coming in 1973, but they were preparing. Convinced that they could count on no one else in the world for

Hugging three Palestinian children in Hebron. They were affectionate, too, in the shy, tentative manner of 6- and 7-year-old boys.

their nation's survival, their defensive posture was in place. At the same time, they knew and resented that they needed US financial and political help, so their attitude towards Americans, at least among the young Israelis I met, was one of disdain.

For the most part, I stayed in Jerusalem, and at age 25, spent much time with these young Israelis, nicknamed *Sabras* after a cactus plant with prickly fruit. "Why don't you speak Hebrew?" they demanded. "Why don't you live here?" they asked disapprovingly. "Yes, you American Jews send money, but we risk our lives so that you will have a homeland if you ever need it!" they declared.

Most often, I was the only American in a group. And most often, they refused to speak the English they knew so well. Although I asked many questions, trying to learn who they were, what they thought and felt, I was asked only one question—ever—during my time there. "Do you like Israel?"

I saw them as a generation not given to introspection, but full of pride bordering on arrogance, and too nationalistic for my comfort. Israel's purpose was their purpose. But I understood.

While everyone was focused on the threat from the Arab nations in 1971, I had begun to get a hint of the depth of the domestic problems facing the country.

In 1971, most Israelis with whom I spoke were totally one-sided in their assessment of the well-being of the Arabs. They said that those Arabs who lived in Israel were happy, because they had good jobs, good housing, and basically a much better life than before Israeli rule. Those Sabras would never have predicted the 1987 intifada, the popular uprising of Palestinians in the West Bank and Gaza Strip in an effort to end Israel's occupation of those territories and to create an independent Palestinian state.

In 1971, there was discrimination among the Israelis. The Ashkenazim, or Northern European Jews, were the "haves" and the Sephardim, or Southern European and Middle Eastern Jews, including those from Iran and Iraq, were the "have nots." The Sephardim received the worst jobs, the most inferior housing. The Sabras showed no sensitivity to that reality.

Back then, the Sabras dismissed the ultra-orthodox Jews as primitive throwbacks to the European *shtetls*, didn't consider them a part of modern Israel, never dreamed they would gain so much power and influence, never dreamed that in 1995, one of them would assassinate their Prime Minister, Yitzak Rabin.

(Fifty years later, the fanatic ultra-orthodox were creating worse problems, had become racists fighting reform within Judaism, even attacking women whom they believed weren't dressed modestly enough. In 2019, The Pew Research Center reported that "When it comes to restrictions on religious freedom, Israel is in the company of countries like Saudi Arabia, Syria, and Iran ... Israel is one of the top 20 most religiously restrictive countries in the world.")

Israel

I thought it might be different on a kibbutz, and so I went to the Kibbutz Mishmar Hanegev, near Beersheba, intending to stay a couple of weeks. Beside the fact that my bus got a flat tire en route from Tel Aviv, and that I had to get a ride on a "fragrant" fertilizer truck from the main road into the kibbutz itself, my bed had no sheets or pillows, there were mice in the room, and people were sick. I went to a meeting—boring. Then to dinner—awful. Finally my three roommates there told me that it was a good kibbutz because there were lots of drugs. And I told them that I lived in Los Angeles and certainly didn't need to come to a kibbutz for drugs. I left the next day.

Not to say that I didn't enjoy many things I did in Israel. I ate fresh pomegranate for the first time. I hooked up with an Israeli guy named Izzy, stayed with him in his apartment, which used to be a sultan's stable, and he took me to the Golon Heights, Safed, Acre, Caesarea, to parties, for drinks or meals to the Artist's Cafe, to the American Colony Hotel, or to Feferberg's, the Eastern European Jewish restaurant opened in 1934. And to the Casbah Restaurant, where I saw Moshe Dayan come in to make a phone call. Izzy and I rode Arab-owned horses. I even watched one of his friends smoking hash at an Arab establishment in the Old City, although he didn't tell me till later that was what it was. The water pipe should have given me a clue!

And he took me through Hezekial's underground tunnel, 1,750 feet long, built in the 8th century BC, to bring spring water to King David's City. We carried candles and sang as we made our way through the darkness and the waist-high water.

But I found the warmth and connection that I was craving was in the older generation, the parents and grandparents of Izzi's friends, the Sephardic Jews who had emigrated from Iran and Iraq. I found joy in the Israeli music. And I found wonder in the biggest, most round, most orange, most beautiful moon I had ever seen, rising over Jerusalem.

1994

By 1994, the landscape had changed. That year, when I finally returned to Israel, 23 years after my first visit, the Gaza Strip and the West Bank city of Jericho were under Palestinian control, and after six years of the Intifada, I took no trips to Hebron, no photos with friendly Palestinian children, who were more likely to be throwing stones than giving hugs.

There was increased use of drugs in the country, particularly Angel Dust and LSD.

In 1994, the society was faced with finding jobs and housing for the 600,000 Jews who had arrived from Russia since 1989 and they had to try to integrate the 20,000 Ethiopian Jews who began arriving *en masse* in 1983 and then in another wave in 1991. To complicate their assimilation, the ultra-orthodox rabbis were trying to force the Ethiopians to convert.

The ultra-orthodox, who then were slightly more than 10 percent of the population, had much greater political power in the Knesset (Israeli legislature) than their numbers would indicate because of the need for the major parties to build coalitions to reach a majority.

And the problems the ultra-orthodox have created for the majority of Israelis are not insignificant. They are anti-Zionists; they believe that the Jews have no business in Israel until the Messiah comes. At excavation sites, they have painted swastikas on the stones because they consider the Jewish archaeologists "Nazis," accusing them of desecrating 2,000-year-old Jewish graves. Until 2014, when Israel passed a law allowing the draft of ultra-orthodox, they did not serve in the army like most others, and would not agree to even some substitute form of public service. Secular Israelis resent the fact that these people live off the very state whose right to exist they deny.

The ultra-orthodox Jews in 2020 comprised about 13 percent of Israel's population, or 1.1 million, and they control marriage and divorce. There are no civil marriages. Jews who wish to marry in Israel must be married by an orthodox rabbi, otherwise the marriage is not recognized by the state. Their only other option is to travel outside Israel for the ceremony, usually to Cypress. If married outside of Israel, their marriages are recognized. I believe it is the only place in the world where marriage is forbidden to some Jews.

Both the Arabs in Israel and the orthodox Jews sometimes have as many as ten to twelve children, far more than the average Israeli. With these greater numbers will come an even greater voice and no doubt greater conflict.

But during my 1994 visit, the cypress trees were taller, the egrets more in number, and I found the voice of the Sabras less strident, more sensitive, reflecting a recognition of the complexity of the issues facing the nation, of the need for compromise. It was evident that both the Sabras and the nation had matured, a consequence of tragic conflicts and world criticism, and of the knowledge that under the most difficult of circumstances, Israel had become a very impressive nation.

And, people were simply nicer. I think that was a result of their optimism, their belief then in a real possibility for peace.

Consequently, Frank and I had a wonderful time during the three weeks we were there. We had dinner with Ethan Bonner, the *New York Times'* Jerusalem Bureau Chief. Went to the Knesset to see the government in action. We rode camels. Swam in the Dead Sea. Hiked in the Sinai Desert in Egypt. Took a room at St. Catherine's Monastery so that after a few hours sleep, we could climb all night to reach the top of Mt. Moses, 7,500 feet above sea level, to see dawn break. (Mt. Moses is supposedly the Mt. Horeb of the Bible, where Moses is believed to have received the Ten Commandments.)

Our way was lit only by the cigarettes of the men with camels, who periodically yelled "*cameel*," in case anyone wanted to give up and get a ride to the top. It was strenuous, but we made it on our own, found a large, relatively comfortable boulder, and as the sun began to rise and warm our faces, a church group from Greece began to sing and chant. Absolutely one of our most memorable travel experiences.

Another of the highlights for me then was the fact that I took a resort scuba lesson in order to go scuba diving with dolphins. Usually, one was able to snorkel or swim with them, but when we arrived, there were two one-week-old babies who they didn't want disturbed. I'm not a strong swimmer. I never, ever dreamed that I would someday put on all that equipment and trust my breath to a clunky can of air. They gave permission for me to scuba dive with the dolphins, but only after I told them I planned to write an article about the experience for the *Boston Globe*. And after I took an introductory scuba diving course at a dive center nearby. I really wanted to hug those babies. Of course, I couldn't catch them.

Particularly haunting at Yad Vashem, the Holocaust Memorial site, was the dark Children's Memorial to the 1.5 million killed during the Holocaust, with its quiet music, lit candles, and their names. So many names.

And then to Megido, which is supposed to be the site of the future Armageddon of the Bible. And to a cemetery, where we saw stones piled high on each grave as is the Jewish custom.

I also bought some stones, with poems painted on them in Hebrew, to give away as gifts. I kept one for myself:

In the desert, there are soft stones in the riverbed
And letters never finished.
Nostalgia for peace.

At the Diaspora Museum, for eight shekels, I got a computer printout of the history of the Dickstein name, and another about Glubokoye.

We were motivated to take this trip by more than the fact that Frank hadn't yet been to Israel. In June of 1992, for Father's Day, the *Boston Globe* had published an op-ed piece I had written about my father. That evening, I got a call from one of my Scranton cousins, whom I hadn't seen since I was a child.

Shirley Dickstein Hollenberg, my Uncle Harry's daughter, had come from Scranton to Boston for that weekend for a bar mitzvah and she saw the article.

After we reconnected then, we became very close. When I told Shirley about my meeting Mark, she told me about Lena Torchin, a Russian relative in Tel Aviv whom her father talked about, and Lena's sister Naomi Wexler, who had died two years earlier but whose husband Yale still lived in Bridgeport, Connecticut. Lena and I began a correspondence, and soon after, I visited Yale and met his daughter, Jeannie Rifkin. Two years later, in 1994, Frank and I went to Israel for Jeannie's daughter's Bat

The author meeting with Lena Torchin in Tel Aviv

Mitzvah at the Congregation Moreshet Yisrael, the only conservative synagogue in Jerusalem, with the party afterward at Jerusalem's King David Hotel. And we went also, of course, to meet Lena.

It was Tuesday, June 28, my birthday, and what a gift I gave myself. After picking up some wine and chocolate, we arrived at Lena's home at 5:00 PM. I was excited. She was excited. We showed pictures, asked questions, talked and listened. Her husband Mendl and Frank mostly listened.

Lena, named after my great-grandmother Chiena, spoke English, Russian, Polish, German, Hebrew, and Yiddish. She told me that her mother's name was Frada Henya. She provided absolute proof that Alla and Mark and their family were really my family, too. Mark Segal's mother, Yelizabeta, was the sister of my grandfather, Chaim Lazar. So the relationship was finally known. Mark and my father were first cousins.

My grandfather was also Lena's mother's brother. Thus, Lena was also my father's first cousin. When we began corresponding, Lena told me that she did not remember my father, but she knew that my grandfather Chaim Lazar was the son of Abram Dickstein.

She confessed to me that no one, not her husband nor her children, knew that she was three years older than she said she was. Born on May 15, 1913, she was actually the same age as her husband. She told me of her daughter Hava and her son Joshua, called Shuki.

Little did I know then that Hava and her husband Reuven, who worked in the foreign department of the Prime Minister's office, would soon spend a year in Boston when he was chosen to be a Wexner Israeli Fellow at Harvard's Kennedy School, or that in following years Frank and I would meet them in Cologne, Germany, or for dinner in Hanoi when we found that coincidentally we would be there at the same time, or that I would go to London to meet Hava in 1997, so we could we spend a few days enjoying the city and one another. We added our flowers at Buckingham Palace to the 60 million left to honor Princess Diana, who had died August 31 in a tragic car accident.

Lena's sister Brocha and her daughter Dvora went to Palestine in 1947, on the ship *Exodus*. When it was denied entry by the British, they and other passengers were sent to Germany, where they stayed until they were eventually allowed to continue on to Israel. At the time, Brocha was six months pregnant with Naom's second child and had been married only five weeks when her husband Naom (Kaplan—her first cousin and Sofya's brother) died in the war. All she had to remember him by were his letters, and when she left Russia, she was so nervous, she had left all the letters under her pillow.

She had her son Zvi, then married again (to a Guzman) after she got to Israel, but was not happy with that husband. In fact, Lena said Brocha had a very miserable life.

Lena talked of how she came to Israel.

"I left home because I heard Menachem Begin speak in Vilna, when he was head of Betar (the Zionist Youth Movement founded in 1923 by Vladimir Jabotinsky). He tried to convince all young Jews to go to Palestine, to build the country, because he said

Declaration 970
The one (Brocha) who is holding this declaration (a *maapil*) is a brave person who left Europe in 1947 and was returned forcibly to Germany from the port of Haifa and is in exile while returning to Israel. (No name is listed.)

The *Exodus* stamp was put on in the Poppendorf exile camp by the people in charge of the camp on July 25, 1947.

Translation: Compliments of Rabbi Israel Becer of Congregation Chofetz Chayim, Tucson, AZ

Europe wasn't safe for them. I told my mother I wanted to go and she said no. I went anyway.

I left on the ship *Parita*, the first ship to come to Tel Aviv, not Haifa, six weeks before the war broke out. I came with only a sack on my back, two dresses which I wore, one pair of shoes, two pairs of underwear, and no photos because we knew we had to throw our packs into the water. It took six weeks, with hardly any food, only some potatoes or pasta and a glass of water per day. It was so hot, there were worms in the pasta.

On the way, the ship stopped in Turkey and we all asked for bread and water. Jewish people there came with little boats and brought us food and drink. I still remember how to say bread and water in Turkish: *Su ekmek*. Mendel was here six years already. Because war broke out in 1939, the day I arrived in Israel, I was allowed to stay even though I had come illegally."

Lena did know a lot about the family. She told me that we had relatives in the small town of Kurinetz, not far from Glubokoye, because her mother always talked about it. I later learned that my grandmother, Socia Zalmon Alperowitz, was from that town.

And in fact, the only information I have about my grandfather's parents came from Lena.

She told me that my great grandfather Abram, born around 1840, had four or five brothers, who were all rabbis. He was the only one who was not, and he was the only one not killed in pogroms. His wife was named Chiena.

She also told me that her parents and grandparents were very religious. That on Shabbat, they went only to synagogue; they did not work, they did not cook, they did nothing. That Abram was a genius who sat all day, every day, studying the Bible, learning the Torah, and that all the Christian people knew him and came to him for advice.

Thus, it was my great-grandmother Chiena, with the help of her daughters, who ran the hotel and restaurant they had at a train station in Scribenetz, not far from Glubokoye and Sharkovshchyzna, their hometown.

Guests at the station often talked about girls and sex and Lena's mother, Frada Henya, listened. She did most all the work there, making kishka, cholent, all the food, and she told Lena not to believe any boys because they would go with a girl, then laugh about it later.

"Chiena died when she was in her 60s from cancer. Abram's second wife was about 50 years old, when my mother was 45, and she colored her gray hair black so she would look younger. My mother and my aunts did not like her."

Abram supposedly had from Rambam an original book he wrote by hand in the 12th century, before the Inquisition. (Ramban, also known as Maimonides, full name Rabbi Moshe ben Maimon, was an astronomer, a philosopher and a physician, and one

Israel

Hava Torchin Avital, Lena's daughter

of the most influential medieval Jewish scholars.) Lena said that either my grandfather Chaim Lazar (the oldest of the siblings, she thought) or his brother Max took the book after Abram died, as his inheritance.

Unfortunately, I've no idea what happened to the book.

After a couple hours of talking, Lena's daughter Hava and her husband Reuven Avital came and took us out to dinner at the Reef, a wonderful restaurant near the water.

Five years after my visit with Lena, in November of 1999, Mark and Dina travelled from Russia to Tel Aviv to meet Lena. Both she and Mark described the meeting as one of the happiest days of their lives.

Unfortunately, I never saw Lena again, but we corresponded often. How lucky I was to find and meet her before she died of cancer in March of 2006 at the age of 93.

Chapter 28
Partisans

*"And when you plough a field, erect a mound of stones on it
as a testament and memorial for brothers who did not attain a Jewish grave."*
—Dr. Mark Dworzecki (1908–1975)
Ghetto survivor, writer

Before World War II, Glubokoye was a thriving community with a large trade center. Jews there were very active and relatively prosperous. They had religious elementary schools called *kheyders*, a *yeshiva*, a Jewish newspaper, theaters, two cinemas, and an orchestra. Also there were organizations to help sick Jews, women, children in need. A Bread for Poor Society provided food for *Shabbos* to poor Jews and those in prison. And one could hear klezmer music at celebrations, and often the sweet notes of a violin, harmonica, or accordion through open windows.

The town of Glubokoye before the war also had numerous Zionist organizations, as well as Bundists and an underground Communist cell. And too, there were the Yiddishists, those who didn't want any Hebrew to be spoken.

The Soviet Army occupied Glubokoye on September 17, 1939, and citizens were forced to adapt to the Soviet ways. But on June 22, 1941, Germany attacked the Soviet Union. By the 24th, Soviet officials, their families, and the Red Army began to evacuate the town, and on July 2nd, the first German soldiers appeared in their green uniforms with swastikas on their sleeves, to begin the occupation of Glubokoye. They established the Glubokoye Ghetto on October 22nd, 1941, when they gave Jews a one-hour notice to vacate their homes.

And thus the terror truly began for the town of Glubokoye—and for my relatives there.

According to the book *Glubokie Ghetto: A Concentration Camp for the Remaining Jews of the Surrounding Liquidated Shtetls*, translated by Eilat Gordin Levitan, in July 1942, German authorities ordered that all survivors of 42 annihilated cities and towns in the area must go to the Glubokoye ghetto. Meanwhile, Christian children threw stones at the Jews. Local hooligans attacked and beat the Jews. Adults placed anti-Semitic slogans on the streets, calling for their annihilation and death. Jews were soon denied any personal property.

The Germans assured the Jews that no one would be killed. But people were killed. Killed if someone fled the ghetto for the forest, or if they were caught with a bit of butter or some fresh berries they may have picked off a bush. Undernourished, they lived in unbearably overcrowded conditions, desperately waiting for a Red Army victory. In anguish, some of these people turned to alcohol. They prayed for miracles. They wept. They killed their infants so that their crying wouldn't reveal their hiding places. Some committed suicide. Murdered bodies were not buried but left exposed, to be eaten by dogs or other wild animals.

But all that was nothing compared to the torture and humiliation that would follow, best described in excerpts from two books in particular:

Throughout the Temporarily-Occupied Regions of the Soviet Union and in the Death Camps of Poland During the War of 1941-1945
edited by Ilya Ehrenburg and Vasily Grossman, Holocaust Library, NY:

"In Borki, 1½ km from Glubokoye, the Germans forced the young to dance at the edge of an open grave and the old to sing songs. After this sadistic mockery they forced the young and healthy to carry the feeble old people and cripples into the pit and lay them down. Only after this were they to lie down themselves, and then the Germans methodically and calmly shot everyone…..The murders were preceded by unimaginable torture: people were cut in half, teeth were pulled, nails were driven into the victim's heads, people were kept naked in the freezing cold and soaked with cold water, beaten with sticks and rifle butts until they lost consciousness…"

And in another book by Dr. Mark Dworzecki, *The Jerusalem of Lithuania: in Struggle and Destruction* (Paris: L'Union Populaire Juive en France, 1948):

"In December, 1941, more than 100 gypsies were brought and before shooting, were stripped naked and kept that way for a long while in the bitter winter cold. Their children were seated naked on the ice. They turned blue. Their faces froze so they couldn't cry. They stiffened and soon thereafter they died. The Germans then drove the gypsies, naked, into the Borok Forest, forcing them to drag along their frozen children. There at the open pits, the murderers ordered them to sing, dance, jump, clap and so on. As they performed they were beaten with whips to make them dance better, sing louder and the young gypsies were forced to laugh. The strains of the original, sad gypsy songs, combined with their crying, yammering, and screaming cut through the air and were carried through the entire forest and rolled far beyond the forest….then, the Germans pushed the unfortunate gypsies into the pits where they had previously thrown their dead children, and there, they shot them."

Dworzecki recounted that in an effort to break the spirit,

> "…the Germans would make merry during work time, and would force the Jews to sing songs, imitate various animals, creep on all fours, dance, jump, kiss their boots… And this, often while they were naked."

Glubokoye partisan units began forming in 1942.

On August 20, 1943, planes in two days dropped bombs, grenades and released some flaming material that set fire to the entire ghetto, killing 3,500 Jews. Many were burned alive. A few escaped by running, concealed by the fire and smoke.

One of the escapees was my cousin Nachama.

The Red Army finally liberated Glubokoye on July 3, 1944.

* * *

When I was young, my father used to go to house or estate sales and come home with boxes of books and comic books. (He also bought and sold antiques.) When I went through his things after he died, I found a black Nazi scrapbook with a swastika on the cover, printed during the war but in perfect condition and with pages mostly blank except for photos of leading Nazis. What to do with it? I certainly didn't want it in my home and I didn't want to sell it and have it end up in the hands of some Neo Nazis. Nor did I want to throw it out, as if that could make history disappear. I finally decided to contribute it to the Holocaust Center of Northern California in San Francisco (now named the Jewish Family and Children's Services Holocaust Center).

The Nazis had long hated Jews and Bolsheviks. In 1930, Hitler wrote, "The Nordic race has a right to rule the world…any cooperation with Russia is out of the question, for there on a Slavic Tartar body is set a Jewish head." (Zvi Gitelman, *A Century of Ambivalence: The Jews of Russia and the Soviet Union, 1881 to the Present*, Indiana University Press, 2001)

Chapter 29
Nachama and Yale

"All the Dachaus must remain standing. The Dachaus, the Belsens, the Buchenwalds, the Auschwitzes—all of them. They must remain standing because they are a monument to a moment in time when some men decided to turn the earth into a graveyard, into it they shoveled all of their reason, their logic, their knowledge, but worst of all their conscience. And the moment we forget this, the moment we cease to be haunted by its remembrance—then we become the gravediggers."
—Rod Serling (1924–1975)
screenwriter and TV producer from Binghamton, NY
"Death's-Head Revisited," (episode 74 of *The Twilight Zone*)

Lena told me about her sister Nachama. Nachama's daughter, Jeannie Rifkin, also shared what she knew of her parents during the war.

Frada Henya, Nachama's and Lena's mother (and also a sister of my grandfather, Chaim Lazar), raised seven children in Sharkovshchyzna, Lena's home town. Only three of the children survived the war, two of them (Brocha and Lena) because they had moved away.

When the Nazis established the Glubokoye ghetto in November of 1941, Frada Henya and four of her children still in Russia were taken from their home in Sharkovshchyzna. They were five of 6,000 Jews forcibly relocated to Glubokoye. Her husband Joshua had just died in his bed at home in Sharkovshchyzna of natural causes. "One of the lucky ones," it was said.

(In the destruction of the Sharkawshchyna Ghetto, which numbered 1,200 Jews... (p. 67, 69)..."they poked out the eyes of the unfortunates with red-hot rods, skinned them alive, broke the fingers, pulled out the teeth (especially if they were gold teeth), cut out tongues and more." (Dr. Mark Dworzecki, *The Jerusalem of Lithuania: in Struggle and Destruction Paris*: L'Union Populaire Juive en France," 1948)

While her family was living in the Glubokoye ghetto, Nachama was on the run with the man she loved, Yale Wexler, and they decided to go to Glubokoye. After a time, Yale went back into the woods and joined a partisan group and Nachama stayed with her mother and her siblings.

When Hitler's officers ordered the Glubokoye ghetto destroyed, the family was hiding in an underground bunker. When the soldiers stormed the area, Frada Henya was faced with a choice: stay there or make a run for it. Nachama begged her mother to grab the other children and run, but her mother said no, she didn't have the strength. And there, they died.

Except Nachama, who ran and hid in a cemetery. There she later met someone from Yale's group who went back to tell Yale she was alive.

The lives lived by partisans in the forests were both heroic and horrific. They built bonfires and sang Jewish partisan songs in both Yiddish and Russian. But they had infections, typhus, sores on their legs and feet. They were hungry, dizzy, suffered bug bites in summer and freezing cold in the winter, and had only tattered rags for bandages after they were shot as they ran through fields of cows and pigs in an effort to escape the Germans.

Those woods were my cousin Nachama's home for three years. She became a partisan. She fought the Nazis. And when a rabbi came to their partisan group, she married Yale.

In 1992, the Organizations of Partisans, Underground Fighters and Ghetto Rebels in Israel published a book in Yiddish, *With Proud Bearing, 1939-1945: Chapters in the History of Jewish Fighting in the Narotch Forests*, edited by Moshe Kalchheim.

Nachama and her husband Yale each have a chapter in that book. Below, excerpts in their words…..

Mendle Torchin, Lena Torchin, Yale Wexler, Shirley Hollenberg, Naomi Wexler

Yale Wexler

"Already having been forced into a ghetto, I had built an underground bunker in Postov in the early days of autumn in 1942. And a group of former soldiers decided to organize an underground group whose task would be to protect ourselves in case of liquidation and prepare ourselves to go into the woods when the time came.

"When the Germans began the destruction of the ghetto, 12 of us went into the bunker and hid for nine days. When we emerged, we saw that the Ghetto was empty of all its Jews and we decided to divide into small groups and look for hiding places on the properties of local peasants. The peasant at whose place my parents had been hiding gave them up to the Germans, who shot them on the spot.

"Winter came and with it the cold. The peasant with whom Nachama and I were staying told us to leave because he was no longer willing to risk his life. We decided to go to the Glubokoye Ghetto. On the way there, Nachama got frostbite on her feet and when we got to the ghetto, she had to be put in the hospital, where they cut off the sole of her right foot.

"In the spring of 1943, I went with some friends into the woods. Nachama remained behind in the Glubokoye Ghetto with her mother and her brothers and sister until the liquidation and during the great slaughter, she had a chance to escape and made it to the woods of Kazhan.

"I myself arrived in the Rusakovsker Pooshtche. There I met up with many more Jews who had gathered there from the surrounding towns. I found mostly families with small children. I found them in a terrible state. Uprooted, cut off, underdressed, hungry. Their situation was precarious. It was winter. It was very cold. All day, every day, they huddled on the ground around a fire. There was no roof over their heads. Most importantly, they had no idea what to do next. And they had to hide from the enemies, the Germans and the Lithuanians (who often collaborated with the Nazis). But they were also frightened of what the Christian partisans would do to them if they came upon them as they foraged for food for their families.

"It's hard to convey what kind of impression it left on me to see these people and I began to think about what I might be able to do to improve their situation, to make the lives of these people a little bit brighter. I was young then. Just out of the army. Full of hopes for a better life. But all I wanted to do was fight and take revenge on those damn enemies of the Jewish people.

"My goal was to join a group of partisans.

"Refused by the Russian partisans commanded by Tsherkasov because we had no weapons, a requirement for membership, a group of us decided to do something that wouldn't require weapons. We learned where a German unit drove through every day. We went there, took from the peasants saws and axes, cut the telephone wires and with the wires, twisted the rails and on top, poured garbage and covered it with sand so that it would look like landmines. We went to Tsherkasov and told him. He didn't believe it and sent his aides to find out what happened to the German unit. His aides came back and reported that a unit that had been sent to the front had been forced to stop for five days until a special group came to take apart the mines. Peasants told the Germans that it was Jews who were responsible for this, which made them very angry.

"I first joined the partisan group in Niyever. My wife was still in the ghetto in Glubokoye and I went to the commissar to talk to him about what one might be able to do for the Jews in Glubok, to bring them out of the ghetto. It took a few weeks before I received an official letter from him with permission to go to the Glubok Ghetto to try to liberate all the Glubok Jews. As we approached Glubokoye, I sent someone I knew to the ghetto with a note for Nachama, asking her it if was possible to get into the ghetto. He returned with a message that one could no longer enter the ghetto because it was now surrounded by Germans. When it got dark, I said, "We don't have a choice; we're going in.

"The messenger, a local peasant, told us that we shouldn't go that night because the Ghetto was surrounded and none of us would get back alive. So we decided to wait another day and see what was going on. In the morning, we heard that all the Jews in Glubok were being taken out of the ghetto. Nachama had escaped and hid in the forest in Kazhan. I found her.

"We then went to the Prozvodstvener Group.

"After liberation, Nachama and I went back to Postov. Nachama immediately went back to our normal family life. With her goodness, her friendliness, she opened our house to everyone. Dozens of people passing through from the Russian forests would find something to eat in our home or a place to sleep. Nachama welcomed them with open arms.

"All the Jews of Postov who came back from the woods and who were mobilized in the Red Army died at the front. I was the only one who remained alive."

Yale became a rabbi in Postov, which enabled him to avoid being drafted.

Nachama (Naomi) Wexler

"One night in the forest, Yale and I found two sisters who first gave us a nice meal. Yale went off to meet with his brother and sister, who were with a group of Jews nearby and I fell into a deep sleep in the hay of the sisters' barn. Soon after I had allowed myself to fall asleep, I heard someone yelling that we had to wake up because the Germans were coming. I ran to the Jews in the forest, and then when they heard the news, we all ran deeper into the forest and hid in a swamp. We sat close to one another and we stopped even breathing. We heard footsteps. After a few minutes, we heard shouting. A small group of partisans was shooting at the Germans and was able to escape.

"After sitting a few days in the swamp in God's mud, we came back to the base of the Jewish detachment. Joseph Glassman, the head of the Jewish detachment, was the first person to greet us. He congratulated Yale on the hard job he did in such a difficult situation to bring everyone back safely and who, in such a fearful time, had the strength and will to take such a difficult journey in order to bring his girlfriend back. He said that when the war ended, he would write a book about everything and he would write about this love between Yale and me.

"It was very much a home atmosphere at the base. People forgot what was happening on the other side of the woods. Each one was thinking to himself, "God knows how long we will enjoy this life, so let us enjoy life for now." We made ourselves have as much fun as we could.

"Then, like a hurricane passing by, the news came. The blockade came to our Narotch woods. We were surrounded on all sides by German divisions. The clouds covered our faces and our hopes and happiness disappeared. In small groups, we started to run in different directions, wherever our eyes were looking because nobody knew a place where we would be safe from the enemy. In our group there were 12 people. One woman was very sick with a high fever, typhus.

"We hadn't gone far from the base when we heard the Germans yelling and shooting. We started running deeper into the swamp and we got to deep water. We couldn't go backward or forward. We just remained standing quietly in the water, but we couldn't stay there safely because the Germans were close and might see us. We could hear already their footsteps and their voices were getting closer and closer, and we couldn't move. We had just one way to avoid capture, to kill ourselves. In all the group, only Yale had a rifle and I had a pistol. People began to argue over who could be shot first, but Yale said he wouldn't shoot anybody.

"'First I am going to kill a few Germans, then we'll see,' " he said.

"A group of Germans walked by where we were, but didn't see us. All night we were sitting in the cold water, tired and hungry and freezing, but we wanted to live so much that it gave people strength to endure. When it started to get light, we began looking for a more comfortable place for us. We stayed in a big trench in the ground for a few days, covered with leaves and branches, without food and water. There were cows in the area, so we knew we were close to houses and a village, and that made us afraid even more.

"On the third day, because we didn't hear any shooting, we climbed out. Yale climbed up a tall tree to look around and didn't see anybody. With our last strength, we walked back to our base."

* * *

In 1947, Yale bribed someone to drive them across the border to Germany so they could leave. Sponsored by a Jacob Hofing, a cousin of Nachama's in Trenton, New Jersey, Yale and Nachama left the Old Country and came to America, landing at Ellis Island on the USS *Ernie Pyle*. With them they had their first child, their daughter Jeannie, 15 months old, who was born in a convent in a displaced persons camp in Eschwege, Germany. She had been delivered by a nun. Her mother was too afraid to go to a German hospital, in case there were Nazis working there

Nachama and Yale initially wanted to immigrate to Israel. But when Jeannie was an infant, she had fluid running out of an ear and a doctor told them that she would probably go deaf. Israel then was a new country, without established medical facilities, so they decided they had better go to America. Once there, a doctor prescribed an antibiotic, Jeannie's ear cleared up, and her hearing was fine.

(In the 1930s, four million Jews lived in America, half of them in New York City. By the end of WWII, five million Jews lived in America, making it the largest Jewish community in the world.)

In America, Nachama became Naomi. She and Yale bought a poultry farm, and they had two more children, Pearl and Abraham. Pearl became an agent for Hollywood actors and Abraham became a podiatrist. When he was 28, Abraham was operated on successfully for ulcerative colitis, but a nurse neglected to pull up one of the bars on his bed and he fell on the floor. His internal stitches opened, peritonitis set in, and he died six weeks later. His son Stephen was one year old.

Sisters Pearl Wexler (Tessler) and Jeannie Wexler (Rifkin)

In 1993, I met Jeannie and her father Yale when I went to their home. Sadly, Naomi had died five years earlier, at age 73 from a heart attack. Yale, almost 80 years old, died a few months after the bat mitzvah in Jerusalem of lung problems. He had smoked most of his life.

In 1941, Nazi-occupied Russia contained four million Jews. By the end of World War II, three million Russian Jews had been murdered. The one million Jews who avoided execution were the lucky ones who were able to escape into the forests or enlist in the Soviet army. Of these three million victims, 800,000 of them were Belorussian. Ninety percent of the Jews in Belorussia had been murdered. (*Jewish Virtual Library*)

By the end of the 20th century, only 600,000 Jews lived in the area that had been Russia and the Soviet Union.

Hitler spoke often of America's elimination of millions of its Native American population and its eugenics movement. *In Mein Kampf*, he wrote "We Germans must emulate what Americans are doing."

In 1907, supported by Theodore Roosevelt and the US Supreme Court, Indiana passed the first sterilization law in human history. Throughout the US, eugenics and forced sterilization were widely embraced—in academia, by corporate funding from such notables as the Kellogg Cereal Company, Carnegie Steel, and Rockefeller's Standard Oil, (which also funded the program Nazi war criminal Joseph Mengele worked at before he went to Auschwitz), and even by feminist Margaret Sanger. Between 1909 and 1960, 60,000 to 65,000 Americans were sterilized under this program in the belief that control of breeding by the state would rid society of the week and unfit, who bred faster. Literature was sent to Germany, to their medical people and scientists, and provided a model for the Nazi's forced sterilization program and a rationale for the murder of millions of people.

However, not all Americans agreed with the country's plan to "improve" society. In the June 1926 issue of *The American Mercury*, edited by H.L. Mencken, lawyer and ACLU member Clarence Darrow, (who defended John T. Scopes in the Scopes "Monkey Trial") argued against the policy in an essay, "The Eugenics Cult."

> "I, for one, am alarmed at the conceit and sureness of the advocates of this new dream. I shudder at their ruthlessness in meddling with life. I resent their egoistic and stern righteousness. I shrink from their judgment of their fellows......."

In addition to forced sterilization and mass deportations, during the height of the American eugenics movement, Calvin Coolidge, soon to be sworn in as president of the United States, was quoted in *Good Housekeeping* magazine in 1921 as saying "Biological laws tell us that certain divergent people will not mix or blend. The dead weight of alien accretion stifles national progress." The Emergency Quota Act of 1921 claimed that "Jews were intellectually inferior to native born whites."

In 1924, the Immigration Act was passed and barred admittance to the US by East Europeans, Jews, Arabs, and East Asians, dooming hundreds of thousands, perhaps millions of Jews who otherwise could have come to America to escape Hitler's Holocaust.

On February 20, 1939, 20,000 Nazis, members of the German-American Bund, attended a rally in Madison Square Garden, where they referred to the Jewish-controlled press and stated that they were fighting for a white, gentile America. Their banners read "Stop Jewish Domination of Christian Americans."

In the 1930s, some called Boston the most anti-Semitic city in the country, home to a network of Nazi supporters who even got money sent from Berlin. Charles Coughlin, a Canadian-American Catholic priest and populist leader who promoted anti-Semitic and pro-fascist views and was one of the most influential public figures in the United States, was said to have his largest following, adherents of primarily Irish-American descent, in Boston, earning the city the name "The Poisonous City" until after the end of World War II.

Chapter 30
Secrets

"However rare true love is, true friendship is rarer."
—La Rochefoucauld (1613–1680)
French writer

The week after Frank and I returned home from Israel, Robert told me he needed to talk to me about something important. He suggested we meet at the reflecting pool at the *Christian Science Monitor*. Since our first trip to Russia, we had become very close friends.

For years, I had gone through periods of worrying and wondering, but as I pieced together bits of conversation, shaping them the way I wanted, using my own hope as glue, I convinced myself that Robert wasn't HIV positive. At that time, before medical research developed the cocktail, it was a death sentence.

(During the 1980s, as part of their "active measures" to influence events in the US, Soviet intelligence spread the rumor that the AIDS virus had been created by American intelligence at Fort Detrick, Maryland. Of course, the CIA also used active measures throughout the world, often to work to overthrow regimes.)

While I fought the urge to double over to deal with the feelings in my tight stomach and weak knees—the last thing I wanted was to make it more difficult for Robert by revealing how upset I was—he told me he had known for five years, that he was probably about halfway through the quiet period of the disease. He said that one of the reasons he hadn't want to tell me about the HIV was because of Natasha, because it meant I was going to have to go through this dying thing with yet another person I loved.

He confessed that he was afraid of dying alone, and said that the hardest part would be knowing when to check out.

"If I ever become severely incapacitated, would you pull the plug for me?"

"Yes, yes, yes, I would."

Then I told him about my own health secret, about my MS. He asked a lot of questions. "Are you scared?"

"Yes, I am."

And then, life intruded with its mundane but demanding details. As we were leaving, Robert noticed that my tire was low and told me I had to go get air. Immediately. I wanted to go sit somewhere alone, maybe by the river, to cry, to pull myself together. So I could walk in the house and talk to Frank as if everything was the same as it had been that morning. Instead, I found myself at a gas station, begging a very fat, sweaty man to put air in the tire, even handing him the quarter because my hands were shaking.

One of the things marriage affords you is a routine, a marital dance, and once you know the steps, you can do it without thought. It is one of the things that can dull a marriage, but that day I was so grateful for it. Robert had asked me not to tell him, and Frank had no idea I was so upset.

The next morning, a poignant email from Robert, filled with hope and gratitude and love.

"...Thank you for being what and who you are. I cried after our talk because you touched me that deeply. You have given me more than I could ever repay..."

I sobbed while I read it, but all tragic and intense moments have their humor. While I was letting out my tears and letting in the pain, my cat Grapefruit was beside me, throwing up.

Chapter 31
1994—Last and 20th trip to Russia

"Most important is what the persistent NESNE outreach spawned. Journalistically, the early conferences were an anomaly. Here was a small US regional newspaper organization meeting with representatives of Pravda, *(the official paper of the Communist Party)* Izvestia *(the Soviet government paper), and other high-circulation national newspapers. For 1982, it was not the fit in our media world."*
—Thomas Winship (1920–2002)
editor of the *Boston Globe*,
chairman of the Center for Foreign Journalists

After the fall of Communism in 1991, I received dozens of phone calls from people looking to do business in Russia. In many cases, I knew exactly who to put them in touch with, but I advised all callers against it, told them about the necessity for bribes, the threats, the violence. I didn't want any of that on my conscience. I loved Russia. I loved the people. I loved going there. But I would not have loved being in business there.

From January 14 to 21, NESNE received a delegation of eight Russian journalists, which finally included women. Three! We took them to NY, as usual, and then Boston. But the tenor of these meetings had changed. We learned that the press was still not serving as an independent watchdog of the government, and that the influence of the larger, central papers had diminished while that of local and provincial papers had increased. We also learned that leading businesses and bankers paid newspapers to interview them.

There were, of course, some questions from Russian delegates about business issues—competition, information gathering, advertising. And press laws and how to achieve accuracy and fairness, since they had no real fact-checking process. But shopping now seemed more important to the delegates than any new information, which was disheartening to our New England people.

In September, Robert and I again went to Russia. The plane ride wasn't bad, seven hours, no sleep for me, of course. Our Helsinki Hotel Pasila was fair, not great. That evening, we went to dinner with Tuija, one of our hosts in Finland, to the Kellarikrouvi Restaurant. Robert and I both had reindeer with mashed potatoes and lingonberrys.

Tuija picked us up the next day and took us to the train for the two-hour ride to Tampere, about 100 miles north of Helsinki. The aerobics class of 35 people lasted 1½ hours, with a warm-up, funk, country western, a cool-down, and some muscle conditioning with abdominal exercises, and finally the relaxation. I was reminded yet again how good Robert was.

On one of our days there, we went for lunch at a Chinese restaurant, where I had mediocre rice and stir-fried vegetables. It seemed that everywhere we went, we heard American oldies. At breakfast in the hotel, they played Paul Anka. At lunch, we had been surrounded by the usual red Chinese decor, yet we heard "Broken-Hearted Melody," "Teen Angel," "Tennessee Waltz."

On the train to Moscow, after almost a fifth of vodka, we talked a lot about dying, about friends of Roberts who had died and how they went, and a lot about his HIV and what was ahead. He said he'd never seen a photo of Natasha, and when I started to describe her smile, I got teary.

Our Moscow hotel was the Russian Army Hotel, within walking distance of the Olimpiyskiy Stadium, built for the 1980 Summer Olympics. It was actually quite nice with a remodeled bathroom and a sitting room. Our suite was clean, sunshine came in, and it was really comfortable except for the fact that very often there was no hot water and we could never figure out when or why it went off or came back on.

I didn't go with Robert to class the next morning. Instead, I went shopping. It was a beautiful day (except after the overnight rain, worms wriggled all over the sidewalk. Big ones!)

With my rubles, I bought Stolichnaya vodka for $1.50 each, Finnish vodka for $6.00, champagne for $3.00. Then I just meandered in and out of stores. One grocery store actually had Tyson Chicken, Sara Lee, and Pepperidge Farm products in the freezer.

One night, we went to Big Sasha's for dinner, and as usual, it was a wonderful evening. And so gratifying for me. A good dinner, piano playing and singing by Sasha and Nadia, and Sasha even playing the accordion. It was so nice to see that they still used my Polaroid and had the dolls I brought Nadia and Dima's radio that he proudly brought out for me to see. Sasha was even wearing a tie I had given him. And there was a 5x7 photo I had taken and had enlarged. Sasha told me it is the only large picture of the family that they had.

But as I looked around, I noticed that the apartment had changed; it had more clutter. Things for the dacha, Sasha said, but it seemed shabbier, older, and dirtier. I saw several cockroaches for the first time there. And Vera had lost something, a spark. Life must have gotten much harder. The children were having problems. Dima had allergies and Nadia had some trouble with her esophagus, got sick when she ate salty things, sauces, almost anything but mashed potatoes and fruit. Apparently, this occurred just after she had measles (or chicken pox, a sickness with red spots, Sasha said). Robert had a hard time believing that Sasha was only 35, Vera 33. Nadia was then 8, almost 9, and Dima 11.

We exchanged gifts and I was given a blue and white ceramic samovar with Petrovka 38 written on it. More important was the warmth of the evening. I found myself overwhelmed with affection and so happy to be with Big Sasha and his family. And so happy that I could share them with Robert.

That night, I dreamed that Robert and I were in a small café, hot and crowded. Candlelight brightened the wooden walls and burnished the faces of the patrons, whose mouths moved in animated but silent conversation. After we ate, he paid as I was reaching into my wallet for money. Instead, I pulled out hundreds of fortune-cookie-sized papers, all written on in my handwriting. Single sentences, solitary words, some numbers. People crowded around me to read the scribbling. Slowly, we made our way past them to the door, then out into the crystal cold night. Robert walked ahead of me, and with each step, expanded the space between us. The snow reached my knees and each of my steps became slower, more difficult, until I could no longer lift my legs. I called out to his distant silhouette, but the wind carried no answer back to me. I, by then a statue, watched him disappear. I understood where the dream came from.

Another night, Valery picked us up and took us to his home for a light supper. His wife Lena was pregnant and due any day. Valery drove a Peugeot and carried a BB gun. When we arrived, he pulled into a security area with what looked like storage spaces with padlocks. It was a garage for which he had paid $1,500.

Then, in his home, the TV was on and it was a terrible, tacky American movie. All the women were bare breasted and making passes at men in back seats of cars. Pathetic. It seemed as if the Russians were importing the worst of American culture, not the best.

The next morning, Sofya's son David and his wife Natasha came to our hotel. I gave them things from Alla and Sofya and we sat and talked for an hour. David said life was better in Russia, while Valery had talked about crime being so much worse, with people substituting water or worse in vodka, etc. A perfect example of how difficult it can be to determine the truth.

When Robert's teaching was finished, I went over to the Olympic stadium to take photos of him giving the exam and then the certificates to the 220 people who had participated in his classes, some from as far away as Kazakstan, Ukraine, Estonia, and Poland.

That evening, we went for a long walk, across the big stone bridge, to the Kremlin, through Red Square down to the Metropole Hotel. It was a beautiful night and it felt so good to be out walking alone. However, unlike in years past, we were cautious and watchful for suspicious people. Happily, none intruded.

We had another bottle of champagne on the train to St. Petersburg, and a bar of Fazer chocolate. Of course.

In the middle of the night, I heard a loud whisper. "Oh, Cynthia, wake up. Look at that." A beautiful black sky, full of beautiful bright stars. We both stared quietly out the window for a long time.

That overnight trip from Moscow to St. Petersburg by train, in Robert's words:

> "Cynthia and I had spent most of the evening drinking vodka and champagne (what a surprise!) in anticipation of the last leg of our journey. I awakened around 3 AM as our compartment was stiflingly hot.
>
> "As I lay there feeling the rhythm of the train tracks beating in time with the alcohol pounding around in my head, I looked out of the window, my face was pressed against the cool glass for the relief it offered. We were so far north that there were no lights as civilization appeared to have never taken root there. The earth and sky were separated only by the line of blackness where the stars seemed to end and eternal blackness, which was the earth, began. In all my life, I have never seen so clearly the majesty of the heavens as represented by the brilliance of the stars vaulting over my head. It seemed that I could even see the rotation of the planet as it moved through this field of light.
>
> "I could not let Cynthia sleep through this, in spite of the fact that one does not wake Cynthia once she finally falls asleep. We both lay there for some time watching the stars seemingly spin while the world turned upon itself. I remember thinking how vain and petty all our cares and concerns are compared to the greater concepts of time and space. Still, we are creatures of this time and space and so our vain and petty concerns are all we have. My life is a testament to the eternal spiraling of life within ourselves and with each other."

As I look back, I think those train rides were my happiest times with Robert.

The train arrived in St. Petersburg around 8:00 AM. After breakfast at our Hotel Rus, we went to the Pavlovsk Palace. Hardly anyone else was there and we were able to wander from beautiful room to beautiful room pretty much on our own, without crowds to hinder our enjoyment and appreciation.

The ruble's value was plummeting. A week earlier, I had exchanged money for 2,600 rubles to the dollar. That day, it was 3,900 and 5,000 on the black market. The next day, 4,000 rubles to the dollar! Incredible when you think it used to cost me $2.60 to buy one ruble.

1994—Last and 20th Trip to Russia

One evening, to the Kirov, which had been renamed the Marynsky Theatre, to see the ballet *The Bayadere*. Long, three acts with two intermissions. We got some juice, and as we walked through the halls, we heard the constant pop of champagne bottles.

Another evening, Mark met us in our hotel lobby and took us to his home. Nina A. came and looked beautiful. We talked business and then had a dinner of great "golden" vodka, caviar, liver and onions, chicken and potatoes, tomatoes from their dacha. Dessert, cake with kiwi, chocolates and tea. As tired as we were, we had a great time.

The train to Helsinki was first-class, clean, and comfortable. Ironically, just as we got into Finland, the sun came out after three dreary, gray days in St. Petersburg.

Our Russian customs inspector was a woman, whom I clumsily and unwisely banged in the knee with my suitcase. She searched through almost everything I had. Looking for money and antiques, I guess, since a dog had already come in to sniff for drugs. She found 10,400 rubles in my wallet, but ignored them. The $4,100, payment for Robert's work and the fitness clothes we had bought for the Aerobics School to resell, which was concealed in my left sneaker, my usual hiding place, went undetected. It was the most thorough search in many years. I think Robert actually enjoyed it, and the inspector actually got pleasant toward the end, probably due to our efforts to speak some Russian to her. Or maybe because she saw my Petrovka 38 police samovar and thought I was connected to the police. Perhaps she thought it was safest to let me pass without further inspection.

Robert's teaching had gone very well, but we wrote off the National Aerobics School as a viable future partner because, understandably, they had no creative business sense. We decided that it was not profitable to return to Russia, even when they paid Robert a stipend, without some kind of a deal, a group, or a sponsor. Or, maybe the best thing was to take his experience and the accompanying press and approach other countries about a fitness program.

Helsinki's Hotel Hesperia was warm and welcoming and dinner was wonderful—chateaubriand for Robert and lamb for me. And champagne, of course, for both of us. We then went to dance at a gay disco club called "Don't Tell Mama."

Ours was most certainly a peculiar relationship. Many times I thought yes, Robert is gay, but would like to have been otherwise, or hasn't come to terms totally with his homosexuality, and his relationship with me allows him to believe that he is bisexual, without having to actually engage in sex. As for me, I liked his compliments, liked dancing and partying with him, liked feeling like the younger me, before the MS diagnosis. But in reality, we were simply friends who flirted with fantasy.

I didn't know then that that—our third trip together—would be both the end of my trips to Russia and the beginning of the unraveling of our relationship.

The Associated Press reported that the life expectancy for men in Russia dropped significantly, from age 62 in 1993 to 59 in 1994.

Eight years after Chernobyl, a *Novaya Gazeta* 1994 report stated that 300,000 people had been involved in the clean-up; one of ten was disabled, over 5,000 had died. In some provinces, the number of suicides by clean-up veterans ran as high as 60 percent.

Gorbachev declared that the Chernobyl disaster caused the end of the USSR.

In 2014, HBO produced a documentary, *Hunted: The War Against Gays in Russia*. It revealed that vigilante gangs hunted gays for sport in Russia. They used the Internet to lure gays to meet up, then beat them.

Same-sex sexual activity between consenting adults in private was decriminalized in 1993 in Russia, homosexuality was declassified as a mental illness in 1999, but there are no laws against sexual discrimination and same-sex marriage is still, at the time of this writing, prohibited.

According to the March 6, 2017, *New Yorker Magazine*, by winter of 2017, 30 journalists had been murdered in Russia over the past 15 years.

Chapter 32
Robert

"The man who fears suffering is already suffering from what he fears."
—Michel de Montaigne (1533–1592)
French Renaissance philosopher

"Robert, I'm sure your mother's death was peaceful. The pain meds really work; they put the person in a peaceful place. Again, I'm so sorry." Cynthia

"I appreciate your note so much. You've no idea how much it means to me. Let's keep in touch from time to time." Robert

Those emails, among the first communication we had in 10 years, were the last words we said to one another.
Robert had called me to tell me his mother was dying of leukemia, and to give me a last opportunity to talk to her. She and I had felt a closeness the very first time we met, when she said to me, "Please, make sure you tell Robert we love him. Please let me know if anything is wrong."

And she and I had kept in touch throughout all those years, although she never acknowledged that Robert and I were no longer in one another's lives. Robert, too, on the phone, spoke as if our long estrangement had never happened, as if we hadn't said such hurtful things to one another that last day.

Over time, I had gained greater insight into the Robert he was trying so hard to hide. That abused, (although never explicit, he hinted often about sexual abuse), scared little boy who had been physically abused and humiliated by his father in front of his friends, who had been drugged and raped by at least one man, who became an angry adult who could become hostile in a heartbeat, who still had nightmares, who still felt the shame. Who felt that his success was based on deception. Who found it too threatening to trust or to sustain intimacy because the person might see the real Robert, the unlovable Robert. The Robert who believed he was unable to truly love. And I came to understand that what he wanted most is what he feared most, and so he created distance the way he knew best—with anger.

Still, we had shared some wonderful times. We went out dancing a lot. We became certified scuba divers together, went diving in St. Maarten and the Bahamas. On the shark-feeding dive, one shark passed so close to me that I could have reached out and touched it. There must have been a hundred of them, reef sharks, all with one objective. Food. On another dive, we explored the eerie, barnacle-crusted passageways of an old sunken ship and on the interactive dolphin dive, we were kissed by dolphins, lips to lips and then with our right arms stretched out, those dolphins spun us around faster than we could blink.

And we decided to write a book together, a book about abuse.

Robert had a client who offered to let us stay for a week at his house on Little Gull Island in Florida, so that we could write without distraction. One night, we drove into Key West, had dinner at a restaurant called La Ti Da, went dancing, and on the way back, driving over the Seven Mile Bridge with the top down, we once again found ourselves staring up in wonder at the night sky.

The next day, over cocktails, after a productive day of writing, Robert turned to me, his face blank, and said, "Remember, we have a pact. You'll be there when I need you?"

I assured him I would.

In addition to our book, we worked on a piece about diving for the *Boston Globe* travel section, which did get published after our return.

But the trip wasn't all fun. My relationship with Robert had settled into one of contrasting components, excitement and anticipation, disappointment and regret, joy and then anger. He tested me unlike any other. Sometimes I felt as if I were in our relationship by myself. If I allowed myself to express my anger, he wouldn't engage and became cold and distant. The fact that he was going to die had given him control over me because compared to that, my anger at whatever he had failed to do after he said he would paled in comparison. The knowledge of his pending death rendered me powerless.

In retrospect, it seems to me that our relationship started to deteriorate when he went on the cocktail and his HIV was no longer a death sentence or a secret. As I saw it, he then needed me less, and I was then less willing to put up with things that made me angry.

And I knew what his pattern was because he sometimes let me know how much he struggled.

In one 1995 email, he wrote:

Robert

"I have eliminated so many former friends these last months. Friends that were a part of the old Robert, the one who manipulated and seduced in order to maintain the face of a compassionate and concerned guy."

And in another,

"Kevin died and I am so saddened by his passing. He was a major part of my life. Did I love him or was he one of those people I used in one of my many attempts to overcome my fear of my heart and mind?"

At the time, I truly believed, because he had shared these insights with me, that I would be the friend he wouldn't do that to.

But gradually, we were no longer close, no longer writing chapters for our book, were no longer even friends. At the time, I didn't understand what was happening. When I repeatedly asked what the problem was, he'd say he was simply too busy with work. The hurt and rejection kept me from recognizing what I already knew, what he in fact had already revealed about himself and his pattern in relationships. What I did recognize, with a great deal of sorrow, was that we were no longer important to one another.

One day, we had a fight. I had been home sick for a week and he had never called to see how I was. When I arrived for my personal training session with him, I showed how disappointed I was over that. He got defensive, things escalated and we both said some nasty things to one another. As I stamped out of his studio, I yelled "Fuck you! I'm done. I am no match for you—I thought I was strong enough".

He made one disguised attempt at reconciliation by sending a businesslike note, which I ignored.

I never saw Robert again.

As years passed, I believed that during our time together, there were many moments of true intimacy, true friendship. I came to understand even more about our relationship. That with me, Robert could pretend he could sustain a loving relationship. That with him, perhaps I was hoping to save him, which I had failed at with my mother.

"Let's keep in touch from time to time."

I hadn't answered that last email back in 2007, thus I never told him that Frank and I were coming to Boston in a couple of weeks.

Did I want to see him? I had considered asking him to get together when I was in town. I was no longer angry. But I was afraid to get pulled back into what might become yet another whirlwind of negative emotions, afraid to take the chance of being painfully pushed away yet again.

Two days before we arrived in Boston, Robert put an end to his fears. On September 19, 2007, he overdosed on pain pills and left a note, saying he'd had enough, that the constant strain on his body and mind due to the HIV had worn him down, and that his mom's passing was the final chapter for him.

He died alone.

But I was there for him at his memorial service.

Robert had often quoted Oliver Wendell Holmes: "Alas for those who never sing, but die with their music still in them."

Robert did sing during his 54 years, and I was there for much of his music. But his song was too short. Much of it was also too dissonant, but when there was harmony, it was exquisite.

> **According to verywellhealth.com, in 2018 the prevalence of HIV in Russia, which has half the population of the US, was almost seven times that of America. By 2019-2020, Russia had a million HIV cases, 1 percent of the Russian population. They are facing this epidemic because of government inaction; belief in conspiracy theories that claim HIV isn't real; discrimination against the gay population. As most of the world was making progress against the spread of HIV, the opposite was happening in Russia.**

Chapter 33
Dealing with the US Government

"When money speaks, the truth keeps silent."
—Russian proverb

Because of changes in Russia, my projects and programs in 1995 took on a different complexion. Russian real estate people came to US and visited the Real Estate Board of New York, the Boston Redevelopment Authority, the Suffolk County Registry of Deeds, and the Suffolk County Land Court. The head of the group was Sergei Kisselev, Director of the Department of Technical Inventory for the government of Russia.

I set up a program for 27 architects and engineers from the Architecture and Construction Department of Moscow Region Government to go to MIT to meet a Professor of Architecture, Les Norford.

Twenty-four beer brewers came to Boston, visited the Commonwealth Brewing Company, had a VIP tour of Samuel Adams Brewery, Anhauser Busch in Merrimack, New Hampshire, Pepsi in Cranston, Rhode Island. For their final night, a dinner at the John Harvard Beer Pub in Harvard Square.

But most unexpected, in May I was contacted by Chuck Ramsey from the Department of Energy (DOE). He had been one of my delegates on the Firefighters Exchange to Russia in 1992. Since then, he had periodically kept in touch and he submitted a proposal for government funding to help the Russian nuclear power industry upgrade safety. When he got approval by Congress to go ahead, he called and asked for my help.

He told me that the G7 nations (at the time, US, Japan, Germany, France, Italy, Canada, and the United Kingdom) were in agreement that the nuclear industry in Russia was in such a sorry state that it jeopardized life as we knew it on this planet and thus they all had allocated funds to help fix it. Since they hadn't had any luck working in Russia "from the top down," or with the Russian nuclear people because no one seemed to be in charge or have authority, and there was no central place in Moscow to oversee the nuclear industry, DOE thought they would try going at it from a different angle—through the Fire Service.

Battelle Pacific Northwest Laboratories, an arm of DOE, sent me a letter of intent to grant my contract, pending negotiations on my hourly rate ($125 per hour then). The work would involve my going to Washington, DC whenever necessary. Ramsey asked me to start the project immediately, saying there was some urgency. Thus, before my official contract was signed, I submitted the requested proposal to the appropriate person in Russia, the man who was head of the Fire Service there, my good friend General Rubtsov. I sent a long letter outlining what DOE wanted to do and requested that the general set up a meeting in two weeks so that Ramsey and Richard Denning, Senior Research Leader from Battelle, could talk about it in person in Moscow. And I told him I would be working on the project. I got an answer in two days with the general's acceptance of the proposal.

Once the US people had their meeting in Moscow, I then got a second letter from Battelle saying: *No contract!* When Ramsey returned, he said he was angry, filled me in on all the politics of the situation, and then told me Battelle would pay me for the work I had done already, but they wanted their own people going forward instead of outside contractors. I'm not sure I believe that he didn't know this all along, but Ramsey was gracious enough to say that none of their people was as qualified as I was.

Nevertheless, I was put in a difficult position regarding the fact that I would not be participating in the project after all. I had two choices re General Rubtsov. Write to him to tell him what happened, or stay silent. That really wasn't a choice. I couldn't speak poorly of my government, so I stayed silent, and to this day regret that he most likely thought I was using him.

The fact that I got paid for setting up the meeting didn't lessen my anger, or belief that I had been the one used because I had the contact they wanted. There was no need

The author and General Rubtsov

for subterfuge, for sending me a letter of intent regarding the contract. If Ramsey had asked me, as a favor, to set up the meeting, I would have done so because I knew how important it was.

That incident reinforced my long-held belief that my work through IPEX, Inc., should remain in the private sector and especially non-governmental, as it always had been.

That year marked Sofya's 90th birthday with a party on Saturday, April 8, 1995, at a Boston restaurant.

Mark and his wife Dina came from Russia, as did Alla's brother David, along with his wife Natasha. Also attending was Yelena Bonner, Soviet dissident and human rights activist herself, and wife of Andrei Sakharov. Dina and Bonner were old friends from college.

Yelena Bonner and Mark Segal

Also that year, a few different undertakings for me. I volunteered at Boston's Children's Hospital to hold and play with the infants. Volunteers weren't allowed to know why the little ones were in the hospital, but it was always clear who the AIDS babies were when I looked at the one- to two-feet-long list of medications hanging on the wall above their cribs.

And I began volunteer work as the International Development Coordinator for GAP, the Great Ape Project, founded in 1993 by Australian philosopher and professor at Princeton University, Peter Singer and Italian philosopher Paola Cavalieri, the editors of the book by the same name, *The Great Ape Project: Equality Beyond Humanity*. I had the opportunity to speak with Jane Goodall, who was one of their first supporters.

GAP's mission then was to work to guarantee the basic rights of life, freedom, and non-torture to the non-human great primates—chimpanzees, gorillas, orangutans and bonobos, our closest relatives in the animal kingdom. Primates who also have culture, consciousness, who suffer pain and who I believe have far greater capabilities than most humans give them credit for. Maybe an even more important mission is to insure their survival. (According to *The Week* magazine, June 8, 2018, since the dawn of civilization, mankind has wiped out an astonishing 83 percent of all wild mammals on Earth, and half of all plants…)

My love for animals grows more passionate with each passing year, having begun with my desire for a monkey and now embracing far more than primates and my beloved cats and dogs.

> *"One day, the absurdity of the almost universal belief in the slavery of other animals will be palpable. We shall then have discovered our souls and become worthier of sharing this planet with them.*
> —Martin Luther King, Jr. (1929–1968)

Paths of Stones

In addition, I participated in the MOVA (Massachusetts Office of Victim Assistance) annual Victim Rights Conference at the State House. The *Boston Globe* had recently published an op-ed piece I wrote about the abuse in my family. Subsequently, I was invited to be a member of a panel at their annual Domestic Violence Workshop on April 25th.

I was initially reluctant, but I finally did agree so that I could explain then that I have never seen myself as a victim, have always felt sorry for my parents, not me. I chose at a young age to believe that the craziness in my house belonged to my parents, not to me; that the awful things they were doing they were doing to each other, not to me; and that they were responsible, not me. I escaped by losing myself in books or my diary, and by creating close relationships with friends (especially Arlene) and with their families. I prided myself on what I now know was an exaggerated sense of independence.

As a child, I think that trying to figure out which parent was right and which parent was wrong was the most confusing issue for me. As an adult, my biggest dilemma has not been figuring out who was right or wrong, but trying to understand how my father could treat me so well in so many ways and my mother so awfully.

Recently, I have looked back into my past with some clarity, feeling strong enough to open the curtain of defenses that has served me so well, and admitted that both my parents did use me as a weapon or as armor against the other one, did manipulate me, did subject me to things which certainly were not in my best interests, but in theirs. Yet I don't blame them. I knew I was loved. And I believe that has been the key to my sense of wellbeing. That, and a feeling of responsibility and a determination to make my life a good life, as if that will somehow show that their suffering and their sorrow was not for nothing.

After hearing me speak, Betsy Graves, founder of the Child Witness to Violence Project at Boston Medical Center, interviewed me for her book, published in 2002, *Children Who See Too Much*. She told a bit of my story in her chapter on how to help children who witness violence.

> **Boris Yeltsin was re-elected President of the Russian Federation on June 16. On September 1, in an address to the Democratic Press Forum, he said, "The Russian state and Russian society have a vital interest in strong, professional and truly free media."**
>
> *Izvestia*: **June 24, 1995**
> **Every year Russia performs approximately 3.5 million abortions, leading the world because of the shortages of contraceptives.**

Izvestia: Sept 1, 1995
Lawlessness on the part of police has become a nationwide problem. Today no Russian citizen can be guaranteed against police brutality. In effect, men in uniform can beat any of us up without any reason, and the most frightening thing is that such actions almost always go unpunished…..It's a paradox, but when the Communists were in power, there wasn't the kind of lawlessness on the part of law enforcement agencies that there is today.

Izvestia: October 25, 1995
15,000 women had died the year before from domestic violence and 57,000 were maimed or physically injured.

Chapter 34
1996—Cambridge, Massachusetts

*"The river is constantly turning and bending and you never know
where it's going to go and where you'll wind up.
Following the bend in the river and staying on your own path
means that you are on the right track.
Don't let anyone deter you from that."*
—Eartha Kitt (1927–2008)
American singer, actress, and dancer

Living so close to Harvard Square enabled Frank and me to walk there and thus go frequently because we were spared the search for parking spaces. Toscanini's Ice Cream shop was a favorite destination, along with the Casablanca Restaurant and the Harvard Book Store.

Sometimes we sat outside and watched Little Brut, a lively, likeable Dzungarian dwarf hamster, race up and down the driveway inside his clear plastic ball. Tambi and Tara brought him to me for my birthday, because I always complained I could never have a pet as a child, not even a hamster. In time, Little Brut learned the sound of my voice and when I called his name, he would pop up out of the hole in the top of his domain, place his tiny front paws on my fingers, and proceed to eat out of my hand.

When it was time to clean his cage, he voluntarily climbed into his plastic ball for his weekly outing on the driveway. Often he'd get running so fast he'd end up ass-over-teakettle, but then he'd quickly right himself and keep on running. In pursuit of freedom, perhaps?

It was then that I would look at him, such a cute little creature, and wonder if he was lonesome, if he was bored, if he would have been better off out in the wild of Mongolia, in his natural habitat. Did he have a better life in my home, free from predators and with a plentiful food supply, or was his an unnatural, unfulfilled life? Did I have the right to keep this little creature in a cage, far removed from his intended environment, simply for my own pleasure?

I now believe that our dominion of other animals, with its roots in Genesis, is immoral, and in fact, diminishes both the planet and our own species. Perhaps if we viewed ourselves as tenants on the earth—tenants tied to the natural world by the very air we breathe, much like a fetus who is dependent upon its mother's umbilical chord—rather than landlords, we'd be more respectful of that which gives and sustains our life.

Little Brut lived only a year and we buried him in our garden, without his cage, under a concrete bench with proud lions for its pedestals. Dogwood trees, azalea bushes, mountain laurel, and all that sustains them then became the elements of his domain. It is a quiet place, a peaceful place, a place where I went to contemplate the very complicated nature of things, to wonder…

Our four-story condo had an outdoor shower on our top deck that I enjoyed whenever the weather allowed. But living in our condo association also had its minuses. Because he was calm and levelheaded, Frank became the person our neighbors contacted when there were problems.

"Can you help me get my kitten who fell off the kitchen counter and is now stuck behind the refrigerator?"

"Can you tell R. that he has to take down the front door that he just put up that is different from everyone else's door?"

But my favorite call for help—and I promise I didn't make this up—was when someone called Frank to complain that "B. is so disrespectful to my wife (whom none of us actually liked very much) that whenever he can, he gets as close to her as possible in public and aims a loud burp directly at her face."

That was one complaint that Frank opted not to mediate.

We had one set of neighbors who had a beautiful Bouvier. We weren't friends with the Singers, and saw Judy only when she was walking the dog or tending to her flower garden. In fact, in the ten or so years that we were neighbors, we never laid eyes on her husband Stu. It turned out we would both move to Tucson, a few years apart, and end up living about two miles from each other. Then we became friends!

And one of our neighbors confessed to me that he had been an Israeli spy during the war. He didn't say which war, and your guess is as good as mine as to whether that was true.

Tambi was living in Boston then and we got together often to play squash. I wasn't bad, but she was great. I don't believe I ever won a game. But it was so wonderful to have her in town, for squash, for dinners out, for long confidential girl talks, for a girl's weekend in Provincetown.

In 1992, I started a book group that met once a month. The 13-member group is still meeting and three of us who belonged from the beginning and have moved away from Boston continue to go to meetings whenever we are in town or via Zoom.

We spent New Year's Eves with Winer and her husband Sol. We visited Kathy and her wife Ronnie out in Pelham, where we had our choice of cats and dogs and goats to shower with affection.

1996—Cambridge, Massachusetts

Frank and I both had big birthdays in 1996. In March, I hired Russian-born Igor Fokin, street performer and puppeteer, to perform at Frank's 60th birthday party at the Charles Hotel in Harvard Square. Fokin, who had come to the US only two years earlier from St. Petersburg, carved his marionettes himself out of wood, painted them, and sewed their clothes. A few months after Frank's party, Igor performed shows as part of the festivities at the Summer Olympics in Atlanta, Georgia.

Sadly, six months after Frank's party, Fokin died of heart failure at age 36, two weeks after his third child was born. In 2001, a sculpture representing one of his marionettes was erected where he usually performed on Brattle Street in Harvard Square.

On my 50th birthday in June, Frank had my party at the Four Seasons Hotel in Boston. Two friends hired a drag queen to impersonate Eartha Kitt, whom I adored and who we had seen at the Café Carlyle in New York.

Every Christmas season, we had a catered open house for about 60 people. But all had to come in costume, according to the theme I had chosen—animals, cats, women, even drag. Under the tree, there was a small gift that I had picked out for every guest.

Besides parties, there was still work, with more Russians coming to America than Americans going to Russia. I organized two programs for City Developers, another for more real estate people.

As for NESNE, four NESNE delegates, sponsored by a new organization in Russia —the League of Journalists of St. Petersburg—went in July to St. Petersburg and Volhov, where they not only met with various newspaper people, but also spent a half-day on a fishing trawler on Lake Ladoga.

They saw billboards, cell phones, the rebirth of religion. They noticed that pedestrians no longer avoided the eye of passing foreigners because they were afraid. They also saw and heard that people were impatient with the pace of reforms.

In November, nine Russian journalists (the tenth delegate was not granted a US visa) arrived for visits to NY City, where they had a meeting with the Committee to Protect Journalists, saw the World Trade Center and Statue of Liberty, and went sightseeing and shopping. And once again, home visits in New England and the conference at the *Boston Globe*, where the discussion topic was "The Role of a Free Press: How Free are We?" They also toured the Naval War College in Newport, Rhode Island, the mansions, and the old Truro synagogue.

The last meeting between NESNE and Russian journalists took place one year later, September 16 to 29. Eight NESNE delegates went to St. Petersburg, Moscow, and Kirishy, a town 71 miles southeast of St. Petersburg.

Discussions then revealed that Russian newspaper circulation had dropped drastically and that the government still had control because most papers were printed by state-owned facilities, which could be closed down anytime the government wanted.

One of the American delegates concluded that it would take an enormous effort for Russia to achieve capitalism and stability.

Although the Russians indicated they wanted to continue the exchange, many NESNE members felt that their value had become questionable, which prompted much debate. Finally, a consensus was reached that it was time to conclude the 15-year-old exchange program and to establish a similar program elsewhere. Perhaps in Cuba? Iraq? Maybe Vietnam?

NESNE had accomplished a lot with Russia. Probably most important and impressive were the three-month exchanges of young working journalists under age 40.

Most notable, Yelena Khanga from *Moscow News* was placed at the *Christian Science Monitor* in Boston. She was very much in demand for interviews, in part because she was a Black woman and many Americans didn't know that there were Black people in the Soviet Union. She was interviewed by the *Washington Post, New York Times, Boston Globe,* and *20/20 TV.*

She went to Los Angeles and met Michael Jackson, interviewed Dianne Feinstein, who was then mayor of San Francisco, also talked to Stevie Wonder on the phone for half an hour. In 1992, she published a memoir: *Soul to Soul: A Black Russian American Family 1865-1992*, which was reviewed in *The Nation* magazine. Five years later, she became a host of a new weekly Russian late-night talk show, *About It*. "It" was sex.

When Sergo Kukhianidze came from the International Desk of Moscow *Pravda* in 1989 to work at the *Cape Cod Times*, he did a piece on John Reed, the author of *Ten Days That Shook the World*. I mentioned Reed earlier, but didn't know till Sergo reported on him that he had died in Moscow from typhus three days before his 33rd birthday, or that he had summered in Provincetown from 1914 to 1916, and wintered in Greenwich Village.

There was one more NESNE exchange program to come, one that was totally unexpected, one that took me to a country I never dreamed I'd visit.

1996—Cambridge, Massachusetts

1997

On June 17, I went to the Glubocker Benevolent Association in Brooklyn, New York, to give a talk about my father's beginnings in Glubokoye and the discovery of my Russian family. Founded in 1893 by immigrants from Glubokoye, there is a Gluboker section in the Mt. Zion Cemetery in Brooklyn. In 1980, the Association erected a memorial in New Montefiore Cemetery, Pinelawn, New York, (Sec 3, Block 14).

> *"Dedicated to all who perished in the three massacres in the ghetto Globoke Poland and in tribute to the partisans who died fighting the Nazis in the forest during the Holocaust of World War II."*
> —The Globoker Survivors in America

The dates mentioned for the three massacres are 9 Nisan 1942, 4 Tammuz 1942, and 19 Av 1943.

Part Seven

Chapter 35
1998—Iran

*"Let me tell you the one thing I have against Moses.
He took us forty years into the desert in order to bring us
to the one place in the Middle East that has no oil!"*
—Golda Meir (1898–1978)
Fourth Prime Minister of Israel

- "I believe the worst dictatorships in the world are in the name of God."
- "Americans think the Persian Gulf is their playground."
- Consumerism is the plague of American society.
- On the grounds of the Shah's Palace: "Please tell people that the Shah's wife was so kind."
- From the man at the store in the Bazaar, where I was shopping for a carpet: "I'm not like the Jews who ask higher prices and you must bargain."
- At Behesht-e Zahra Cemetery, we saw the grave of a 13-year-old who was honored because he strapped a grenade to his midriff and crawled under an Iraqi tank to detonate it.
- In front of a Mecca memorial with photos of dead at the pilgrimage, the words of Ayatollah Khomeini: "Israel should be eliminated from the world."
- Graffiti outside a restaurant, in English: "Love my dick."
- And from a pretty parakeet on the street, who, in return for a small sum of money for its handler, chose and gave me my fortune: *You should not hesitate in your work.*

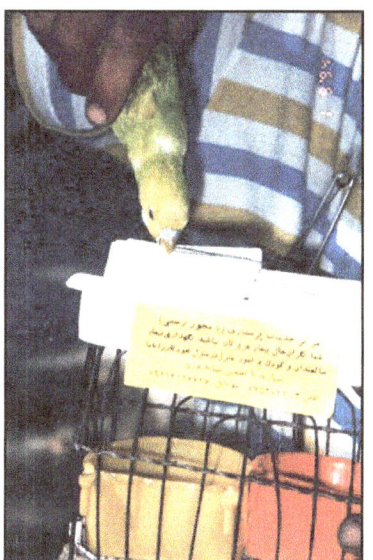

Parakeet choosing the author's fortune

And it was my work that took me to Iran. I heard or saw the above words in June of 1998, when Maura Casey, associate editor of *The Day* newspaper in New London, Connecticut and I spent ten days in Tehran laying the groundwork to establish a journalism exchange program between NESNE and Iran. We discussed what we at NESNE envisioned and personally extended invitations to newspapers to participate.

Prior to the visit, I had spent months working up a budget, fundraising, and making appropriate contacts to prepare for the trip. The plan was to invite Iranian journalists to America and then have a delegation of New England journalists go to Iran.

NESNE's attention turned to Iran after the election of President Mohammad Khatami and his interview with Christiane Amanpour on CNN in January of 1998, when Khatami called for "dialogue and understanding between the two nations" and the "exchange of professors, writers, scholars, artists, journalists, and tourists."

At the suggestion of the organization Internews, which already had people on site in Iran, and with funding from The Ploughshares Fund, George Soros' Open Society Institute, the Rockefeller Foundation, and support from Harvard's Nieman Foundation, Brandeis University, the *Boston Globe*, the *New York Times,* and various newspapers and individuals, NESNE did what was necessary to create a program to once again foster greater understanding and communication between the US and a hostile nation, to once again make a difference.

After anxious waiting, we received our Iranian visas only the morning of our departure. Just before we were to leave the plane, we had to put on our scarves. I first struggled to pull the headband across my scalp, to get all the hair off my face. I must have been a vision, and my frustration must have showed, because several men started to laugh and when I looked at Maura, she had tears running down her cheeks from laughing so hard. Frankly, I never got the hang of it.

In Tehran, Maura and I met first with the Director General of the Ministry of Culture and Islamic Guidance, Hossein Nosrat, who encouraged us and enthusiastically gave us names and phone numbers of fourteen editors at papers that might be receptive to the exchange.

Days later, because we had had some difficulty taking street photos because of police interference, he also gave us a letter of introduction from the Ministry of Culture:

To all Disciplinary Forces
Tehran Province and Bazaar Branch
Please Maura Casey and Cynthia Dickstein are newspaper writers from America.
They want to prepare photos and report on Tehran. Please cooperate with them
From 6/06 – 6/13
Signed by Nosrat, Director, Foreign Department

1998—Iran

Before we began to make calls to set up all our professional meetings at the recommended newspapers and magazines, we went to the Imam Khomeini Shrine and Mausoleum on June 4th, the anniversary of his death. Because we carried cameras and had not yet received our press passes or Nosrat's letter, we had some difficulty getting inside. Five different checkpoints refused to allow us entry, until the sixth let us in, thanks to the efforts of Persheng Sadegh-Vaziri, our guide and interpreter who was affiliated with Internews. A group of women in chadors and carrying walkie-talkies examined our cameras and patted us down. We then handed over our passports and received journalist ID cards for that day. (In 2017, that Shrine was attacked by Islamic terrorists.)

At the Shrine's women's entrance, we were handed a plastic bag with handles to put our shoes in. Inside, we were firmly instructed to sit in a straight line on the huge Persian carpet, under enormous crystal chandeliers. Several times, security women walked up and down the line, demanding that someone move forward or back a few inches. Other women came by offering water, with ice, in a red plastic cup to all who asked. And we were each given a *mohr*, a prayer stone for us to rest our foreheads on when it was time to bow.

The thousands of men and women were separated, of course.

Huge banners of Ayatollah Khomeini surrounded us, and in the background, we heard the men chanting and cheering as they repeated: *"Long live the Revolution!" "Down with Israel!" "Down with America!"*

(Women's voices were not allowed to be heard in religious settings.)

Women in prayer at the Khomeini Shrine and Mausoleum

The first speaker we heard was Hassan Rouhani. (Little did we imagine then that he would become president of Iran in 2013.) Unfortunately, there was no way Pershang could translate fast enough and loud enough for us to understand what was being said. We were told to keep a very low profile, and she in fact said to the women surrounding us, when they asked, that we were Canadian.

"It will avoid any potential problems, as well as the many questions that will inevitably follow if they learn you are Americans."

She also said that the reason for the current anger toward America was the support for Israel. No news there.

At other times, Maziar Bahari, a Canadian-Iranian journalist and filmmaker, was our interpreter. He took us to the Carpet Museum, which was exquisite, and to the Shah's Palace. As we did every day, regardless of who we were with, we asked lots of questions. We learned from Maziar that many young people in the country smoked opium and used heroin. If caught selling it, one was hanged. Regarding religion, Maziar told us that he knew many agnostics who were more comfortable without religious practice. In fact, he said that not being religious was a kind of status symbol in Iran. However, by law you could be killed if you were found to be an atheist.

The billboard on a main thoroughfare in Tehran pictured a profile of a veiled woman and proclaimed in big, bold letters, in English, "*Hejab is Dignity.*"

Hejab is proper Islamic dress. It is the loose clothing, dark colors preferred, that women must wear to cover all bare skin except their face and hands. Some chose to wear the traditional chador, which resembles a long, loose, shapeless sheet; others put on ankle-length cloak-like garments. All were required to wear the veil to cover their hair. Make-up was forbidden.

When the Shah outlawed the veil in 1933, he was using women to fight against religion. The Shah's police beat women for wearing the chador. But then, when Ayatollah Khomeini took power, his police beat women for not wearing the veil. Under Khomeini, men on motorcycles slashed women's hands or sleeves with sharp razors to punish them for their improper appearance.

To our Western sensibilities, that veil, required in Iran for all females over nine years old, symbolized oppression, symbolized the religious patriarchy, symbolized anything but dignity.

And for the days that I had to wear it, I felt annoyed, angered, even amused at times. Anything but dignified.

Islamic religious leaders have traditionally taught that women are ruled by almost ungovernable passions, which is why they must be protected by fathers, brothers, and husbands. Because their emotional natures incline them to be sinful, they must dress as they do because they are the cause of sinfulness in men.

But the status of women in the Iranian society is complex. Behind those veils, many women are anything but passive. Their own voices cry out the contradictions and create for the curious Westerner a collage of contrast and confusion.

According to John Simpson in his book, *Inside Iran*, Persian women have never been "the meek inhabitants of the inner rooms," as have women in Arab countries. They have traditionally played an equal part in family life and often a dominant one. Yet it wasn't until 1962 that women won the right to vote.

Maura and I were very much interested in the lives of women in Iran, and requested and were granted interviews with a cross-section of women outside of journalism.

"Regarding the veil, it is obligatory by law. Without it, a woman can be sentenced to lashes or prison. But in our struggle for Islamic rights, dress code isn't important for us because we live in a country where we women don't have the right to exist. We live in a country where a man can kick out a wife whenever he wants. We live in a country where mothers have no rights to their children. We must gain primary rights first."

We were told this by Shirin Ebadi, attorney, law professor, writer, human rights monitor, married mother of two children, and the author of a book about children's rights in Iran, published by UNICEF in England.

Shirin Ebadi and the author

Shirin, whose name in Farsi means "pleasant" or "delicate," was indeed very pleasant. But this woman who, shortly before our visit, was featured on a *60 Minutes* segment as the attorney charging a father with murdering his daughter, this woman who had received death threats because she was very vocal in her crusade on behalf of women in her country, was not delicate when it came to fighting for what she believed in—that women of Iran have to know their rights and start asking for them.

She took off her veil as soon as we were inside her home.

"Let's start with the position of women in Iran. In law, they have a very bad situation. Compensation for women is half of that of men because legally, a woman is regarded as half a man."

"Inequality extends to other things. A man can take four wives. Divorce is a man's right and he can do it without any reason. The law limits when a woman can divorce a man. Pre-nuptials giving the right to divorce are a recent phenomenon. But we must fight for rights in law, not in pre-nuptials or temporary legal documents.

"After divorce, the man gets custody. Boys can stay with their mothers up to the age of two years, girls up to seven, but then they have to go to the father. After a woman takes another spouse, she loses her right to custody, no matter how old the children are."

"So, not only do mothers have no rights regarding their children, the children have no rights. A girl of nine years old can declare her own consent to get married, but below that age, the father or grandfather can force her to marry the husband they have chosen. This is exactly like slavery.

"When a man wants to be physically abusive to his wife, he does it in the house, not on the streets. For example, in one of my cases, my client was beaten regularly, but there were no witnesses until her husband did it once at a party. The children, ages 10 and 8, came to court and testified that their father beat the mother so much she had to be hospitalized. The court did not accept that (court always means judge, since there is no jury). The judge ruled in the man's favor because the husband apologized and said he wouldn't do it again."

Shirin said that for reasons such as these, the feminist movement in Iran was very strong, unlike during the Shah's time, when feminism was weak. "Women speaking out is one of the solutions to the problems in society. Traditional women and intellectual women are struggling together now. Now I am optimistic about the future."

Although she didn't know it at the time, Shirin had good reason to be optimistic, and pessimistic. In 2003, she won the Nobel Peace Prize, the first Iranian and Muslim woman to win the prize in its then 102-year history. Six years later, her medal was stolen by authorities from her safe deposit box in Iran and her bank accounts were frozen. With her safety in question, she has lived in exile in the United Kingdom since 2009.

* * *

"There are no advertisements in Iran using women.
Here a woman has dignity, human status."
—M. Ebtekar

Thirty-eight-year old Masoumeh Ebtekar was Vice President and Head of Environment, and one of three of President Mohammed Khatami's VP's. (She later became the highest-ranking woman in the government from 2017 to 2021, when President Rouhani appointed her VP of Iran for Women and Family Affairs.) She was also a mother of two sons, ages 10 and 15 then. We met in her office where a small flag of Iran sat on her

1998—Iran

Masoumeh Ebtekar was vice president and Head of Environment, and one of three of President Mohammed Khatami's vice presidents

desk and a magnificent stuffed peacock hung on the wall behind her. She chose not to sit behind the desk, but at the head of a long conference table, where her staff served us juice and tea.

I had just recently read an interview with her in which she addressed the need to fight the "acute problem of pollution in Iran." At the time, Tehran was one of the world's most polluted cities. Only in Beijing, Calcutta, and Delhi was the air pollution worse. (Several surveys in 2018 listed Iran's city of Zabol, near the Afghan border, as the most polluted city in the world.) Ebtekar was used to being quoted. As a student with excellent English, known as "Mary" to the Americans, she was the official interpreter and spokeswoman of those who took the hostages in the American Embassy in 1979, something she preferred not to discuss.

"The role of women in political affairs and in government was defined in the early stages of the Revolution by Khomeini. He made it clear that not only should religion not serve as an obstacle to women's participation in Islamic affairs, but Islam invites both men and women to work together to build the future of their society ... Women are now entering the political sphere in greater numbers.

"The most important challenge facing women in Iran is to sustain the model of the Moslem woman in spite of changes in society. Women want a healthy competition between the sexes, a balanced sharing of responsibilities as intended under Islam. They need to make sure that there is no power struggle between men and women, no confrontations like the feminist movement produced in the West."

"Our society is also religious, yet we have so much more violence than you do here in Iran. Why do you suppose that is?" I asked.

"It is the mentality of the American people. US society may have a religious tendency, but you have the culture of Hollywood, MTV, regular TV. It is not a religious culture, not an ethical culture. There are signs of moral degradation in every film that comes out of Hollywood. The media shape the mentality, and as long as the media don't feel responsible, it will be a problem. Yes, in America you have freedom of expression, but freedom has its limits and should be defined within the interests of the general population. Since it isn't so defined, you have drug addiction and the destruction of the family."

She also talked about US materialism.

"You Americans are not culturally oriented, but rather special-interest oriented. Your free speech is not about freedom; it is all about advertising and business, about getting greater audiences. Driven by a consumer culture, you are losing future generations.

"After all, what kind of role models do you have when Elvis is a hero, when your president poses with Michael Jackson?"

* * *

"In any organization, any family, the main role here in Iran is the woman's. Their leadership is hidden. We call it leadership from the shadows. After the Revolution in 1979, many men lost their jobs, stayed at home, and got depressed. Their wives found work and held the families together. Yet women are considered *zaifeh*, the weak sex."

Fereshteh, the mother of three, was a prominent children's filmmaker in her 40s. Very soon after meeting her, it became obvious that she was a strong woman and an astute businesswoman who was very comfortable being in charge.

Hers had been a traditional marriage. She had felt no attraction to the man from the beginning. But her mother said to try; the prospective husband was rich. Fareshteh said he had loved her, but was selfish. She waited to divorce him until a time when there would be no hard feelings. It took 16 years, and she managed only with the help of her mother-in-law, who finally told her son there was no sense in being married to a woman who does not love you. Fereshteh walked away from a beautiful home, asked for no money, no child support. She wanted—and got—only custody of her children.

1998—Iran

Fareshteh accompanied us to the Ayatollah Khomeini's home, where we had been granted permission to visit by the Ministry of Culture and Islamic Guidance. We stood in front of the one room that was on view, the room where the Ayatollah spent his days receiving guests, addressing his people, saying his prayers. A small room, about 10 by 14 feet, it was simple, reflecting the man and his beliefs. Still there on the Persian carpet were a pair of his beige sandals and a pair of his black slippers.

The turquoise walls had only small patches of paint on them. Most of the paint had been scratched off, down to what looked like plaster and concrete, by peoples' fingernails, people clawing in their desperate grief after his death. The long marks were still visible.

Khomeini was placed for viewing in an open wooden coffin. His funeral was a frenzy of millions of people trying to touch him, trying to literally get a piece of him. They tore his white shroud to pieces and were so out of control that they pulled him out of the casket. Fereshteh told us his dead body had been packed with ice and when it dripped from the box, people drank it.

Then she began to sob.

The Imam had a great sorrow in his heart for all the people of the world, not only Moslems. He felt that all should have a better life, that the leader should live like the poor people, not the rich.

Khomeini made it clear that whenever he spoke about other nations, he spoke about their governments, not the people themselves. He said America wanted to control other countries, but all countries should obey only God, not America. That's why the American government was like Satan, because it wanted to control people.

Fareshteh, whose name means "angel," would have controlled every moment of our time if we had let her. As we were driving back to our hotel, she came up with all sorts of plans for the remainder of the day, which we had already scheduled. As I tried to politely decline, she asked, only half jokingly, "Is this how you obey your husband?"

"*Obey* is not part of my marriage vows," I replied.

"Here in Iran, women pretend to agree with their husbands, but they usually have a better idea. It is good to pretend to obey, you get lots of good things, such as jewelry and trips."

"Well, did you obey your husband?" I asked.

"No," she said matter-of-factly. "He wasn't qualified."

* * *

"Yes, I can call myself a feminist in my situation. But feminism has a bad connotation here in Iran, and there are various points of view within the movement."

Roza Eftekharg was the cultural editor of *Zanan*, a woman's magazine. An attractive woman, she was single, had never been married, and lived alone. She said that for a woman to live alone in Iran was unusual, that it had not yet become a tradition, although more were doing so then than 20 years ago. It was happening because of economic problems, because marriage became more difficult for young people.

"What about homosexuality in Iran?" I asked.

"You cannot talk about homosexuality with either men or women; it is not yet discussed. But there are secret reports that it exists.

"We do have a report in our magazine about transsexuals in Iran. The cases we have found are mainly men trying to be women. The Ministry of Health gave them permission and financial help for the sex change. Cases were approved when three to four psychologists and hormone experts saw that the men had a problem. It is safe to talk about it because it is medical.

"We had an article about feminism and mentioned that lesbianism is not a phenomenon of feminism, but goes back centuries to Plato, who wrote about it. Consequently, we were charged with spreading prostitution by encouraging immoral activity. The charge was politically motivated, and we were exonerated."

Finally, "Is there anything you would like to say to women in America?"

"I want to ask American women to think about our problems in a just way, just as we look at women's issues in America, such as lesbianism, as social phenomenon we can discuss in a just way. We are coming from two different cultures, and we have to look at each other's cultures without political opinions or prejudices.

"We still have some traditional prejudiced views of America. We can rationalize it somehow because Iran was a colony and America was the master and Iranians still feel some hostility. The conservatives use the slogan *Death to America* from 20 years ago to justify their existence, without it they are not legitimate. We insist on independence and Islamic values, it doesn't mean we want death to anyone."

* * *

During my time in Tehran, along the sidewalks women in their hajib walked past propaganda billboards, one particularly large one designed to represent the American flag. In both English and Farsi, it read *Down with the USA*. Instead of stars, there were skulls in the upper left-hand corner, and at the bottom of the red stripes, rockets were descending.

The women didn't even glance at the billboards. Under their proper Islamic dress, some were wearing jeans, many had fashionable shoes—Timberlands, Nike sneakers, pumps, or platforms. Others carried Chanel handbags. Older women in their black chadors showed no hair; younger ones did, as a sign of protest. When I looked closely, I saw that a few had manicures. Some were even wearing lipstick.

I saw many similarities between Iran and the USSR. The personality cults of Lenin and Khomeini; the existence of the black markets; the desire for American-made jeans, fashions, and culture. In Tehran, there was a Chicago Bulls decal on the back of a van. There were street signs advertising Polo, Boss, Nike, Adidas. Mickey Mouse tee-shirts were for sale in shops. And there was even a Hallmark card shop. (Often, when shopkeepers learned we were Americans, their faces changed and we almost physically felt their dislike.)

Back in their day, Russians feared the KGB. Iranians feared the brutality of the Shah's secret police, the Savak. Under Communism, men wearing red armbands patrolled the Russian streets to maintain order. In Iran, there were Komitehs, similar groups who attempted to regulate behavior to ensure conformity.

Each country treated its Jews poorly. Between 1979 and 2021, the number of Jews in Iran decreased by 90 percent, leaving only around 8,500, mostly elderly. (worldpopulationreview.com)

But each country elected a reformer. Mikhail Gorbachev in the USSR, Mohammed Khatami in Iran. In fact, Iranians referred to Khatami as the "Gorbachev of Iran." Unfortunately, in spite of those elections, things in each country did not change enough to keep the hard-liners from regaining power.

However, there was one area where there was absolutely no comparison between the two countries. The food in Iran was fresh, fine-looking and full of flavor. Just fabulous!

And the Persian rugs in the Carpet Museum were the most magnificent I'd ever seen.

After our trip to Tehran, we extended formal written invitations to the publications we visited, asking them to send delegates to the first part of our proposed exchange program. Seven never responded; one said he could not come because of academic commitments; another could not participate because of problems with the Taliban. The five below were brave enough to accept:

- Ms. Kamelia Entekhabifard, reporter, Zan newspaper
- Mr. Mohammad Atrianfar, editor, Hamshahri newspaper
- Ms. Shahla Sherkat, editor Zanan magazine
- Mr. Karim Arghandehpour, editorial board member Salam newspaper
- Ms. Mojgan Jalali, editor Iran News English Daily

Prior to their arrival, I also wrote letters of invitation to ex-President Jimmy Carter and to Senator Edward Kennedy. Unfortunately, neither was available to work it into their schedules to meet our Iranian delegates.

In Iran, the hard-line press reported on their visit that NESNE was affiliated with the CIA and Zionists, and that the trip of the Iranians to the US was a subterfuge, an attempt by the Great Satan to influence and interfere in Iran's press and further its efforts to overthrow the Islamic republic of Iran. (In 2021, approximately 10,000 Jews lived in Iran.)

Of course, none of that was true. The program I had arranged involved visits to newspapers—the *Boston Globe*, the *New York Times*, and other regional papers. Visits to universities—Columbia, Brandeis, and Harvard—where the actual two-day conference was held at the Kennedy School. The program also included a press tour of the United Nations, and the Iranians spoke at the Asia Society. Sightseeing included the Statue of Liberty, Ellis Island, and a gospel brunch.

They also were invited to visit George Soros at his home on Park Avenue, because his Open Society Foundation was one of the funders. In spite of being born to a Jewish family in Hungary and having to pose as a Christian child to survive the occupation, Soros is still falsely accused of collaborating with the Nazis during the war. Even though he had given away 32 billion dollars around the world to help build democracy, in 2023, at 93 years old, he was still vilified by activists on the right in the US and by nationalist leaders in Europe. He is still believed today to be a part of a Jewish liberal plot to dilute the white world with immigrants, to want to do away with borders, to financially control the world.

I can't resist adding that while in Tehran, we were the recipients of gracious hospitality, all the delicious food we could eat, no matter the time or place, but especially when in someone's home. Multi-billionaire George Soros graciously served the Iranians and me tea and—potato chips. He also gave the delegates signed copies of his book, which they threw away before they got back to Iran, fearful that they would be punished for having met with the Jew who is "leading efforts to take over the world."

NESNE, a regional organization of New England newspapers, had pulled off two historic firsts! In 1983, a journalism exchange program with the USSR that lasted 15 years, and then with Iran in 1998, when there had been no Iranian journalists in any official capacity in the US since before the hostage situation in 1979. Unfortunately, NESNE delegates never got invited to go to Iran, despite our best efforts. It became clear that it wasn't safe for a newspaper there to invite Americans, and thus that exchange program was short-lived.

However, the trip to Iran, the visit of their delegates, the entire experience has stayed with me all these years. The aftermath proved to be both joyful and tragic.

Maura Casey and I bonded in Iran in ways that just aren't possible in our day-to-day lives. We still talk about what an incredible adventure it was, about what we accomplished, what we saw and did, and how much we laughed over the silliest things.

1998—Iran

Maura Casey and the author

I never got used to putting on the headscarf in any way that was even remotely flattering.

After her work at *The Day* in New London, Connecticut, Maura went to work for the *New York Times*. She now does independent writing and editing for individuals and organizations and she comes to visit Tucson (where I now live) when she can. And when she does, we laugh some more.

I became friends with the youngest Iranian delegate, Camelia Entekhabifard, who was imprisoned on trumped-up charges shortly after her return to Tehran. She spent three months in prison, being interrogated daily while blindfolded, accused of spying, of prostitution, alcohol consumption, spreading atheism, and working for the CIA and Radio Free Europe. Her work and her interviews were seen as threatening to the government, in particular her attempts to interview Salman Rushdie. I don't believe her participation in the NESNE delegation contributed to her arrest, although I'm sure it didn't help.

Once released, she managed to come to America and knew that it was unsafe for her to return to her home. She now divides her time between New York City and Dubai. I adore Camelia, and continue to see her if she is there when I am in New York. I am so proud of what she has accomplished. She got a master's degree from New York University's School of Journalism, then another master's from Columbia University School of International and Public Affairs. As her website states, she currently reports on Iran and Afghanistan for AP, Reuters, *Le Monde Diplomatique*, *al-Jazeera*, *al-Arabiya*, the *New York Times*, the *Huffington Post*, the *Village Voice*, and *Mother Jones*, among others. She is now editor-in-chief of the *Independent Persian*, the first international newspaper published in Persian. *Camelia, Save Yourself by Telling the Truth* is the title of the book she wrote shortly after her NESNE visit.

I stayed in touch with our interpreter Maziar Bahari after our Tehran visit, until right after the conference, when he interviewed me for Radio Free Europe. Like Camelia, Maziar also went to prison. He was arrested in Tehran on June 21, 2009, while he was a reporter for *Newsweek*, and held in the notorious Evin Prison for 118 days. He was accused of espionage, to which he confessed on TV after physical and psychological torture and solitary confinement. Following an international campaign that called for his release, he was allowed to go to London to join his wife a few days before the birth of his child. He has not returned to Iran. He wrote the book, *Then They Came for Me*, which was made into the movie *Rosewater*, written and directed by Jon Stewart.

Finally, the conference would not have been as successful as it was if it weren't for Chris Stevens at the Iran Desk, Northern Gulf Affairs, at the State Department, who I contacted in the run-up to the Iranians visit to ask for help. The INS (Immigration and Naturalization Service) routinely subjected Iranians to a high level of scrutiny when entering the US—fingerprinting, mug shots, lengthy interviews. This was not the way we wanted to begin the delegation's visit. In the months leading up to the Iranians' arrival, I spoke or wrote to Chris often, to update him on who was coming, dates, program, and so on, and he was always polite and pleasant and professional. He got their visa application process amended to make it easier for them to apply, and then he managed to get waivers so that the delegates did not have to go through any of the usual unwelcoming arrival procedures.

Chris went on to be appointed Ambassador to Libya.

Where he was killed at the American Consulate in Benghazi, in September 2012.

August, 1998 Russia devalued the ruble, to take effect on Nov 1. Subsequently, nearly 1/3 of the country's population fell below the poverty line.

According to Bill Browder, author of the book *Red Notice*, "In Soviet times, the richest person in Russia was about six times richer than the poorest. ….by the year 2000, the richest person (in Russia) had become 250,000 times richer than the poorest person."

First Chechen War 1994 to 1996, Second Chechen War 1999 to 2000

May 7, 2000: Vladimir Putin was inaugurated as President of Russia after Yeltsin handed over power to him. Less than one year later, all three federal TV networks were controlled by the State. In time, Putin pushed the Parliament to pass anti-gay legislation, and to restrict protests.

October 7, 2006: Russian journalist Anna Politkovskaya was shot dead in the elevator in her apartment building. Suspicion since then has been that she was assassinated under Putin's orders in response to her reports about human rights violations—torture and terror—in Chechnya under pro-Moscow, corrupt President Ramzan Kadyrov.

Part Eight

Chapter 36
Becoming a Political Talk Show Host

"What draws us into the desert is the search for something intimate in the remote."
—Edward Abbey (1927–1989)
American author
From *A Voice Crying in the Wilderness*

On the morning of 9/11, Frank was on the Isle of Wight, an island in the English Channel, visiting a friend. My niece Renee called me and told me to turn on the TV. We watched together in silence as the World Trade Center buildings collapsed. After we finally hung up, I got a quart of chocolate ice cream from the freezer and sat again in front of the screen, watching. And eating. All day.

Then, on September 18th, 2020, she called to tell me that Ruth Bader Ginsburg had died. I told her not to call me anymore. And then I brought out the ice cream.

Two weeks after the Twin Towers fell, Frank and I flew to Tucson to close on the home we had bought that we initially intended to be a winter get-away. One winter we drove out across country, listening to the *Tortilla Curtain* by T. Coraghessan Boyle. Our little cat Vodka had died a few months earlier, but we took her sweet sister Grapefruit with us. She listened to the big semis we passed, screaming what sounded like feline obscenities to each one. But on leash, she calmly walked up Beale Street in Memphis—I hope enjoying the music coming from the storefronts—and then to the Mississippi River, where she stared long and hard at a landscape she had never before seen and could hardly have imagined. She also became familiar with Tucson's landscape, until her heart failed two years later.

My entertainment was somewhat different. Frank was looking forward to the drive more than I, so I decided I had to create some way to occupy myself as we passed and sometimes stopped at the highway exits with their multiple and monotonous motels, fat-laden fast-food restaurants and grim gas stations.

I created anti-President Bush flyers that I taped on every door inside every stall in every restroom I visited, most gleefully in Midland, Texas, where he lived—while Frank sat in the car with the motor running - like the get-away driver during a bank heist —nervously worrying and waiting for his wife to emerge unscathed.

Paths of Stones

After a few seasons in Tucson, after we had grown to love the cacti, the desert creatures, the summer monsoons, and the spectacular sunsets, we decided we wanted to live there full-time and sold our place in Cambridge. MaryAnne, my college friend from Canastota, often came to visit from her home in Carlsbad, California, and we always made her mother's recipe for Italian sauce. We also took a road trip throughout New Mexico, which allowed us to spend more time together than we had since college.

A few years later, Renee and her husband Thumper moved to Las Cruces, New Mexico, four hours away. Almost every year, Tambi from the West Coast and her younger sister Tara from the East Coast have come to either Renee's or our house for the holidays, so we have all been able to remain close.

After working 21 years with NESNE, I resigned in 2005, closing a creative and challenging chapter in my life. A chapter that gave me pride—and my wonderful husband Frank. I also stopped my work with OASES and IPEX.

* * *

But before I leave that work behind, a few more things that I haven't mentioned.

In the wake of the 1986 Chernobyl nuclear accident, after contacting both government and private agencies and leading scientists, IPEX produced and mailed out a fact sheet about the disaster, to inform the public about radiation levels, the advisability of travel to the USSR, potential food contaminations, and appropriate precautions.

For a few years, we presented a panel at the Annual Conference of the New England Slavic Association at Harvard. I chaired the 1985 session, "Breaking Barriers: US/USSR Exchanges". Our main speaker then was Andrei Parastayev, First Secretary for Public Exchanges, Soviet Embassy, Washington.

In 1989, we sponsored a performance of Russian music by violinist Michael Appleman and pianist Diane Huling.

I put together a slide show and talk, "Faces and Façades of the USSR," which I presented at the Women's Educational and Industrial Union in Boston (Feb 1989), as well as many other venues. In addition, I taught a course on Russia at Boston Adult Education and participated as a panel-member in the 21st Annual International Careers Forum at the Boston University School of Law.

And in 1990, we sent Rosamond Purcell, photographer of the book, *Illuminations: A Bestiary with Scientific Text* by Stephen Jay Gould, to Russia to photograph artifacts from both the collection of Peter the Great at the Kunstkammer Museum of Ethnography and from the Museum of Zoology, USSR Academy of Sciences.

Many proposals for exchange programs suggested by the Russians didn't work—exchanges for animators; for raising chickens and processing them; for criminal medical doctors; for perishable food transportation systems; and for setting up the production, processing, and utilization of truffles.

Talk Show Host

But my work and candid conversations over 26 years with Iranians, Soviets/Russians, and Americans proved that myths and misunderstandings can be dispelled, and lasting personal and professional relationships can be established with the "enemy."

It took a little time in Tucson for me to figure out what to pursue next. Frank had retired in 1992 and we did a lot of traveling, but I wanted to become connected to the community. I sat on some non-profit boards, did some volunteer work, and started a political book group. Then I was asked to host a talk show on Access Tucson, the local public access TV station.

Before I agreed to host *Political Perspectives* in 2006, I had been on TV only briefly—once when my Brownie troop appeared on the TV Ranch Club hosted by Bill Parker (originally from Canastota!) on WNBF in Binghamton and then when some of my delegations and I were interviewed by Soviet TV in Moscow. I wasn't comfortable in front of a camera.

During the four years that I hosted the show, Frank kindly said I grew into the role of interviewer and moderator, became more relaxed. Those were years when George W. Bush was president, when we on the political left thought he was the worst thing that had ever happened to the country, when we never imagined a Donald Trump. I did my part to protest the Bush administration's policies by the topics I chose for the show, topics such as "Separation of Church and State"; "Nuclear Power: Worth the Risk?"; "Is Big Media Failing Democracy?"; "Private, For-Profit Prisons"; and "Politics and Christian Fundamentalism."

Sol Littman, the first Director of the Canadian Branch of the Simon Wiesenthal Center, who later became a visiting scholar at the Arizona Center for Judaic Studies at the University of Arizona, spoke about Universal Health Care in Canada. Mort Rosenblum, former Chief International Correspondent for the Associated Press addressed the fear that Big Media was failing democracy. Amanda Simpson, who later was appointed a senior technical adviser with the Department of Commerce under President Obama, the first transgender appointee to the Federal Government, talked about transgender realities. Leslye Obiora, law professor at the University of Arizona who had been Executive Cabinet Minister for Mines for the government of Nigeria, her place of birth, told our viewers about the "New Scramble for Africa" by countries all seeking influence and profit there. Retired US Army Brigadier General John Adams, who served as a military intelligence officer, as a military attaché in S. Korea, and a US military representative to NATO, gave us his opinion about "America's Image in the World" at that time.

I was fortunate to interview Gabby Giffords, then running for the 8th Congressional District seat, about the challenges of serving in the Arizona State House and Senate. She was intelligent, articulate, and warm, which made the attempt on her life five years later, in 2011, and the bullet wounds inflicted in her brain all the more tragic.

Reporter and writer Chuck Bowden, who spoke at length about border issues and crime in Mexico, was one of my favorite interviews. I think he delighted in the crusty, curmudgeon affect that he projected, but he knew his stuff, was passionate about that stuff, and his writing reflected that. Sadly, we lost him too soon, when he died in his sleep at age 69 in 2014.

My guests were too many to mention, but I was privileged to speak with all of them, to learn from them, and to enjoy them.

Until recently, as a member of the organization, I served for two years on the Equity Committee for Social Venture Partners Tucson: "… an ever-expanding community of engaged philanthropists dedicated to building the capacity, strength, and impact of nonprofits in addressing social problems." We created a "Diversity and Inclusion Resources" online library which I curated, whose goal is to provide information about racism and inequality.

And now, since 2014, I continue to voluntarily serve as a mentor editor for The Op-Ed Project, whose mission is to work "with universities, think tanks, foundations, nonprofits, corporations, and community organizations across the nation, scout and train under-represented experts (especially women) to take thought leadership positions in their fields (through op-eds and much more); connect them with our international network of high-level media mentors; and vet and channel the best new ideas and experts directly to media gatekeepers across all platforms."

Chapter 37
Mystery Solved

"The grandson of the cousin of a grandmother's cousin is still something for a Jew. If you're family, then you're family, as the saying goes."
—Tevye, in *"Fiddler on the Roof,"* inspired by the works of Sholem Aleichem (1859–1916) Yiddish author and playwright

A few months after we got our dog, back in 2007, (we already had two cats, Zeke and Zoe, to replace Vodka and Grapefruit), we met a couple at a Tucson farmer's market who said they also had a Havanese and belonged to a puppy "playgroup." Barbie Adler and John Nemerovski asked if we wanted to join. We did, and for years, our affectionate little Tito enjoyed Saturday or Sunday morning playtime with his peers.

On an 82-degree Sunday evening, February 28, 2010, one of the women from the doggie group, Anne Bowden (wife of Jan Zwartendijk, whose father, a Dutch diplomat

Barbie Adler and John Nemerovski

from the Netherlands based in Kaunas, Lithuania, saved 2,345 Lithuanian Jews during the Holocaust by issuing them visas to leave the country.), had a birthday party at Barbie and John's home and invited us. We didn't know most of her friends, so as people filed in, Ann told us a bit about everyone.

"That's Seymour (Si) Reichlin and his wife Ellie. They moved here from Boston," Ann said. "He is retired now, but way back in 1972, Tufts Medical School described him as a world-renowned leader in the field of neuroendocrinology and disorders of the thyroid gland. He is apparently considered the father of neuro-immuno-endocrinology."

After a while, I went up to Dr. Reichlin, and on a whim, told him I had Reichlins in my family (which I had learned while pursuing genealogy after meeting Mark twenty years earlier) and asked where his family was from in the Old Country.

"A small town not far from Minsk," he countered. "I doubt you've heard of it. Glubokoye."

Stunned silence.

Finally, "That's where my father was born!"

He hesitated while staring at me. "We must be related," he said, eyes wide and questioning.

We immediately sat down to talk, to share family details, and suddenly I learned who those two little girls were who came to America so long ago with my father and my grandmother.

I leaned across the table, took his hand, and whispered "Si, I have your mother's passport."

Si listened in shock, shook his head, got teary-eyed, grabbed my arm, and took me to every table so he could proclaim, "This is my cousin. Can you believe it? Cynthia is my cousin!"

And how did this come to be that Si and I were related?

Well, it is all about Nachama, (a different Nachama than Naomi), my grandfather's sister. She married a Saul Reichlin, and they had two children, Harry and Freida. Harry was Si's father, which means Si and I are second cousins, because his grandfather married my grand-aunt.

But there is so much more to the story.

When Si's grandfather Saul was in the Russian army, he came home unexpectedly on a short leave. It was very late in the night when he arrived and not wanting to disturb his sleeping wife and children, he slept in a hay wagon out in the street. As a result, he got a cold, followed by pneumonia, and then death. He was only 21 years old.

After Saul died, my grand-aunt Nachama remarried in 1898 to a Joseph Rosen, who had been married to a Rebecca Rabinowitz in 1890 and had two children. After Rebecca died, her mother Freida raised these girls in Glubokoye. Two little girls, named Chiena and Basia, later Celia and Betty, became stepdaughters to Nachama.

Mystery Solved

(Was my Glubokoye guide Yakov Rabinowitz Pelkin, whose wife's name was Frieda, related to Rebecca and Frieda Rabinowitz? It wouldn't surprise me.)

Nachama and Joseph Rosen had three children together.

Nachama died on November 10, 1906.

But the story still isn't over. Lo and behold, Nachama's son later married his step-sister Celia Rosen. Again, Celia, as you now know, was one of those little girls passing illegally as my grandmother's daughters when they left Russia for America in December of 1910.

Almost 100 years later, her son Si and I discovered one another in Tucson, Arizona. At a birthday party. All because of the breed of our beloved dog, Tito.

Tito Che Dogvara

Chapter 38
Si

"America was not the land of milk and honey, but it was the only place where they could be free. Learned men were janitors, but they came here for their children."
—Si's mother, Celia Reichlin (1899–1975)

In the years since we met, Si's wife Ellie died from cancer, I got to know their children, and he and I have spent a lot of time going to lunch and talking. A lot of talking. We got to know one another's present and past, we compared notes, shared family memories.

On January 4, 2016, over lunch at the Arizona Inn, I interviewed Si in an attempt to fill in some blanks, to get his full story.

Si was born on May 31, 1924, at Doctor's Hospital, New York City. His full name is Seymour Reichlin, no middle name, and he was named after his father's father, who was Shlomo, or Saul Reichlin.

Si's bar mitzvah was on Saturday, May 8th, 1937. Among the many guests were two of my uncles—Samuel Dickstein and Herman Dickstein. Si remembers my Uncle Herman, remembers that he had a deep resonant voice, that he was very nice to Si, and that his daughter Lorna was a sweet girl. But Si (as well as the rest of my family) had little respect for Herman when he divorced his wife Lydia after 45 years of marriage.

Si was graduated from high school in February when he was 15, went to City College, and at 17, transferred as a sophomore to Antioch College. At age 19, in 1943, he enlisted in the Army Medical Corps. After one year, they discharged him to go to medical school, which was paid for by the GI Bill.

When I asked him if he ever experienced anti-Semitism, he cited the fact that he graduated at the top of his class, applied to 16 medical schools, and was accepted into only one, Washington University.

He also remembered that as a nine-year-old child, he was verbally attacked in the street by a man who shouted out to him, "You dirty little Jew."

Si was six when he started thinking he wanted to become a doctor. By the time he was nine, he knew for sure. He had asthma as a child and was often seeing doctors. At his appointments, he always asked medical questions and his path in life was clear. Si went on to achieve great things in his professional life. He became president of the

Endocrine Society and was elected to the American Academy of Arts and Sciences. He was most proud though, the day he graduated from medical school, when he looked out into the audience and saw Herb (his brother) and Natalie (his sister), and his parents, two immigrants with minimal education, who were then able to say, "Our son, the doctor."

He was 27 when he married 22-year-old Ellie Thurman Dameshek, whose father was the first president of the American Society for Hematology and who for many years was the world's most famous hematologist. Si said his happiest times were when his children—Seth, Annie, and Doug—were young. If there was one lesson he'd like his kids to have learned, it is: "Be a good person, so you have no regrets."

His saddest moments have to do with death and grieving—when he saw his father slowly dying and knew that all the burden was on his mother, and when his sister was dying. Si's mother went to the hospital every day to see her. Finally Natalie said to Si, "Please, tell her to leave, I can't die with her here." Si, of course, didn't tell his mother the truth, simply said it was too distressing for Natalie to see how sad her mother was.

When I asked Si if there was anything in his life he would change, he thought for a long moment, and then said, "No, I have accomplished everything I am capable of doing."

In 1975, Si's mother Celia was interviewed by her niece, Si's brother Herb's daughter, much the same way I interviewed Si, and he gave me a copy of the interview. Celia remembered that the tsar's portrait hung on a wall in her grandmother's house, and that every Sabbath, people collected food to share with the poor. On Purim, people made candies and nutcakes, put them on a platter, and went from one house to another, where people took something off and put something else on.

When young, Celia believed that she was one of the Chosen People. She also remembers that the "Russian peasants went on killing sprees and killed Jews."

She said that after his wife, my grand-aunt Nachama, died in 1905, her father left for America to avoid the draft. Jews were so persecuted in the army that they would maim themselves so as not to be drafted.

She told about being brought to America with her sister by a woman (my grandmother), who got so sick on the ship that they "thought they would have to drown her." Celia was 11, although the passport said she was younger.

She remembered that a man came up to them at Ellis Island, a man Celia and her sister did not recognize. He said he was their father and took them to live on 103rd Street in Harlem, in a railroad flat with a long, narrow hallway, where he had a wife and son, and where two Russian brothers also lived.

Celia said she was lonely, missed her grandmother, and felt that her new stepmother resented and hated her. And perhaps there was reason for her to be angry. Celia's father had never told his wife-to-be that he had left five children behind in Russia. Celia was never allowed to play, although the boys were; she couldn't read books, had to constantly clean. Of her stepmother, she said "she was just dreadful".

Celia commented that Jews always helped other Jews from the Old Country, that there was a group in town affiliated with Glubokoye that provided burial plots to all, so that no one had to end up in Potter's Field.

And she told this story. One day, her father met his stepson, Harry Reichlin, walking down a street in NY. Apparently Joseph had no idea Harry had come to America. And since Celia was 13, it was expected that she " would be his sweetheart." She was told she was engaged and she said she didn't know any better. Celia graduated from public school in 1915, Harry brought her flowers, and soon after she married him.

At the time, she was a milliner, but Harry bought first one deli, then others, (one was the 91st St. Deli at 2444 Broadway in 1936) and she had to quit her work to help in the stores. She never got over that she couldn't continue designing hats, and she hated working in the delicatessen shops. Eventually, Harry and Celia, with her prodding, bought a cottage at Ocean Beach, Fire Island.

She said of Si: "He was a junior rabbi at the synagogue; he elevated us, he never left us out."

When Si's father Harry died in 1967, Celia moved to Miami Beach, Triton Tower on Collins Avenue and 28th. She then said, "I feel I will always walk alone and live in the past." But she lived until she was 93, when she died in her sleep. Alone.

Si also told me she was outgoing, gregarious, socially conscious, liberal, and very affectionate. And that Celia sang beautifully. He also said she was a "tumbler," a lively person who stirs things up, gets the party going. She used to dress up in costumes and put on funny shows for the neighborhood kids.

Si's father was born in August of 1893, in Glubokoye. He was deep into politics and music, although he had no talent himself. He mostly worked and if he wasn't working, he read the newspaper. A few times he took Si to the 2nd Avenue Jewish Theatre. And he was a good cook. He was very liberal, and held on to money that people had collected to send to HIAS (Hebrew Immigrant Aid Society). He also bought his kids gifts on Christmas so they wouldn't feel left out.

Si said his father talked little about Russia, mostly about working for his grandfather and delivering seltzer water. And he resented his mother (Nachama) for sending him away. At age 15, he went to live with his grandparents. He came to America when he was 19 and worked as a paperhanger, then for a deli man named Rosenbaum. He went into the US Army and went to cooking and baking school in Alabama. That is where he actually learned English and became a naturalized citizen.

But Si said his father Harry was a controlling person, had a mean voice, and his parents weren't a happy couple. He was never physically abusive to his wife, but they used to fight a lot over money. It got so bad that the three children went to them and said their arguments were making the kids unhappy. That helped.

When his father was running his stores, he criticized his staff unmercifully and often publicly. Si could see that they were humiliated and he told his father he shouldn't do that, especially in front of other people. But the irony was that he insisted his kids treat the staff respectfully, taught them how to treat people less fortunate. Also, Si said his father was affectionate, and Si always knew both parents loved him.

Si's mother, Celia Rosen Reichlin (age 19), one of the little girls my grandmother brought to America as her own, on her wedding day, March 15, 1919.

Celia, years later

Si

Standing: Herb, Natalie, Si
Front: Parents Harry and Celia Reichlin

Brothers Herb and Seymour Reichlin

Paths of Stones

Harry died at age 73 from complications of coronary artery disease (which Si also has). He was 56 when he had his first symptoms. Both he and Celia are buried at the Workmen's Circle Cemetery on Long Island in the section devoted to Glubokoye.

Joseph, Si's mother's father, lived till he was 83, but he got paranoid toward the end of his life and accused his third wife Sadie of having an affair. Si said if you knew Sadie, you'd know just how out of it he was with that suspicion. He remembers no good times with his grandparents, and in fact, when he showed me pictures, they looked very stern. They had no English, Joseph was remote and Sadie hardly spoke.

Betty, Celia's older sister, married a man named Norman Pohl, a dress manufacturer whose company was named Norman Modes. They eventually moved to Long Beach, Long Island. Betty and Celia were close, but there was still resentment on Celia's part, bickering and competing, perhaps fueled by the fact that Si thought his mother was in love with Betty's husband Norman, and probably would have liked to have married him if it had been possible.

Si loved his Aunt Betty, said she was a character. She was phobic about food and cleanliness and her kids adopted the same phobias.

Si's sister, Natalie, was born four years before Si (May 29, 1920) and his brother Herb came along a year and a half after Si (November 8, 1925).

Natalie died in 1980, a few months short of her 60th birthday, from a rare pancreatic tumor, the first of its kind diagnosed at New England Medical Center, where ironically Si was Chief of Endocrinology. She lived four years after the diagnosis. Natalie had worked as a microbiologist and married a lawyer named Dave Storper. Sad story—her husband and her best friend were having an affair before she got sick. And when Natalie was in the hospital having chemotherapy, her husband had her served with a *get*—a Jewish divorce document. Si has not spoken to him since.

Herb joined the army in September 1944, and on January 9, 1945, was part of the infantry that attacked the Germans in the Battle of the Bulge. (The battle had begun on December 16th, 1944 and lasted until January 25th, 1945.)

In his words:

> "The heavy machine gun squad I was in had five men. We took turns carrying the gun, the tripod mount, and the steel cans of ammunition, our feet freezing in wet leather boots as we trudged through the foot-deep snow, our hands like frozen claws, in woolen knit gloves, clasped on the metal. No decent food for weeks. Exhausted from lack of rest and constant shivering.
>
> Late in the day, a German plane buzzed us in a Luxembourg village. Then, in the field beyond, there was sudden artillery fire from 88s. That's when I was hit by a steel grenade."

(On December 26th, Frank's older brother Rufus died in the same battle, two weeks before Herb was injured.)

Sixty-three years after that combat day, I attended a reunion of my 90th Infantry Division for the first time and through an amazing meeting with a replacement to my squad learned that every one of the men in my squad had been wounded or killed that day. Who was wounded? Who was killed? I will never know.

I lost an eye and part of my skull and it took a year and a half to rebuild and mend my shrapnel-torn face and body, but I am still glad I enlisted and was there at the Bulge."

Si told me that the family didn't hear anything from Herb after he enlisted, until five months later in February, when they received word from the Red Cross that he was in a hospital in England. He had lost his left eye and part of his skull, including his left frontal lobe, and also a baby finger. He was unconscious for six weeks. The army discharged him with a rating of 90 percent disabled. He had almost died and he was in and out of hospitals for the next nine years due to his life-threatening injuries.

After the army, Herb went to Antioch College, where he majored in mathematics and statistics. He worked as a computer analyst, was Program Director for Information Technology for Pennsylvania State University Health Department, got married, and had six children, who were raised Christian. Herb wears a patch over what was his left eye.

Herb also remembered my Uncle Herman. "Short legs, long torso, kind of a phony. He wanted to be a powerful man. My father didn't like him too much." (Herbert Reichlin died on April 8th, 2024, at the age of 98.)

Si mentioned that we had a distant cousin by marriage, Manny Rosen, who wrote the song "King Heroin," performed originally by singer James Brown. Manny identified himself as a humorist, poet, and writer. He also was at one time a pro boxer, worked as a longshoreman and was a counter man at the Stage Deli in midtown Manhattan for 32 years. What he wasn't, according to Si, was a nice man.

On the other hand, Si is not only a nice man, he is very talented. An internationally famous doctor whose 100th birthday will be in May 2024, he is still a writer, a researcher, a musician, and a sculptor. A true Renaissance man. During Trump's presidency, he began to create what he called *Occhios*, Trump and his people, all with long noses to represent the lies. *Trumpocchio*, holding the pussy cat, was the first one he did.

Si's collection of Trump and his fellow "occhio" partners in crime

Trumpocchio, holding the cat, was the first one

My favorite is this tall white one, representing Trump Tower, with all Trump's sheep in MAGA hats desperately following while he holds the January 6, 2021 flag in one hand and Lady Liberty in a stranglehold in his right hand

Si

Shortly after I interviewed Si, I had a get-together of cousins at our house, all of whom had worked alone and/or with each another on genealogy. We represented five of the six lines of descendants from my great-grandparents.

Eva Rosen, Cheryl Sofer, the author, Dana Korby and Si Reichlin

2012
The Magnitsky Act was passed by Congress to punish Russian officials responsible for human rights abuses by denying them entrance into the US and our banking system. It specifically targeted those blamed for the death in prison in 2009 of lawyer and auditor Sergei Magnitsky. Magnitsky had uncovered and testified about massive corruption by Interior Ministry officers who had stolen $230,000,000 from the state. Arrested, subjected to torture and deplorable living conditions for a year while in detention, he was ultimately denied medical treatment and died screaming in pain. In retaliation for the Magnitsky Act, Russia banned US adoption of Russian orphans.

2014
Eduard Shevardnadze died when he was 86 years old. Earlier in his work life, when he had a job overseen by the KGB, he was known to have been very cruel and to torture prisoners. Yet even before Gorbachev, it is said that he recognized that the Soviet system was failing and that corruption was a real problem. After he left his government position in Russia, he returned home to Georgia and became president. He survived an ambush, which killed two of his bodyguards, and two car bombing assassination attempts. But he didn't survive the anger of his citizens, who witnessed rampant crime and corruption that they blamed on him, and he was forced to resign in 2003.

2015
We started hearing about a Russian disinformation campaign, about them using bloggers to spread pro-Kremlin propaganda, some from a 24-hour site where hundreds of people worked to flood the Internet with pro-Putin comments or simple, straight-out lies.

2016
We had suspicions the Russians had meddled in our election, working to elect Donald Trump, etc. In 2017, the *New Yorker* published an article about this on March 6, by Evan Osnos, David Remnick, and Joshua Yaffa. And in 2018, from special counsel Robert Mueller, we learned more about just how far they had meddled in that election.

With the 2020 presidential election coming up, we were learning more and were fearful about their influence.

Chapter 39
Michael

"When those you love die, the best you can do is honor their spirit
for as long as you live. You make a commitment that you're going
to take whatever lesson that person or animal was trying to teach you,
and you make it true in your own life.
It's a positive way to keep their spirit alive in the world,
by keeping it alive in yourself."
—Patrick Swayze (1952–2009)
American actor
From the book, *The Time of My Life* (2009)

Besides seeing Michael whenever I went back east to Canastota, New York, I also got together with his sister Marie and his mother. His mother and I often went out to Graziano's Restaurant to sit at the bar, where we had martinis and mimosas. In later years, when it was more comfortable for her to stay home, she always had vodka and grapefruit waiting for me at the house, where I was pleased to see a framed photo of me. We had heart-to-heart talks and she confided family secrets,

Michael's mother Mary Villari
and his sister Marie Villari Campanie

shocking secrets that I have never revealed. I introduced Frank to her, and to Michael and Marie, because they had been and continued to be such a meaningful part of my life.

Michael understood me very well. He once told our friend MaryAnne, "Cynthia is always happiest when she is with someone she loves."

I always wished there were some way I could help Michael find love like I had with Frank, find that contentment and peace. I wrote him letters, told him how much I cared, how important he was to me, how smart he was, how life was too short to lose himself in alcohol (his replacement for drugs), how he couldn't hide from his unhappiness. But I think that I always knew that I couldn't change the path that he was on, and that he wouldn't.

What I didn't know was how to define the love I felt for him. It wasn't romantic anymore. It wasn't the love one feels for a parent or a sibling or a child. And it was more than one feels for a friend. I told him once I didn't have the vocabulary to describe the depth of my feelings, the kind of connection I felt with him.

In 2008, he was diagnosed with lung cancer. Each time I saw him, he was thinner. Each time I saw him, I feared it would be the last.

On October 15, 2013, Marie called me.

Michael hadn't kept his promise to me to be there when we got old.

His most recent diagnostic tests showed just how far the cancer had spread and his prognosis was dire.

One morning, he went outside with a cup of coffee to sit on his patio. How long did he sit there? Was he depressed, angry, scared, resigned? Did he listen to the birds? Did he enjoy the warmth of the sun on his face?

What was he thinking before he put the rifle to his head and pulled the trigger?

With no warning to anyone—and no note.

A year after his death, Marie, Michael's brother Peter, and I spread Michael's ashes at his parents' tombstone. I poured some of those ashes into my hand first, to feel closer to him, and before I dropped them onto the green grass, I silently said my last goodbye to Michael, whispered the same words we both told one another over so many years. *I love you, always have, always will.*

To A Stranger

Passing stranger! you do not know how longingly I look upon you,
You must be he I was seeking, or she I was seeking, (it comes to
me as of a dream,)
I have somewhere surely lived a life of joy with you,
All is recall'd as we flit by each other, fluid, affectionate, chaste, matured,
You grew up with me, were a boy with me or a girl with me,
I ate with you and slept with you, your body has become not yours
only nor left my body mine only,
You give me the pleasure of your eyes, face, flesh, as we pass, you
take of my beard, breast, hands, in return,
I am not to speak to you, I am to think of you when I sit alone
or wake at night alone,
I am to wait, I do not doubt I am to meet you again,
I am to see to it that I do not lose you.

Walt Whitman
(1819–1892)

Chapter 40
Sofya Turns 100

"Live for one hundred years, learn for one hundred years."
—Russian Proverb
(Век живи — век учись.)

March 28, 2015

Not much would get me to leave sunny Tucson to go to Boston during one of the worst winters they had ever had. But how often does one get to go to a 100th birthday party for someone? And how often is that someone a relative who lives alone, who looks fabulous and who dances at her party?

The cold, harsh winter wasn't finished with New England yet, but it was warm and welcoming inside the St. Petersburg Café in Newton Center, where seventy people, sixteen of them family, two of whom had come from Moscow, attended the party to help Sofya celebrate, and to honor her.

And honored she was, with special greetings from President Obama and First Lady Michelle, from the Ice Skating Federation of Russia because Sofya had been a judge for them many years ago, and from New Jersey governor Chris Christie. Alla's son Leonid lived then in Ft. Lee, New Jersey, and arranged for the letter from Christie.

When Leonid told me where he lived, I said "Oh, I know the town."

"Have you been there?" he asked.

"No, but I know of it because of the disastrous bridge closing that caused days of traffic tie-ups, because of Governor Christie."

"I wrote to him," Leonid replied.

My political, impolite self responded without thinking. "I hope you told him what to do to himself?"

"No," Leonid said. "I like him."

Let's just say we left it at that.

Sofya, elegant in a plum-colored, jeweled shell, with a sheer cover-up of the same color draped over a black, floor-length, pleated skirt, was beaming. And never more so than when she heard the congratulations from the Federation of Russian Figure Skating. Both the president of the Federation and the General Director sent a certificate honoring her "*for the exceptional anniversary of your birthday. Sincerely, and from the bottom of our hearts, we thank you for many years of productive and unselfish effort for the good of the Federation of Russian Figure Skating. And we wish you enthusiastically the very best of what life has to offer."*

The Russian champagne (which might better be called syrup because it is so sweet), cranberry vodka, and wine flowed freely, as did the many courses of Russian food—St. Petersburg potato salad, pirogues, mushrooms, meat, and more, and a beautiful birthday cake.

Some family members, Leonid and Nina Polonsky (Sofya's niece,) and their adult twin daughters, Olga and Anna, are professional classical musicians who came to the States from Russia. They all played music for Sofya. Also, Leonid's 11-year-old daughter Maya played *Bach's Invention 2 in C Minor* on the piano.

I sat at the family table, bookended by Maya and the Polonskys. I hadn't seen Maya since she was a baby, and she had become a lovely young girl. After she played her piece, she stood, microphone in hand, to tell everyone that Sofya, her great-grandmother, was a role model, and that she wished her not only 100 more years, but only happiness during those years.

Leonid and Maya's mother, Irina, had been divorced some years ago, and Leonid had remarried. Maya has a half-sister, Leona, six years younger. The two girls clearly adore one another. Toward the end of the evening, Maya's grandmother came up to me, put her hand on my arm, and said simply "thank you for loving Maya." With much effort, I was able to hold back tears.

The party was very well organized. Large, three-paneled boards held photos of Sofya and family and friends. And there was a short video shown of highlights from her life. As I watched, I thought of the stories she had told me of her life, of the sad and difficult times she had endured. And I marveled at how beautiful she was as a young girl, and how good she looked that night, in spite of the hardships.

I truly hoped the memory of this party, at least, would give her peace.

Mark, who was then 94 and failing, wasn't able to come, but the tribute from him and Dina was heartfelt.

> *"Today we gather to celebrate our loved one Sofya Khikevitch on her anniversary. From our heart with simple words let us congratulate you for who you are and for the fact that you are with us. Sofya is caring and feminine, independent and hardworking, and everything in life that she has achieved, she achieved herself. Nothing came easy to her.*
>
> *Sofya, do not get sick, do not get old, do not have sorrow, do not be bored. We wish you to celebrate many, many more birthdays with us."*

Sofya Turns 100

But Mark died two years later at his home on August 2, 2017 at age 96. He is buried in the Jewish cemetery in St. Petersburg. Shortly before his death, he said of his years, "the body ages, but the soul remains young."

Sofya celebrated five more birthdays and died on December 13, 2020, three months short of her 106th.

Mark and Sofya

Sofya and family, her 100th birthday.
Standing, L to R: Leonid Polonsky, Margarita Morozov (Simon's sister), Irina Khilkevich (Simon's wife), Simon' Khilkevich (David's cousin), David Khilkevich (Alla's brother), the author, Leonid Makarovsky (Alla's son), Leona Makarovsky (Leonid's daughter) Julius Frumin (Alla's husband)
Seated (L to R): Nina Polonsky (Sofya's niece), Olga Polonsky (Nina's daughter), Ubix Koncz (Olga's son), Maya Makarovsky (Leonid's daughter), Sofya Khilkevich, Alla Makarovsky (Sofya's daughter), Ella Dragilewa (Leonid's 2nd wife) , Natasha Kirsanova (David's wife)

Chapter 41
The Adventures

"It is only in adventure that some people succeed in knowing themselves—in finding themselves."
Andre Gide (1869–1951)
French novelist and essayist

On a Monday morning in November of 2017, I woke up with my entire left side tingling, feeling like pins and needles, and tight pressure around my entire body between my waist and my chest, which I later learned is something called the "MS Hug." It is often described as feeling like being squeezed by a boa constrictor. I knew exactly what was happening and I also knew how very lucky I had been to have gone 23 years without another MS episode. I was optimistic that since so much time had elapsed between flares, my MS would remain relatively benign.

Back in 1994, Dr. Caplan had given me cause for optimism. He said that I would probably have more episodes but he expected that they would most likely have no damaging effects.

Why? Because I was female, men do worse. My age—I was older when the first symptoms appeared. The types of attacks I had—muscular problems seemed to be more problematic. And I had no lingering symptoms from all my episodes.

Over all those years, I told very few people about the MS. I didn't want the disease to take up any space in my life.

It didn't.

And thus I got the adventure I was so desperate to experience since I was young.

Frank and I took many trips. To Vietnam, Cambodia, and Thailand.

To Africa. To Rwanda, South Africa, Morocco, and Kenya, where the sun set in shimmering splendor behind august acacia trees, where a magnificent moon marched over the horizon at dusk, where nature bathed us in her beauty and her bounty.

The safari in Kenya, where I was served chilled champagne after the daily afternoon drive when we heard the baboons barking; the hippos laughing; the Masai cows mooing and shaking their bells, creating a field of wind chimes; the bird calls; the croaking of the frogs; the distant braying of a zebra—and where in front of the campfire

Cynthia and Wendy Berenson, friends on the author's safari in Kenya and a later trip to Viet Nam / Cambodia

one night, under a full moon, arriving one at a time, eight men, all wearing the traditional red *shuka* tied at the shoulder, their ears pierced and stretched, their bodies adorned with bright beaded belts and bracelets, earrings and necklaces, began to chant, a rumble, almost a roar, coming deep from their chests, and then they jumped, each trying to go higher than the other, their twig-like legs carrying them a foot or more off the ground, the dance they have been dancing since the beginning of their memory.

To the Sahara Desert of Morocco where, alone, in the hotel lobby, across from five Moslem men who were kneeling on their small rugs, their heads bent to the floor in prayer, I did my Tai Chi.

And where I finally got to at least hug a monkey, and my friend Jane Ragle, traveling with us along with her husband, also got a hug from a different sweet creature.

Two strenuous treks in Rwanda with grandchildren Hannah and Owen, to see the mountain gorillas, to watch the little ones bounce around, beat their chests, wrestle and playfully pester their parents. To look deep into the eyes of the adults and viscerally feel our connection, our ancient link. And on another day's trek to hear the primal screams of the chimpanzees from high up in the trees, to feel those screams reverberate in my chest.

To China and a tour on the Yangtze River with grandchildren Andrew and Emily.

A zoo in Cape Ferrat, where I fed a porcupine, which might be the most gentle of creatures, and massaged the hand and then the foot of a gibbon when she reached out beyond the bars of her cage. I wondered why she was in a cage alone, which is not the norm for primates. I searched for a person in charge. No luck. Perhaps the gibbon had

The Adventures

Monkey happiness

Jane Ragle, baby goat tenderness

Grandchildren Hannah Stebbins and Owen Lemoine with our wonderful Rwandan guide, Jimmy Bilima

Granddaughter Emily Stebbins and grandson Andrew Lemoine in Shanghai

been raised as a pet and was then given to the zoo when she became too much to handle. It was the closest I got to that monkey I wanted so badly as a child.

A zipline ride in the rainforest of Costa Rica, where we went twice to attend Delia's daughters' weddings.

Cabo San Lucas, where I stood within a few feet of dozens of whales as they came close to shore to rub the barnacles off their bellies. Also in Mexico, a mummy museum near San Miguel de Allende and a steep climb to the 79-foot-high top of the Kukulcan Pyramid of Chichen Itza in the Yucatan. (No one has been allowed to climb it since 2006, when a woman fell to her death.)

And a wonderful *National Geographic Lindblad* cruise to the Arctic, the Norwegian archipelago of Svalbard and Longyearbyen, (home to a global seed vault), where we saw a record number of polar bears, as well as walruses and whales. And a white fox while we hiked on the tundra. The fox apparently wasn't afraid of humans, since not twenty yards from us we apparently inspired him to pee in front of us. Stephanie was one of our friends who accompanied us on that trip.

Weeks of hiking and driving in Arizona's and Utah's spectacular canyons where I fell in love with the ravens and where on my first visit to the Grand Canyon, Frank and I read Walt Whitman poems to one another before bed in our log cabin. And in Death Valley, an afternoon spent at the remote, flat Racetrack Playa, with its mysterious moving rocks and boulders that leave long tracks on the dried up dirt bed. No other

The Adventures

people there then, no cars, no footprints. Just Frank, Tito, and me, three mortal visitors at an almost three-mile-long stretch of silence and solitude, peace and perpetuity.

Frank and I visited Italy and France several times. Delia and John had divorced in 1993 and the man she was seeing at the time was an international financier and had a yacht. They met us in Italy at the Four Seasons Hotel in Milan where we were staying. As soon as we saw one another Delia and I ran across the lobby to give each other long, affectionate embraces. There are truly no friends like dear old friends!

Stephanie Sklar, Arctic trip

The last time in France, when we stayed for a month, we brought Tito who, in the black beret I had custom-made for him, accompanied us to every restaurant for every meal. He was given a bowl of water even before we were asked if we wanted anything to drink.

Also in France, the opportunity in Nice to eat several times at my very favorite restaurant, La Reserve de Beaulieu, serving food since 1880.

Tito charming the Parisians

Over the years, I took my nieces and Frank and I took our grandchildren on trips when they graduated from high school.

As I mentioned earlier, Tambi went to Russia with me. I took her sister Tara on an entirely different kind of trip, to Paris and London, where the men tripped over themselves to get her attention because she was so beautiful, asking her if she was a movie star or a model. And where I for the first time experienced what older women talk about when they say we become invisible. Although I did have one unattractive man approach me, about 20 years older than I, much to Tara's undisguised amusement.

Tara Davis

We went to the center of champagne country, Reims, and we toured the Taittinger Champagne Cellars; we had champagne and chocolates at every meal except breakfast, and of course went to Versailles, theater in London to see *Miss Saigon* and did our share of museums in both cities.

Frank has three children—Dianne, Karen, and Mark—each of whom has two children.

Frank's daughter Dianne, her husband John Lemoine, and their sons Owen on the left and Andrew on the right. The dog is Gordy.

The Adventures

Frank's daughter Karen Stebbins (center), her daughters Emily on the left and Hannah on the right

Frank's son Mark, his wife Laura, and daughters Samantha on the left and Meghan on the right

Our two youngest grandchildren, Samantha and Meghan, whom we took to Paris and the Riviera in August 2022

Other Family

Frank's brother Edmund and partner Patti Zenna

Frank's half brother Richard with the author's cat Zoe

The Adventures

The author's niece Renee and her husband Ron Davis, better known as "Thumper"

The author's grand-niece Tara and David Popkin

Their daughters Ava and Mia Popkin

Brittany Edwards and the author's grand-niece, Renee's daughter Tambi Yu, married February 25, 2023

At home, besides becoming certified as a scuba diver, I learned to play squash and to cross-country ski. To knit and do needlepoint and to write in calligraphy. To ride horses.

And I even got to pretend to be a man in drag. Knowing that we were going to dine at the New York restaurant Lucky Chengs, where everyone was a female impersonator or trans-woman, I had dressed in a short, black leather skirt, high leather boots, and long feather earrings. I asked the waiter if I could borrow his napkin and order book. I then went to a table of six, asked them if they enjoyed their dinner and if I could get them anything else. No, they were happy, they said. Several minutes later, I went back, and said "So, did you know?"

One guy slammed the table and said, "I told you" to his friends.

"How did you know? "I asked.

"Your goiter. You don't have a goiter!"

* * *

I saw many performers, too many to list, but among them: Bobby Short at the Carlyle in New York, Neil Diamond at the Los Angeles' Troubadour, Bob Marley and the Wailers, the Rolling Stones, and Bob Dylan in Boston, Elvis Presley in Binghamton shortly before he died. And I was lucky to see Pavarotti perform in New York and

The Adventures

Rudolf Nureyev dance in Los Angeles. I don't remember the venue; all I remember were the magnificent movements of Nureyev's body and his exotic, extraordinary face.

The only adventure I regret, really regret, not pursuing was going underwater in scuba gear in a cage in South Africa to see the great white sharks. Frank turned white himself when I suggested I might do it. My musical regret—I never heard Leonard Cohen or Freddy Mercury in person. But I listen to their voices almost daily.

On May 17, 2004, Massachusetts became the first state to legalize same-sex marriage and at 12:01, couples began filling out applications. Frank and I drove the few blocks to the Cambridge Courthouse to witness history in the making, to see the crowds waiting and the police in riot gear marching by to discourage any disruptions.

What about children? If Frank and I had been younger when we got together, I might have had one or more children, happily. But, I have never regretted not having them, because in their place, I lived and loved the life I've had, which I couldn't have done if I had been a mother.

And over the years, I've had small children to love. Renee's two daughters, Tambi and Tara, and now Tara's two girls, Ava and Mia, have provided more joy than I could ever express. And Frank and I have six adorable grandchildren to love, to watch with pride as they took their first steps and then, in what took too short a time, their walk into adulthood.

A few years ago, I had a DNA test done with saliva through Ancestry.com. The analysis revealed that I am:

- 50% European Jewish
- 48% Eastern European and Russian
- 2% Other

Among the "Other," 1% Middle Eastern descent, and less than 1% each from Central Asia, Finland, Great Britain, and Africa, specifically South Eastern African Bantu!

Sofya also had her DNA tested too, through 123 and Me. Alla's son Leonid arranged for it and then called me to walk me through downloading my raw data at Gedmatch so that we could make a comparison. Our chromosome readings revealed that Sofya and I fell halfway between first cousins and second cousins. According to all my genealogy research, she and my father were first cousins, so the DNA tests validated that and confirmed that she and I were first cousins once removed.

Chapter 42
Putin

> *"If those in charge of our society—politicians, corporate executives, and owners of press and television—can dominate our ideas, they will be secure in their power. They will not need soldiers patrolling the streets. We will control ourselves."*
> —Howard Zinn (1922–2010)
> Historian, author, professor, playwright, and activist

That violent Russian October Revolution in 1917, with its promises to workers and peasants. All for what?

For a 74-year oppressive Communist rule? For a gleam of light during Gorbachev's era, when he worked to end the Cold War and the war in Afghanistan, prepared for open elections, and allowed unprecedented freedom of speech and press? But that light was extinguished by Chernobyl, the Armenian earthquake, the failure of the campaign against alcohol and political opposition. For the elderly living quietly on pensions to suddenly have to deal with black marketers, shootings, gangsters under Vladimir Putin, a KGB foreign intelligence officer for sixteen years, and then President of Russia who has high domestic approval ratings in spite of his despotism—because he has brought stability, his people say?

For a president who is an autocrat with absolute power, a killer of opponents, dissidents and investigative journalists from supposed accidents, shootings and poisonings, many officially reported as heart attacks, all of which resulted in Russia becoming one of the most dangerous places in the world for reporters. (According to Mediaite.com, by 2019, 26 Russian journalists had been murdered by Putin during his reign.) Who through corrupt capitalism looted his country to become one of the richest men in the world, by late 2007 reputed to be worth 40 billion dollars and in 2016 named by *Forbes Magazine* the most powerful man in the world?

The failed coup of 1991 led the West to be optimistic about democracy taking root in Russia, myself included, but political freedoms and reforms granted in the 1990s disappeared under Putin. When he came to power, appointed prime minister in the summer of 1999, then in March 2000 elected as president, all democratic reforms stopped. No fair elections. (The last free election in Russia was in 1990.) The independent media, doing very well in the early 1990s, pretty much disappeared. Within a year of his election, the state took over all TV channels, most radio stations and newspapers, which now disseminate propaganda and a distortion of reality. And Russia's neo-Nazi movement became one of the most violent on the continent.

Putin refurbished Lenin's tomb in 2011 so that his citizens could still line up to see a reminder of what so many believe were the good days. He has worked to rehabilitate Stalin for his defeat of fascism and is said to toast Stalin on his birthday every year. On May 9th, Victory Day, for decades a celebration of the end of WWII, Russian citizens now see more tanks and uniforms in Red Square, meant to remind the people of the greatness of Stalin's USSR. A Levada Center poll in 2017 asked Russians to name "the 10 most outstanding people of all time and all nations."

Stalin came in first. In large part because he turned an agrarian society into an industrial superpower in a generation, they said.

In 2012, the *Moscow Times* reported that there had been more German-run Jewish ghettos in the USSR and Eastern Europe during WWII than previously believed, 200 more, to add up to 1,100 in total.

Very few Jews live now in Poland, Romania, Hungary, or Ukraine, but there are still substantial numbers of Jews living in Russia. The FSU (former Soviet Union) in 2021 had the seventh largest Jewish community in the world, with Israel and the US the top two. Also in 2012, a Jewish Museum and Tolerance Center, chronicling the history of Jews in Russia (http://mievr.ru) opened in Moscow. The museum is the largest Jewish museum in the world, with a focus on centuries of the history of Jews and Jewish life in Russia. It was reported that Putin donated one month of his salary to its construction.

But that same year, a YouTube video was made with Jewish music, the purpose of which was to show that opposition to Putin was being led by Jews. And Andrei Sakharov's historic dissidence is dismissed by saying that his Jewish wife, Yelena Bonner, had influenced him. What was historically primarily government anti-Semitism has now been joined by well-organized grassroots anti-Semitism.

Belarus, now independent, has built its first nuclear power plant, named Astravets. They began loading fuel into the first of its two nuclear reactors in August 2020. They expect construction on the second reactor to be operational in 2023. One hundred miles from Glubokoye, the first reactor began licensed operation on June 10, 2021.

At the end of the last century, Belarus had lost 90 percent of the Jewish population it had at the beginning of the century—from 5.2 million to 600,000 Jews.

Chapter 43
Write the Story

"For the dead and the living, we must bear witness.
For not only are we responsible for the memories of the dead,
we are also responsible for what we are doing with those memories."
—Elie Wiesel (September 30, 1928 – July 2, 2016)
Writer, professor, political activist, Holocaust survivor

On that Arctic cruise I mentioned, I often stood alone at the bow of the ship, thinking of my Russian family, watching the ice drift, appreciating the clear, clean air, and actually enjoying being cold for perhaps the first time in my life. And one of those times, as if it flew in on a breath of that air, an understanding, almost a command. *Write the story!*

I ran back to my cabin, grabbed pencil and paper and started outlining, scribbling down ideas and events as fast as I could, trying to keep up with the racing stream of thoughts in my head. And so began this book.

How reliable are our memories? My journals provided what I wanted and didn't want to remember, the truth as I perceived and understood it at the time. And as I looked back while writing, I decided that truth was more important than loyalty.

And I began to think about what can happen in a generation.

Things can remain the same.

My father hid under the tables or chairs when Cossacks came; in grade school, we had duck and cover. And now, schools have drills to practice what to do if an armed shooter enters their building and we already have armed guards in some schools. And there is talk about arming teachers.

There was domestic violence in my father's home in Russia, and then in mine in America.

Russia under Putin no longer has a czar, is no longer Soviet, but it is still a dictatorship. His cruelty, by design, I believe, has come to resemble that of Stalin.

And we all know that while there are no pogroms or ovens, anti-Semitism is still alive and well there. Alive and well in countries, such as Poland where the far right has amassed more power. Alive and well and on the rise even here in America; the country where former president Donald Trump has successfully amassed his base of

White supremacists. (In 2018, swastikas were spray-painted on the walls of my high school in Binghamton.)

But things also change in a generation.

Like knowledge. According to a study in 2018 by the Conference on Jewish Material Claims Against Germany, 31 percent of all Americans and 41 percent of all Millennials believe that two million or fewer Jews perished in the Holocaust, instead of the actual six million. Just under 50 percent of all Americans don't know what Auschwitz was and 11 percent of all Americans haven't heard of the Holocaust. Since Holocaust awareness and knowledge is lacking, too many Americans now have no concept of the hell people went through then and the terror they experienced.

To the contrary, my childhood fear was that my life would not be enough, because my mother's life wasn't enough. So this book is a validation for me. I see that my life found its direction, found what was actually there all along, followed its thread. I got what I wanted, and so very much more than I had hoped for.

The very absence of boredom. Rewarding and uncommon work; world travel; the steadiness of strong, enduring, loving friendships; and a very happy marriage with a devoted partner; the joy of a close family and of extended families I never knew existed. Those family discoveries, as I mentioned earlier, the result of my work, a trip to Israel, twenty trips to the Soviet Union and Russia; two improbable, inconceivable coincidences, and Tito, our precious little dog.

Tito

Taavi

In January 2019, we got another Havanese puppy, whom we named Taavi, which means "beloved" in Hebrew. Did I ever dare to dream that I would have two dogs at once! Who sleep with me. And who cuddle!

The author's 4th birthday

The author and Frank on her 75th birthday

Yes, I am responsible for some of my life's journey, but for the most part, my parents created the foundation that enabled it. My mother was a loving, nurturing mom until she started drinking. My father went to third grade; he made sure I went to college. He worried about money every day of his life; I have never worried, thanks to him, thanks to what I inherited from his hardships, his hard work, and the self-confidence he instilled in me.

So as I look back at my life and the things that I did, I first see that small Jewish child, only one generation away from the shtetl, who used to walk her neighborhood alone. That small child who used to sit on the grass and wait for the train to roll by, going she knew not where, so she could wave to the engineer. And then I think—that little girl grew up and did all that she did? And I feel neither pride nor satisfaction, but happiness, and simply grateful wonder.

The End

Afterword
2020 to 2024

2020

These days, I think it is appropriate that I grew up when *The Twilight Zone* was so popular, in the town where its creator lived, because now, that's what life is beginning to feel like. I sit in the house to be safe. I look out at the flowers, at the birds, at the bees, all going about their business as if life were normal. But it is a seductive trap, an illusion. Nothing is normal.

There are enemies out there shattering our sense of safety. The world is not safe with Donald Trump as president; with Russian interference in our elections on social media. The world is not safe with the rise of far right extremist groups and the political and racist/anti-Semitic violence they commit. The world is not safe with climate change that could cause three million species to go extinct by 2070 and that now creates both severe weather events across the world changing the landscape and livelihood of affected communities, and disasters that kill so many people.

At the time of this writing, the worst enemy is a virus that can kill us if we venture carelessly into that beauty outside, into what we used to know as our normal lives. So now, the only truly safe place is in our homes for fear of the Covid-19 and its variants.

They call it "staying in place," or "self-quarantine." Frank and I began our self-quarantine on March 14th, 2020, seven weeks after the first confirmed case of Covid on January 20th. It was then three months before I ventured anywhere, and that was only to go to the vet to get a prescription filled for Tito. I phoned when I arrived, they brought the bag out and put it halfway between their door and the car, then I retrieved it and ran back into the car. And that was the first day I wore a mask, even for those few seconds. Since that March, I go only to the vet when necessary and no one visits here except on Saturday mornings, when our puppy-group friends Barbie and John bring their dog Moxie to play with Tito and Taavi outdoors. We wear our masks and we keep our distance.

We get groceries delivered and are learning to clean the house ourselves. People are suffering. Starving due to unemployment. Most wear masks when they go out in public, except for a group of too many crazies who demonstrate loudly and sometimes violently, because they believe that being told to wear a mask "takes away our freedom."

Paths of Stones

And today, we have President Trump, so very undeserving of the title, who also not only verbally minimizes the seriousness of the virus, but holds open air campaign rallies and refuses to recommend wearing masks.

But Frank and I are among the lucky ones. Retired, financially secure, compatible, still in love and happy together after more than 30 years. We stay in touch with loved ones by Zoom. We have two cats and two dogs who have demands—food, affection, lap time, play time—and who keep us entertained and distracted from the depressing news. And we have ice cream every night, for comfort, after we watch that depressing news and worry about the upcoming presidential election.

Our world has shrunk, but at the same time, it has in some ways become bigger. We take the time to notice things never noticed before—the beauty of a male tarantula, the dozens of little silver lizards dashing about daily, the roadrunners, and the night sky, which we now always stare at together in wonder before bed. And we see more bobcats, javelinas, and coyotes as they pass by the outside perimeter of our wall.

However, many of my closest friends have been or are suffering, although none from Covid. MaryAnne was diagnosed with Parkinson's Disease. Not long after, both her husband and her brother died the same week. Kathy (Holmes), my close friend since 1968, was diagnosed with dementia and had to be admitted to a facility. Linda (Winer) has had several surgeries for her sciatica; she still has quite a bit of discomfort. Debbie had a stroke, from which she has happily and unexpectedly recovered quite well. Arlene was recently diagnosed with Sjögren's Syndrome. And Delia continues to struggle to breathe after decades of COPD.

But my MS is stable.

My bleached-blond short hair is now long and growing in pure white.

I continue serving as mentor editor for the OpEd Project.

And I also took a Zoom class in Yiddish and learned the alphabet, enjoying the familiar sounds of my childhood.

> *"There is a quiet humor in Yiddish and a gratitude for every day of life,*
> *every crumb of success, each encounter of love...*
> *In a figurative way, Yiddish is the wise and humble language*
> *of us all, the idiom of a frightened and hopeful humanity."*
> —Isaac Bashevis Singer, writer
> (1904–1991)

Afterword, 2020-2024

November 7th, 2021

After almost a nail-biting week of watching TV day and night to follow the presidential election, I awoke this morning to learn that Joe Biden had made it and was now the President of the United States. I cannot remember the last time I wasn't anxious. I was happy. I felt relief. And joy. America was safe.

Or so I thought. On November 9th, when Trump was saying he had not lost, implying he would not relinquish the presidency, an organization called RefuseFascism.org felt the need to run a full-page ad in the *New York Times*, signed by many notables, including Cornel West and Noam Chomsky, stating: "In the Name of Humanity We Refuse to Accept a Fascist America; We Pledge our determination to prevail over a regime that imperils the people of the world and the earth itself."

Hence, relief was short-lived.

2021 and 2022

Trump, the most vindictive and incompetent president this nation has ever had, did willingly leave the White House, but he left with too many followers and too many documents. Did he destroy classified documents? Reveal national secrets for his own benefit? Perhaps to Russia's Putin? Will Trump continue to assert that the election was rigged and that he really didn't lose? He worked to launch a coup on January 6th, 2021 to encourage Vice President Pence to lie about the electoral vote count and thus pronounce Trump President. Pence refused, but people died during the riot and the storming of the Capitol.

Will Trump's threatening to run again for president in 2024, in spite of the many lawsuits he is facing, continue to create more insurrection, to inspire white supremacists, and incite shootings, to abolish what is left of our democracy, the democracy my family and so many millions of immigrants emigrated to to fulfill their dreams and create free and productive and happy lives here for their children?

We now go back to a state of stress and worry.

> **Russia's one reformer, Mikail Gorbachev, died at the age of 91 on August 30, 2022.**
>
> **The current popular opposition leader in Russia, Aleksei Navalny, whom I like and respect, is in prison after recovering from a botched murder attempt in Germany by Putin in 2021. Navalny chose to return to Russia and was arrested immediately. In failing health, he is now denied treatment, placed in what he calls a concrete cage, and it is suspected that**

he is given things to make him ill in the hope that he will die in prison and thus spare Putin the rage of Navalny's supporters.

Putin invaded Ukraine in February 2022, attacked civilians, schools, homes, and hospitals, and with no concern for his own soldiers' safety from radiation, trashed the Chernobyl nuclear facility inside and out and destabilized Ukraine's reactors at Zaporizhziah, the largest nuclear plant in Europe. American and European governments, organizations, and companies continue to send aid to Ukraine, and McDonalds and other businesses have closed down their operations in Russia in protest. Sanctions are in place against Russia and luckily, Ukraine has an heroic and admirable leader, Volodymyr Zelenskyy. Jewish. Still, the war continues. With no end in sight.

As does HIV in Russia. In December 2022, the *Moscow Times* reported that at the end of 2021, the country had the fifth highest infection rate in the world.

And on October 7, 2023, Hamas attacked Israel, starting a bloody war in Palestine with no end in sight.

2022-2024

As for COVID, vaccines were developed and we got ours. But still too many refuse to take them, still stating crazy conspiracies that the government is inoculating us with microchips, that the inoculation will magnetize us, and more. And perhaps new variants will occur that may be resistant to the vaccines we have now.

We no longer have to remain in quarantine and are free to go out, with or without masks. I still wear mine always, except when we go out to restaurants.

Seymour "Si" Reichlin, MD, and the author

Afterword, 2020-2024

Recently, we went to one to celebrate Si's 98th birthday, a truly happy occasion for a cousin I truly love. I think I can honestly say that learning the stories of my ancestors, meeting many of them, and finding Si and connecting to his branch of the family has brought me indescribable joy, and has been as close to a miracle as one could reasonably wish for.

Still, 2022 was a sad year, a heartbreaking year.

I lost my dear Delia Skiffington, a friend of 57 years. She died in May from COPD. I desperately wanted to be with her at the end, as I had been with Natasha, but couldn't get there in time. In December, her daughters held a spreading of ashes for family and close friends high up in the mountains of Costa Rica that Delia loved so much during the 40 years she lived there, and that evening, they organized a Celebration of Life for her in San Jose. I believe she would have been happy that I went and read a tribute to her.

Back East, in September, I was lucky to see Kathy. Remember, she and I had gone to Woodstock together. When I arrived at her facility, she was barely conscious, hardly able to speak, but she smiled when she saw me, grabbed and squeezed my hand, and whispered, "My pal." And then I could barely speak.

She died three days later.

Frank and I had a close mutual friend, one of Frank's closest, actually, Jack Thomas, a fellow journalist with the *Boston Globe*. After a year-long fight against cancer, he died shortly after Kathy.

On September 1st, our precious Tito, without whom this book would not have been written, left us. As the vet stood by, Tito and I were lying on the bed face to face, inches away from one another, looking into each other's eyes. Until there was no life left in his and mine were filled with tears. As were Frank's.

And shortly after, I learned from a mutual friend in Siberia that my closest Russian friend Sasha (who never met me there without flowers) had died from what she called a brain disease. A few weeks earlier, after being out of touch for more than 15 years, he had sent me a photo of himself holding a huge bouquet of flowers and waving. How sweet, I thought when I saw it, that he is saying hello after all this time. When I heard of his death, I realized the wave was most likely a goodbye. So many of my nice memories of my times in Russia included him.

I do have wonderful memories of Russia—beautiful places seen, extraordinary and exciting experiences, so many good friendships, and family found.

My work for so many years was an effort to improve relations between the United States and Russia. And there were times when I was (naïvely) optimistic about the country's welfare and future.

The war in Ukraine continues. Now I look at the deaths and devastation Putin has brought to Ukraine since 2022 in his effort to conquer that country, those nice memories are overshadowed by his depravity, and the tears of thousands of people in Ukraine who have lost homes and loved ones since his invasion and who have no indication of when or how it will end.

And on February 16th, 2024, what I feared but was almost certain would happen, popular reform opposition leader and organizer of anti-government demonstrations Alexei Navalny died in Penal Colony IK-3 north of the Arctic Circle, about 1,200 miles northeast of Moscow, where he had been sent two months earlier. He had been jailed since January 2021 before he was sent to the brutal Arctic Circle prison.

His mother was told that the cause of death was sudden death syndrome and was refused possession of her son's body for nine days.

Despite Kremlin denials, it is almost certain that Putin was behind the death of the 47-year-old man who was so courageous that he posed a serious threat to Putin's leadership and popularity.

After Navalny's death—or probable murder—Ukrainian president Volodymyr Zelenskyy said, "...it's absurd to perceive Putin as the supposedly legitimate head of the Russian state. He is a thug who maintains power through corruption and violence."

I'm angry, and I suspect it is the same feeling generations of my Dickstein ancestors had toward the cruel Russian leaders—when the tsarist government sanctioned Cossack killings, the Soviet government sanctioned pogroms, and Stalin's government sanctioned the murder of so many Jews. To that list, I can add Vladimir Putin. And so it continues.

But such is life. Love and loss. And all too often, evil.

The End

Jews put stones on tombstones to show that someone was there, and that the person's memory lives on in and through us.

Dear Ancestor

>Your tombstone stands among the rest
>Neglected and alone
>The name and date are chiseled out
>on polished marbled stone.
>It reaches out to all who care
>it is too late to mourn
>You did not know that I exist
>You died and I was born.
>Yet each of us are cells of you
>in flesh, in blood, in bone.
>Our blood contracts and beats a pulse
>entirely not our own.
>Dear Ancestor, the place you filled
>one hundred years ago
>Spreads out among the ones you left
>who would have loved you so.
>I wonder as you lived and loved
>I wonder if you knew
>That someday I would find this spot
>and come and visit you.
>   —Author Unknown

Chaim's siblings were Cynthia's great-aunts, great-uncles and cousins (Dickstein ancestors)

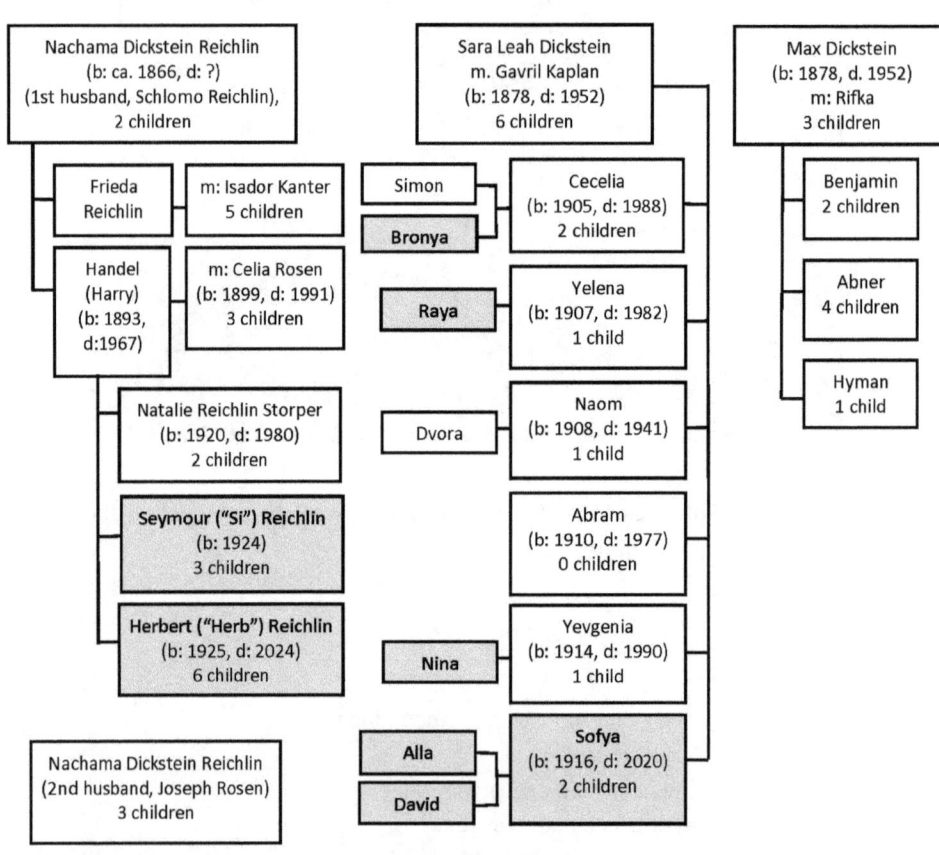

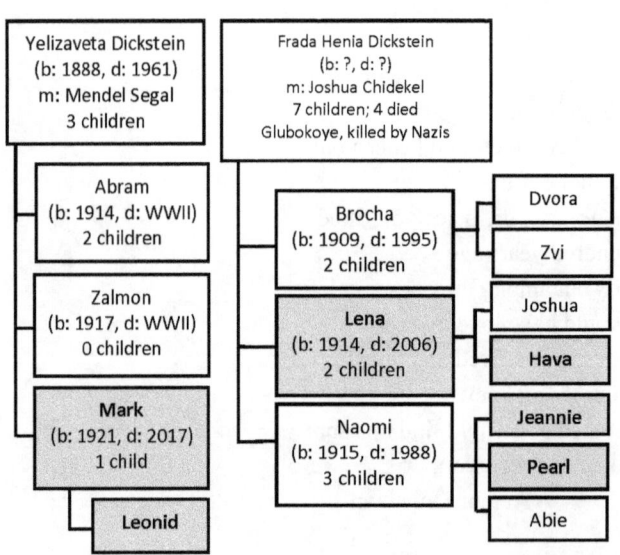

Russian Descendants of the Dickstein Family
(partial family tree)

Five generations, most spouses not included
The author has met people whose names are bolded and/or in shaded boxes.

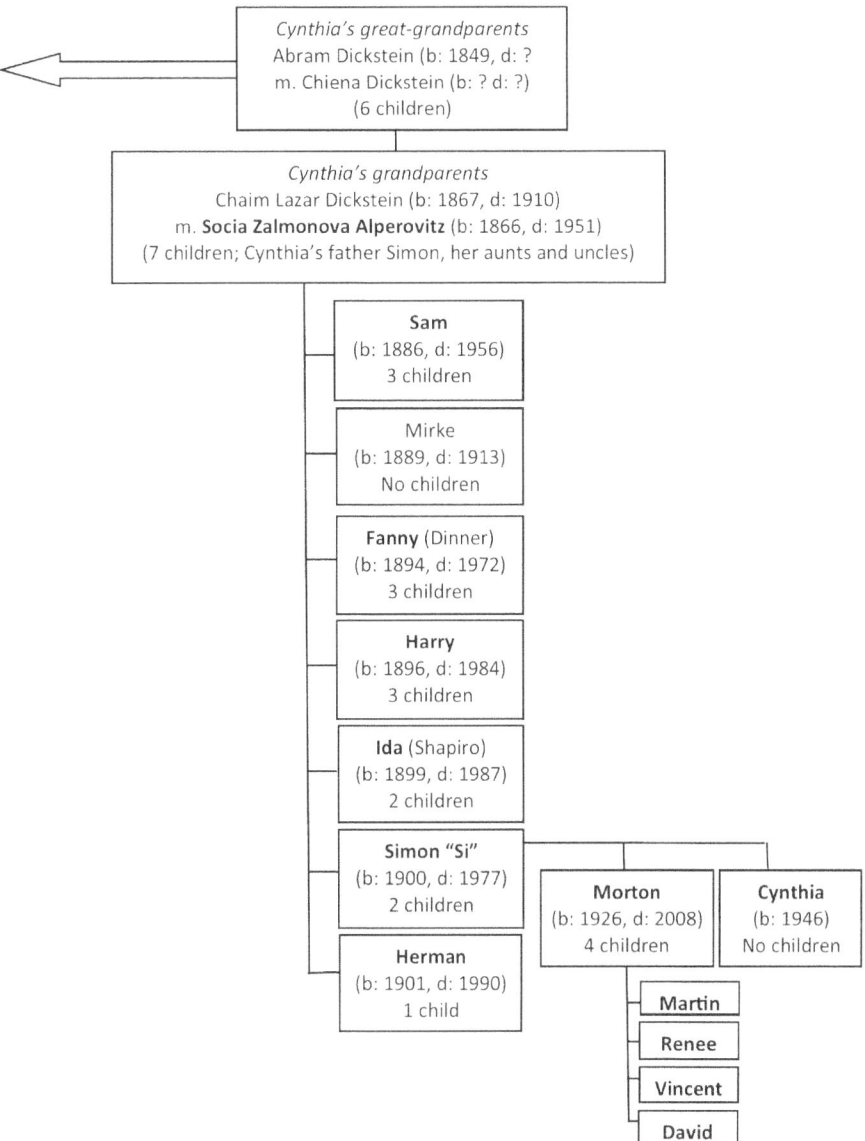

Simon's Sayings

IN YIDDISH

Abi gezunt   As long as you're healthy

Alter Kocker   Old fart

A shaynem dank dir im pupik   Thanks for nothing; many thanks in your belly button

Bubbeh   Grandmother

Bupkis   A lot of nothing

Chazzer   Pig

Farklempt   Too emotional to talk, overcome with emotion

Faygala   Little bird (Male homosexual)

Gai in drerd un bakn beygl   Go to hell and bake bagel

Gai feifen afen yam!   Scram! (Go peddle your fish elsewhere).

Gai kukken afen yam!   Get lost, beat it, (Go shit in the ocean)

Gevalt   Heaven Forbid

Gib a kuk   Give a look

Gonef   Thief

Hak mir nit keyn tshaynik   Prattle pointlessly, stop nagging, (Don't bang on my teapot)

Ich hob es in drerd   To hell with it

Ketzeleh (Catsella)   Little cat, or kitten

Kush mich in toches   Kiss my ass; stop annoying me

Kvetsh   Whine or complain

Maidel   Unmarried girl, teenager

Mamzer   Bastard

Meshuge   Crazy

Nebbish   A nobody or simpleton

Oi vai iz mir   Woe is me

Pisher   Male infant, or a nobody

Ponem   Face

Pupik   Belly button

Putz   A fool

Schlemiel   An inept person

Schmatta   Rags, unfashionable clothes

Schmuck   Vulgar term for penis, in slang a stupid, obnoxious, detestable person

Shaineh maidel   Pretty girl

Shames   Sexton in a temple

Shaygets   A male gentile

Shlump   A pathetic human being

Shmendrik   Nincompoop

Shmegegge   A petty person, one who is untalented

Shikker   Drunkard

Shlimazel   Someone with bad luck, fails at everything, inept

Shmeykhl vi a vantz   Smiles like a bedbug

Shtetl   Small Jewish town or village in Eastern Europe

Shtetlekh   Plural of shtetl

Shtup   Push, shove; fuck

Tchotchkes   Bric-a-brac

Toches   Ass

Ver geharget   Drop dead, get killed

Yahrtzeit   Anniversary of a death

Glossary of People

SOVIET / RUSSIAN

A., Nina. Poet, academic, active in women's issues in Russia. Visited the United States on a lecture tour established by OASES. Friend. Met in 1987.

Afanasyev, Viktor (1922-1994). News editor, academician. Editor of *Pravda* newspaper, the main political publication of the Communist Party in the USSR for 21 years. Forced into retirement in 1989 by Gorbachev for his lack of support in *Pravda* for *glasnost* and *perestroika* and for its strong criticism of Yeltsin.

Alexeyeva, Marina. Journalist. Participant in NESNE American Soviet Journalism Exchanges. In 1993, Director of the Union of Journalists, St. Petersburg.

Andropov, Yuri (1914-1984). Chairman of the KGB from 1967-1982, Fourth General Secretary of the Communist Party of the Soviet Union. Served only 15 months before his death.

Barenboim, Peter (1948-). Attorney and writer. Member of the Board, Union of Soviet Advocates.

Belyaev, Alexander (1953-). Politician. Chairman, St. Petersburg City Council of People's Deputies, who defended against the coup attempt in 1991.

Belyansky, Lev. General. Deputy Minister of the Bureau of the Soviet Ministry of the Interior, Deputy Chief of the Main Directorate. Met in 1988 to present the OASES Law Enforcement Exchange proposal, which he approved.

Beria, Lavrenti (1899-1953). Soviet politician. Chief of Soviet Security and Secret Police (NKVD) under Stalin during WWII. Known sexual predator. Arrested by Premier Khrushchev in 1953, convicted of treason, shot to death while begging for his life.

Bickauskas, Egidijus (1955-). Lithuanian politician, Deputy of the Supreme Council of the Republic of Lithuania.

Bobryashov, Valery. Law enforcement. Member of the hosting delegation for the American-Soviet Law Enforcement Exchange in Russia in 1990.

Bogdanov, Pyotr (1882-1939). Head of Internal Affairs of Moscow City Committee from 1986 to 1991.

Bonner, Yelena (1923-2011). Human rights activist, wife of Andrei Sakharov. Bonner's mother was a Jewish Communist activist. She attended Sofya's 90th birthday celebration in Boston.

Bouzykin, Alexander or "Little"Sasha. Police, Major Criminal Investigation Department. Participant in our first Soviet American Law Enforcement Exchange. In 1990, Soviet police told the American delegation that Bouzykin was KGB.

Brezhnev, Leonid (1906-1982). General Secretary of the Central Committee of the Communist Party of the Soviet Union for 18 years, 1964 to1982.

Brushlinsky, Nikolai. Director of Moscow Fire Safety Foundation, Professor, Fire Technical Institute, established in 1906.

Bugayev. General, Deputy Head of the Political Department in Investigation, Ministry of the Interior. Met in 1989 on first American-Soviet Law Enforcement Exchange Program.

Chernenko, Konstantin (1911-1985). Ukrainian. Soviet politician. Fifth General of the Communist Party. Time in office was only 13 months before he died of emphysema and heart failure.

Dmitri. Tee-shirt designer and supplier to OASES delegations.

Dzerzhinsky, Felix (1877-1926). Bolshevik revolutionary and Soviet politician. Leader of the secret police, first the Cheka and then the OGPU. Ruthless toward political opponents and thus nicknamed "Iron Felix." A 15-ton statue of him in front of KGB headquarters was taken down by protesters in 1991 after the failed coup. Dzerzhinsky's father was Jewish, his mother Polish. He was raised Catholic.

Fetisov, Boris. Deputy Head of the International Department of the Union of Journalists.

Fyodorov, Svyatoslav (1927-2000). Ophthalmologist. Pioneer of refractive surgery, created the Radial Keratotomy procedure. Director of Moscow's Institute of Eye Microsurgery. Died when his four-seater helicopter crashed outside of Moscow.

Gagarin, Yuri (1934-1968). Soviet pilot and astronaut. First human in space when he orbited the earth in 1961. Died in 1968 in a plane crash during a routine training flight.

Gogol, Nikolai (1809-1852). Writer. Severe depression led him to starve himself to death.

Gorbachev, Mikhail (1931-2022). Soviet politician. Eighth and last General Secretary of the Communist Party of the Soviet Union. Instituted policies of *glasnost* and *perestroika* and oversaw the dissolution of the USSR.

Grigoryus, Fishas. Lithuanian lawyer, activist and adviser to the Lithuanian Parliament prior to independence.

Grinenko, Anatoly. Department Head of the KGB Central Archives, oversaw rehabilitation of those murdered by Stalin.

Hiie, Tiaa. Estonian, friend of Natasha Bourso-Leland. Helped establish the 1989 Law Enforcement Exchange program in Tallinn.

Hitler, Adolph (1889-1945). Chancellor of Germany, leader of the Nazi Party. Believed that the Aryan race was superior to all, that Jews were the evil enemy. Initially wanted to expel them, went on to exterminate them during the Holocaust. After losing WWII, he and his wife committed suicide; he shot himself, she took poison.

Ivanova, Olga. Fitness professional. Founder and Director of the National Aerobics School in Moscow.

Karbainov, Alexander (1945-). Major General, Head of the KGB Center for Social Contacts.

Glossary of People

Karpov, Evgeny. Delegate on the last two Russian/US Firefighters Exchanges. Had been a firefighter in Mongolia.

Kazenas, Zinas (1936-2019). Lithuanian photojournalist. Was actively involved with Sajudis, the reform movement for independence from the USSR.

Kerensky, Alexander (1881-1970). Lawyer and revolutionary, key political figure in the February Russian Revolution of 1917 and the provisional government that was established afterward. First Minister of Justice, then Minister of War, and finally the second Minister-Chairman. After the October Revolution of 1917, his government was overthrown by Lenin and the Bolsheviks and he spent the rest of life in exile in France and the US, where he worked for the Hoover Institute.

Khasbulatov, Ruslan (1942-2023). Chechen economist and politician. Chairman of the Supreme Soviet of the Russian Federation from 1991 to 1993. Initially a Yeltsin ally, they clashed, a power struggle ensued, which resulted in the dissolution of Parliament in 1993.

Khilkevitch, Grigory. Sofya's third husband.

Khodorkovsky, Mikhail (1963-). Oligarch and businessman, oil tycoon. Accused the Kremlin of corruption, charged with fraud and jailed from 2005 to 2013, under what many say were politically motivated charges. Defended by Genrikh Padva. Once the wealthiest man in Russia, he was exiled after his jail sentence, and now resides in Switzerland.

Khomenko, Ivan (Vanya) (-1937). Sofya's first husband, executed by Stalin.

Khrushchev, Nikita (1894-1971). Soviet Statesman. First Secretary of the Communist party of Soviet Union 1953-1964. Premier from 1958-1964. Responsible for de-Stalinization of the Soviet Union, promoted reforms, ousted from power in 1964.

Kirov, Sergey (1886-1934). Russian Bolshevik leader. Head of the Communist Party in Leningrad. Shot by a gunman. Stalin was suspected of calling for the assassination, but there has never been any proof.

Kisselev, Sergey. Director of the Department of Technical Inventory for the government of Russia.

Kotlyar, Mark. Jewish. Leader of the Kiev refuseniks. Applied to emigrate in 1977; left in 1990 to live in Los Angeles.

Kozhemyaka, Genrikh Vasilyevitch. 52-year-old homeless man on Red Square.

Kukabaka, Mikhail (1936-). Belarusian dissident.

Kurkov, Anatoly. Chief of Administration for Leningrad Ministry of Internal Affairs. Met in 1989, told the Law Enforcement delegation that they were the first American police to ever visit the headquarters, the administrative center for Leningrad.

Laurinciukas, Albertas (1928-2012). Lithuanian journalist and writer. Chief editor of the newspaper *Tiesa* in Lithuania. Established in 1917, it was the official paper of the Communist Party of Lithuania. Shortly after Lithuania declared independence from the USSR, it became a privately owned publication in 1992. It ceased to exist in 1994.

Landsbergis, Vytautas (1932-). Lithuanian. President in 1990, first head of state after Lithuania's declaration of independence from the USSR, also served as head of the Lithuanian Parliament.

Lenin, Vladimir (1870-1924). Communist revolutionary. Leader of the Bolsheviks. Head of Soviet Russia from 1917-1924.

Lipin, Anton (1968-). Friend, son of Stanislav Lipin, Irkutsk, Siberia.

Lipin, Stanislav (1932- 2018). Naturalist, doctor of biological sciences, Institute of Epidemiology and Microbiology. Often travelled to Northern Siberia to study wildlife. Friend.

Lukyanov, Anatoly Ivanovich (1930- 2019). Communist politician. Poet. Chairman of the Supreme Soviet from 1990-1991, accused of conspiracy during the Soviet coup attempt. Arrested and held in prison for 15 months, during which time he denied the charges. His defense attorney was Genrikh Padva.

M., Sasha (??-2023). Teacher and interpreter. Friend.

Matsak, Yuri. Russian. KGB. Head of the Organized Crime Department. Met in 1990.

Matveev, Vikenty. Journalist. Columnist for newspaper *Izvestia*. Repeat delegate to NESNE Journalism Exchange programs.

Medvedev, Roy (1925-). Russian. Writer, historian, human rights activist, dissident. Critical of Stalin, he was published abroad until after Gorbachev came to power.

Misjura, Galina. Russian. Interpreter and guide for Intourist. Friend.

Monakhov, Valery. Russian. Educator. Vice Director of the Herzen Institute in Leningrad.

Novozhilov, Natalia. Fitness professional. Owner and director of the Minsk Fitness Club "Bagira". Partner in the OASES Aerobics Exchange in 1993.

Oboudikian, Alexander or "Big Sasha." Russian. Major, Ministry of the Interior. Became friends with him and his family in 1990.

Oboudikian, Dima. "Big Sasha's" son.

Oboudikian, Nadia. "Big Sasha's" daughter.

Oboudikian, Vera. "Big Sasha's" wife.

Ortega, Luis (1937-2012). Born in Spain. Painter and engraver. Two years after his birth, his parents were killed in the Spanish Civil War and he was adopted and brought to Russia. His work is found in museum collections in over 30 countries worldwide.

Padva, Genrikh (1931-). Jewish. Deputy Chief of the Union of Attorneys for the USSR before the breakup of the Soviet Union. Vice president of the International Union of Attorneys. Member of the Union of Soviet Advocates (made up of only Jews). Considered one of the leading defense attorneys in Russia.

Pankov, Gennady. Russian journalist. Editor of *Leningradskaya Rabochy*, a worker's paper. One of the first to be a delegate in the NESNE Soviet Journalists Exchange

Glossary of People

Pelkin, Yacov Rabinovitch (1924-). Russian, Jewish. Oldest Jew living in Glubokoye in 1992.

Politkovskaya, Anna (1958-2006). Journalist, writer, human rights activist, murdered in the elevator of her apartment building in Moscow. No evidence of who ordered her assassination, angered the Soviet government by her aggressive reporting during the Second Chechen War. She survived several poisoning attempts and was assassinated on Putin's birthday.

Rasputin, Grigori (1869-1916). Russian mystic, faith healer. Tsar Nicholas II's wife, Tsaritsa Alexandra, believed that Rasputin could heal her son Alexei, who had hemophilia. Many believed that Rasputin had too much influence with the monarchy, and he was murdered by a group of nobles.

Romanov, Anatoly. Russian Major General and Railroad Chief, met in 1991. Suggested exchange of US and Russian railroad police.

Rubtsov, Vyacheslav. General and Chief of the Moscow Fire Central Service. Headed the OASES Russian Fire Service delegation that visited the US in 1991. Friend.

Rutskoy, Alexander (1947-). Russian politician and former military officer. Vice President of Russia under Boris Yeltsin from 1991 to 1993. He broke with Yeltsin, was then accused of corruption. In 1993, he declared himself acting President of Russia. Weeks later, Yeltsin's forces took back the Parliament building and Rutskoy was dismissed as vice president, was imprisoned for almost five months before being granted amnesty.

Sakharov, Andrei (1921-1989). Russian. Nuclear physicist, father of the Soviet hydrogen bomb, dissident and 1975 Nobel Peace Prize winner. Protested Soviet invasion of Afghanistan in 1979 and was subsequently exiled to the closed-to-foreigners city of Gorky, on the Volga River, where he remained almost seven years.

Samoilov, Mikhail (??-1991). Police Captain in Moscow Criminal Department. Killed while on duty. Funeral attended by OASES US Law Enforcement delegation.

Shevardnadze, Eduard (1928-2014). Georgian. Politician and diplomat, Prime Minister for Foreign Affairs under Gorbachev, President of Georgia after dissolution of the USSR.

Simm, Herman (1947-). Estonian. Militia Colonel in charge of the Estonian Defense Ministry's security system for Estonia. Met in 1989 OASES Law Enforcement Exchange.

Smirnov, Valery. Russian. University researcher on electric brain waves.

Smirnov, Nadia. Wife of Valery Smirnov.

Soshnikov, Ivan Sergeevich (1914-1988). Russian painter.

Stalin, Joseph (1878-1953). Soviet Georgian. Birth name Joseph Dzhugashvili. Soviet Revolutionary; General Secretary of the Communist Party of the Soviet Union 1922 to 1952; Premier from 1941-1953. His totalitarian government was responsible for the deaths of millions of his own people, either through execution or starvation due to the Party's policies.

Sverdlov, Yakov (1885-1919). Jewish. Bolshevik party administrator, played an important role in the 1917 October Revolution.

Tibar, Marko (1933-2014). Estonian. Minister of the Interior.

Timofeyev, Lev (1936-). Economist, dissident journalist, novelist.

Timofeyeva, Sofia. International Exchanges facilitator.

Tomashev, Yuri. Russian. Major General, Ministry of the Interior, leader of the 1991 Russian Law Enforcement delegation to the US.

Tsupsman, Leo. Estonian. Chief of Police in Tallinn, Estonia. Met during 1989 Soviet American Law Enforcement Exchange visit to Estonia.

Tovstonogov, Georgy Alexandrovich (1915-1989). Russian. Leader of the Tovstonogov Bolshoi Drama Theater, named after him in 1992.

Trotsky, Leon (1879-1940). Jewish, born in the Ukraine. Marxist Revolutionary, exiled in 1929 for his political beliefs. Assassinated in Mexico with an ice ax upon orders from Stalin.

Tsar Peter the Great (1672-1725).

Catherine the Great (1729-1796).

Tsar Alexander II (1818 -1881, when he was assassinated).

Tsar Alexander III 1845-1894).

Tsar Nicholas II (1868-1918, when he was assassinated)

Tuija. Finland. Physical fitness trainer. Aerobics Program host in Finland, 1994.

V., Natasha. Russian. Interpreter in Minsk during the 1993 Aerobics Exchange.

Vaisvila, Zigmas (1956-). Lithuanian. Politician. Leader of Lithuania's Green party, deputy of the Supreme Council of Lithuania. In 1990, was among those who signed the Act of Re-Establishment of the State of Lithuania.

Valdayev, Alexander. Russian. Deputy Minister of the Interior, Colonel, Chief of Moscow Metro Police and leader of one of the Soviet's law enforcement exchange visits to the US.

Vinogradov, Vladimir. Russian. KGB Deputy Head of their Central Archives.

Vishnevsky, Sergei (1930-1985). Russian journalist. *Pravda* commentator on American affairs. Served as its correspondent in Washington, DC in the 1960s. Reported on the 1963 March on Washington when Martin Luther King gave his "I Have a Dream" speech. Participant in NESNE Journalism Exchanges in 1983 and 1984.

Yegorov, Anatoly. Russian. Colonel and Chief of Moscow Criminal Investigation Department and head of first OASES American-Soviet law enforcement delegation to the US in 1990.

Yegorov, Valentin. Broadcast media administrator, North America desk at Gosteleradio.

Yelizov, Valery. Russian. Interpreter, guide from Soviet Union of Journalists for NESNE Journalism Exchange programs. Friend.

Glossary of People

Yeltzin, Boris (1931-2007). Politician. First President of the Russian Federation 1991-1999, during a time of widespread corruption. Left office very unpopular in the country.

Yezhelev, Anatoly (1932-2012). Russian journalist, head of the Leningrad Union of Journalists. Instrumental in creating new Russian press bill in 1990.

Zassoursky, Yassen (1929-2021). Russian. Professor of Journalism. President of Faculty of Journalism at Moscow State University; Dean of the Faculty of Journalism from 1965-2007.

Zhirinovsky, Vladimir (1946-2022). Russian ultranationalist politician, called fascist by some Western media. Jewish father, which he denied for many years. Anti-Western, supported Donald Trump in his presidential bid in 2016 and that same year, proposed building a wall around Russia to keep out Muslims.

Zubkov, Ivan. Russian journalist. Vice-Chairman of the Board of the Union of Journalists. Head of Russian delegation in 1985 Journalism Exchange in Russia.

AMERICANS / OTHERS

Andrews, Roy Chapman (1884-1960) Explorer, adventurer and naturalist. Director of the American Museum of Natural History. Found the first known fossil dinosaur eggs in the Gobi Desert and thought by many to be the inspiration for the movie character Indiana Jones.

Baker, Veronica Worth. (1955-) Interpreter for the 1980 program for Blind and Deaf in Poland and Russia.

Bourso, Tamara (1946-). Natasha Bourso-Leland's younger sister. Also owner of two Boston restaurants, Dali and Cuchi Cuchi.

Bourso-Leland, Natasha (1944 -1984). Director of Citizens Exchange Council, member of OASES. Friend.

Caballero, Cristina. Founder and President of Dialogue on Diversity, Inc. Participant in the OASES/Women's Peace Initiative American/Soviet Women's Police Conference in 1989.

Caldwell, Paul. Fire chief at Chester Fire Department from 2005 to present.

Campanie, Marie Villari (1952-). Michael Villari's sister.

Collingwood, Fran (1917-2008). Companion to Simon Dickstein.

Damino, John (1947-). Police Captain, Albany NY, when he was twice a delegate on the OASES Law Enforcement Exchanges. Adjunct Faculty for Schenectady County Community College.

Daniloff, Nicholas (1934-). Journalist arrested by the KGB and jailed in Moscow in 1986, accused of espionage. He was allowed to leave the country 21 days later, without charges.

Dukakis, Michael (1933-). Retired Politician, served as 65th governor of Massachusetts from 1975-1979 and again from 1983-1991.

Ebadi, Shirin (1947-). Iranian lawyer, human rights activist, and 2003 Nobel Peace Prize recipient.

Fallaci, Oriana (1929-2006). Italian journalist, war correspondent and author. Partisan during WWII with the Italian anti-fascist resistance movement.

Goldwater, Barry (1928-2012). Politician. Five-term Arizona senator, Republican nominee for president in 1964 election which he lost in a landslide to Lyndon B. Johnson. Although his father was Jewish, he was raised Episcopalian; the first person of Jewish descent to run for president. Died from a stroke and Alzheimer's.

Grinnell, Debbie (1948-). Environmentalist. Worked with C-10 Research and Education Foundation in Newburyport, MA, to conduct radiological monitoring of Seabrook Nuclear Power Plant, as well as plant safety and security. Co-leader on 1986 and 1987 OASES/League of Women Voters Programs in the USSR. Friend.

Grundstrom, Frank (1936-). Journalist. Vice President, *Boston Globe*. President of the New England Society of Newspaper Editors (NESNE). One of the original creators of the Journalism Exchange Program with the Soviet Union. Married to Cynthia Dickstein.

Hildt, Barbara (1946-). Five-time State Legislator in the Massachusetts House of Representatives. Leader of the American-Soviet Women's Policy Conference in 1989.

Howard, Larry (1919-1985). NESNE delegate and *Providence Journal* Associate Managing Editor. Died of a heart attack in Armenia.

Jackson, Sr., Jesse (1941-). American civil rights activist, Baptist minister, and Democrat politician.

Jeffrey, Mildred (1910-2004). Political and social activist, awarded the Presidential Medal of Freedom by President Clinton in 2000.

Lauter-Klatell, Nancy. Associate Professor of Early Education at Wheelock College, Leader of OASES Early Childhood Development Program to the USSR in 1990.

Liberace (1919-1987). American pianist, singer and actor, at one time the highest paid entertainer in the world.

Lowenthal, Scott (1953-). Police officer with Metro North Railroad Police, participated twice in the Law Enforcement Exchange programs in Russia. Went on to be a sergeant with the MTAPD. Currently retired.

Mata Hari (1876-1917). Dutch exotic dancer and courtesan who spied for France in WWI. Convicted of being a double agent and spy for Germany also, she was executed by firing squad in France.

Matruski, James (1942-1965, age 23). Marine, killed in a plane crash minutes after takeoff from El Toro Marine Corps Air Station, CA, destination Vietnam. Cousin of Cynthia Dickstein.

McCabe, William (1937-2009). Commissioner of Public Safety for the Commonwealth of Massachusetts. Served as Chief of Police at Emerson College and was a Lieutenant Colonel with the Massachusetts State Police.

Glossary of People

Mead, Margaret (1901-1978). American cultural anthropologist and author.

Montague, Robert (1953-2007). Physical fitness trainer, Aerobics Exchange Instructor in Russia. Friend.

Norall, Paco. Interpreter, accompanied the first OASES Law Enforcement Exchange Program in the USSR in 1989.

Nye, Bill. Policeman. Proposed an OASES law enforcement exchange, led the first-of-its-kind delegation to Russia in 1989. Retired Chief of Police in East Aurora, NY.

O'Donnell, Eugene. Prosecutor, Queens and Brooklyn District Attorneys' Office. Nationally recognized expert and lecturer on policing issues. Delegate on OASES 1990 Law Enforcement Exchange trip to Russia. Currently professor of law and police studies at City University of New York's John Jay College of Criminal Justice.

Redmont, Bernard (1918-2017). Journalist. Dean of College of Communication at Boston University. Accused of being a Soviet spy, which he denied, landing on the McCarthy-era blacklist for a decade. Worked then for Agence France-Press and the Canadian Broadcasting Company. Eventually hired by CBS News and other American news outlets, before he became dean at Boston University.

Schmidt, Wayne. Consultant and former Executive Director of Americans for Effective Law Enforcement, based in Chicago. Participant in 1989 Law Enforcement Exchange.

Shannon, James (1952-). American politician. Democrat, served as Attorney General of Massachusetts from 1987-1991.

Soros, George (1930-). Business magnate, philanthropist, author. Hungarian Jew who escaped the Holocaust, eventually came to America to become a very successful investor. Created the Open Society Foundation, one of the funders of Iranian Delegation of Journalists in the US, 1998. Also funded millions of dollars to Russian scientists and education in Russia after the collapse of the USSR.

Sproviero, Susan. Retired hospital administrator. Participant in first OASES Law Enforcement Exchange in 1989. Friend.

Stabenow, Debbie (1950-). Politician. Senior US Senator from Michigan, a Democrat, elected in 2000. Delegate in 1989 for the American/Soviet Women's Policy Conference, sponsored by OASES and the Women's Peace Initiative.

Villari, Michael (1946-2013). Landscaper, lover, and friend.

Weiss, Leona (1902-1955). First wife of Simon Dickstein.

Weld, William (1945-). Attorney, businessman and politician. Governor of Massachusetts from 1991-1997, received OASES Soviet Police Delegation in 1990.

Glossary of Terms and Abbreviations

Arbat - Pedestrian street in the center of Moscow, lined with souvenir stalls, street musicians, artists, restaurants and bars.

ASCE, Inc. - American Soviet Cultural Exchanges, Inc.

Ashkenazi Jews - Those whose ancestry can be traced to Central Europe.

Babushka - Kerchief for the head or an elderly Russian woman.

Bagna - Russian sauna.

Beriozka - State-run retail stores in the USSR, foreign currency only.

Birobidzhan - Jewish Autonomous Region in Eastern Siberia.

Bolshevik Party - Political party in Russia that led the 1917 revolution.

Bundists - Members of the Bund, the European Jewish socialist movement founded in Russia in 1897.

Catsella (Ketzeleh) - Kitten in Yiddish.

CEC, Inc. - Citizens Exchange Council, Inc.

Cheka - Soviet secret police created in 1917.

Chernobyl - Catastrophic nuclear power accident in 1986.

Del - Traditional Mongolian coat-like garment.

DOE - US Department of Energy.

Dom Knigi - House of Books on *Nevsky Prospekt*, St. Petersburg.

Dezhurnaya - Woman stationed on each floor of Soviet hotels to monitor events or provide guests needs.

Glasnost - Openness and transparency in the Russian government, policy promoted by Mikhail Gorbachev in the mid-1980s.

Glavmosavtotrans - Main administration of Motor Transportation, Moscow.

Huppah - Wedding canopy Jewish couple stand under during the wedding ceremony, symbolizing the home they will build together.

Intourist - Official state travel agency of the Soviet Union, founded in 1929. Privatized in 1992.

IPEX, Inc. - International Professional Exchanges, Inc.

Izvestia - Newspaper established in 1917 which published the official views and policies of the Soviet government until 1991.

KGB - Main security agency for the Soviet Union, 1954-1991. Mission was internal security, intelligence and secret police.

Kheyder - Jewish elementary school, primarily for boys, in Eastern Europe.

MEEI - Massachusetts Eye and Ear Infirmary.

NESNE, Inc. - New England Society of Newspaper Editors.

Ministry of the Interior - Federal executive body responsible for security and law enforcement inside Russia's borders.

Nevsky Prospekt - The main street running through the center of St. Petersburg, Russia.

NKVD - Interior Ministry of the Soviet Union, ruled by the Communist Party, from 1934-1943.

Novodevichy Cemetery - Most famous cemetery in Moscow, opened in 1898. Burial site of celebrated Soviets and Russians, including cosmonauts, writers, politicians and government leaders.

OASES, Inc. - Organization for American Soviet Exchanges, Inc.

Okhrana - Secret police of the Russian empire, considered a symbol of Tsarist oppression, from 1881 until 1917, when it was disbanded. Allegedly fabricated and distributed the anti-Semitic *Protocols of the Elders of Zion*.

Pale of Settlement - Western region of Imperial Russia, created by Catherine the Great in 1791, where Jews were allowed to live. Outside the Pale borders, Jews were mostly forbidden.

Pamyat - Neo-Nazi, ultra-nationalist organization formed in Russia in 1980 to promote Orthodox Christianity, to disseminate anti-Semitic and anti-Western propaganda. Stated mission is to preserve Russian culture.

Partisans - People who joined resistance movements during WWII against Nazi Germany and its allies. Estimated number of Jewish partisans was 20,000-30,000.

Pelmeni - Russian meat-filled dumplings.

Perestroika - Reform of the economic and political system of Russia, of the Communist Party, instituted primarily by Mikhail Gorbachev in the mid-1980s.

Pogrom - Organized massacre, especially of Jews.

Pravda - Official newspaper of the Communist Party of the USSR, from 1912-1991. The print edition is now run by the Communist Party; the online Pravda.ru is privately owned.

Protocols of the Elders of Zion - A 1903 Russian anti-Semitic text describing a Jewish plan for global domination. Disseminated internationally, proven to be fake by *The Times* of London in 1921; still available and in print and believed by many to be a genuine document.

Refuseniks - Usually Jews and called Prisoners of Zion, who were the Soviet citizens who had applied to emigrate and were refused.

Samizdat - Literature secretly written, copied, and circulated in the former Soviet Union and usually critical of practices of the Soviet government.

Glossary of Terms and Abbreviations

Saratov - Large city and major port on the Volga River, about 522 miles southeast of Moscow.

Shtetl - Small village in Eastern Europe, primarily Yiddish-speaking Jewish market towns.

Solovetsky Stone - Monument across from KGB headquarters erected in 1990 to honor victims of Soviet political repression. Stone is from the Solovetsky Islands, the location of Solovki prison camp, part of the Soviet Gulag System.

Spetsnaz - Special military units controlled by military intelligence. Highly trained, elite, top-secret commandos.

Topchans - Couch-like furniture used in Central Asia for sleeping on at night and sitting on during the day.

Triple Cities - Also called Greater Binghamton area, made up of Binghamton, Johnson City and Endicott.

Yahrzeit candle - Memorial candle that burns for 24 hours; Jewish custom to light it in memory of the dead, on the anniversary of their death.

Yom Kippur - Holiest day of the year in Judaism, observed by a 25 hour period of fasting and prayer and repentance, usually in a synagogue.

Zakuski - Russian appetizers.

38 Petrovka Street - Main Moscow Department of the Russian Interior Ministry; Moscow Criminal Police.

Bibliography / Works Cited

Agayev, M., *Novel with Cocaine*, Dutton Adult, 1984.

Allen, Seema Rynin, *Comrades and Citizens: Soviet People*, Victor Gollancz Ltd, London, 1938, The Left Book Club.

Black, Edwin, *IBM and the Holocaust*, Crown Publisher, 2001.

Black, Edwin, *War Against the Weak: Eugenics and America's Campaign to Create a Master Race*, Four Walls Eight Windows, 2003.

Bogen (originally Katzenbogen), Alexander (Shura), "The Onset of the Partisan Units in the Forest of Naroch," from *With Proud Bearing, 1939-1945: Chapters in the History of Jewish Fighting in the Naroch Forests*, edited by Moshe Kalcheim, published in Yiddish by the Organization of Partisans, Underground Fighters, and Ghetto Rebels in Israel, Tel Aviv, 1992 and translated into English by Eilat Gordin Levitan, naroc_partisans, kehilalinks, jewishgen.org.

Bray, Mark, *Antifa, The Anti-Fascist Handbook*, Melville House Publishing, 2017.

Browder, Bill, *Red Notice: A True Story of High Finance, Murder, and One Man's Fight for Justice*, Simon and Schuster, 2015.

Browssat, Alain and Klingberg, Sylvia, *Revolutionary Yiddishland: A History of Jewish Radicalism*, Verso, 2016.

Carey, Sarah C., *US Soviet Exchanges – The Kinds of Exchanges That Have Taken Place; What Works: How Can They Be Made More Effective?*, Institute for Soviet American Relations, August 18, 1983.

Conor O'Clery, *Moscow, December 25, 1991: The Last Day of the Soviet Union* Book Review, DemocracyJournal.org 2011.

Dickstein, Cynthia, "Blind and deaf in the USSR unlike the USA," *Boston Sunday Globe*, November 2, 1980.

Dickstein, Cynthia, "Despite years of dramatic change, Soviet Union remains the same." *The New London Day*, August 13, 1989.

Dickstein, Cynthia, "Inside Lithuania: eyewitness report of freedom rally," *Sunday Cape Cod Times*, April 29, 1990.

Dickstein, Cynthia, "In father's image," *Boston Globe*, June 21, 1992.

Dickstein, Cynthia, "Giving national tragedy a name," *Cape Cod Times*, May 4, 1993.

Dickstein, Cynthia, "The eternal connections of friendships," *Boston Globe*, July 24, 1993.

Dickstein, Cynthia, "Aunt Ida's final wish," *Boston Globe*, January 1, 1994.

Dickstein, Cynthia, "Going back to the beginning," *Boston Globe*, January 28, 1994.

Dickstein, Cynthia, "Breaking the silence," *Boston Globe*, March 20, 1994.

Dickstein, Cynthia, "Battered mother, shattered child," *Boston Globe,* February 3, 1995.

Dickstein, Cynthia and Montague, Robert, "In the realm of the fishes," *Boston Sunday Globe*, July 14, 1996.

Dickstein, Cynthia, "Iran, its anger waning, echoes back to the USSR," *Boston Sunday Globe*, August 9, 1998.

Dickstein, Cynthia, "Iran's fighter for women's rights," *Boston Globe*, October 11, 2003.

Dickstein, Cynthia, "The comfort of the pineapple bed," *Boston Globe*, August 12, 2010.

Dickstein, Cynthia, "Abortion: Who Should Decide?" My Commentary: https://www.youtube.com/watch?v=f1Q2Xh8cmTs.

Dobbs, Michael, "Russian Arc," *Democracy Journal.org*, Spring 2012.

Dworzecki, Dr. Mark, "The Jerusalem of Lithuania: in Struggle and Destruction," Paris: *L'Union Populaire Juive en France*, 1948.

Ehrenburg, Ilya and Grossman, Vasily, editors, *The Black Book: The Ruthless Murder of Jews by German-Fascist Invaders Throughout the Temporarily-Occupied Regions of the Soviet Union and in the Death Camps of Poland During the War of 1941-1945,* Holocaust Library, NY, 1986.

Gessen, Masha, *The Man Without a Face: The Unlikely Rise of Vladimir Putin*, Riverhead Books, 2012.

Gitelman, Zvi, *A Century of Ambivalence: The Jews of Russia and the Soviet Union, 1881 to the Present*, Indiana University Press, 2001.

Goldstein, Phyllis, *A Convenient Hatred: The History of Anti-Semitism*, Facing History and Ourselves, 2012 www.facinghistory.org.

Groves, Betsy McAlister, *Children Who See Too Much*, Beacon Press, 2002.

Grosvenor, Gilbert H., *National Geographic Magazine*, "Young Russia – The Land of Unlimited Possibilities," November, 1914.

Hartman, Thomas, a review of *After the Empire* by Emmanuel Todd, buzzflash.com, 1976.

HBO documentary, "Hunted: The War Against Gays in Russia," 2014.

Kaiser, Robert G., *Why Gorbachev Happened: His Triumph, His Failure, and His Fall*, Simon and Schuster, 1991.

Kendall, Russell, *Russian Girl: Life in an Old Russian Town*, Scholastic, Inc., 1994.

Khanga, Yelena, *Soul to Soul: A Black Russian American Family 1865-1992*, W.W. Norton & Co Inc., 1994.

Kick, Russ, *100 Things You're Not Supposed to Know: Secrets, Conspiracies, Cover-Ups and Absurdities,* Hampton Road Publishing Company, 2014.

Kogos, Fred, *A Dictionary of Yiddish Slang and Idioms*, Castle Books, 1978.

Bibliography / Works Cited

Levin, Linda Lotridge, *To Understand: The History of a 10-year dialogue between New England and Soviet Editors*, published by the *Boston Globe*, 1993.

Levitan, Eilat Gordin, translator, *Glubokie Ghetto: A Concentration camp for the Remaining Jews of the Surrounding liquidated Shtetls*, eilatgordinlevitan.com.

Lew, Mike, *Victims No Longer: Men Recovering from Incest and other Sexual Child Abuse*, Nevraumont Publishing Co, 1988.

Medvedev, Dmitry Nikolaevich, *Stout Hearts: This Happened Near Rovno*. Translated from Russian by David Skvirsky, Moscow, Foreign Languages Publishing House, 1961.

Mieville, *China*, October, Verso, 2017.

O'Cleary, Conor, *Moscow, December 25, 1991: The Last Day of the Soviet Union*, Public Affairs, 2011.

Osnos, Evan, Remnick, David and Yaffa, Joshua, "Active Measures," *The New Yorker*, March 6, 2017.

Rajak, Zvi and Michael, *The Destruction of Globokie (Hlybokayo, Belarus)*, translated by Eilat Gordin Levitan, published in 1956 in Buenos Aires.

Reed, John, *Ten Days that Shook the World*, Transcribed from a 1919, 1st Edition, published by BONI & Liveright, Inc. for International Publishers, the publishing house of the Communist Party, USA.

Shevardnadze, Eduard, *The Future Belongs to Freedom*, The Free Press, 1991.

Slezkine, Yuri, *The Jewish Century*, Princeton University Press 2004.

Suvorov, Viktor, *Spetsnaz: The Inside Story of the Soviet Special Forces*, W. W. Norton and Company, Inc., 1988.

Timofeyev, Lev, *Russia's Secret Rulers: How the Government and the Criminal Mafia Exercise Their Power*, New York: Alfred A. Knopf, 1992.

Todd, Emmanuel, *The Final Fall, On the Decomposition of the Soviet Sphere*, Karz Publishers, 1979.

Weiss, Arnine Cumsky and Miller-Lanning, Darlene, *Jews of Scranton*, Arcade Publishing 2005.

Wex, Michael, *Born to Kvetch: Yiddish Language and Culture in All of its Moods*, Harper Perennial, 2006.

RECOMMENDED READING

Alexievich, Svetlana, *Secondhand Time: The Last of the Soviets*, Random House, 2016.

Anderson, MT., *Symphony for the City of the Dead: Dmitri Shostakovich and the Siege of Leningrad*, Candlewick, 2015.

Brent, Jonathan and Naumov, Vladimir P., *Stalin's Last Crime: The Doctor's Plot*, John Murray Publishers LTD, 2003.

Canduci, Alexander, *The Greatest Lies in History*, Metro Books, 2009.

Daniloff, Nicholas, *Two Lives, One Russia*, Houghton Mifflin Co, Boston 1988.

Des Pres, Terrence, *The Survivor: An Anatomy of Life in the Death Camps*, Oxford University Press, 1976.

Duffy, Peter, *The Bielski Brothers: The True Story of Three Men who Defied the Nazis, Saved 1,200 Jews, and Built a Village in the Forest*, HarperCollins Publishers, Inc., 2003.

Entekhabifard, Camelia, *Camelia: Save Yourself by Telling the Truth, A Memoir of Iran*, Seven Stories Press, 2007.

Fallaci, Oriana, *A Man* (her autobiographical recall about her relationship with Aleksandar Panagoulis, Greek political activist,) Simon & Schuster, 1980.

Freemantle, Brian, *KGB, Inside the World's Largest Intelligence Network*, Holt, Rinehart and Winston, 1982.

Macintyre, Ben, *The Spy and the Traitor*, Crown Publishing Group, 2018.

Makine, Andrei, *Dreams of My Russian Summers*, Arcade Publishing, translated from French, 1995.

Massie, Suzanne, *The Land of the Firebird: The Beauty of Old Russia*, Simon & Schuster, 1980.

Medvedev, Roy, *Let History Judge, The Origins of Stalinism*, Columbia University Press, 1989.

Montefiore, Simon Sebag, *Stalin: The Court of the Red Tsar*, Vintage Books, a division of Random House, 2003.

Okrent, Daniel, *The Guarded Gate: Bigotry, Eugenics and the Law that Kept Two Generations of Jews, Italians and Other European Immigrants Out of America*, Scribner, 2019.

Patenaude, Bertrand, *The Big Show in Bololand: The American Relief Expedition to Soviet Russia in the Famine of 1921*, Stanford University Press, 2002.

Redmont, Bernard, *Risks Worth Taking: The Odyssey of a Foreign Correspondent*, University Press of America, 1992.

Reichlin, Herbert, *Command Blunders: The XYZ's that Caused France and Germany to Lose WWII*, Book Baby Publisher, 2024.

Reichlin, Seymour, *Video History Project*, The Endocrine Society, YouTube, 2010.

Recommended Reading

Salisbury, Harrison, *The 900 Days: The Siege of Leningrad*, Harper and Row, 1969.

Schmemann, Serge, *Echoes of a Native Land: Two Centuries of Life in a Russian Village*, Alfred A. Knopf, NY, 1997.

Shore, Marci, *The Taste of Ashes: The Afterlife of Totalitarianism in Eastern Europe*, Broadway Books, 2014.

Website: www.jewishgen.org/yizkor/hlybokaye/hly032.html.

Weiner, Tim, *The Folly and the Glory: America, Russia, and Political Warfare, 1945-2020*, Henry Holt & Company, 2020.

Wyman, David, *The Abandonment of the Jews: America and the Holocaust 1941-1945*, Pantheon, 1984.

Zinn, Howard, *A People's History of the United States*, Harper & Row, 1980.

Acknowledgements

To those who contributed and/or inspired:

Rebecca Akpan
Patricia Andrate &
    Hank Walker
Jacqueline Ballantyne
Carolyn Brown
Ruby & Bill Buchsbaum
Paul Calderwood
Heidi Carlson
Maura Casey
Peter Cronk
Emilia Farrell
Julius Frumin

Harold Garfinkle
Stephen Golden &
    Susan Tarrence
Cande & Tom Grogan
J. Lisa Jones
Simon Khilkevich
Nina Klose
Anton Lipin
Laurie Mann
Bill Nye
Gerard O'Neill
Jane Ragle & John Smith

Isadore Shapiro
Nancy & Joe Sharkey
Judy Singer
Stephanie Sklar
Kendall Taylor
Mark & Niza Uslan
Valery Yelizov
Michelle Young
Andi Ziegelman
Howard Zinn

To many, but by no means all, cousins who have shared their family stories and information so that I could write this book:

Natalie Reichlin Storper
    Natalie's Children
      Barbara Storper
      Dan Storper

Herb Reichlin
    Herb's Children
      Siobhan Bowler
      Lucy Reagan
      Liz Reichlin
      Andrew Reichlin
      James Reichlin
      Evan Reichlin
        Skinner

Seymore Reichlin
    Si's Children
      Seth Reichlin
      Annie Reichlin
      Doug Reichlin

Yale Wexler
    Yale's Children
      Jeannie Rifkin
      Pearl Wexler
      Abie Wexler

Sofya Khilkevitch
    Sofya's Children
      Alla Makarovsky
      David Khilkevitch

Hava & Reuvan Avital
Robert Dickstein
Stanley Dickstein
Dana Hill
Matt Hollenberg
Shirley Hollenberg
Raya Kaplan
Karen Kirshner
Leonid Makarovsky
Nina Polansky
Jeannie Rifkin
Eva Rosenn
George Saiger
Mark Segal
Cheryl Sofer
Lena Torchin
Pearl Wexler
Linda Wilson
Bronya Zilberman

Paths of Stones

To my oldest friends on this journey, some still here, some sadly gone, all of whom have enriched my life beyond measure:

Ernest Ahrens	Marion R. Copeland	Tim Leland
Cynthia & Teddy Berenson	Geraldine Denterlein	Peter McHenry
	Judith Feher	John Priber
Natasha Bourso-Leland	Linda Winer Feldman	Arlene Nelson Sahr
Debbie Breen	Cleve (Corky) Ford	MaryAnne Setticase
Debby Brown	Debbie & Chan Grinnell	Lena Sirotin
Marie Campanie	Victor Gurewich	Delia Devens Skiffington
Gail Casale	Julie Hatfield	Susan Sproviero
Karen Coen	Ted Holmberg	Sylvia Stearns
Alan Cohn	Kathryn Holmes	Jack Thomas
Dottie Cohn	Steven Jacobs	Michael Villari
Larry Cohn	Tom Lattyak	Peter Villari

And to close family, who are both the soft and the strong threads in my life:

Frank Grundstrom, my beloved husband
Renee & Ronald Davis
Tambi Yu and Brittany Edwards
Tara Davis & David Popkin
   Ava & Mia Popkin
David Simon Dickstein
Diane & John Lemoine
   Andrew & Owen Lemoine

Karen Grundstrom Stebbins
   Emily & Jim McMeeken
   Hannah Stebbins
Mark & Laura Grundstrom
   Samantha & Meghan Grundstrom
Ed Grundstrom & Patti Zenna

To the Setticase and Villari families of Canastota, NY, who welcomed me like a member of the family.

To Armen Dedekian, Vice President of IPEX, who contributed essentially to all of our projects, and who was always ready to gladly lend a hand when needed.

To Barbie Adler and John Nemerovsky, who, through their invitation to puppy play group with Tito enabled me to meet my cousin Si, and who put me in touch with Kira Henschel at HenschelHAUS Publishing. Kira guided me through the necessary steps to prepare the manuscript. She recommended changes or additions and did the editing and layout. She is professional, gracious, and a pleasure to work with.

About the Author

Cynthia Dickstein began her professional career working for Ealing Corporation in Cambridge, MA doing advertising and public relations. After later receiving a master's degree in teaching the blind and then working for Braille Institute in Los Angeles for five years, she worked in the private sector and organized non-political international, cultural, and professional exchanges for 25 years.

She first worked for Citizen Exchange Council, Inc., based in NY, then served as the president of the Organization for International Professional Exchanges, Inc., (OASES) a private, non-profit organization in Cambridge, MA, which was renamed International Professional Exchanges (IPEX). Concurrently, she served as the Director of the Foreign Exchange program of the New England Society of Newspaper Editors Foundation (NESNE) from 1984-2005.

Ms. Dickstein is also a freelance writer who has been published throughout New England, most frequently on the op-ed page of the *Boston Globe*.

In 2001, she moved to Tucson, where for several years she served on the Board of Access Tucson and then became the host of their talk show *Political Perspectives*. She was a member of the philanthropic organization Social Venture Partners, Inc., where she was the curator of their Diversity and Inclusion Resource online library. Currently, she is a mentor editor for the Op Ed Project. She lives with her cherished husband Frank, their sweet cat Zeke, and their spirited dog Taavi.

Cynthia's email: cdickstein@gmail.com

www.ingramcontent.com/pod-product-compliance
Lightning Source LLC
Chambersburg PA
CBHW060332010526
44117CB00017B/2810